# Regional Trade Integration and Conflict Resolution

This volume addresses the growth of regional trade agreements (RTAs), which have mushroomed since the 1990s, and considers their potential as a tool for reducing inter- and intra-state conflict.

Exploring the links between trade, conflict and peace in different and varying contexts, this book maps the extant RTAs in the region, analyses the factors that hinder or promote regional trade integration and considers their economic and political impacts. Presenting a series of case studies in four regions: South America; the southern African region; South Asia; and South East Asia, the authors consider three key questions:

- What is the significance of the recent and rapid development of RTAs for peace building both within and between countries?
- To what extent do RTAs engender inter- and intra-state conflict?
- To what extent are trade and RTAs hostage to conflict and is regional political stability a precondition for economic integration?

*Regional Trade Integration and Conflict Resolution* will be of interest to students and scholars of trade, international relations and conflict studies. It will also be of interest to policy makers and non-governmental organisations (NGOs).

**Shaheen Rafi Khan** is Research Fellow at the Sustainable Development Policy Institute (SDPI), Islamabad, Pakistan.

# Routledge Advances in International Political Economy

# Regional Trade Integration and Conflict Resolution

Edited by Shaheen Rafi Khan

Routledge
Taylor & Francis Group

LONDON AND NEW YORK

First published 2009
by Routledge
2 Park Square, Milton Park, Abingdon, Oxon OX14 4RN

Simultaneously published in the USA and Canada
by Routledge
270 Madison Avenue, New York, NY 10016

*Routledge is an imprint of the Taylor & Francis Group,
an informa business*

Typeset in Times New Roman by
RefineCatch Limited, Bungay, Suffolk
Printed and bound in Great Britain by
TJ International Ltd, Padstow, Cornwall

*British Library Cataloguing in Publication Data*
A catalogue record for this book is available from the British Library

*Library of Congress Cataloging-in-Publication Data*
Regional trade integration and conflict resolution / edited by Shaheen
Rafi Khan.
    p. cm.—(Routledge advances in international political economy ; 14)
    Trade blocs—Developing countries.   2. Developing countries—
Commercial treaties.   3. Developing countries—Foreign economic
relations.   4. Peace-building—Developing countries.
5. Regionalism—Developing countries.   I. Khan, Shaheen Rafi.
  HF1418.7.R443 2008
  382′.911724—dc22                        2008018392

ISBN 10: 0–415–47673–9 (hbk)
ISBN 10: 0–203–88980–0 (ebk)

ISBN 13: 978–0–415–47673–7 (hbk)
ISBN 13: 978–0–203–88980–0 (ebk)

# Contents

# Figures

# Tables

# Contributors

**Hernán Blanco** is Executive Director and Founding Partner of RIDES, Santiago, Chile.

**Oli Brown** is a project manager and policy researcher for the International Institute for Sustainable Development's (IISD) Trade and Investment, and Security programmes.

**Edmundo Claro** is Associate Researcher at RIDES, Santiago, Chile.

**Peter Goldschagg** is Associate Researcher at RIDES, Santiago, Chile.

**Shaheen Rafi Khan** is Research Fellow at the Sustainable Development Policy Institute (SDPI), Islamabad, Pakistan.

**Hank Lim** is Director of Research at the Singapore Institute of International Affairs (SIIA), Singapore.

**Mzukisi Qobo** is Research Fellow at the South African Institute of International Affairs (SAIIA).

**Alejandra Ruiz-Dana** is a researcher at the Recursos e Investigación para el Desarello Sustenable (RIDES), Santiago, Chile.

**Faisal Haq Shaheen** is Visiting Research Associate at the SDPI, Islamabad, Pakistan.

**Azka Tanveer** is Research Assistant at the SDPI, Islamabad, Pakistan.

**Moeed Yusuf** is a consultant on Economic Policy at the SDPI, Islamabad, Pakistan.

# Foreword

## Flat world or a world of regions?

While many have talked about globalisation and some suggest we live in a 'flat' world, regionalism has been a phenomenon that has been less remarked upon and studied. Yet, even with the lower costs of travel and transport, and the wonders of technology, there are still costs and constraints such as time and culture that lead globalisation to be incomplete. Thus, in a less than fully global world, there are many reasons that regionalism has continued and indeed grown.

The European Union (EU) has provided the boldest and perhaps most advanced example of regionalisation in the world. Yet we may equally note different efforts to link and prefer regional ties in North and South America, in Africa and across Asia.

Many of these are overlapping groups. For example, in Asia alone, there is the Association of South East Asian Nations (ASEAN), that brings together the ten states of Southeast Asia; ASEAN+3, with the North East Asian countries of China, Japan and South Korea; the East Asia Summit, with the foregoing plus India, Australia and New Zealand; and the still wider Asia-Pacific Economic Cooperation (APEC) process.

For these reasons, there is evidence to suggest that we live not in a flat world in which all points are equally accessible, but in a world of regions, with differing circles of proximity and identification. Such thinking underscores the current talk about the rise of Asia to a greater equality with North America and the EU.

While this book deals with regionalism in different parts of the world, allow me in this context to share some observations drawn from an Asian perspective.

## Asian regionalism and trade

More and more people predict the rise of Asia with economic, political and other dimensions. However, this is not an assured and guaranteed outcome, as the crisis of 1997 showed us. Much depends on the policies and choices that Asians make in facing the challenges ahead and dealing with potential conflicts. In this context, trade and the avoidance of conflict are key pillars.

Trade has been a central policy for many Asian states not only to drive its rise, but also to address diverse attendant challenges such as education and equity for the poor, and industrialisation and economic competitiveness in the private sector.

Given the modern patterns of trade, Asians have traditionally traded more with the developed economies than with each other. International trade remains of key importance to Asia, and many have hoped for progress in the Doha Development Round and the equitable representation of their interests and perspectives in the World Trade Organization (WTO).

Yet Asia has also witnessed a rising tide in regional trade agreements (RTAs). While early efforts among Asian economies like the Japan–Singapore Economic Partnership Agreement were doubted by both those within and outside the region, regional free trade and economic agreements have proliferated from the early 2000s. Today, there are few Asian states that are not involved in one or more trade agreements, either bilaterally or as a sub-regional group.

Some question these free trade agreements (FTAs) for their efficacy and efficiency, suggesting that an unwieldy and incoherent 'spaghetti bowl' of agreements has resulted. Notwithstanding this, we can see that these FTAs serve as political signifiers of the growing ties and sense of regionalism among Asians, and underline a real and underlying economic integration that already exists in Asia.

This growing regional trade integration can be seen in the rise in the volume of intra-Asian trade. A large part of this trade is in intermediate goods, with the final product meant for export to non-Asian markets, especially the US and EU. This signifies the creation of a regional production base as private sector actors rationally leverage on different competitive strengths in different Asian states, rather than producing any product exclusively and less efficiently in a single country.

Additionally, a growing part of the intra-Asian trade is not for export but meant for consumers within Asia. For this reason, as the US faces economic difficulties ahead, there is some talk of a decoupling of their economies such that Asia can and will keep growing even if the US is adversely affected. My own analysis is that such talk is perhaps premature. While Asian consumption is growing with the rise of a middle class, there is still considerable interdependence and exchange with non-Asian economies, especially the US and EU. What may be truer is that the dynamics in these interregional relationships are changing and becoming more equal as Asia grows and becomes more integrated.

## Trade and conflicts

Peace or at least the avoidance of conflicts is a second important pillar in the rise of Asia. Differences over trade can and will be likely to arise. While the importance of trade is almost universally recognised, particular groups and sectors may well face losses, and drive political and social sensitivities to liberalisation. There can and have been disagreements on other issues too, such as the environmental impacts of trade in certain goods, or their impact on human and labour rights. Or about standards of safety, technical requirements and other areas.

Such differences over trade arise at different levels and scales and can lead to wider political differences and tensions between states. The resolution of such differences in the WTO has been developed and increasingly strengthened.

Yet regional approaches to trade dispute resolution are also needed in Asia and other regions. Efforts should be made so that trade relations can be dealt with in a wider context of relations and the need to avoid increasing tension and possible conflict between states.

Wider and more fundamental conflicts must also be managed and avoided at the regional levels, between neighbours and near neighbours. These include the political and security tensions that exist in Asia and other countries. Some relate to historical differences, narrow nationalism, ethnic differences (or indeed commonalities) and territorial claims. Others even more dangerously perhaps relate to political hegemony presently or in the future, whereby security, trade and other concerns are brought together in a heady and potentially dangerous brew.

What is the role of regional trade integration in such conflicts? This is one of the difficult questions that this volume makes an effort to address. This is most welcome.

Many regional schemes for cooperation and integration have proceeded on the faith that interdependence in the economic field can potentially soften political tension and competition between states. This has been the rationale in Asia and ASEAN, whether stated or implicit. Similarly, some see the intra-Asian efforts such as the ASEAN+3 as an effort to engage China as an emerging power, and the China–ASEAN FTA as, conversely, China's effort to reach out to its southern neighbours.

Bilaterally too, the high levels of investment and trade between neighbours often belies a relationship that can be tense, in other dimensions. Relations among the Indo-Chinese states and Thailand, between Singapore and Malaysia, and between these two triangulated with Indonesia, and perhaps most famously between Japan and China show this pattern.

This volume is therefore to be welcomed for more closely and critically examining the relationship between regional economic integration and conflict, not only in Asia but also across the world. For as economic and other ties bring us closer together, there are both opportunities for closer cooperation and greater understanding, as well as dangers for increased frictions and envy between neighbouring states. The studies in this volume therefore bear close study for the observations they make and the implications they draw out about the reality of the world we live in, that is increasingly interconnected but not at peace.

Simon S.C. Tay
Chairman
Singapore Institute of International Affairs

# Preface

Economic interdependence as a means to attain peace is becoming increasingly important, as the evolving global security paradigm grows weary of purely military solutions to inter- and intra-state tensions. A concrete articulation of this is regional trade agreements (RTAs), which mushroomed globally during the 1990s. The 'rush to regionalism' generated considerable debate. While Jagdish Bhagwati dismisses these agreements as 'spaghetti bowl situations', at the other end of the spectrum, scholars and policy practitioners view RTAs as World Trade Organization (WTO)-plus arrangements to spur global trade. They also add potential value in inverting the historical dictum, 'trade follows the flag'. In other words, RTAs have political relevance in as much as they can promote regional peace. Inspired by the example of the European Union (EU), aid donors and the international community have been particularly keen to promote regional economic integration in the developing world, anticipating both trade liberalisation and political stability.

This may be a reasonable expectation in the north given the enabling institutional environment. Southern dynamics are far more unstable, with the possibility that RTAs can actually implode; they can either trigger conflict, or they may not even be able to get off the ground in the absence of certain political preconditions. The range of possibilities suggests the need for empirical research to shed light on these questions. However, most of the existing literature is preoccupied with conducting a theoretical debate on the issue. There are relatively few attempts to test the theoretical premises through empirical studies. In an effort to address this deficiency, we have examined the issues of regional and bilateral trade and peace building under varying contexts and in different regions. The volume provides useful insights for students from a southern perspective, providing a counterweight in the debate, which has thus far revolved largely around Eurocentric premises and insights.

For instance, the evidence suggests possible reverse causality, with prior political conditions determining the scope for economic integration. Further, even the best-designed RTA can abort in the absence of trade and economic complementarities – the RTA can end up diverting rather than creating trade. These are important distinctions as they differentiate between those RTAs (mostly northern) that are politically and institutionally grounded, and those (mostly southern) that lack an enabling environment. The message is that the optimism generated by the 'rush to regionalism' needs to be tempered with reality.

This volume explores the trade–peace–conflict linkage through a case study approach. Four regions: South America; the southern African region; South Asia; and South East Asia are the subjects of the case studies. The three key questions addressed are:

- What is the significance of the recent and rapid development of RTAs for peace building both within and between countries?
- To what extent do RTAs engender inter and intra-state conflict?
- Conversely, to what extent are trade and RTAs hostage to conflict? In other words, is regional political stability a precondition for economic integration?

The contrasting theoretical premises provide an introduction and a context for examining peace or conflict outcomes in disparate regions of the world. The investigative part of the study includes a mapping of extant RTAs in the region, an analysis of the factors that hinder or promote regional trade integration, and the consequent economic and political impacts. These aspects are examined in more depth at the bilateral level, between two countries in each region. The concluding section attempts to draw out synthesising as well as differentiated messages.

This book is the result of a two-year research collaboration involving four regional institutes and one northern institute. The International Development Research Centre (IDRC) funded the initiative. The Sustainable Development Policy Institute (SDPI), the Recursos e Investigación para el Desarello Sustenable (RIDES), the South African Institute of International Affairs (SAIIA) and the Singapore Institute of International Affairs (SIIA), Singapore and the International Institute for Sustainable Development (IISD) engaged in the research. SDPI and the IISD coordinated the global effort, in particular organising the consultative process from inception to stakeholder workshop to peer reviews. The research partners presented their initial findings at the WTO Ministerial in Hong Kong, followed by consultative workshops in Calgary, Canada and Johannesberg, South Africa. This book represents the final stage of the research process.

Shaheen Rafi Khan
Research Fellow
Sustainable Development Institute

# Acknowledgements

The book is a collective effort and it needs a collective acknowledgement. The authors would like to extend warm thanks to the International Development Research Centre (IDRC) for funding the initiative and for showing extraordinary patience and support while the research was underway. In particular, they would like to thank Dr Gerd Schonwalder, Marie-France Guimond, Mano Buckshi and Bill Carman from the Centre who guided and encouraged us in their various capacities. In particular, we thank them for providing a research environment that allowed articulation of Southern voices but in a manner that was detached and objective.

# Acronyms

| | |
|---|---|
| ABACC | Brazilian–Argentine Agency for Accounting and Control of Nuclear Materials |
| ACM-ECS | Ayeyawady-Chao Phya-Mekong Economic Cooperation Strategy |
| ACPHR | AU Commission on Human and People's Rights |
| ADB | Asian Development Bank |
| AEC | ASEAN Economic Community |
| AEM | ASEAN economic ministers |
| AFTA | Andean Free Trade Area |
| AFTA | ASEAN Free Trade Area |
| AIS | Andean Integration System |
| ANC | African National Congress |
| APEC | Asia-Pacific Economic Cooperation |
| ARATS | Association for Relations Across the Taiwan Strait |
| ARF | ASEAN Regional Forum |
| ASC | ASEAN Security Community |
| ASCC | ASEAN Socio-Cultural Community |
| ASEAN | Association of South East Asian Nations |
| ASEAN-ISIS | ASEAN Institute of Strategic and International Studies |
| ASEAN-MBDC | ASEAN-Mekong Basin Development Cooperation |
| ASP | ASEAN Surveillance Process |
| ATPA | Andean Trade Preferences Act |
| AU | African Union |
| BIMSTEC | Bangladesh, India, Myanmar, Sri Lanka, Thailand Economic Cooperation |
| BJP | Bharatiya Janata Party |
| CACM | Central American Common Market |
| CAN | Andean Community |
| CARICOM | Caribbean Common Market |
| CBM | confidence building measure |
| CENTO | Central Treaty Organisation |

| | |
|---|---|
| CEPA | closer economic partnership agreement |
| CEPT | Common Effective Preferential Tariff |
| CCP | Chinese Communist Party |
| CIS | Commonwealth of Independent States |
| CLMV | Cambodia, Laos, Myanmar and Vietnam |
| CMC | Common Market Council |
| CMG | Common Market Group |
| COE | Committee of Experts |
| COHA | Council on Hemispheric Affairs |
| COMESA | Common Market for Eastern and Southern Africa |
| COP | Committee of Participants |
| CSCD | Committee on Studies for Cooperation in Development in South Asia |
| CU | customs union |
| DMZ | demilitarised zone |
| DRC | Democratic Republic of Congo |
| DSM | dispute settlement mechanism |
| EACCU | East African Community Customs Union |
| ECLAC | Economic Commission for Latin America and the Caribbean |
| ECOWAS | Economic Community of West African States |
| EFTA | European Free Trade Association |
| ELN | National Liberation Army |
| EPA | economic partnership agreement |
| ESAP | Economic Structural Adjustment Programme |
| EU | European Union |
| FARC | Colombian Revolutionary Armed Forces |
| FATA | Federally Administered Tribal Areas |
| FDI | foreign direct investment |
| FOCEM | Fund for Structural Convergence of MERCOSUR |
| FLS | front-line states |
| FTA | free trade agreement |
| FTAA | Free Trade Agreement of the Americas |
| GAM | Gerakan Aceh Merdeka (Free Aceh Movement) |
| GATT | General Agreement on Tariffs and Trade |
| GDP | gross domestic product |
| GEL | general exception lists |
| GEMS | Global Environment Measurement System |
| GIO | Government Information Office |
| GMS | Greater Mekong Sub-region |
| GNP | gross national product |
| GPS | global positioning system |
| GQEC | Golden Quadrangle Economic Cooperation |
| IAC | internal armed conflict |
| IADB | Inter-American Defense Board |

| | |
|---|---|
| IAEA | International Atomic Energy Agency |
| ICG | International Crisis Group |
| IDRC | International Development Research Centre |
| IISD | International Institute for Sustainable Development |
| IL | inclusion list |
| IMF | International Monetary Fund |
| IPA | Integrated Programme of Action |
| IPI | India–Pakistan–Iran (gas pipeline) |
| IPKF | Indian Peace-Keeping Force |
| IR | international relations |
| ISI | Inter-Services Intelligence |
| JI | Jemaah Islamiya |
| KMT | Kuomintang |
| KNU | Karen National Union |
| LAC | Latin American and the Caribbean |
| LAFTA | Latin American Free Trade Association |
| LAIA | Latin American Integration Association |
| LDC | least developed country |
| LMA | Lloyd's Market Association |
| LOC | line of control |
| LTTE | Liberation Tigers of Tamil Eelam |
| MAC | Mainland Affairs Council |
| MDC | Movement for Democratic Change |
| MERCOSUR | Southern Common Market |
| MFN | most favoured nation |
| MILF | Moro Islamic Liberation Front |
| MNR | Movimento Nacionalista Revolucionario (Nationalist Revolutionary Party) |
| MOMEP | military observer mission to Ecuador–Peru |
| MQM | Muttahida Qaumi Movement |
| MTL | Mini-three-links |
| NAFTA | North American Free Trade Agreement |
| NAM | Non-Aligned Movement |
| NATO | North Atlantic Treaty Organisation |
| NEPAD | New Economic Partnership for Africa's Development |
| NIE | newly industrialised economy |
| NGO | non-governmental organisation |
| NHBP | no haste, be patient |
| NTB | non-tariff barrier |
| NUC | National Unification Council |
| NWFP | North West Frontier Province |
| NWFZ | nuclear weapon free zone |
| NYS | National Youth Service |
| OAS | Organization of American States |

| OECD | Organisation for Economic Cooperation and Development |
| OPSD | Organ for Politics, Security and Defence |
| PLA | People's Liberation Army |
| PLEM | proactive liberalisation with effective management |
| PRC | People's Republic of China |
| PTA | preferential trade agreement |
| RAW | Research and Analysis Wing |
| REC | regional economic community |
| RIDES | Recursos e Investigación para el Desarello Sustenable |
| RISDP | Regional Indicative Strategic Development Programme |
| RISNODEC | Research and Information System for the Non-aligned and Other Developing Countries |
| RISP | Regional Integration on Support Programme |
| RO | rules of origin |
| ROC | Republic of China |
| ROW | rest of world |
| RSS | Rashtriya Swayamsevak Sangh |
| RTA | regional trade agreement |
| SAARC | South Asian Association for Regional Cooperation |
| SACU | Southern African Customs Union |
| SADC | Southern African Development Community |
| SADCC | Southern African Development and Coordinating Conference |
| SAFTA | South Asian Free Trade Agreement |
| SAGQ | South Asia Growth Quadrangle |
| SAIIA | South African Institute of International Affairs |
| SAPTA | South Asian Preferential Trade Agreement |
| SARC | South Asian Regional Cooperation |
| SARS | severe acute respiratory syndrome |
| SDPI | Sustainable Development Policy Institute |
| SEATO | South East Asia Treaty Organisation |
| SEF | Strait Exchange Foundation |
| SEOM | senior economic officials meeting |
| SIIA | Singapore Institute of International Affairs |
| SIPO | Strategic Indicative Plan for the OPSD |
| SMC | SAFTA Ministerial Council |
| SME | small and medium enterprise |
| SMIC | Semiconductor Manufacturing International Corporation |
| TAC | Treaty of Amity and Cooperation |
| TEL | temporary exclusion lists |
| TSM | Taiwan Semiconductor Manufacturing |
| UANC | United African National Congress |
| UEMOA | Union Economique et Monetaire Ouest Africaine |

| | |
|---|---|
| UMC | United Microelectronics Corporation |
| UN | United Nations |
| UNCTAD | United Nations Conference on Trade and Development |
| UNSC | United Nations Security Council |
| USAID | United States Agency for International Development |
| USNCI | United States Nation Council on Intelligence |
| VHP | Vishva Hindu Parishad |
| WHO | World Health Organization |
| WTO | World Trade Organization |
| ZANLA | Zimbabwe African National Liberation Army |
| ZANU | Zimbabwe African National Union |
| ZANU-PF | Zimbabwe African National Union-Patriotic Front |
| ZAPU | Zimbabwe African People's Union |
| ZAPU-PF | Zimbabwe African People's Union-Patriotic Front |
| ZCIA | Zimbabwe Chamber of Informal Economy Association |
| ZCTU | Zimbabwe Congress of Trade Unions |
| ZIPRA | Zimbabwe People's Revolutionary Army |
| ZOPFAN | Zone of Peace, Freedom and Neutrality |

# 1 Introduction

*Oli Brown, Shaheen Rafi Khan and*
*Faisal Haq Shaheen*

## Regional trade agreements: building peace or promoting conflict?

Over the last 15 years regional trade agreements (RTAs) have become defining features of the modern economy and a powerful force for globalisation. As of July 2007 more than 380 RTAs had been notified to the World Trade Organization (WTO) of which nearly 205 were active (see Table 1.1 for a list of selected RTAs).[1] All but one WTO member, Mongolia, are engaged in an RTA of one sort or another (Crawford and Fiorentino 2005: 1).

The example of the European Union (EU) as an economically successful trade agreement and peaceful political arrangement has much to offer the world. While the EU is the product of a unique political and economic landscape, other RTAs also have the potential to build peace and prosperity.

However, RTAs can also be divisive and exclusive, and their terms can embed regional tensions and power imbalances. Particularly when negotiated between countries of differing economic power, trade agreements can exert powerful leverage on the political stability of the economically weaker partner. Poorly designed and implemented RTAs can lead to heightened tensions between countries and increase the risk of inter-state conflict. At the same time, the political and economic adjustment costs involved in pursuing regional trade integration can undermine local livelihoods and create winners and losers, spurring competition between groups and leading to intra-state conflict.[2]

The repeated frustrations of multilateral trade negotiations have resulted in renewed energy being directed towards regional trade integration as a more flexible way of liberalising trade and pursuing other strategic goals. In the 13 months between January 2004 and February 2005, 43 RTAs were notified to the WTO. In the words of Jo-Ann Crawford and Roberto Fiorentino of the WTO, 'this [is] the most prolific RTA period in history'.[3] For some WTO members preferential trade now represents over 90 per cent of their total trade. While some agreements count as few as three member nations, the majority have ten or more signatories.

*Table 1.1* Acronyms for selected prominent RTAs

| Acronym | Stands for | Acronym | Stands for |
| --- | --- | --- | --- |
| **AFTA** | ASEAN Free Trade Areas | **EFTA** | European Free Trade Association |
| **ASEAN** | Association of South East Asian Nations | **GCC** | Gulf Cooperation Council |
| **CACM** | Central American Common Market | **LAIA** | Latin American Integration Association |
| **CAN** | Andean Community | | |
| **CARICOM** | Caribbean Community and Common Market | **MERCOSUR** | Southern Common Market |
| **CEFTA** | Central European Free Trade Agreement | **MSG** | Melanesian Spearhead Group |
| **CEMAC** | Economic and Monetary Community of Central Africa | **NAFTA** | North American Free Trade Agreement |
| **CIS** | Commonwealth of Independent States | **SADC** | Southern African Development Community |
| **COMESA** | Common Market for Eastern and Southern Africa | **SAPTA** | South Asia Preferential Trade Agreement |
| **EAC** | East African Community | **SPARTECA** | South Pacific Regional Trade and Economic Cooperation Agreement |
| **EAEC** | Eurasian Economic Community | **UEMOA (WAEMU)** | L'Union Economique et Monetaire Ouest Africaine (West African Economic and Monetary Union) |
| **ECO** | Economic Cooperation Organization | | |

Source: IISD–SDPI in-house, 2007.

Crawford and Fiorentino's 2005 study argues that there are four main emerging trends in regional trade integration:[4]

1   Countries are increasingly making RTAs a central objective of their trade policy, which may take priority over multilateral trade objectives.
2   RTAs are becoming more complex, in many cases establishing regulatory regimes that go beyond multilaterally agreed trade regulations.
3   The emergence of trade agreements between key developing countries may be evidence of strengthened 'south–south' trading patterns.
4   RTAs are generally expanding and consolidating. On the one hand there are a growing number of cross-regional RTAs, which account for a large proportion of the total increase in RTAs. On the other hand, regional trading blocks that span continents are in the making.

The debate on RTAs has tended to revolve around the somewhat narrow topic of what the trend means for multilateral trade liberalisation; whether RTAs are a 'stumbling block' or a 'stepping stone' to multilateralism.

However, as the EU shows, trade agreements can presage deep and profound economic, social and political changes. Aid donors and the international community have been particularly keen to promote regional integration in the developing world as a stepping stone towards greater interdependence, trade liberalisation and stability. Yet, while the process promises much in terms of greater interdependence and stronger relationships between countries, it also presents very real dangers.

In attempting to introduce the relationship between RTAs and violent conflict we chart the development of RTAs around the world, and question the extent to which the trend is an endogenously or exogenously driven process. We investigate some of the non-trade concerns that are being bundled into modern RTAs – particularly those that attempt to use trade agreements as a vehicle for good governance and interdependence as mechanisms to encourage peace. Finally, we attempt to assess the positive and negative impacts of RTAs on peace and security around the world.

---

**Acronym soup: a word on terminology**

There are a number of different types of trade agreement and a variety of ways to describe them. As these phrases are often interchangeable and confusing it is worth briefly noting what we understand by them in this chapter.

- A free trade agreement (FTA) is where each party to the agreement reduces tariffs and other non-tariff barriers to trade but maintains its own trade policy vis-à-vis third parties.
- A preferential trade agreement (PTA) is the same thing but the term highlights the point that the lowered trade barriers between partners are preferential to those offered to third parties.
- A customs union (CU) is more politically ambitious requiring as it does a common external tariff and the harmonisation of external trade policies.
- Regional Trade Agreements (RTAs) simply refer to any of the three above when concluded within a regional group.

---

## Understanding the growth of RTAs

RTAs are signed for a number of reasons. Increasing trade flows may be part of the story, but there are often other geostrategic and political motives at play. The socio-economic and political 'drivers' of regional trade integration can be divided into 'internal factors' (drivers that originate from within a particular region) and 'external factors' (drivers that come from outside a region or nation).

### Internal factors

*New markets and trade opportunities*: Typically, by expanding access to regional markets, RTA agreements promise increased and low cost intra-regional trade. They can also help promote foreign direct investment (FDI), improve economic growth, improve a country's balance of payments position and bring new skills and technology. MERCOSUR, the RTA concluded between the countries of southern Latin America, is credited, for example, with significantly increasing regional trade flows in the decade during 1990–2000. Exports between MERCOSUR members rose from US$4.1 billion to US$17.6 billion while imports grew from US$4.2 billion to US$17.9 billion. During 1995–2000, exports of every MERCOSUR state to other members showed an upward trend.

*Geostrategic and political interests*: While economic interests may be the principal engines driving the growth of RTAs, such agreements are also increasingly being guided by political, strategic and security concerns. The fact that the negotiation and commitments of RTAs tends to be less transparent than multilateral trade negotiations makes such an approach easier. There are several examples of south–south RTAs that reflect a combination of economic and security goals. The Association of South East Asian Nations (ASEAN), for example, was initially created as a response to the perceived spread of communism in the region in the 1960s.

*Growing frustration with multilateral trade negotiations*: There is mounting scepticism in the ability of negotiations under the framework the WTO to deliver sufficient progress towards trade liberalisation. The perception is that negotiating trade agreements within smaller blocs is both more flexible and quicker than attempting to bring the 152 members of the WTO to consensus. In addition, RTAs can be more specific to the needs of a particular region than the 'lowest common denominator' solution often offered at WTO negotiations.

*Counterbalancing the negotiating power of other blocs*: Regional blocs are a powerful tool to negotiate common interests both within and outside the WTO. Increasingly, many developing countries are realising that their interests may best be served by integration with like-minded countries that have similar economies. In the case of the Latin American countries, regional integration has been used to counterbalance the negotiating power of the US while it sought to expand the North America Free Trade Agreement (NAFTA) to the Free Trade Agreement of the Americas (FTAA). The formation of trading communities such as ASEAN, MERCOSUR and the Andean Community (CAN) are clear examples of bloc building efforts to bolster a particular region's resilience against other regional and global trading blocs.

*Building on socio-cultural similarities*: Sharing a common language and culture can encourage closer integration. While differing in terms of development and prone to intra-regional conflicts, the Commonwealth of Independent States (CIS), which emerged from the collapse of the Soviet Union, was brought together, at least in part, by socio-cultural similarities.[5]

*Reducing illegal trade and smuggling*: RTAs can establish the institutions for shared information and action to reduce illegal trade in drugs and weapons. Meanwhile, common tariffs for trade between members help to undermine the economic incentive for smuggling. MERCOSUR, made up of Argentina, Brazil, Paraguay and Uruguay, was created with the explicit goal of providing a platform for member states to discuss common security issues such as drug trafficking.

### External factors

*'Exporting' the model of regional integration*: EU delegations are actively encouraged to help 'export' the EU's model of regional integration. This is backed up by EU funds to support regional organisations such as the African Union and the Pacific Forum with the specific expectation of contributing to the prevention, management and resolution of violent conflicts (Council of the European Union 2004: 3). The same is true of the US. According to Edward Mansfield of the University of Pennsylvania, both the Clinton and Bush administrations have made spreading regional economic agreements a foreign policy priority (Mansfield 2003: 14). In July 2005, for example, Louis Michel, the EU Commissioner for Development and Humanitarian Aid, signed an agreement to provide €30 million to the Common Market for Eastern and Southern African (COMESA) as part of the EU's five-year €223 million Regional Integration Support Programme (RISP).[6]

*Pursuing strategic bilateralism*: In the case of India and Pakistan, the fear that this region could continue to be unstable has motivated regional and global players such as ASEAN and the US to try to encourage a more stable (trading) relationship between the two countries.

## RTAs and peace building – the visionary ideal

The links between international trade and security have been recognised for centuries. As the French philosopher the Baron of Montesquieu said in 1748, '[peace is a] natural effect of commerce' (Humphreys 2004: 8). The Italian economist Vilfredo Pareto argued in 1889 that CUs could help to achieve peace between countries.

At the most basic level, equitable trade promotes prosperity and reduces poverty. But beyond that, free trade has also been seen as a vehicle to promote internationalism and end war. 'For the disbanding of great armies and the promotion of peace' wrote John Bright, one of the leaders of the Anti-Corn

Law League in 1840s Britain, 'I rely on the abolition of tariffs, on the brotherhood of the nations resulting from free trade in the products of industry' (Sturgis 1969).

Recent empirical studies also seem to confirm the adage that countries that trade with each other (on equitable terms) are less likely to fight each other (Humphreys 2004: 8; Mansfield 2003: 222). Trade can be a powerful driver of growth, reducing poverty and creating jobs. In theory at least, there are a number of ways that regional trade integration can support peace:

1   Given the relatively small size of many economies in the developing world, and their dependency on a handful of primary commodities, regional trade integration offers poorer countries mutual development gains through pooled resources, expanded markets, increased regional trade and investment, and greater economic diversification.
2   Economic integration makes conflicts more costly for individual states. Attacking a neighbouring economy becomes just as damaging as attacking one's own.
3   Through interdependence, nations can use trade to access one another's resources, instead of using violence to capture them.
4   Regional groupings such as MERCOSUR and the South Asian Association for Regional Cooperation (SAARC) can serve as aspirational clubs and can play a stabilising role for countries on their borders.
5   RTAs provide non-military ways to resolve disputes and promote understanding and dialogue between countries. Many agreements have instituted dispute settlement mechanisms to mediate economic conflicts that have also been used for managing political conflicts.

In practice several economic and trading arrangements have been established with the explicit purpose of preventing conflict between or within states. For instance:

•   Concerns about the threat of the spread of fundamentalism motivated the governments of Egypt, Morocco and Tunisia to negotiate regional agreements with the EU.
•   MERCOSUR was originally established to reduce tensions between Argentina and Brazil. It also helped to avert a possible coup in Paraguay following reaffirmation by the presidents of the MERCOSUR member countries that democracy was a necessary condition for membership.[7]
•   The Stability Pact for South-Eastern Europe was created in 2000 to create a free trade area designed to promote economic recovery and integration in the war-devastated Balkan region.[8]
•   In December 2004 Israel and Egypt signed a trade protocol with the US designed to accelerate the two countries' rapprochement. The deal creates five special zones where Egyptian goods will have free access to US

markets, as long as 35 per cent of the goods are the product of Israeli–Egyptian cooperation.[9]

## RTAs and good governance

Moreover RTAs can play a role in promoting elements of good governance such as budget transparency, careful fiscal management and an independent judiciary. A notable trend in north–south trade agreements is the increasing inclusion of non-trade commitments as part of the agreement. The 2000 Cotonou agreement between the EU and countries of the African-Caribbean-Pacific region is a case in point. It lists three so-called 'essential elements': respect for human rights, democracy and the rule of law. If contravened, these conditions can lead to suspension of cooperation – including the cancellation of preferential access.[10]

Similar conditions are being currently attached to the trade agreements that are to succeed the Cotonou agreement. Known as economic partnership agreements (EPAs), the EU is negotiating these trade agreements with blocs of African, Caribbean and Pacific countries. Former EU Trade Commissioner Pascal Lamy argued that trade agreements should contain even more extensive conditionality. He suggested that the agreements should allow the EU to ban any imports that do not meet the EU's 'collective preferences'. The term is deliberately broad and vague but would likely enable trade sanctions in cases of human rights abuse, poor governance or rigged elections.

In short, rich countries are using trade agreements as an inducement for largely unrelated governance concerns. That this is possible at all is indicative of their negotiating power. South–south RTAs have not gone as far down this path, perhaps because negotiations tend to be less one-sided and are focused on extracting trade concessions rather than other commitments.

Nevertheless several south–south RTAs do include such provisions. The trend seems to be catching on. Table 1.2 lays out the governance and security commitments in six current south–south RTAs. The majority of RTAs establish some degree of dispute resolution between signatories. The Economic Community of West African States (ECOWAS) and the Southern African Development Community (SADC) go further; signatory countries agreed to cooperate on specific security concerns and establish ways of mitigating conflict between members. The agreements also contained weak provisions on respect for democracy, human rights and the rule of law. The links between good governance and peace are well established. If south–south RTAs can encourage 'good governance' this could add a new dimension to their role in building peace between and within countries.

*Table 1.2* Good governance conditionality in south–south RTAs

| Agreements | NON-TRADE CONCERNS | | | | | | | | | | | | | | Dispute settlement | | | Others |
|---|---|---|---|---|---|---|---|---|---|---|---|---|---|---|---|---|---|---|
| | Security clauses | | Conflict mitigation resolution within member states | Coordination of stance on international issues | Civil society involvement | Social/ cultural aspects | Transparency | Democracy | Governance | Respect for rule of law | Human rights | Gender issues | Property rights | Anti- corruption | Consultation | Arbitration | Decision by established body | |
| | General security exception | Cooperation on specific security concern | | | | | | | | | | | | | | | | |
| **NORTH–SOUTH AGREEMENTS (MODEL AGREEMENTS)** | | | | | | | | | | | | | | | | | | |
| Association Agreement between EU and Chile | ○ | ● | × | ○ | ● | ● | ● | ● | × | ○ | ● | ○ | × | × | ● | ● | × | × |
| COTONOU Agreement | × | ● | ● | ● | ○ | ● | ○ | ● | ● | ● | ● | ○ | ○ | ○ | ○ | ● | ● | × |
| **SOUTH–SOUTH AGREEMENTS (BY REGION)** | | | | | | | | | | | | | | | | | | |
| *North and South America* | | | | | | | | | | | | | | | | | | |
| Caribbean Community and Common Market (CARICOM) | ○ | × | × | ○ | × | ○ | × | × | × | × | × | × | ● | × | ● | ● | × | ● |
| Common Market between Argentina, Brazil, Paraguay and Uruguay (MERCOSUR) | × | × | × | × | × | × | × | × | × | × | × | × | × | × | ● | × | ● | × |
| *Africa* | | | | | | | | | | | | | | | | | | |
| Economic Community of West African States (ECOWAS) | × | ● | ● | × | × | ● | × | ○ | × | ○ | ○ | ○ | × | × | ● | ● | ● | × |
| Southern African Development Community (SADC) | ○ | × | ● | × | ● | ○ | × | ○ | × | ○ | ○ | × | × | × | × | ○ | × | × |
| *Asia* | | | | | | | | | | | | | | | | | | |
| South Asia Free Trade Agreement (SAFTA) | × | × | × | × | × | × | × | × | × | × | × | × | × | × | ● | × | ● | × |
| SAARC Preferential Trading Arrangement (SAPTA) | × | × | × | × | × | × | × | × | × | × | × | × | × | × | ● | × | ● | × |

● Mentioned in sufficient detail to be implemented under the agreement
○ Mentioned in agreement but with minor detail; no implementation procedure provided
× Not mentioned in agreement
Source: SDPI in-house compilation, 2006.

## RTAs and conflict – the occasional reality

Regional trade integration is progressing fast, propelled by a growing number of regional trade agreements and the encouragement of many Organisation for Economic Cooperation and Development (OECD) countries. For example, in December 2004, the members of MERCOSUR and the CAN signed an agreement for closer economic and political integration, to be called the Union of South American Nations, with an explicit nod to the trail blazing role of the EU.[11]

But there is no compelling reason why south–south RTAs should follow the same trajectory as the EU. The first thing to note is that an RTA may not be much of a 'brake' on conflict. Even when war is costly and the option of a negotiated bargain exists, rival states can nevertheless go to war, propelled by incentives to misrepresent or keep information private, commitment problems after a settlement, or indivisibility of issues. Certainly, there are many examples of conflict between members of RTAs:

- border clashes between Armenia and Azerbaijan, members of the CIS;
- the outbreak of war in the Great Lakes with foreign involvement in the Democratic Republic of Congo (DRC) from Angola, Namibia, Rwanda, Uganda and Zimbabwe, all members of COMESA; and
- the Iraqi invasion of Kuwait and violent border clashes between Egypt and Sudan, all members of the Council of Arab Economic Unity.

The EU's genesis was a unique set of circumstances: the devastation of the EU's productive capacity after the Second World War and the determination of its political leaders to banish any future prospect of war. Other regions may not be willing, or able, to pursue certain aspects of integration, such as opening labour markets and allowing the free movement of people across borders.

Most important, and in contrast to many other regional agreements, the EU and its predecessors have provided a means of redistributing income from rich to poor countries. This has proved to be an effective compensation mechanism for the losers from trade liberalisation: facilitating economic integration, promoting partnership between countries and preventing the marginalisation of certain groups and countries. Following the fall of the Iron Curtain, the EU concluded bilateral trade agreements with the Eastern European countries that helped stabilise them and prepared them for eventual inclusion as new member states.

So, while many liberal economists claim that RTAs build stability and encourage peace, there is also a convincing case for the reverse: that RTAs may even increase the chances for instability and conflict both between and within countries.

## Instability and conflict between countries

There is no rule that says regional integration is an automatic force for mitigating tensions or conflict. Without careful negotiation and implementation, regional integration between countries of widely differing size, wealth and influence can cement inequalities, create tensions and trigger conflict. This is perhaps particularly likely if there is a lack of transparency and accountability in the negotiation of the agreement and its subsequent implementation.

Nor does membership of a trade institution automatically create bonds of trust. Envy can result from trade imbalances and result in the creation of social networks of memberships, resulting in social unrest. Trade ties can actually provoke hostilities between states. Gains are rarely felt proportionally and large inequalities in the relative distribution of gains can shift the balance of inter-state power. There may also be tensions between members of the RTA and non-members who may find that trade diversion within the RTA results in lost markets. In a sense trade 'gives people something to fight about'.

Neither are trade institutions necessarily the best mechanism to mediate disputes – especially if those disputes have wider social and political dimensions. In conflict prone areas, international institutions built around trade agreements can have adverse effects on conflicts among member states by mismanaging crisis situations and worsening conflict intensity, or producing rivalry among states due to their relative social positions (Hafner-Burton and Montgomery 2005).

During the 1980s and 1990s the EU encouraged rapid regional integration and structural adjustment policies on Francophone West Africa, urging the free movement of goods but not people and without providing for a redistributive wealth mechanism that would have helped surmount the adjustment costs of trade liberalisation and integration. Some analysts argue that this uncompromising process, which drove up unemployment and undermined government social programmes, can explain much of the subsequent instability in Francophone West Africa.[12]

Finally, there is also a concern, though one without much empirical investigation, that trade integration may help to facilitate the illegal trade in conflict resources such as blood diamonds and illegal timber. It may also increase access to weapons. After all trade agreements are about reducing barriers to trade: the increased trade that can result can be both legal and illegal.

## Instability and conflict within countries

RTAs typically involve concessions to greater liberalisation. Trade liberalisation can result in painful adjustment to new tariff barriers, new regulation and the influx of fierce new competition. Over the short term trade liberalisation can lead to industrial contraction, unemployment and social unrest. If new market opportunities fail to materialise, this can set a trend of increased poverty and economic instability over the long term.

In addition, trade liberalisation creates winners and losers. The resulting increased wealth disparities can create tensions and lead to conflict. A reduced tax base as well as reduced receipts from duties on exports and imports can severely strain government revenues and undermine health and education spending. The costs of integration itself can be a further burden. In the case of the former East African Community the establishment and cost of suitable organisations to oversee trade integration proved to be contentious both within and between countries (Wu 2005: 476).

In general, economic integration can be socially destabilising and promote processes of change that erode established identities, undermine established ways of conducting national politics and reduce state capacities to provide for poor and marginalised segments of the population. Such socio-cultural challenges of integration are one element in the Zapatista rebellion in Chiapas.

RTAs can help to reinforce both the perception and reality of trade domin-ance by an external power. Public perceptions of trade dominance can be a powerful force. Examples of such sentiment can be seen in the anti-globalisation riots of Seattle and Genoa or in the way US headquartered franchises based in developing nations are treated during times of protest against US foreign policy. In extreme circumstances, such strong domestic opinion can undermine peaceful relations between countries.

Finally, RTAs can generate high expectations of increased economic growth, new job opportunities and reduced poverty. However, RTAs between countries that are reliant on the export of primary resources and that have relatively undiversified economies can fail to live up to their proponents' rhetoric.

Countries tend to exclude key goods from liberalisation agreements. When those countries trade in a similar, and narrow, basket of goods the net economic impact of the RTA can be limited. For example, West Africa's reliance on cocoa and palm oil leaves little else to trade between countries. Consequently, mismanaged expectations coupled with the adjustment costs of joining an RTA can lead to the perception that governments have let their citizens down.

## Dissecting the rush to regionalism

The rise of the RTA is an important feature of the global economy, which is altering the political chemistry of entire continents. RTAs are increasing both in number and in ambition. We are now seeing a complex, overlapping web of trade agreements stretching across the world.

The received wisdom is that regional trade integration can be a powerful force for peace. Building interdependence between countries, creating eco-nomic incentives for peace and developing non-military means for resolving disputes are all goals of the proponents of trade integration. Using trade as the cement, RTAs help to bind countries' interests to a common future.

However, in the light of recent experience, this assumption requires scrutiny. The many conflicts between member countries of RTAs imply that regional trade integration is not an automatic brake on conflict. That said isolationism is also a risky strategy. A study by the US State Failure task force found that the likelihood of state failure is affected by international influences, particularly the openness to international trade and membership of international organisations. Those countries outside regional integration processes, or with no obvious regional 'club' to join, such as Myanmar, Afghanistan or Turkmenistan, are arguably more likely to suffer state failure and further isolation.[13]

This book is the result of an 18-month multi-regional study that investigated the promise of regional trade integration for conflict prevention. Research institutions in Chile, South Africa, Pakistan and Singapore investigated the institutional, political and economic implications of south–south RTAs and trade integration in each of their regions. The following questions directed their analysis:

1    What is the significance of the recent and rapid development of RTAs for violent conflict and peace building both within and between states?
2    How can RTAs be negotiated in a way that reduces inter- and intra-state tensions and helps construct institutional barriers to violent conflict?
3    What range of non-trade provisions (such as on the rule of law, respect for human rights) are being included in southern RTAs? And how effective are these provisions at improving domestic governance and reducing the risk of future conflict?
4    What are the threats and opportunities when building trade links and formalised trading relationships between countries previously at war or risk of war?

The book is divided into two sections. The first section takes a regional focus and looks at the institutional dimensions of trade integration, asking what it means for regional conflict prevention.

The second section focuses on country case studies in each of the regions. These case studies analyse in more detail the role of trade in conflict prevention and confidence building between countries with a history of tension and conflict: China and Taiwan; Peru and Ecuador; Pakistan and India; Zimbabwe and its neighbours.

The concluding chapter attempts to weave together the key messages from the regional analysis and country case studies. It addresses two fundamental questions: Is trade a cause or effect of peace? And how can the international community best contribute to the process of developing peaceful trading links between countries emerging from or at risk of violent conflict?

## Notes

1 http://www.wto.org/english/tratop_e/region_e/region_e.htm (accessed 3 June 2008).
2 Violent conflict is understood in this context as encompassing both violent conflict and destabilising but non-violent disputes between and within states.
3 See Crawford and Fiorentino (2005).
4 Ibid.
5 The CIS was created in 1991 and closer economic union was signed in 1993. At present the CIS consists of Azerbaijan, Armenia, Belarus, Georgia, Kazakhstan, Kyrgyzstan, Moldova, Tajikistan, Turkmenistan, Uzbekistan and Ukraine. See http://www.cisstat.com/eng/cis.htm (accessed 21st September 2005).
6 Europa press release, 20 July 2005 (accessed 19th September 2005). The RISP ran between 2002 and 2007. See http://europa.eu.int/rapid/pressReleasesAction.do?reference=IP/05/991&format=HTML&aged=0&language=EN&guiLanguage=en (accessed 11 June 2008).
7 See http://www.state.gov/r/pa/ei/bgn/1841.htm (accessed 11 June 2008).
8 Council on Hemispheric Affairs, press release 'Argentina–Brazil relations: urgent challenges come to the forefront', 12 July 2005, http://www.coha.org (accessed 20 September 2005).
9 BBC 'Egypt and Israel seal trade deal', http://news.bbc.co.uk/1/hi/business/4095011.stm (accessed 11 June 2008).
10 ECDPM (2001).
11 Euractiv 'First steps taken towards a south American EU', 8 December 2004, http://www.euractiv.com/Article?tcmuri=tcm:29-133262-16&type=News (accessed 11 June 2008).
12 Interview by author in Brown (2005: 13).
13 Goldstein *et al.* 'State failure task force: phase III findings', 2000. See http://www.cidcm.umd.edu/publications/papers/SFTF%20Phase%20III%20Report%20Final.pdf (accessed 11 June 2008).

## References

Brown, O. (2005) 'EU Trade Policy and Conflict', Geneva: International Institute of Sustainable Development (IISD).

Council of the European Union (2004) 'Council common position concerning conflict prevention, management and resolution in Africa', SN 1010/04. Brussels: Council of Europe.

Crawford, J. and Fiorentino, R. (2005) 'The changing landscape of regional trade agreements', *Discussion Paper 8*, Geneva: WTO.

ECDPM (European Centre for Development Policy Management) (2001) *Cotonou Infokit: Essential and fundamental Elements* (20), Maastricht: ECDPM.

Hafner-Burton, E. and Montgomery, A. (2005) 'War, trade and envy: why trade agreements don't always keep the peace', presented at the International Studies Association Annual Conference, Honolulu, Hawaii.

Humphreys, M. (2004) 'Economics and violent conflict', in D. Brack (ed.) *Trade, Aid and Security: Introduction, Background and Conceptual Framework*, Cambridge, MA: Harvard University, IISD/IUCN.

Mansfield, E.D. (2003) 'Preferential peace: why preferential trading arrangements inhibit interstate conflict', in E.D. Mansfield and B.M. Pollins (eds) *Economic Interdependence and International Conflict: New Perspectives on an Enduring*

*Debate*, Ann Arbor: Michigan Studies in International Political Economy, University of Michigan pp. 222–236.

Sturgis, J.L. (1969) *John Bright and the Empire*, London: University of London.

Wu, J. (2005) 'Trade agreements as self protection', *Review of International Economics*, 13:3, 472–484, Oxford: Blackwell Publishing.

# 2 Regional integration, trade and conflicts in Latin America

*Alejandra Ruiz-Dana, Peter Goldschagg, Edmundo Claro and Hernán Blanco*

## Introduction

Free trade often has conflict connotations. These connotations stem from different takes on the subject. Different media, particularly newspapers, refer constantly to the positive and negative ramifications of trade; they also tend to polarise public opinion on the subject. In fact, free trade is part of an intricate web of complexities that can yield more than the two sides of the proverbial coin. In other words, the outcome is never black and white. Hence studies, such as this one, which attempt to identify potential links between trade and conflict, as well as the incidence of conflict resolution in the context of increased interdependence, are important.

### Views on conflicts and prevention

Conflicts often stem from disagreements between two or more parties. These disagreements arise out of perceived threats to a party's interests. In the context of diplomatic relations, the tension brought forth by disagreements can give way to international armed conflict, involving two or more states. We refer to these tensions as externally driven confrontations.

Internal armed conflict (henceforth referred to as IAC), is defined by the Geneva Convention as occurring in the territory of one of the parties. To qualify as an IAC, a conflict must take place 'between a [High Contracting Party's] armed forces and dissident armed forces or other armed groups which, under responsible command, exercise such control over a part of its territory as to enable them to carry out sustained and concerted military operations'.[1] On the other hand, internal disturbance and tensions, such as riots, isolated and sporadic acts of violence and other acts of a similar nature, are not considered IACs.[2]

The term 'internationalised armed conflict' describes internal hostilities that are rendered international. More specifically, the term includes 'war between two internal factions, both of which are backed by different states; direct hostilities between two foreign states that militarily intervene in armed conflict in support of opposing sides; and war involving foreign intervention in support of an insurgent group fighting against an established government' (Stewart 2003: 315). While distinguishing this type of conflict from an IAC makes analytical sense, in practice, IACs are seldom free from foreign involvement, although such involvement is not always immediately obvious (Stewart 2003: 316).

Confidence building measures (CBMs) constitute measures taken to reduce military tensions between a set and sets of states, before, during or after actual conflict. The European experience indicates that efficient CBMs draw upon two elements: (1) 'stability and predictability in the region' and; (2) 'the existence of a shared political culture amongst the states in question' (Bromley and Perdomo 2005: 6). The first element is rarely found in Latin America (see Figure 2.1); despite a shared political culture, distrust and animosity characterise relations between neigbouring countries, such as Peru and Ecuador, Chile and Bolivia, Argentina and Brazil. Most CBMs in Latin American are reached at presidential reunions that imply personal commitments understood as 'governmental policies', instead of 'state policies' (Bromley and Perdomo 2005). Presidential voluntarism does not translate into an ability to fulfill commitments – much less where good governance is relatively, if not wholly, absent.

In the virtual absence of successful CBMs in Latin America, some exceptions are worth mentioning. The Tlatelolco Treaty of Non-Proliferation (1967) was sustained by the fear and concern that arose in the aftermath of the Cuban Missile Crisis; it made the threat of nuclear war real. The treaty was ratified by 11 states at the time of its inception, in 1969. Argentina and Brazil chose not to be parties to the treaty since their mutual animosity had embroiled them in an arms race. However, the treaty did pave the way for a future CBM between the two countries. The Joint Declaration of Nuclear Policy, signed in December 1986, opened communication channels for consultation and the exchange of information on nuclear matters. The precedent led to the eventual creation of the Brazilian–Argentine Agency for Accounting and Control of Nuclear Materials (ABACC).[3]

Future CBMs will need to take into account a wide range of threats to security. The Organization of American States (OAS) took a step in the right direction by adopting the Declaration on Security in the Americas in October 2003. The declaration states that different perspectives regarding security threats and priorities are to be recognised. Its scope includes a wide array of non-traditional threats to security, including transnational organised crime, corruption, asset laundering, illicit trafficking in weapons, extreme poverty and social exclusion, HIV/AIDS and other diseases and environmental degradation. Trade also falls in the genre of 'non-traditional' threats to security. Therefore regional trade agreements (RTAs) and regional integration initiatives constitute legitimate CBMs. In the following sections, we will explore the extent to which selected RTAs have contributed to trade promotion and conflict mitigation.

*Figure 2.1* Map of South America.

### *Why have MERCOSUR and the Andean Community (CAN) been selected?*

This chapter focuses on MERCOSUR (Southern Common Market) and the CAN. Both represent the most important regional integration agreements in Latin America. The agreements include countries with a long-standing history of bilateral conflicts that have come together voluntarily under an institutional arrangement that seeks to foster political and economic interdependence.

The MERCOSUR is the world's fourth largest integrated economic block. Representing 67 per cent of Latin America's land area,[4] 47 per cent of its population and more than half of Latin America's gross domestic product (GDP);[5] it is the most progressive trade integration scheme in the developing world. MERCOSUR's model of 'open regionalism'[6] aims to create a common market in the mid-term future. International relations scholars view the model as a crucial step to overcome the historic agenda of grievances, mutual distrust and diverging interests within the region (notably by linking the Southern Cone's rival regional powers, Brazil and Argentina). They compare it to the European Union (EU) – the most important example of peace and regional political stability through economic integration (O'Keefe 2005).

The CAN, endowed with supra-national organs, embodies institutional depth. The hemispheric block – with 120 million people and a GDP of US$260 billion in 2002 – is beset with various inter-state and intra-state conflicts. The most prominent example of inter-state conflict is the persistent border dispute between Peru and Ecuador. Examples of intra-state conflicts are the guerrilla conflict in Colombia and the indigenous movement in Bolivia. The analysis of these two regional blocs, with their distinct profiles and contexts, will help us understand the relationship between integration, trade and conflicts in the region.

The second section reviews the general conditions and trends in relation to regional integration, trade, and conflicts in Latin America and the Caribbean. The third section analyses the specific cases of MERCOSUR and the CAN. The fourth section concludes with recommendations.

## Regional trade integration and conflict

In Latin America, trade integration initiatives are more likely to be based on political rather than economic considerations. As Kacowicz puts it: 'In contrast to the common theoretical assumption, the order of causality has been reversed in Latin America: economic interdependence became the consequence, not the cause, of political cooperation and of economic integration' (Kacowicz 1998: 28). The political component in the equation is what determines the outcome. The situation is similar to South Asia in some ways. Khan *et al.* (2007) argue that trade flows are contingent upon political agreements; in fact, the regional integration process (culminating more often than not in an RTA) follows the ebb and flow of regional politics.

Both historical and extant intra-regional trade flows in Latin America have been low. A quick glance at regional trade statistics illustrates this point. In 2004, intra-regional commerce in the MERCOSUR and the CAN constituted 12.9 and 10.4 per cent of total trade respectively (CEPAL 2005: 106). This is in contrast to what the two regions export to other Latin American nations (15.4 and 16.8 per cent), the United States (18.3 and 46.6 per cent), and the EU (23.0 and 11.0 per cent) (Kacowicz 1998). If economic integration were, indeed, the salient motivation for MERCOSUR and the CAN, these numbers would have been reversed.

The level of intra-regional trade is also explained by the expected efficiency gains from trade. These are very low as '[t]rade among similar Latin American economies often heightens competition in primary goods, driving down profits. It does little to increase technology or productivity, since competition among manufacturing firms remains meager' (Aggarwal and Espach 2003: 20–21). This situation also makes bilateral trade agreements between neighbouring Latin American countries a rarity. Chile remains the lone exception. It has opted for bilateral agreements with its neighbours instead of joining their trade blocs. Both political and economic reasons motivate this stance. On the one hand, Chile prefers the flexibility of choosing at will without having to subject itself to supra-national rules. On the other, 'Chile's stable and fast-growing economy and its increasing consumer market give it leverage over its poorer Andean neighbors, while the competitiveness of its exports and international corporations serves it well in the much larger Argentine and Brazilian markets' (Aggarwal and Espach 2003: 27). Such bilateral trade remains low nevertheless. In 2005, only 11.3 per cent of Chile's exports were aimed at South American markets; Central America and the Caribbean received 1.7 and 0.4 per cent, respectively.[7] Chile's predisposition to favour partners outside of the region and its relative success has invited criticism and retaliation by its neighbours. As a case in point, Bolivia refuses to sell natural gas to Chile.

### *Historical background of conflict*

Historically, wars in Latin America have taken place due to foreign intervention (wars of independence) or internal struggles (revolutions). In addition, recurring disputes – often associated with unresolved border issues, erupt sporadically and continue to the present day. The 1995 clash between Peru and Ecuador over a section of the Amazon River basin is an example. Most tensions associated with geopolitical ambitions of certain regimes have cooled down, but others have increased recently. Venezuela's president, Hugo Chávez, is promoting a Boliviarian project whose aim is to accelerate South American integration and, in his own words, draw a 'new geopolitical map ... to counterbalance the global dominance of the United States' (Wagner 2005). Chávez has been stocking up on weapons, buying them from Russia and Spain. Most observers express concern that such stockpiling goes beyond a revamping of Venezuela's military and that these purchases may affect the balance of power in the Andean region.

However, the consensus is that the region 'no longer represents a global threat in terms of security' (Narich 2003: 1). Indeed, Latin America is often held up 'as an example for the rest of the world when one deals with traditional security issues'.[8] There is both an historical and ethno-religious context to the absence of violent conflict. In the first place, the continent enjoys considerable religious and ethnic homogeneity. Simón Bolívar, leader of the independence movements in South America, appealed to the region's common cultural heritage to seek the union of American states in 1826. His call sparked an inter-American cooperation process that eventually led to the creation of the OAS in 1948, a predecessor to the United Nations (UN) (and, according to some, much more effective than the latter).

Prior to the OAS, the Inter-American Defense Board (IADB) was established in 1942 to coordinate security efforts in the region as a collective response to the Second World War. The IADB is the oldest international organisation of its kind in the world and is linked to the OAS through the latter's general secretariat. Other unprecedented diplomatic efforts include the formation of the Tlatelolco Treaty. It set the standard for all nuclear weapon free zone (NWFZ) agreements. Direct conflict mediation has also achieved hallmark status. The Rio Protocol of 1942, for example, put an end to the first war between Peru and Ecuador (*c*.1939–1941).

Although the 1960s and 1970s were particularly turbulent, '[t]he strengthening of democracies and the creation of trade blocks in the 1980s and 1990s in Latin America contributed to an atmosphere of growing trust and cooperation' (Narich 2003: 6). Simultaneously, the military's role diminished dramatically in the Latin America. The end of the Cold War in 1989 marked the end of global bipolarity and the beginning of international and regional approaches to issues of security and economic concern. Latin America ceased to look up to the United States as the command and control centre for regional security matters, mostly because the economic incentives to do so were withdrawn and, as expected, the political justification no longer existed. In the absence of a powerful benefactor, the challenges ahead seemed daunting for the individual Latin American states. Their reaction, prompted by emerging globalisation, was manifested in the shape of integrated responses.

### Current conflict trends

With the exception of the 1995 war between Peru and Ecuador, IACs have been few in Latin America since the 1990s. As mentioned, the uniqueness of the inter-American cooperation system deters an escalation into full-scale war. Topographical and geographical restraints, weak military institutions and socio-economic factors also limit the capacity to engage in open warfare (Saavedra 2005). However, tensions and disputes continue to persist and merit analysis. With this in mind, a distinction is made between traditional and non-traditional disputes.

Traditional disputes are ancient in nature. They comprise border/frontier disputes and other areas of historical tension between states. These disputes 'have a higher probability of [leading states] to war than other kinds of disputes' (Dominguez *et al.* 2003: 14). Non-traditional disputes are due to new or modern threats to security as a result of the weakening of the state and the consequent rise in internal delinquency and violence. Examples include terrorism and drug trafficking. Hence, these disputes are associated with the spillover effects of an internal problem that has been unsuccessfully contained by the afflicted state. The problem, then, becomes internationalised and, consequently, requires an international response.

'Whereas interstate conflict has generally been limited in contemporary Latin American history . . . intra-state violence has always been a great problem' (Narich 2003: 7). Again, ideological and institutional factors are behind this occurrence, which, in turn, also explains the relatively low levels of defence spending in the region. Intra-state violence or turmoil is mostly explained by persistent political and economic instability. The most visible and damaging of these intra-state conflicts is Colombia's civil war. The intensity of the conflict there is such that some spillover effects are already evident in the neighbouring countries (as discussed shortly).

According to a report by the US National Council on Intelligence (USNCI), the main threat to security in the region is posed by the failure of governments to alleviate extreme poverty in spite of 'the greater integration into the global economy in the past decade' (USNCI 2004: 78). Such failure sparks populism and radical indigenous action. Recent estimates indicate that 'violence has increased in Latin America as a result of poverty-induced criminality. In the year 2000, the crime rate in Latin America was twice the world average (22.5 per 1000 versus 10.7 per 1000)' (Narich 2003: 7). Addressing this violence presents a formidable challenge for many Latin American regimes.

### The origin and evolution of RTAs in Latin America

Latin American countries have a long-standing, but erratic history of regional integration. Prior to the Second World War, desultory attempts at regional integration were motivated by the great freedom fighter, Simón Bolívar. The focus later switched to more pragmatic development-oriented economic goals. Inspired by the economist Raúl Prebisch, regional integration initiatives in the 1960s were conducted within the framework of 'import substitution industrialization' (Ocampo 2001). The Latin American Free Trade Association (LAFTA), established in 1960, aimed to overcome the inherent scale limitations of the small domestic markets by allowing industries to become competitive on a regional level. The initial enthusiasm waned when sensitive sectors (automobiles, textiles, agriculture) came up for discussion; eventually, across the board industrial rationalisation was aborted. By 1980, the less ambitious Latin American Integration Association (LAIA, *in Spanish ALADI*), which was largely structured around bilateral trade preferences had replaced LAFTA (Hufbauer and Kotschwar 1998: 12).

Partly due to the limited progress on LAFTA's economic front, six of its original members (Bolivia, Colombia, Ecuador, Peru, Chile and later Venezuela) established a sub-regional trade arrangement – the Andean Pact – in 1969. Although very ambitious politically, it was supported by supranational arrangements and institutionally viable. However, the pact did not achieve much by way of tariff reduction and trade promotion, collapsing shortly after Chile pulled out in 1976. The sub-region then fell into an extended (ten-year long) recession. Subsequent sub-regional arrangements also did not fare much better. The Central American Common Market (CACM) proved to be a paper arrangement, neutralised by political and military conflicts in the 1980s. The Caribbean Common Market (CARICOM) never came close to being a common market due to its member states' reluctance to reduce trade barriers. The oil price hike in 1973, followed by the debt crisis and the global economic downturn, induced a deep recession and a severe contraction of intra-regional trade.

The move towards a new wave of regionalism took place in the early 1990s. The inward-looking policies had been largely discredited throughout the 1980s, to be replaced by the neo-liberal 'Washington Consensus'. This was a major paradigm shift that promoted 'open regionalism' as the most viable option for developing states to integrate effectively within a global economy marked by increasing interdependence, liberalisation and competition for investments. A former exponent of the import substitution strategy, the Economic Commission for Latin America and the Caribbean (ECLAC) now became the foremost proponent of the new regionalism. A spate of market-oriented reforms followed in the shape of privatisation, deregulation and budget consolidation. These reforms profoundly reshaped the political-economic landscape of Latin America.

Except Cuba, all Latin American countries are now part of some regional bloc, ranging from bilateral and plurilateral free trade areas to customs unions (CUs) with ambitions of becoming a common market. Key among these initiatives are the CACM, CARICOM (revived), and the Andean Pact (now known as the CAN), as well as an increasing number of other free trade agreements: Chile–Mexico (1991); Colombia–Venezuela (1992); Mexico, Costa Rica, El Salvador, Guatemala, Honduras and Nicaragua (1992); the Group of Three – Colombia, Mexico and Venezuela (1993); and Chile–Venezuela (1993). Figure 2.2 shows the tangle of relationships resulting from multiple and overlapping preferential trading arrangements, referred to as a 'spaghetti bowl'.

By far the most important arrangement in the 'open regionalism' context is the MERCOSUR. MERCOSUR is embedded within a new policy frame-work; prior to joining, the signing members (Brazil, Argentina, Paraguay and Uruguay) were all democracies, with market-based economies. The arrangement has worked well. Politically, it has diffused tensions between Argentina and Brazil. Economically, it has stimulated intra-regional trade and growth by dismantling tariff barriers, reflecting a region-wide tendency, as evident in Figure 2.3.

However, removing non-tariff barriers has proved more difficult, as has the forging of a common external trade policy. The common external tariffs still include a broad range of exceptions to sensitive products, in spite of MERCOSUR's formal status as a CU since 1995.

MERCOSUR has rapidly acquired international legal status and a formal

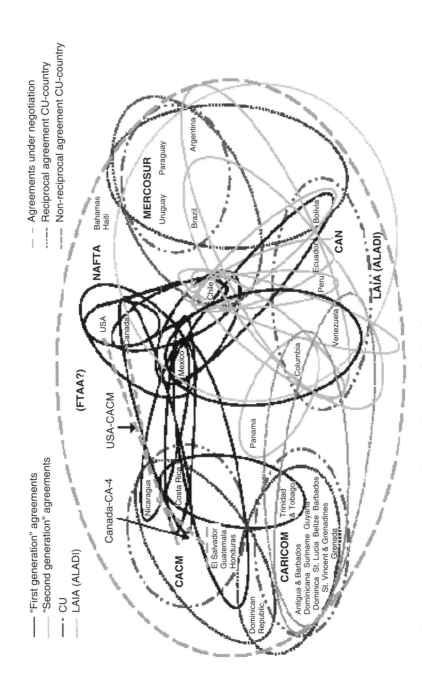

*Figure 2.2* Trade agreements signed and under negotiations in the Americas.

Source: Adapted from Estevadeordal LAIA (2002: 5).

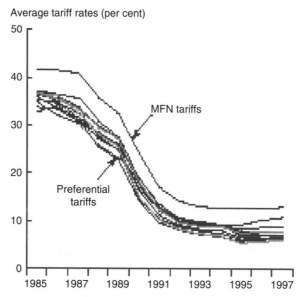

Average tariff rates (per cent)

*Figure 2.3* Development of tariffs in Latin America and the Caribbean (LAC).
Source: World Bank (2005: 68).

structure. However, in institutional terms, it is relatively less developed compared to its Latin American counterpart, the CAN. Its rules are not well harmonised and there is a relative absence of autonomous governing bodies; in effect, MERCOSUR still remains an incomplete CU (Gratius 2005: 286). Its decision-making process remains exclusively intergovernmental, based on the principle of unanimity.[9] We analyse the impacts on conflict resolution processes in the third section.

### Latin America's basic regional trade profile

Overall, countries in Latin America exhibit similar patterns of inter- and intra-regional trade flows, as indicated in Table 2.1. The exception is Mexico, a North American Free Trade Agreement (NAFTA) member. Over 90 per cent of its exports go to the north (primarily to the US, but also to the EU and Japan).[10] In contrast, LAC exports are almost equally divided between the north and the south. With regard to the latter, in 2004, 21.2 per cent of the continent's exports were directed to other developing countries while 27.3 per cent stayed within the region. The recent increase in inter-regional trade across the south has been triggered by the high Chinese growth rates and the recovery staged by the Asian tigers after the 1997 crises.

In contrast, as evident in Table 2.2, Latin America's intra-regional trade flows have been erratic. During the 1990s, trade within the four customs unions (CAN, MERCOSUR, CARICOM and CACM) was Latin America's

*Table 2.1* LAC (excluding Mexico): Export structure by major destinations (in percentages of total exports)

| Regions / World | 1980 | 1990 | 2000 | 2004 |
|---|---|---|---|---|
| LAC – North | 56.8 | 63.8 | 57.8 | 51.5 |
| North America | 30.3 | 33.1 | 36.6 | 30.8 |
| European Union | 25.7 | 29.2 | 20.6 | 20.4 |
| Japan | 0.9 | 1.6 | 0.6 | 0.3 |
| LAC – South | 43.2 | 36.2 | 42.2 | 48.5 |
| Intra-regional | 26.4 | 18.2 | 31.0 | 27.3 |
| Inter-regional | 16.7 | 18.0 | 11.2 | 21.2 |
| World | 100.0 | 100.0 | 100.0 | 100.0 |

Source: ECLAC (2005).

*Table 2.2* Intra-regional trade per sub-region (exports of goods as a proportion of GDP)

| | 1980 | 1985 | 1990 | 1997 | 2003 |
|---|---|---|---|---|---|
| LAC | 16.4 | 10.6 | 14.4 | 21.1 | 16.0 |
| CAN | 3.7 | 3.2 | 4.1 | 12.1 | 9.0 |
| MERCOSUR | 11.6 | 5.5 | 8.9 | 24.9 | 11.9 |
| CACM | 23.1 | 14.4 | 14.1 | 13.3 | 20.7 |
| CARICOM | 8.3 | 11.3 | 12.4 | 16.7 | 21.3 |
| NAFTA | 33.6 | 43.9 | 41.4 | 49.1 | 55.0 |
| FTAA (34) | 33.6 | 43.9 | 41.4 | 49.1 | 60.1 |
| ASEAN (10) | 17.4 | 18.6 | 19.0 | 24.0 | 22.7* |
| EU (15) | 55.6 | 59.9 | 64.9 | 62.9 | 62.7 |

Source: ECLAC, International Trade and Integration Division, based on official data.

Note: * Coefficient corresponds to the year 2002.

primary growth engine, peaking in 1997 (IADB 2000: 3). With the onset of the global financial crisis, intra-regional trade declined steadily until 2002.[11] Subsequently, it picked up but remains low in relative terms – compared to the EU and NAFTA.

## The cases of MERCOSUR and the CAN

MERCOSUR and the CAN are the two main regional integration schemes in South America. The review of both cases offers the opportunity to identify similarities and differences. Whereas in the case of MERCOSUR the focus is on trade and bilateral conflicts, in the CAN case the focus shifts to trade and internal conflicts.

## MERCOSUR

*Current trade performance and integration outcomes*

MERCOSUR was initially founded with the ambitious goal to 'accelerate the process of economic development in conjunction with social justice' by amplifying each member's respective market through regional integration.[12] Until 1998, MERCOSUR was one of the most successful integration projects in the developing world, characterised by a remarkable commitment to reciprocal trade liberalisation that resulted in a sixfold increase in intra-regional trade. However, the integration process appears to have lost its early momentum. More than a decade after the Treaty of Asunción came into force, the Southern Cone's initiative looks shaky. In particular, the economic turmoil experienced in the 1999–2002 period demonstrated its vulnerability.

External shocks, such as the Asian crisis, led to severe macro-economic disturbances and a drop in foreign direct investment (FDI) flows in the Southern Cone. MERCOSUR's rudimentary institutional structures were unable to produce the economic and monetary cooperation required to withstand these shocks. In the absence of a mechanism to deal with trade imbalances, unilateral moves, such as Brazil's uncoordinated currency devaluation in 1999, created strong tensions among the regional trading partners, endangered the integration process and the future of the customs unions (Paiva and Gazel 2003: 119). As a result, intra-MERCOSUR trade plummeted to 12.9 per cent of the regions global exports in 2004, in contrast to the 25.3 per cent level registered in 1998 (CEPAL 2005: 106). Although a slight improvement (12.9 per cent)[13] occurred in the wake of Argentina's economic recovery, overall MERCOSUR's intra-regional trade coefficient is considerably lower than its global comparators (except the Andean community, see Table 2.2).

Institutional factors are not the only reason for MERCOSUR's poor trade performance since 1999. Vaillant points to the unequal distribution of benefits as a crucial obstacle to trade growth and full economic integration (Vaillant 2005: 60). Thus far, only Brazil has profited from intra-regional trade. The three smaller countries, Argentina, Uruguay and Paraguay, have been unable to access Brazil's markets. Such inequities tend to make regional integration efforts counterproductive. Non-tariff barriers (NTBs) and rules of origin (RO) procedures act as an incentive to locate investment and production in the dominant market while leading to deindustrialisation in the peripheral ones. The constant disputes and conflicts between Brazil and Argentina on the subject of asymmetries and inequalities have to be seen in this context. To date, they have hindered the formulation of a common trade policy as a precursor to the longer term goal of a common market.

Despite such asymmetries Paraguay and Uruguay, the two smallest players, continue to adhere to MERCOSUR since they see benefits in integration. However, the windows of opportunity are small. Uruguay, has taken advantage of the free access to the Brazilian and Argentine markets. It has also extracted concessions from Argentina and Brazil by employing its veto power. In an effort to address its regional partner's concerns, Brazil has channelled investment in their direction, particularly towards Argentina during the 1990s. Its oil and gas company, Petrobras, is a leading investor. Argentina has also invested in Brazil, especially in connection with various industrial products. These cross-investment currents have also extended to Paraguay and Uruguay.

Still, such strategies cannot offset asymmetrical economic power within the region. Like Chile, Uruguay is contemplating a lone-player policy and has entered into negotiations with the US, outside the MERCOSUR framework. Paraguay has even less leverage within the framework and can only fulminate against regional economic disparities.

MERCOSUR's guiding lights and managers appear to have learned their lessons from the recent turbulent years. An important advance in this regard has been the response to the long-time demand of MERCOSUR's smaller states, Paraguay and Uruguay, to implement a cohesion fund and a MERCOSUR Parliament (Parlasur). These actions aim to strengthen the social dimensions of the integration process and to reduce inequalities. The creation of a Permanent Court of Dispute Settlement in 2002 was another step in the right direction. Last but not least, the block has re-emphasised its commitment to macro-economic and monetary cooperation. As Espino and Azar point out, 'although, this progress is very slow and fragmented', it represents an important 'chance of stepping forward to build a shared space for sustainable development' (Espino and Azar 2005: 4).

*Trade and economic aspects*

Despite the identified shortcomings in MERCOSUR's institutional framework and trade performance, its overall purpose of creating a common market has been steadily reaffirmed. Indeed, MERCOSUR's integrative common market goal is by far the most ambitious of all Latin American economic integration schemes.

In order to advance and institutionalise the process of economic and monetary integration, the four member states have created two collegiate and inter-governmental organs. The Common Market Council (CMC) – comprising foreign ministers and the ministers of economic affairs – is MERCOSUR's highest policy-making body, responsible for compliance with the strategic economic objectives of the Asunción Treaty and its subsequent protocols. The Common Market Group (CMG) – coordinated by the Ministries of Foreign Affairs – represents its executive body, charged with the implementation of CMC's consensual decisions through the initiation of practical measures for trade promotion, the coordination of macro-economic policies, and negotiations with third parties. The CMG is assisted by ten working groups in the areas of trade and customs issues; standards; trade related monetary and fiscal policies; infrastructure; energy policy; and the coordination of macro-economic policies. A special Trade Commission was established by the Ouro Preto Protocol (1994), to function under the ambit of the CMG. This commission is responsible for the technical negotiations required to design and enforce common trade policy instruments.

## Non-trade aspects

Although MERCOSUR has evolved – in spite of its political roots – as a predominantly commercial initiative, based on the successful implementation of a trade liberalisation programme, it has gradually incorporated a variety of non-trade issues in its agenda. Referring to the inherent 'trade and cooperation linkage', which distinguishes its integration scheme from a purely free trade agreement, such as NAFTA, the block seeks a broad cooperation process in a wide range of socio-political areas (such as education, justice, environment, energy, technology, health and foreign policy). Addressing these areas is considered crucial for the establishment of a 'community sense' and a regional identity, based on shared values and principles (Costa Vaz 2001).

### LABOUR ISSUES

In order to mitigate the societal impact of greater economic integration, MERCOSUR's labour ministers proposed the creation of a Social Charter for MERCOSUR two months after the signing of the Asunción Treaty (1991). This charter addresses labour issues and improved working conditions. Later, the Protocol of Ouro Preto created the Economic and Social Consultative Forum. Made up of national representatives of the different economic and social sectors, the forum serves as an advisory board to the CMC. The creation of the MERCOSUR Socio-Labour Commission (1999), through the proposal of the Working Group No. 10, has been a significant advancement. Designed as a mandatory consultant of the CMG, the commission established a Labour Market Observatory and which successfully led to a CMC Resolution on Professional Qualifications.

### DEVELOPMENT AND POVERTY ALLEVIATION

The CMC's decision to establish a structural fund of US$100 million per year, to address the problem of asymmetries and inequalities within the block, was a momentous one. The main objective of this Fund for Structural Convergence of MERCOSUR (FOCEM) is to develop competitiveness; to encourage social cohesion, particularly in the smaller economies and least developed regions; to support the functioning of the institutional structure; and to strengthen the integration process. Presently, the fund is undercapitalised in view of the large number of people living below the poverty line in the Southern Cone (approximately 95 million according to ECLAC 2003).

ENVIRONMENT

Following upon the statement of intent in the Asunción Treaty, MERCO-SUR's member states expressed the need to complement the free movement of goods and services with appropriate environmental measures. After a significant delay, the block signed a 'Framework Agreement on the Environment in MERCOSUR' in 2001. This framework aims to foster regional sustainable development through the harmonisation of national environmental standards, the sharing of information on environmental emergencies, and research promotion for clean technology. Entering into force in June 2004, the agreement focuses on the intra-regional elimination of environmental NTBs; the implementation of a bloc-wide system of environmental information sharing; the creation of guidelines for environmental emergencies, as well as for international environmental standards; and the introduction of a region-wide system of eco-labelling. On 20 July 2006, the MERCOSUR Council, the highest technical body within the block, issued Decision N 14/06: 'Competitiveness For Program Complementation – Directives for Environmental Management and Cleaner Production', evidence of a growing environmental awareness within MERCOSUR as a whole.

*Conflict resolution mechanism*

As the regional integration process proceeds towards the integration of policy disciplines, there is an increasing need to embed them in a strong and supportive institutional framework, which is capable of resolving disputes arising from treaty obligations. A key imperative, driven by MERCOSUR's distinctive intra-regional power asymmetries, is that the dispute settlement mechanism serves not only to prevent the escalation of retaliation measures, but also guarantees that the bloc's weaker states can effectively push the stronger ones to comply with their obligations.

In the early stages of the integration process, the governments were reluctant to establish an independent judicial body, preferring a flexible and cost-effective inter-governmental process based on political negotiations and an ad hoc tribunal. The Protocol of Brasilia for the Solution of Controversies (1991) provided two diplomatic measures (consultations and claims), but only one arbitration procedure. While consultations are supposed to settle minor disputes through direct negotiations, claims are designed to resolve more awkward conflicts. Such claims need to be initiated by a national section within the Mercosur Trade Commission. If the plenary session of the commission does not resolve the case, it is sent to a technical committee, which issues a non-binding recommendation to the Trade Commission. If there is still no consensus, the claim may be forwarded to the CMG, which may, as a last step, activate the arbitration mechanism. The arbitration proceedings finally take part under an ad hoc tribunal composed of three members. After a series of negotiations under the intervention of the CMG, mandatory and final determinations are issued. In the repeated event of non-compliance, retaliation may be the ultimate response.

This minimalist jurisdictional architecture, based on consensus and diplomatic cooperation, proved to be effective at the initial stages when interdependence was relatively low and political commitment high. Its short-comings became apparent in the aftermath of Brazil's currency devaluation in 1999: when Argentina imposed unilateral trade barriers in order to protect its domestic market from the flood of Brazilian manufactures, the affected private parties had no institutional bodies within MERCOSUR they could revert to in order to redress their grievances (O'Keefe 2003). Other claims were raised by the smaller states, lacking sufficient political leverage to ensure their unrestricted market access. In a climate of retaliation, the absence of an independent supra-national court with permanent arbitrators becomes a serious hindrance to intra-regional trade.

In order to minimise such trade disruptions and its political ramifications, the Protocol of Olivos (2002) introduced a number of innovations. Among these, the establishment of a post-decision control mechanism and the cre-ation of a permanent review court were the most noteworthy (Pena and Rozenberg 2005: 9). The post-ruling control strengthens the obligatory nature of the arbitration decisions by invoking possible compensation in case of a member state's non-compliance. The Permanent Review Court has a twofold responsibility: reviewing the tribunal's decision; and providing an alternative to ad hoc arbitration, where the parties may submit their disputes directly to the court without having to go through the arbitration process. In a recent case, the tribunal met in Montevideo, Uruguay, to arbitrate the ongoing dispute between Argentina and Uruguay over a water-contaminating pulp mill plant to be installed close to the Uruguay River, a natural border between both countries. The tribunal, assembled in early September 2006, included legal representatives from both countries and a neutral arbitrator. The result-ing ruling appears to have satisfied both parties (López-Dardaine 2006). Admittedly these are preliminary initiatives, but they pave the way for strengthening supra-national arbitration institutions in the Southern Cone.

### *Intra- and inter-state conflicts within the context of MERCOSUR*

MERCOSUR came together in 1991 in almost ideal circumstances. Tensions among member states had declined noticeably. In conjunction with their neighbours, the member states had intensified efforts to settle territorial disputes,[14] and conflicts in the field of trade and investment were miti-gated through enhanced political cooperation and the institutionalisation of CBMs. As mentioned, the concept of 'open regionalism' underpinned the integration process (emphasising external opening, privatisation, deregulation and democratic governance). This approach reduced implicit and explicit security threats. MERCOSUR's firm diplomatic intervention in Paraguay's constitutional crisis (1996) earned it external credibility as a stable region

(Strűmberg 1998: 12). In fact, such intervention effectively put an end to the persistent threat of military coups in the whole region (Vasconcelos 2001: 136). O'Keefe noted that the so-called 'democracy clause' in the Treaty of Ushuaia (1998) provided 'a way to strengthen weak democracies by requiring liberal democracy and respect for human rights as a condition for entry and continued access to the benefits of membership' (O'Keefe 2005: 212).

However, notwithstanding MERCOSUR's democracy clause, the diverse CBMs and the changed political culture, new security issues emerged in the wake of closer economic integration and open borders. Social and political conflicts, induced by the trade in narcotics and international terrorism, become more prevalent and produced spillover effects. The need for a concerted regional response is clearly evident but not forthcoming. A major obstruction is the combination of interdependency and inequality within the region (Bodemer 2002: 415). Hafner-Burton and Montgomery's condition that 'trade institutions can keep the peace ... when they create ties among states with relatively equal social positions within the international political economy' is far from being fulfilled in the Southern Cone (Hafner-Burton and Montgomery 2005: 32). The lacunae in macro-economic and monetary integration are a symptom of the glaring inter-state asymmetries, which inhibit further progress towards conciliation and integration. Compounding these asymmetries are the diverging foreign policy objectives, expressed inter alia by Argentina's efforts to counteract Brazil's lobbying for a seat in the United Nations Security Council (UNSC) (Brown *et al.* 2005: 20). The popular backlash against globalisation and free trade in Latin America has stalled the politico-economic convergence process even further. There has been a re-emergence of nationalistic rhetoric and a revival of old protectionist import-substitution nostrums.

The MERCOSUR undoubtedly exemplifies the positive connection between regional economic integration and security, yet the process is far from being complete. Only by strengthening it with efficient conflict-solving mechanisms and instituting a fair and equitable distribution of benefits for all, will its members be able to secure peace in the long-term future.

## CAN

The CAN comprises four member nations: Bolivia, Colombia, Ecuador and Peru.[15] It has its roots in the Andean Pact, a trade bloc formed in 1969, within the framework of the LAFTA:

> Together with CARICOM, it formed part of the second wave of integration processes in Latin American and the Caribbean. Its goals were to improve the conditions for participation of the less developed countries encompassed by the LAFTA agreements, while simultaneously aiming at the gradual formation of a Latin American Common Market.
>
> (Malamud 2005: 9)

As it stood, LAFTA left much to be desired. The Andean Pact attempted to compensate for its inefficiencies by fostering further integration. The pact did not make much headway either. Venezuela's entrance in 1973 and Chile's withdrawal in 1976 created disarray among the members. They countered through institutional initiatives such as the creation of the Court of Justice and the Andean Parliament in 1979. However, these institutions lacked real weight – in neofunctionalist terms, 'form took precedence over substance' (Malamud 2005: 10–11). Nonetheless, they set the institutional groundwork for a viable regional bloc.

Currently, the affairs of the CAN are coordinated by the Andean Integration System (AIS). This constitutes a set of bodies and institutions 'designed to allow for an effective coordination between them in order to maximize subregional Andean integration, promote their external projection and strengthen the actions related to the integration process'.[16] A total of six ruling bodies including the Andean Presidential Council, and six community institutions govern community affairs. '[T]he legal principle of direct effect and the pre-eminence of community law evokes a level of formal institutionalization, only behind the European Union' (Malamud 2005: 11). Still, the CAN has not been uplifted by its network of institutions. Malamud argues that the member countries are 'naïve regarding their faith in supranationality' (Malamud 2005: 16).

The CAN has recently initiated a systemic approach to an Andean security policy, formalised in the 'Lima Declaration' of November 2001 and complemented with the Guidelines for the External Security Policy of the Andean Community adopted in July 2004. This is in addition to efforts such as intelligence sharing and ending arms trafficking. While these provide some regional sense of security, they do little to forestall internal conflict. Indeed, a new instability cycle has emerged in the central Andes. Michael Weinstein refers to the 'massive protest marches, roadblocks, the taking of official installations, regional rebellions, government alienation and an attempt by governments to extend their powers in an unconstitutional manner' (Gonzalez and Luis 2005: 1–2). In all the member countries, with the exception of Venezuela, subversive groups run riot, revealing the substantial capacity of the indigenous population for mobilised action.

Similarly, treaties and declarations have done little to erase tensions caused by border disputes. The case of Ecuador and Peru demonstrates that '[b]oundary-related conflict occurs even between partners to preferential trade agreements' (Dominguez *et al.* 2003: 18). Border disputes between these two countries date back to 1840, 'based on the imprecise borders drawn by Spanish authorities during colonization' (Cooper 2003). The 1939–41 war was settled with a demarcation of the border by a third party (a Brazilian mediator, Braz Dias de Aguiar) whom Ecuador did not accept. Subsequently, despite a status quo agreement in 1992, war broke out between the two countries again in 1995. International intermediaries, mostly from South America, negotiated a resolution to the chagrin of some nationalist groups.

Currently, there is insufficient evidence to link reduced tension and political instability with CAN membership. Nor does it explain why, despite such membership, intra-regional commerce is low, constituting only 10 per cent of total trade. However, this figure was registered in 2004, after declining for two consecutive years (CEPAL 2005: 109). While intra-regional trade flows fall below what would be expected in a trading bloc, they are still significant compared to those recorded prior to the establishment of the Andean Free Trade Area (AFTA). The bloc's overall trade performance does more to justify its continuation. An extenuating factor is that political affinity (or its absence thereof) does not explain trade preferences. Thus trade flows between Colombia and Venezuela, the largest in the CAN (at 75 and 65 per cent respectively), belie the tension existing between the two countries (Cooper 2003).

## Colombia and the CAN

CONTEXT

Colombia is currently home to the most intense and complex IAC in the region, with a history of conflicts dating back to the nineteenth century. The recent conflict is associated with the guerrilla movement that emerged in the 1960s, in the aftermath of '*La Violencia*', a civil war that took place between 1946 and 1959. Initially a political and ideological (Cooper 2003) movement that sought an end to socio-economic injustice perpetuated by a corrupt government, it has now become a full-fledged civil war pitching the left-wing guerrillas, right-wing paramilitary groups and the Colombian government against each other. Attempted peace negotiations have not been fruitful. These tend to break down because of the 'zero-sum mentality in which only one victory is acceptable' (Azcarate 1999: 31). Unfortunately, the breakdown of negotiations does not signal a cool-down period, but a return to business as usual.

ECONOMIC CONSEQUENCES

Besides the loss of human lives (nearly 7,000 people died between July 2002 and June 2003), this IAC has serious economic consequences. The cost of the conflict has been monetised at 1.34 per cent of GDP for the period of 1991–2001, rising to 1.91 per cent in 2001 (Caballero Argaez 2005: 28). Also, starting in 1980, a drop in productivity has caused the rate of expansion of the GDP to go down after registering a constant growth at 5 per cent for the last 30 years. Clearly, violence heightens uncertainty and raises the costs of doing business. According to one estimate, an increase of 1 per cent in the homicide rate is enough to drop private investment by 0.66 per cent (Echeverry *et al.* 2001). The attendant expected drop in long-term growth is estimated at 8 per cent of GDP (Caballero Argaez 2005: 28). Also, the informal economy has expanded. This is mostly due to the conflict's shift from political and ideological objectives to pecuniary ones (Ballentine and Nitzschke 2003: 6). This new paradigm redefines the conflict as a fight for the control and influence of forest areas dedicated to growing and processing cocaine (Azcarate 1999: 22–23). The combatant pool has also increased to include drug dealers and farmers. Thus, the incentives to engage, rather than disengage, make the web more intricate than it used to be 40 years ago. In other words, the absence of causes and lowered social inhibition result in 'criminal inertia' (Echeverry *et al.* 2001).

IAC AND INTEGRATION

How does the conflict in Colombia fit in the CAN scenario? According to Andrew Hurrell, 'the liberalization of economic exchanges facilitates illicit flows of all kinds, especially when this liberalization forms part of a more general shift in power from the state to the market. Such illicit activities may then spill over into inter-state relations' (Hurell 1998: 540). For instance, Ecuador has received about 6,000 refugees displaced by the conflict (Ramirez 2004: 3). A reported 1.3 million people were displaced in the 2001–2004 period. Venezuela, Brazil and Peru have also experienced negative repercussions from the drug trade originating in Colombia.

A truly regional approach to solving the problem has been absent for two reasons. First, Colombian heads of state refuse to recognise the internationalisation of the conflict; for fear that doing so has trans-territorial implications and could, consequentially, lead others to challenge their sovereignty. Former President Andrés Pastrana made an exception when he attempted to promote peace diplomacy. 'Faced with the "internationalization of the conflict", that is to say a situation that began to be understood as a threat to the peace and security of the region and hemisphere, [Pastrana's] government opted for an "internationalization of the peace" ' (Ramirez 2004: 3). The subsequent peace negotiations took place in 1998 and 2002, but without much success. During these negotiations, the Colombian Revolutionary Armed Forces (FARC) was severely criticised, prompting their withdrawal.

The second factor relates to external recrimination and lack of accountability. Ecuador and Peru 'have blamed Colombia for not doing enough to contain its armed conflict and prevent irregular armed groups and refugees from crossing the border. In August 2002, Ecuador imposed travel restrictions on Colombians and stepped up security along its northern border (ICG 2004: 5). In January 2006, an alleged invasion of Ecuador's aerial space by Colombian military forces reignited tensions between the two countries. Keeping in mind the backdrop of the Andean Plan of Cooperation against Drug Trafficking and Criminal Activities (approved in June 2002), there is little to be said in defence of Colombia's neighbours. Much as they like to complain about the situation in Colombia, Ecuador and Peru have done little to halt the flows of arms trafficking originating in their territories.

Venezuelan support for Colombia's main rebel groups, FARC and ELN (National Liberation Army) is not as farfetched as it sounds, given Chavez's apparent sympathy towards rebel groups. Overall, inter-Andean solidarity has been marred by distrust and lack of cooperation.

## Bolivia and the CAN

With a GDP of $10.06 billion (2005 estimate)[17], Bolivia is the poorest country in South America. An estimated two-thirds of its 9.2 million people live in poverty.[18] The International Monetary Fund (IMF) supported structural adjustment programmes in the 1980s and 1990s. These programmes failed to alleviate poverty despite a recorded economic growth of 3.8 per cent in the last decade (CAFOD 2005). The income inequalities associated with such growth fuelled mass resistance, particularly by indigenous groups, against Bolivia's ruling class. The political ramifications of such resistance were evidenced in the ousting of President Gonzalo Sánchez de Lozada in November 2003 and the resignation of former President Carlos Mesa Gisbert in June 2005. The latter witnessed over 800 protests during his term in office (Albro 2005: 1).

While political participation by those who have long been disenfranchised by the system (i.e. indigenous groups) is an important step towards a representative democracy, it also has had detrimental impacts. In economic terms, it has deterred foreign investment (FDI flows have dropped from $US1,044 million in 2002 to $US160 million in 2003).[19] Politically, the mass unrest has triggered sharp internal divisions. These divisions pit the wealthy side of the country, the lowlands or *cambas*, against the poor side, the *collas* or western highlands.

Popular unrest has its roots in the 'water war'. The war originated in the city of Cochabamba, in April 2000, in response to the privatisation of the water services (the consortium was led by International Water Ltd, a subsidiary of a US-based corporation, and Edison SPA, Italy's largest private energy services provider). The steep rise in costs (for some users, the rates went up by 300 per cent)[20] angered the citizens of Cochabamba, who took to the streets in protest. Initially, the Banzer administration sought to put the protest down by force, which only increased its intensity. Eventually, the Bolivian government cancelled the contract without compensating the investors. The success of the water war can be attributed to a broad coalition of *cocaleros*, students, workers unions, and even middle-class professionals. Contrary to popular belief this was not an ethnic war waged by poor, indigenous Bolivians. Rather than *un problema de indios* (an Indian problem), the war had a national and popular dimension.

The sale of natural gas, a newly discovered and vast resource, has fuelled unrest on a similar scale. The gas is located in the lowlands, where an elite minority has claimed it as its own. This sentiment is not shared by most Bolivians, who believe that this resource is a national patrimony and, as such, belongs to all Bolivians. They consider the sale of gas to foreigners as a threat to their sovereignty – a one-way deal. As evidence, multinational companies have profited from the income generated by the sector, taking in as much as 58 per cent, while government revenues have dropped (CAFOD 2005). The decision by President Sánchez de Lozada to approve the sale of liquefied gas to Mexico and the United States provoked a popular and violent uprising, resulting in the loss of 67 lives and considerably more injuries (CAFOD 2005). After reaching a referendum in July 2004 in favour of more state control over the industry, the country was swept up in another political crisis over the passing of a controversial hydrocarbons law. More than three weeks of protests demanding the nationalisation of gas ended with the resignation of President Mesa in June 2005 (CAFOD 2005). Most Bolivians expect the newly elected president, Evo Morales, to uphold the law despite these threats and dissenting opinions from the business groups in Santa Cruz. The president himself prefers a middle ground: joint venture partnerships.

INDIGENOUS UPRISING AND THE MORALES EXCEPTION

Indigenous communities, representing 70 per cent of the population, are increasingly gaining political recognition (Gonzalez 2006). Their success derives from an assertion of cultural practices combined with an openness that allows these communities to cooperate with others with similar grievances and aspirations.

The results of the 2005 presidential elections reflect their political achievements. For the first time in Bolivia's electoral history, an indigenous person, Evo Morales, won the presidential race. He beat out the candidate of the Movimiento Nacionalista Revolucionario (MNR – Nationalist Revolutionary Party), the party whose political prominence dates back to 1952. As president, Morales faces formidable challenges. He has to determine the fate of Bolivia's natural gas resources and oversee key legislative measures. These measures relate to a referendum on departmental autonomy for the region of Santa Cruz and Tarija, and a new constitution that fully takes into account the rights of indigenous people. As expected, both measures have drawn criticism from both sides of the political spectrum. On one hand, *cruceños* argue that Bolivia's population is predominantly *mestizo* (of mixed race) and that the indigenous discourse is self-serving (ICG 2003: 16). On the other, some indigenous activists believe that foreign oil companies are behind the referendum and that their real intention is to generate 'a violent reaction by indigenous movements, in order to justify external military intervention' (Gonzalez 2006). While the nature of these accusations is questionable, they nonetheless illustrate the conflicting forces at play. Mediating these will become a paramount task for the new president if he is to prevent any further polarisation that could lead to civil unrest. For now, the risk of revived violence and institutional destabilisation has come to a halt thanks, mostly, to the same democratic processes that invested Morales with the presidency.

IAC AND INTEGRATION

At first glance, the link between Bolivia's internal problems and the trade and integration processes it is currently engaged in is not clear. Within the CAN, Bolivia was the first country to liberalise its trade in 1985. It also maintained the lowest tariff schedules in the bloc.[21] The country currently directs a respectable 22 per cent of its free on board exports to the CAN.[22]

This profile is at odds with a grassroots movement demanding the nationalisation of natural resources, on the premise that the current exploitation arrangements benefit foreigners and a Bolivian minority. According to a Pew study, only 15 per cent of Bolivian respondents believed that growing trade and business ties were very good for the country, in contrast with 62 per cent, who thought it was beneficial to some extent.[23] In another Pew study, 47 per cent of respondents believed that anti-globalisation protests were a positive influence.[24] On the other hand, economic models on FDI, debt rating and entrepreneurship, seem to indicate that a negative attitude towards globalisation is detrimental for the economy (Noland 2004: 14). One thing is clear; in the absence of the political stability needed to safeguard their interests, foreign players need to tread cautiously. Prior to the 2004 hydrocarbons referendum, Brazil's Lula travelled to Bolivia to defend the interests of Petrobras, which controls two oil refineries (the only ones currently operational) and 25 per cent of Tarija's natural gas reserves (Zibechi 2005: 2). If Bolivia's trade partners are to ensure a smooth flow of goods and services, they will have to take measures to assist the country in its efforts to overcome its political and economic difficulties. At the very least, Bolivia's partners should avoid arrangements that could do Bolivia's cause a disservice by further incensing its people.

## Conclusions and recommendations

The following paragraphs recapitulate the content of our analysis. Conclusions and recommendations are provided at the end of the section.

### *MERCOSUR*

The MERCOSUR constitutes the region's most important and successful integration effort in the region. Its formation was motivated by the need to strengthen diplomatic relations between member countries, particularly Brazil and Argentina; second, the members aspired to enhance regional competitiveness and, thereby, promote regional development. Since its inception in 1991 to the mid-1990s, MERCOSUR achieved impressive growth in intraregional trade. The elimination of trade barriers was mainly responsible for such growth. After the Asian crisis, the bloc's performance has been somewhat erratic. More recent setbacks, such as Brazil's currency devaluation and Argentine crisis, further stalled integration efforts.

In general, MERCOSUR's trade performance is negatively affected by several factors. First, NTBs remain. Their removal is subject to individual members' perception of product sensitivity and their internal policies. These factors hinder the formation of a CU and a common external policy. Second, MERCOSUR's member countries are not willing to defer to a supra-national authority, preferring to manoeuvre the process at their own will. To compensate for the resulting low level of institutionalism, several decision-making bodies or committees, such as the CMC, have been created. There is only one arbitration procedure and it is, at the same time, a last-resort mechanism that is cumbersome to activate. Moreover, unilateral disregard for these resolution mechanisms has been the rule, rather than the exception. An attempt to overcome this systemic failure was made through the enactment of the Protocol of Olivos, but it is still behind in its efforts to develop a reliable system of international commercial arbitration.

MERCOSUR was given an initial boost by Argentina and Brazil's willingness to leave their differences behind and put an end to their bilateral nuclear arms race. Political conflicts are now suppressed by shared expectations/confidence building measures. For instance, the democracy clause establishes democratic governance as a precondition for enjoying membership rights and benefits. However, the extant inter-state conflicts are rarely political in nature. These tend to arise out of the unequal distribution of benefits and unilateral economic policies. The level of integration achieved thus far has actually caused deindustrialisation in Argentina, Paraguay and Uruguay, due to tariff-base liberalisation – with their manufactures being displaced by Brazil. These are factors that deter full integration.

## CAN

The Andean Pact was formed to fill the void that LAFTA left behind. Institutionally, the CAN has few peers in the developing world. Its supra-national bodies take precedence over domestic law, effectively curtailing unilateral digressions. The AFTA was recently completed with Peru's accession. Intra-regional export flows have been erratic since the formation of the bloc. Historically, the flows reached their highest level in the 1990s, after integration efforts were reactivated following the sluggish trends of the 1980s. Currently, intra-regional trade has been growing steadily and constitutes around 10 per cent of total trade. Commerce has not been halted by tensions among neighbours. Bilateral trade between Venezuela and Colombia continues despite disagreements over how the guerrilla crisis is being handled. Ecuador and Peru maintained trade links throughout their territorial dispute, although the flows experienced a significant upsurge after the dispute was settled.

The Andean bloc has experienced relative peace since the last inter-state conflict in the region, between Ecuador and Peru, was resolved in 1998. However, latent threats to security continue to persist, reflecting the high military spending in the region, non-traditional security concerns and the high incidence of intra-state conflict. If unresolved, intra-state dynamics have the potential to spill over borders. In this regards, CAN members are grappling with the problems of migration and arms trafficking.

Recent disagreements arose in the context of the bilateral trade agreements some of the CAN members are negotiating with the US. According to Hugo Chávez, the president of Venezuela, these agreements nullify the authority of the CAN, as its conditions seek to override the community's law. He, subsequently, withdrew from CAN, causing the bloc to experience a major internal crisis.

In order to identify the links between trade and conflict in Latin America, there needs to be a systematic tracking and analysis of related events. This study attempts to fill the void, but also leads us to question its usefulness. That is, how practical is the attempt to correlate RTAs with conflict given that we do not know what the life-span of an RTA is? When Venezuela withdrew from the CAN, it shook the bloc's core and some observers feared its eventual demise. Although members of the CAN and MERCOSUR hope to eventually merge into a single bloc, the fact that both regions are mired in their own difficulties and tug of wars could have a negative effect on the formation of a South American Free Trade Area. Each country participates in the regional and global markets according to expected gains; proximity is less relevant today thanks to globalisation and advances in technology. For this reason, Chile has remained unengaged in the regional processes surrounding it. Hence, we suggest that putting too much emphasis on RTAs as precursors to regional peace and economic development might tempt us to overlook other, more promising possibilities.

With the above in mind, we make the following recommendations:

- To enhance the integration process, the existing conflict/dispute resolution mechanisms must be redesigned. They must have supra-national authority so as to ensure independent judgement. In theory, some of the existing mechanisms were designed to fulfil this criterion, but the practice reflects another reality. A serious overhaul is needed, one that is based on renewed commitments, rather than an old model that has already demonstrated its futility.
- Trust is present in a relationship only when the interested parties continuously work towards its consolidation. An action taken unilaterally will easily break the trust that takes years to build. A country with such inclinations should not sign an RTA in the first place, as its actions will affect regional morale and give way to tensions between members. Moreover, trust is essential to induce transparency and ensure compliance. With this in mind, member countries should demonstrate a willingness to subject themselves to third-party verification and oversight. The more harmonised policies and cooperation are, the less the potential for regulatory interference.
- No foolproof way of avoiding conflicts exists, particularly in the face of

power disparities. In the 1980s, the EU accepted countries that were considered 'backwards' in relation to the majority of its members (Spain, Portugal and Greece). These countries were not left to their own devices because the EU understood that improving their situation was in its best interest. Regional aid was, therefore, provided to help bring these countries closer to the northern European average. A similar approach could be taken, especially in the case of the MERCOSUR, to address asymmetries.

- As in the case of the EU, asymmetries tend to be subsumed as interdependence increases. The greater the interdependence, the less likely that a conflict will escalate. However, the reality is that both the MERCOSUR and the CAN direct most of their exports to external markets, the US and the EU in particular, which reduces the level of interdependence among member countries. It is, therefore, necessary to strengthen regional institutions so as to augment the competitiveness of member countries. A country or regional bloc cannot effectively compete in the absence of reliable institutions, for it is these same institutions that serve as guarantors and reduce the cost of doing business.

- Today's security concerns are often related to organised crime. No regional approach to these issues has been adopted yet. Blame games, sovereignty discourses, and well-intentioned rhetoric must be set aside in order to coordinate an effective strategy to address new security challenges. This is of utmost importance given that the spillover effects transcend boundaries and their cumulative effects can be devastating. Moreover, an effective strategy requires continuous cooperation and reviews to remain so; it is never static. The fact that even a well-designed security machine, such as that of the US, can fail should serve as a reminder of the need to be meticulous in this regard.

- Both the MERCOSUR and the CAN could benefit greatly from each other's experience. The CAN has lessons to share in terms of institutionalisation, whereas the MERCOSUR has greater commercial leverage and could help pinpoint competitive strategies for Andean countries to adopt. Such complementarity suggests the possibility of creating a South American Free Trade Area.

## Notes

1  See Protocol II to the Geneva Convention, Article 1(1), (1977).
2  Ibid.
3  See http://www.abacc.org/engl/abacc/abacc_history.htm ABACC (n.d.).
4  MERCOSUR is comprised of Brazil, Argentina, Paraguay and Uruguay as full members. Chile, Bolivia, Venezuela, Peru and Ecuador participate as associate members.
5  Without Mexico.
6  Regional economic integration that is not discriminatory against outside countries; typically, a group of countries that agrees to reduce trade barriers on a most favoured nation (MFN) basis.

7 See 'Chile trade facts and figures', http://www.chileinfo.com/index.php?accion= info_comercial (accessed November 2005).

8 Narich further elaborates on this point by stating: 'Indeed, Latin Americans were key worldwide pioneers of ideas and institutions that have succeeded in reducing the incidence of warfare and also in strengthening the expectation that neighboring countries will not go to war with each other.'

9 Marques-Pereira (2002/2003: 45) notes the absence of supra-national institutions in the MERCOSUR and points out the lack of clarity regarding the precedent of community law over domestic law; only the constitutions of Argentina and Paraguay recognise such precedence.

10 See ECLAC (2005).

11 Ibid.

12 'Antecedentes del MERCOSUR', http://www.mercosur.int/msweb/portal%20 intermediario/es/index.htm (accessed December 2005).

13 ECLAC (2005).

14 Such as in the case of Argentina and Chile.

15 Chile was among the original five signatories, but it later withdrew.

16 See 'The Andean integration system', http://www.comunidadandina.org/ingles/ sai/que.html (accessed December 2005).

17 See 'The World Fact Book: Bolivia', http://www.cia.gov/cia/publications/factbook/ geos/bl.html (accessed January 2006).

18 See 'Country profile: Bolivia', http://www.state.gov/r/pa/ei/bgn/35751.htm (accessed February 2006).

19 United Nations Conference on Trade and Development (UNCTAD) http:// www.unctad.org/Templates/Page.asp?intItemID=2921&lang=1 (accessed January 2006).

20 See Shultz (2000).

21 Tariff barriers to internal trade have been phased out.

22 See 'Estadísticas: Indicadores económicos de la Comunidad Andina', http:// wwww.comunidadandina.org/estadisticas/documentos_indicadores.htm (accessed November 2005).

23 See 'Support for free trade: Miami protests do not reflect popular views', http:// pewglobal.org/commentary/display.php?AnalysisID=74 (accessed December 2005).

24 See 'World publics approve increased international trade, but concern for problems of global economy', http://pewglobal.org/commentary/display.php?Analysis ID=68 (accessed February 2006).

## References

ABACC (Brazilian–Argentine Agency for Accounting and Control of Nuclear Materials) (n.d.) 'History of the ABACC'. Available from http://www.abacc.org/ engl/abacc/abacc_history.htm. Accessed 28 February 2006.

Aggarwal, V.K. and Espach, R. (2003) 'Diverging trade strategies in Latin America: an analytical framework', *The Strategic Dynamics of Latin American Trade*, Stanford, CA: Stanford University Press. Available from http://ist-socrates.berkeley.edu/~basc/pdf/articles/. Accessed 18 November 2005.

Albro, R. (2005) 'The future of culture and rights for Bolivia's indigenous movements', New York: Carnegie Council on Ethics and International Affairs. Available from http://www.cceia.org/media/fellowPaper_albro2.pdf. Accessed 22 February 2006.

Azcarate, C.A. (1999) 'Psychosocial dynamics of the armed conflict in Colombia',

*Journal of Peace and Conflict Resolution* 2:1. Available from http://www.trinstitute.org/ojpcr/2_1colombia.htm. Accessed 31 October 2005.

Ballentine, K. and Nitschke, H. (2003) 'Beyond greed and grievance: policy lesson from studies in the political economy of armed conflict', New York: International Peace Academy. Available from http://www.ipacademy.org. Accessed 23 October 2005.

Bodemer, K. (2002) 'The Mercosur on the way to a cooperative security community?', in P. Giordano (ed.) *An Integrated Approach to the European Union – Mercosur Association*, Paris: Editions de la Chaire Mercosur, 403–417.

Bromley, M. and Perdomo, C. (2005) 'CBM en América Latina y el Efecto de la Adquisición de Armas por parte de Venezuela', *Real Instituto Elcano*. Available from http://www.realinstitutoelcano.org. Accessed on 10 and 11 November 2005.

Brown, O. *et al.* (2005) 'Regional trade integration, violent conflict and peace building', working paper for the IDRC Research Initiative. Winnipeg, Canada: IISD.

Caballero Argaez, C. (2005) 'La estrategia de seguridad democrática y la economía Colombiana: un ensayo sobre la macroeconomía de la seguridad', Banco de la República (Colombia). Available from http://www.banrep.gov.co/docum/ftp/borra234.pdf. Accessed on 11 November 2005.

CAFOD (Catholic Agency for Overseas Development) (2005) 'Why focus on Bolivia?' Available from http://www.cafod.org.uk/news_and_events/features/focus_on_bolivia/why_focus_on_bolivia. Accessed 25 February 2006.

CEPAL (Comisión Económica para América Latina y el Caribe) (2005) *Panorama de la Inserción Internacional de América Latina y el Caribe: Tendencias 2005*, Santiago: UN/CEPAL.

Cooper, T. (2003) 'Peru vs. Ecuador: Alto-Cenepa war, 1995', *ACIG Central and Latin American Database*. Available from http://www.acig.org. Accessed 11 November 2005.

Costa Vaz, A. (2001) 'Forging a social agenda within regionalism: the case of Mercosur and the FTAA in a comparative approach', unpublished working paper.

Dominguez, J.I. *et al.* (2003) *Boundary Disputes in Latin America*, Washington, DC: United States Peace Institute. Available from http://www.usip.org. Accessed 20 November 2005.

ECLAC (Economic Commission for Latin America and the Caribbean) (2003) *Economic Indicators 2003*. Available from http://www.eclac.cl/publicaciones/xml/8/13618/EconomicIndicators2003.pdf. Accessed 2 February 2006.

ECLAC (Economic Commission for Latin America and the Caribbean) (2005) 'Latin America and the Caribbean in the world economy: trends 2005', *Bulletin FAL*, 230.

Espino, A. and Azar, P. (2005) 'Mercosur: are we there yet? From cooperation to integration', working paper. Montevido: Latin America Gender and Trade Network Interdisciplinary Centre for Development Studies, Uruguay.

Estevadeordal, A. (2002) *Traditional Market Access Issues in RTAs: An Unfinished Agenda in the Americas?*, preliminary draft presented at the seminar Regionalism and the WTO, Ginebra, 26 April, Washington, DC: Integration, Trade and Issues Division, Integration and Regional Programs Department, Banco Interamerican. de Desarrollo.

Gonzalez, G. (2006) 'War on terror has indigenous people in its sights', *Inter Press Service News Agency*. Available from http://ipsnews.net/news.asp?idnews=28960. Accessed 18 February 2006.

Gonzalez, M. and Luis, E. (2005) 'El "Etnonacionalismo": Las nuevas tensiones interétnicas en América Latina', *Real Instituto Elcano*. Available from http://www.realinstitutoelcano.org. Accessed 10 November 2005.

Gratius, S. (2005) 'EU–Mercosur relations as a learning experience for bioregionalism', in R. Seidelmann and W. Grabendorff and (eds) *Relations between the European Union and Latin America; Bioregionalism in a Changing Global System.* Berlin: Stiftung Wissenchaft und Politik, pp. 279–318.

Hafner-Burton, E. and Montgomery, A. (2005) 'War, trade and envy: why trade agreements don't always keep the peace', working paper presented at the International Studies Association Annual Conference, Honolulu.

Hufbauer, G. and Kotschwar, B. (1998) 'The future of regional trading arrangements in the Western Hemisphere', working paper. Washington, DC: Peterson Institute for International Economics.

Hurell, A. (1998) 'Security in Latin America', *International Affairs*, 74:3.

IADB (Inter-American Development Bank) (2000) 'Periodic note on integration and trade in the Americas'. Available from http://2005.sice.oas.org/geograph/westernh/idb2000.pdf

ICG (International Crisis Group) (2003) 'Colombia and its neighbors: the tentacles of instability', *IGC Latin America Report*, 3. Available from http://www.crisisweb.org. Accessed on 22 November 2005.

ICG (International Crisis Group – Las Divisiones en Bolivia) (2004) 'Demasiado hondas para superarlas', *Informe Sobre América Latina*, 7. Available from http://www.crisisweb.org. Accessed 22 November 2005.

Kacowicz, A.M. (1998) 'Regionalization, globalization, and nationalism: Convergent, divergent, or overlapping?' working paper 262, Notre Dame, IN: The Helen Kellogg Institute for International Studies. Available from http://www.nd.edu/~kellogg/wps/262.pdf. Accessed 18 November 2005.

Khan, S.R. *et al.* (2007) 'Regional integration, trade and conflict in South Asia', Winnipeg, Canada: Sustainable Development Policy Institute. Available from http://www.iisd.org/pdf/2007/tas_rta_south_asia.pdf. Accessed 11 June 2008.

López-Dardaine, M. (2006) Personal communication.

Malamud, A. (2005) 'Spill over in European and South American integration: an assessment', LASA 2001 meeting paper, Lisboa, Portugal: Centre for Research and Studies in Sociology (CIES-ISCTE). Available from http://136.142.158.105/Lasa2001/MalamudAndres.pdf. Accessed 18 November 2005.

Marques-Pereira, B. (2002/2003) 'Processus de développement régional en Amérique Latine', Syllabus DEVL 013, Brussels: ULB Presses Universitaires de Bruxelles.

Narich, R. (2003) 'Traditional and non-traditional security issues in Latin America: evolution and recent developments', occasional paper series, 42, Geneva: Geneva Centre for Security Policy (GCSP).

Noland, M. (2004) 'Popular attitudes, globalization and risk', working paper, 04-2, Institute for International Economics. Available from http://www.iie.com/publications/wp/wp04-2.pdf. Accessed 3 March 2006.

Ocampo, J.A. (2001) 'Raúl Prebisch and the development agenda at the dawn of the twenty-first century', *ECLAC Review*, 75, 23–37.

O'Keefe, T. (2003) 'A resurgent Mercosur: confronting economic crises and negotiating trade agreements', *North–South Agenda*, papers no. 60, January. Florida: The Dante B. Fascell North–South Center at the University of Miami.

O'Keefe, T. (2005) 'Economic integration as a means for promoting regional political stability: lessons from the European Union and Mercosur', *Chicago-Kent Law Review*, 80, 187–213.

Paiva, P. and Gazel, R. (2003) 'Mercosur: past, present and future', *Nova Economia*, 13: 2, 115–136 IADB.

Pena, C. and Rozenberg, R. (2005) 'Mercosur: A different approach to institutional development', federal policy paper, FPP–05–06, Ottawa: Canadian Foundation for the Americas.

Ramirez, A. (2004) 'The role of the international community in Colombia', Accord: An International Review of Peace Initiative, 14. Available from http://www.c-r.org/accord/col/accord14/roleofinternational.html. Accessed 18 November 2005.

Saavedra, B. (2005) 'Transnational security crime in Latin America: building up cooperation in the Andean Ridge', CSRC discussion paper. Available from http://www.da.mod.uk/CSRC/documents/Special/csrc_mpf.2005-10-17.5799702381/05 (54).PDF. Accessed 18 January 2005.

Shultz, J. (2000) 'My response to Bechtel', letter in *Weekly News Update on the Americas*, 556. Available from http://www.1worldcommunication.org/bolivia.htm#TEXT%20OF%20STATEMENT. Accessed 16 January 2006.

Stewart, J.G. (2003) 'Towards a single definition of armed conflict in humanitarian law: a critique of internationalized armed conflict', *International Review of the Red Cross*, 85: 850, 313–350. Available from http://www.rcrc.org. Accessed 11 November 2005.

Strűmberg, T. (1998) 'Did regional integration save democracy in Paraguay?' working paper, Oslo: Bertil Ohlin Institutet. Available from http://www.ohlininstitutet.org/304c_uppsats/304ctidvinnare.4d. Accessed 11 November 2005.

USNCI (United States National Council on Intelligence) (2004) 'Mapping the global future: report of the National Intelligence Council's 2020 Project'. Available from http://www.cia.gov/nic/NIC_globaltrend2020.html. Accessed 31 October 2005.

Vaillant, M. (2005) 'Mercosur: Southern integration under construction', *Internationale Politik und Gesellschaft* 2, 52–71.

Vasconcelos, A. (2001) 'European Union and Mercosur', in Mario Telò (ed.) *European Union and New Regionalism*, Burlington, VA: Ashgate, pp. 135–152.

Wagner, S. (2005) 'Summit in Venezuela: accelerate South American union'. Available from http://www.venezuelanalysis.com/news.php?newsno=1564. Accessed on 2 February 2006.

World Bank (2005) *Global Economic Prospects*, Washington, DC: World Bank.

Zibechi, R. (2005) 'Two opposing views of social change in Bolivia', IRC Americas Program special report, 14 December. Washington, DC: Center for International Policy (CIP).

# 3 Regional integration, trade and conflict in southern Africa

*Mzukisi Qobo*

## Introduction

Regional trade integration, in the strict sense of the concept, is a relatively new development in southern Africa, although Africa's post-colonial leaders had, in the early 1960s, called for integration of Africa's political and economic structures. The story of regionalism in sub-Saharan Africa is marked by failure, with lack of political will an oft-cited reason. The sub-continent has had to contend with many challenges in the process of regional integration and cooperation. This chapter will examine these challenges, focusing on the intersection of trade and security in the southern African context.

The southern African region became an institutional construct in the form of the Southern African Development Coordinating Conference (SADCC) in the late 1970s (this structure was later renamed Southern African Development Community (SADC)), with the expressed purpose of providing a counter to the hostile apartheid regime in South Africa. By this time a large number of countries in the sub-region had obtained their independence from colonial powers, and South Africa was seen as the last bastion of colonialism in the continent, a situation that made the political environment in southern Africa fraught with security tensions. The backdrop of apartheid South Africa and heightened Cold War tensions that played themselves out in southern Africa shaped the formation of the region.

This chapter discusses the nature of political and economic relations amongst SADC country members, looking specifically at the intersection between trade and security. The existing literature on southern Africa tends to treat various dimensions of regional integration and cooperation separately. There is very little work done on the linkages between trade, security and development. Yet southern Africa is a good example of a region that captures the complex dynamics of trade and security. The security aspect, in particular, has been salient both before democracy and after apartheid, whereas the trade dimension is relatively new and took on prominence after South Africa was integrated into the formal structures of the region.

The discussion of trade and security issues in this chapter draws both on academic and policy research. It should be underlined from the outset that on both fronts – trade and security – progress in the region has been tortuously slow and much of this reflects the weak institutional capacity of SADC member countries. The strengths and weaknesses of the organisation mirror those of the individual member countries. There is, however, a considerable scope for SADC's institutions and policy architecture to improve.

This chapter is divided into five sections. The second section provides a critical overview of the broader debate on trade and security, focusing mainly on the implications for the study of regions. It feeds into the main theme this chapter attempts to develop, namely that regional relations based on trade and security cannot be understood in isolation from domestic level challenges, including the nature of institutions, the political culture and the relationships between various societal actors, especially the state–society nexus. The experience and expectations of state actors who facilitate political and economic relations at regional and international level are shaped heavily by their domestic political context, institutional experiences and the nature of social relations and networks at the domestic level. Hence this chapter also considers the impact of intra-state experiences on regional level interactions and conversely.

The third section highlights some of the tensions that exist within the region, and the nature of regional organisations, including their overlapping memberships in the wider southern African region.

The fourth section considers pertinent issues of trade integration and security cooperation in SADC. The discussion centres on the two most critical areas: the SADC Protocol on Trade, and the Organ for Politics, Security and Defence (OPSD). Areas of tensions and cooperation in relation to trade and security are discussed. Regarding the SADC Protocol on Trade, I consider both the structure of trade complementarities and the nature of rules of origin (RO) as examples of how trade can generate tensions within the region. This questions the standard liberal-trade assumption that trade relations foster harmonious social relations that could automatically generate peace. On the OPSD, I draw examples from the Great Lakes conflict to demonstrate how institutional weaknesses at domestic and regional levels can create fertile conditions for conflict.

Related to this point is the fact that even though trade relations existed among all the countries that were part of the conflict, it did not stem the tide of violent conflict, and perhaps even promoted it via resource competition. In examining this case, the countries involved and the institutional mechanisms that were in place, the question that I pose – and seek to answer – is what is the appropriate institutional design that could help foster deeper trade relations and ensure sustained peace in regions that were previously mired in violent (inter-state) conflict?

The last section draws summary conclusions from the study and points to some of the policy considerations that could improve our understanding of the relationship between trade and security and the institutional designs that could be explored to create a strong positive association between trade and security in a regional context.

# Trade and security: a critical review of theory

## *The benign trade–security nexus*

The case for a positive relationship between trade and security gained strong currency in the liberal-trade paradigm, propounded strongly by Mansfield and Pevehouse (2000). These scholars have made a noteworthy contribution in taking the trade–security debate away from generalities and broad conceptualisation to the more specific context of preferential trading partners – bilaterally and regionally. Their proposition is that the 'conflict-inhibiting' effect of preferential trade will grow larger and stronger as trade flows rise, and that 'heightened commerce will be more likely to dampen hostilities between PTA [preferential trade agreement] members than between other states' (Mansfield and Pevehouse 2000: 781).

The assumption is that increased commercial relations create a climate for peaceful co-existence or, simply put, the more countries trade, the more peaceful towards one another they become. This is hardly a novel proposition. Since the late seventeenth century, liberal philosophers such as Charles Louis de Secondat Montesquieu, John Stuart Mill and Jean-François Melon drew a close association between the expansion of commerce, the spread of gentleness or civilisation and taming of violent passions.[1] Montesquieu[2] argued that 'the natural effect of commerce is to lead to peace. Two nations that trade together become mutually dependent . . .'.

In further expounding this theoretical proposition, Albert Hirschman[3] points out that 'international commerce, being a transaction between nations, could conceivably have also a direct impact on the likelihood of peace and war: once again the interests might overcome the passions, especially the passion for conquest'. Following this argument, peace can be regarded as an outcome or dividend of good commercial behaviour. In this respect, today's proponents of the thesis that trade equals the absence of conflict draw a conclusion that, with increasing interdependence among nations, bound together by common commercial interests or a balance of interests, conflict is levelled out.

This view is deeply rooted in the European intellectual tradition as it was there that the rise of commerce and the formation of nation-states were co-reinforcing. Ironically, this was also the region that gave rise to the most destructive (global) conflicts in recent history. Indeed, the late nineteenth century was a time of great optimism for liberal theorists but this gave way to the carnage of the First and Second World Wars. Arguably a major contributing factor was the lack of formal institutional mechanisms for regulating resource competition amongst industrialising nation-states – states built on mercantilist notions of state-craft. It was not until after the Second World War that such institutional mechanisms were put in place (the General Agreement on Tariffs and Trade (GATT); the European Union (EU)), and with relative success. This recent historical experience in institution-building lends substantial weight to the liberal proposition, at least from the standpoint of Western history.

However, applied to other contexts, especially where the state was more an external imposition than an organic development, this perspective is unconvincing. For example, in most instances, states in sub-Saharan Africa were forged through the crucible of conflict, according to Buzan and Weaver, 'without exception based on inter-state rivalry, and many of them were born into war' (Buzan and Weaver 2003: 17). In contrast, during Europe's transition from feudal societies to modern nation-states, the political elite used taxation in the process of state-building and socio-political change. On the other hand, most of sub-Saharan Africa's elite did not use fiscal policy instruments to build cohesion among citizens.

The liberal free-trade-peace thesis has been contested by some scholars, who argue that interdependence can also increase the risk of militarised disputes. They suggest that asymmetric dependence in trade relations can create conditions that could give rise to conflict. Indeed, it is possible that such unequal trade arrangements, where benefits are seen as accruing disproportionately to one member or a select group of countries, without compensatory mechanisms to assuage the sense of deprivation, can create resentment and cause strains in regional relations. At the heart of Barbieri and Schneider's argument is that symmetric ties may promote peace while asymmetric trade dependence could lead to conflict (Barbieri and Schneider 1999: 387–404). Conflict could be a function of skewed distribution of material power in a regional context, which in turn could establish grounds for the emergence of hostilities or lead to strained relations, especially if there are no compensatory measures extended by the hegemon. If the regionalisation process is seen to proceed in a way that reduces gains for other countries and creates a space for hegemonic assertion by a strong country, resentment is likely to arise among countries that perceive themselves to be in a position of disadvantage and vulnerability in relation to the dominant country.

Arguably, one of the key reasons for the failure of the East Africa community integration project in the late 1960s was Kenya's perceived domineering role. Kenya was seen as benefiting disproportionately from the customs union (CU) at the expense of the other two countries (Tanzania and Uganda). Other political factors also came into play, including tensions between Tanzania's Julius Nyerere and Uganda's Idi Amin, which saw the former engineer a coup that edged Amin out of power. The fact that commercial relations existed between these countries did not restrain political actors from engaging in violent conflict. It would however be facile to suggest that these tensions resulted from trade-generated disparities but the telling point is that economic relations are on their own insufficient for forging harmonious relations.

Barbieri criticises the liberal view that 'leaders are deterred from engaging in conflict with important trading partners for fear of losing the welfare gains associated with trade'. It is not always the case that the economic welfare trade generates outweighs the benefits of engaging in conflict. Such a linkage assumes a universal or standard conceptualisation of benefits, and this fails to take into account the composition of the state and the nature of the relationship it has with civil society in different contexts. Similarly, Buzan and Weaver (2003) suggest that the nature of the links between trade and security are governed by internal institutional conditions. Regions made up of weak states will be different from those made up of fairly strong states: weak and strong states are defined based on the degree of internal cohesion of the state and the degree of socio-political cohesion between the state and civil society (Buzan and Weaver 2003: 22). While, as they suggest, 'Sub-Saharan Africa contains predominantly pre-modern states', there is a degree of differentiation and signs of 'modern' state construction in some cases in southern Africa. Without doubt, most of the continent's states conform to the image of pre-modernity, with weak institutionalisation and relations with civil society constituted in neo-patrimonial terms.

## Regional political geography before 1994

Western European state-systems failed to take root in sub-Saharan Africa.[4] As Chabal and Daloz argue, the state in sub-Saharan Africa has an edifice that conforms to the Western template, yet its workings derive from patrimonial dynamics, characterised by a lack of 'emancipation' of the state from clientelistic social networks, informalisation of politics and personalisation of public service (Chabal and Daloz 1999: 8).

Much of southern Africa mirrors the failure of nation-state building and the lack of rules-based socio-political cohesion between the state and civil society. The new political elite in the region, after achieving independence, inherited state structures that were largely underdeveloped. Even the formation of a regional institutional entity (SADCC), which responded to the security challenges posed by apartheid South Africa in the 1970s, acted fitfully well into the 1980s.

The organisation was a politically directed effort aimed at dealing with essentially non-economic challenges. As such, it was less demanding of its members and accorded greater weight to the sovereignty of national governments, relative to supranational structures (Anglin 1983: 709). This sovereignty did not go far in defining the precise form the relationship between the state and civil society would take and, because the Western bureaucratic state model was relatively new, had the political elite as its primary security reference point rather than the citizens. As Anglin noted, 'national sovereignty was fundamental to SADCC's *modus operandi*'.[5] This logic, especially in its preoccupation with national interests and economic autonomy, is still pervasive even though SADCC evolved into SADC in 1992.

It is this form of sovereignty – characterised by Jackson as 'negative sovereignty' – where state elites in southern Africa are bent on safeguarding their security. This form of sovereignty is deliberately limited to the legality of the state's existence and does not confer responsibility or obligation upon state elites towards their subjects; the 'liberty' possessed by the state is in relation to the former colonial state and is especially articulated with respect to independence from external interference (Lal 1994: 81).

Lal observes, 'while paying lip service to the ideal of liberty in their relations with their subjects, their actions belied their commitment to this norm'.[6] This point also features in Jackson's observation of quasi-states when, paraphrasing J.S. Mill, he suggests that 'an independent government which is responsible to other sovereigns can still harm its subjects either deliberately or through negligence or incompetence' (Jackson 1991: 11). In this spirit, supranational entities such as SADC do not deserve their designation since their modus operandi does not protect individuals from the excesses of the state.

In more specific terms, SADCC's core objectives were framed around political initiatives designed to reduce dependence on South Africa and to achieve collective self-reliance and balanced development among member countries. But in reality the region was structured as a security complex in which states were singularly concerned with their survival and sought to maximise their aggregate power through regional cooperation.

Following the Realist perspective, security was considered a derivative of power; the *raison d'être* of the state was seen in terms of maximisation of its security vis-à-vis other states in the region. This political orientation blends well with economic nationalism or – more narrowly, neo-mercantilism, where each state is fixated with maximising its aggregate economic power in relation to other states. These two dynamics are still very entrenched in southern Africa's political and economic thinking. In the realm of politics, they are expressed in the form of a regional security complex.

Buzan defines a security complex as involving 'a group of states whose primary security concerns link together sufficiently closely that their national securities cannot realistically be considered apart from one another' (Buzan 1991: 190). This suggests both interdependence of rivalries and interdependence of interests. It is a form of containment of potential conflicts among contiguous states, and this can be both positive and negative.[7] Furthermore, as Mohamed Ayoob notes: 'The Third World state elites major concern – indeed, obsession – is with security at the level of both state structures and governing regimes' (Ayoob 1995: 6).

The fact that SADCC members saw apartheid South Africa as a common enemy and a threat to their political and economic well-being strengthened the basis for cooperation and sustained the regional body for another decade, until its transformation into the SADC. South Africa had since the 1970s engaged in systematic destabilising campaigns using its military force against neighbouring countries suspected of harbouring members of the African National Congress (ANC) – then a liberation movement – and its military wing. Evidently, the character of the security complex that existed in the region at that time was negative and shaped the contours of future relations between South Africa and regional partners post-apartheid.

## Post-apartheid relations in southern Africa

As the apartheid era ended in the early 1990s, it was widely expected that regional relations would be reconstituted in ways that would accelerate political modernisation and economic growth. In a fit of optimism, it was hoped that post-apartheid South Africa would play the role of a pivotal or hegemonic state, as well as an engine of growth for the entire region. However, apartheid ended over ten years ago, and with its overtly adversarial relations between South Africa and countries in the region, southern Africa remains fraught with political (especially security) and economic challenges. In the security context, latent tensions exist on many fronts within various countries, including those between the ruling elite and civil society, resulting from the incomplete process of state-building, lack of socio-political cohesion and the organisational weakness of state bureaucracy. Tensions also exist, broadly, between other countries in the region and South Africa because of its hegemonic image, as well as perceptions around the division of spoils in trade relations. Another line of tension exists between different groups and alliance structures in the region. This was evident in the military intervention in the Democratic Republic of Congo (DRC) by three SADC member countries (Angola, Namibia and Zimbabwe), ostensibly to defend the DRC from attacks by Rwanda and Uganda with the involvement of rebel movements.

Two key factors explain the uneasy relationship between South Africa and its regional partners. The first has to do with perceptions and envy; and the second, which is discussed in detail below, concerns the character of its trading relationship with regional partners. It is here that questions bearing on the relationship between trade and security may have relevance.

The lingering legacy of apartheid has cast regional relations in a negative light. Some elites in the region also harbour deep resentment against South Africa. Partly, the resentment is generated by a prospering South Africa amidst an almost generalised state of regional poverty and underdevelopment – a situation to which South Africa contributed during the apartheid era. Between 1980 and 1988 the total cost to the region of apartheid is estimated at US$60 billion, measured in terms of lost gross domestic product (GDP), with about one million deaths and millions of people displaced (Ostergaard 1990: 51). This purportedly amounted to three times the gross external resource inflows in the form of grants, soft loans, export credits and commercial loans over the nine-year period. These costs were unevenly distributed, with Angola and Mozambique shouldering a large proportion. About 1.5 million people in these countries were displaced as refugees to other countries.[8]

As Ahwireng-Obeng and McGowan have suggested, state elites in the region had expectations that the new South Africa would feel a moral obligation to 'engage southern Africa in a positive manner' (Ahwireng-Obeng and McGowan 1998: 12). Given the huge cost that South Africa's apartheid policies inflicted on the region, the sense of entitlement that regional elites have with respect to South Africa's largesse is not entirely misplaced, especially since South Africa's dominance of economic (trade) relations continued post-apartheid. As Table 3.1 shows, the trade complementarity within the region is heavily weighted in favour of South Africa.

The indices reflected Table 3.1 reveal asymmetric complementarity between South Africa and the majority of SADC countries, which South Africa's political elite put down to lack of supply capacity in neighbouring countries. An International Monetary Fund (IMF) working paper by Khandelwal on regional integration in Southern Africa also reveals that the extent of product complementarity within SADC is very low. In its measurement, the product complementarity index ranges from 0 (which signifies no complementarity) to 100 (which express full complementarity). According to Khandelwal's calculation, using UN-COMTRADE database, 'there is complementarity between South Africa's exports and the imports of the rest of the region, but not vice versa' (Khandelwal 2004: 16).

On reflection, this suggests two things. First, the structure of trade in the region follows a mercantilist framework, where the gains of trade are seen as generated solely through exports, and because South Africa is a structurally dominant economy such an arrangement serves its interests. Second, this could also mean that, in spite of the prevailing mercantilist manner in which trade relations between two or more countries are structured, South Africa is able to find markets for its products in the neighbouring region, while the reverse is not the case as a result of supply-side constraints (structural limitations) in other countries. Or it could be both.

Nevertheless, as Khandelwal suggests, the trade imbalance raises concerns regarding polarisation as 'investment may be attracted towards the larger and more industrially diversified economies in the region'.[9] This also clearly demonstrates that the level of integration within the region is quite shallow and, as such, extant trade integration is a weak basis for creating strong conditions for sustained peace in the region. Indeed, trade relations understood as a zero-sum game, as is the case in the region, do not augur well for harmonious relations or sustained peace.

Alluding to the dangers of mercantilism, Douglas Irwin points out that concern with zero-sum gains in the context of Anglo-Dutch rivalry for the East India trade routes generated militarised disputes in Europe in the seventeenth century (Irwin 1991: 1296). The *raison d'être* of state during this period, Irwin suggests, was to maximise its aggregate welfare and relative power vis-à-vis other states.[10] As we observed earlier, this nationalistic mindset and approach towards economic relations has persisted in southern Africa well into the establishment of SADC in 1992 and beyond. In part this was influenced by then prevailing pan-Africanism and the quest for political independence and economic self-sufficiency in the colonial aftermath.

Nonetheless, the establishment of SADC in 1992 marked an important phase for regionalism in southern Africa, and portended a gradual shift away

Table 3.1 Bilateral complementarity indices in SADC

| Exporting country | Importing country | | | | | | | | | | |
|---|---|---|---|---|---|---|---|---|---|---|---|
| | Bots. | Mal. | Maur. | Moz. | Namib. | SA | Swaz. | Tanz. | Zamb. | Zimb. | Average |
| Botswana | – | 7.5 | 11.3 | 17.8 | 9.6 | 13.0 | 9.7 | 7.4 | 7.8 | 8.9 | 13.0 |
| Malawi | 13.7 | – | 9.3 | 18.4 | 11.6 | 11.6 | 13.0 | 9.3 | 8.1 | 6.6 | 11.3 |
| Mauritius | 16.8 | 11.3 | – | 21.3 | 14.6 | 15.3 | 15.8 | 12.0 | 10.3 | 8.9 | 14.0 |
| Mozambique | 23.2 | 21.8 | **26.7** | – | 23.9 | 24.6 | **26.2** | 20.8 | 19.5 | 19.1 | 22.9 |
| Namibia | 22.8 | 14.0 | 20.5 | 24.8 | – | 17.1 | 18.8 | 11.5 | 21.0 | 11.3 | 18.0 |
| South Africa | **53.9** | **48.5** | **54.1** | **59.4** | **54.1** | – | **55.1** | **51.3** | **51.0** | **49.9** | **53.0** |
| Swaziland | 27.9 | 20.4 | 23.5 | **30.0** | **29.9** | 22.0 | – | 20.6 | 19.0 | 17.6 | 23.4 |
| Tanzania | 16.4 | 13.1 | 20.2 | 20.2 | 13.4 | 13.2 | 13.3 | – | 8.9 | 7.1 | 14.0 |
| Zambia | 19.0 | 12.9 | 19.3 | 23.2 | 14.9 | 16.6 | 14.2 | 12.8 | – | 11.9 | 16.1 |
| Zimbabwe | 13.7 | 14.0 | 18.4 | 20.4 | 10.6 | 11.5 | 11.5 | 10.6 | 9.1 | – | 13.3 |

Source: From IMF Working Paper, WP/04/227; IMF Staff Calculations using UN-COMTRADE data.

Note: Angola, DRC and Lesotho were excluded due to lack of data. Seychelles, even though included here, left SADC towards the end of 2004; bold denoting a fairly good measure of complementarities is as original table.

from old, exclusively politically driven regionalism, which had been defined largely by excessive state interventionism, and the suffocation of markets within the context of the Cold War and apartheid in South Africa. As by far the largest economy in the region, with relatively well-developed institutions and sophisticated productive forces, South Africa was initially welcomed as a member of SADC by most regional governments. This prompted some African scholars to predict the dawn of a new era for the region, characterised by political and economic modernisation. Asante observed that 'Southern Africa can look forward to the closer integration of the dominant economy of the subcontinent into the economic and political structures of the region' (Asante 1997: 12).

In his take, Azam suggested that South Africa's regional role could propel growth in southern Africa in pretty much the same way that the Asian tigers (Hong Kong, South Korea, Singapore and Taiwan) led the way for Malaysia and southern China (Azam 1995: 12). Azam further suggested that, because of South Africa's future role in southern Africa, the region 'might become the main pole of Africa's development in the medium-term'.[11] Similarly, Western countries hailed South Africa's enhanced participation in the regional economy as an important development that would help stem the tide of economic decline and poor governance and anchor regional economies on a sustainable growth path.

South Africa's reintegration into the region heralded the evolution of regional ties from the minimalist project coordination type towards regional economic integration, especially in trade. This was initially seen in a positive light, and it was hoped that it would facilitate the development of neighbouring economies – which the previous apartheid government stifled – through developmental transfers and enhanced access to South Africa's relatively large market. The bilateral deficits that these countries had with South Africa gave more force to such expectations.

Trade relations in southern Africa were formalised through the signing of the SADC Protocol on Trade, which most countries in the region initially expected to be an instrument that would equalise economic gains in the region. In this respect, trade relations and the benefits associated with them were not seen from the point of view of a fully liberalised trade regime in the region, but through mercantilist lenses. As such there was reluctance amongst most countries in taking major liberalisation obligations, and South Africa was generally expected to make generous offers in its liberalisation schedule in order to address the existing developmental asymmetries in the region, which it later did, albeit under a generally protectionist and defensive climate.

In essence, there was not much reflection on what exactly countries were committing to and what the implications of regional economic integration would be in their national economies. The old SADCC structure (including the Summit of Heads of State and Government, the Council of Ministers, Sectoral Commissions, the Standing Committee of Officials and the Secretariat) became the institutional edifice of the new SADC.[12] It was an attempt to modernise SADC without having to re-think its purpose or take a long-term view of its role in the region and in international relations.

There was also no substantial transformation of regional relations as they existed pre-apartheid and during the Cold War era. It is therefore fair to conclude that the security-complex milieu was not decisively shifted for the region to conform to new global economic challenges, which required, amongst other things, liberalisation of trade and close integration into global markets. That the intended trade liberalisation process in the region was not genuinely driven from below by private economic agents posed major difficulties for the project. Indeed, political considerations overshadowed economic exigencies.

### *The SADC Trade Protocol*

The SADC Trade Protocol was thus signed in 1996 against the backdrop of political changes in South Africa's relations with its neighbouring region, and as the basis on which the region would ensure its economic growth and development as well as positive integration into the global economy. The SADC Trade Protocol was aimed at liberalising intra-regional trade in goods and services with the ultimate view of establishing a free trade area for SADC through an asymmetric tariff phase-down process. The Protocol came into force in September 2000, after the necessary number of signatories was achieved. The DRC is the only country that has not acceded to the Trade Protocol, and Angola has yet to put forward a tariff offer. Incidentally, these are the countries that have had the most frequent incidence of conflict in the region.

Since ratification, the implementation process has been slow. Apart from the fact that neighbouring countries were far less prepared to engage in deeper and meaningful liberalisation of their trade, at the heart of the hiatus in the SADC trade protocol has been South Africa's lack of positive leadership in the early phase. It is believed by other SADC member countries as having been preoccupied with its own short-term interests in the region and demonstrating very limited sensitivity towards its neighbours, conceding, however, that the tariff phase-down is asymmetric in favour of poor countries in the region.

Some of the often cited examples of South Africa's lack of leadership include stringent RO, especially in textiles and clothing, the automotive sector and other manufacturing sub-sectors, which some studies have pointed to as having created a gridlock in the liberalisation process; the existence of other non-tariff barriers; high tariffs in certain product lines such as tobacco and sugar; and tariff escalation in others, for example wood products. The view that South Africa's approach has been somewhat mercantilist is consistent with the sense of grievance other countries in the region and beyond have towards South Africa.

South Africa's approach during the negotiations on the SADC Trade

Protocol played strongly to domestic groups – and was motivated by its domestic growth concerns and anxieties regarding the competitiveness of its domestic industry. In this sense, instead of taking a lead in opening its borders, it fostered relations of rivalry by stringently insisting on protectionist measures. This has, however, aggravated political sensitivities in the region, with potentially corrosive effects on the political influence that South Africa could hope to exert in future.

A climate charged with political insecurity and anxieties regarding the role of the regional power could significantly weaken the platform for fostering long-term peace and security. Although, conceptually, the linkage between regional trade and security is not a solidly grounded one, it should not be an impossible task to examine the prospects, or lack thereof, of peace dividends in an integrating area based on empirical observation. In southern Africa, such an examination should entail the extent to which the design of the regional trade agreement (trade protocol) facilitates deeper integration amongst various countries, fosters harmonious relations and contributes positively in creating a general climate of peace on a sustained basis rather than generating possibilities for reversal.

South Africa's claim to the status of 'security manager' in southern Africa, although not officially pronounced, is not uncontested, especially by countries such as Zimbabwe, which had previously enjoyed a status of a regional hegemon before South Africa was re-integrated into SADC. While regional power centres or pivotal states can give coherence to regional security, as Ayoob suggests, they also have the potential to increase the conflict level if their legitimacy is not accepted or their claims for primacy are under dispute (Ayoob 1995: 59).

Some SADC countries have, as a way of countervailing South Africa's dominance, opted for an alternative centre through which to formalise their commercial relations. Zambia, Zimbabwe, Mauritius and Malawi, all SADC members, are simultaneously participating in the Common Market for Eastern and Southern Africa (COMESA) free trade agreement (FTA) arrangement in a move that is viewed as a snub to a South African-centred SADC (Lee 2003).

Furthermore, these countries are currently negotiating economic partnership agreements (EPAs) with the EU under a different regional configuration, which does not include any of the Southern African Customs Union (SACU) members.[13] In a study conducted among business actors in the region there was a strong view that Tanzania, an SADC member country also active in efforts to establish an East African Community Customs Union (EACCU) and political federation, should integrate closely with COMESA.[14] While politically it may make sense for Tanzania to plug itself into SADC processes, business actors in the country are conscious of the fact that greater benefits could be realised elsewhere – COMESA specifically. It has not escaped private economic agents that a regional trade integration scheme has to open more opportunities for commerce – something that SADC is struggling to achieve – rather than creating a gridlocked enclave.

One of the crucial points in the SADC Trade Protocol concerns RO. For example, the initial rule, which required a change of tariff heading, was replaced by rules that required detailed technical processes, much higher domestic value-added and lower permitted import content (World Bank 2005: 65). This was done without any evidence that existing rules were ineffective and needed to be tightened. There are two major reasons advanced by South Africa in particular: the first is a barely veiled mercantilist one and emphasises the need to curtail trans-shipment through customs loopholes; and the second is ostensibly utilitarian, and views these as instruments to force industrial development in the region. These have been heavily criticised by trade practitioners and independent studies in the region.[15]

This exotic protectionist instrument did not only reveal the extent to which South Africa has at times thrown around its weight in the region to benefit its interests, but also the general lack of commitment to liberalisation. A recent World Bank study on trade, regionalism and development, has noted that 'specifying rules of origin on a product by product basis offers opportunities for sectoral interests to influence the specification of the rules in a protectionist way' (World Bank 2005: 70).

The design of these RO creates variation along product lines. For example, in some products, the requirement would be a simple change of tariff heading; in others it would be a change of tariff chapter; and in others it would be specification for a particular technical process or requirement for levels of value addition in order to qualify for preferential treatment.[16] This creates confusion for already incapacitated customs officials, and also holds the potential to slow down momentum in regional trade integration and give rise to mistrust and tensions in the region. Given the political sensitivities that already existed in the region, the design of the existing trade arrangement in SADC is far from promoting harmonious relations and creates unnecessary political strains in a region already racked by tensions.

Apart from these complex RO, there are other deeper problems in the region, whose roots lie in the institutional domestic setting and structural shape of the economies. Some of these problems include a lack of will by political principals who are obsessed with short-term gains, poor support given to technocrats, weak institutional instruments to implement agreed-upon policies both at the national and regional levels, and overlapping membership and competition between various regional integration schemes with geographical contiguity. Table 3.2 below shows the extent of overlapping membership – a situation that represents a resource drain on poor countries as they have to participate actively in various structures, pay membership dues and implement agreements.

### *SADC Protocol mid-term review*

The failure of regional trade integration has been a subject of interest amongst African scholars and political economists since the early 1980s.

*Table 3.2* Overlapping membership

|  | SACU | COMESA | EACCU | SADC |
|---|---|---|---|---|
| Botswana | X |  |  | X |
| Lesotho | X |  |  | X |
| Madagascar |  | X |  | X |
| Malawi |  |  |  | X |
| Mauritius |  | X |  |  |
| Mozambique |  |  |  | X |
| Namibia | X |  |  | X |
| South Africa | X |  |  | X |
| Swaziland | X | X |  | X |
| Tanzania |  |  | X | X |
| Zambia |  | X |  | X |
| Zimbabwe |  | X |  | X |

Source: Adapted from a TSG report on the SADC Protocol mid-term review, 2005.

From the outset, such efforts were directed through political means and geared towards political objectives, namely creating Africa's economic and political union. The ideological focus was pan-Africanism. It was only late in the 1990s that a serious effort to integrate into the global economy was undertaken, and regional integration schemes began to take a more outward shape. Even so, there are still strong shades of ideology in the integration processes across the sub-Saharan sub-continent, with economic rationale heavily subjected to political expediency. Regionalism in southern Africa is still struggling to make a decisive shift from inward orientation to external integration.

It is doubtful that Europe's functionalist and linear model of integration and security arrangements – epitomised in the EU – is appropriate for Africa's circumstances. Africa's state forms and the shape of its institutions do not provide propitious conditions for such complex systems. It should not be supposed that these states can achieve at the regional level what they have failed or been unwilling to achieve at the domestic setting, namely, institutionalisation. As Lal observes, 'it is unlikely that that third world nation-states are going to give up their adherence to this principle [sovereignty] and to the extant system of nation-states for some more cosmopolitan or supranational form of international society' (Lal 1994: 82).

In early 2004 SADC leaders adopted a Regional Indicative Strategic Development Programme (RISDP) which, unrealistically, aims at achieving an SADC CU by 2010, despite the generally slow pace of implementation of the SADC Trade Protocol.

SADC's RISDP views the attainment of an FTA in 2008 'as a step towards achieving a Customs Union and subsequently a Common Market.'[17] This objective, as the RISDP points out, would be achieved on the basis of greater commitment to the implementation of the SACU Protocol on Trade, appropriately designed RO and greater harmonisation of customs rules and procedures, including standards. The RISDP sets out ambitious targets – very much along the lines of the EU model – for achieving deeper integration.[18] These are:

- completion of negotiations for the SADC CU: 2010;
- completion of negotiations for the SADC common market: 2015;
- diversification of industrial structure and exports with emphasis on value-addition: 2015; and
- establishment of an SADC monetary union: 2016.

This strategy does not seem to have taken into account the ground realities: for example, the existence of multiple integration schemes and overlapping membership; the new SACU agreement finalised in 2002; and the continuing EU EPA negotiations, the outcome of which could significantly alter the nature of integration in southern Africa. Furthermore, there is no mooted institutional mechanism to speed the integration process set out in the RISDP.

The SADC Trade Protocol's mid-term review took place during the latter half of 2004 and was meant to infuse momentum in the liberalisation process. This review was essentially designed to be a stock-taking exercise, focusing mainly on market access, trade flows, tariff phase-down schedules, non-tariff barriers and the pattern of trade flows since 2000. It was meant to look at the progress made so far in these dimensions and propose ways of fast-tracking liberalisation in the sub-region.

Without getting into fine detail on the outcomes of the review, a number of concerns were raised by the report, including what the report calls a situation where 'a much larger degree of implementation existed'. Countries such as Zimbabwe, Malawi and Zambia have substantially delayed implementation of their tariff phase-down schedules; in some instances there have been difficulties with implementing revised, product-specific RO; and in some cases there is poor communication with the private sector.

There are ongoing debates in the region as to the logic of deeper trade integration in an area with so little in common with respect to economic interests, and whether other forms of cooperation focusing on development projects, political cooperation and harmonisation of regulatory systems would not be more appropriate. For example, SADC has more than ten other protocols to foster cooperation in other areas, including mining, infrastructure, energy, environment, and on politics, security and defence.

Since there is a lack of both conceptual and institutional linkage between various protocols – especially related to trade and economic integration on the one hand, and politics and security on the other – it would be difficult to test empirically the liberal-trade-peace assumption that increased trade could generate peaceful outcomes. Even though the level of intra-regional trade is much lower than what one would find in developed countries, still there are trade flows between different countries in southern Africa, both formally and informally, and it does not appear that this has any direct bearing on the state of politics or security.

As suggested in this chapter, more indirectly, trade relations that are fashioned along neo-mercantilist lines have heightened political tensions, but this has not led to actual conflict. This could also be attributed to the fact that there is an institutional arrangement in place, to which politicians have given more attention, to manage issues related to politics, security and defence in the region.

## The organ of politics, security and defence

The history of the southern African region is coloured by political tensions that later took on a very strong security or military dimension. This was evident from the early efforts in establishing SADCC, the same year that apartheid South Africa announced its 'Total Strategy', designed primarily to maintain white rule in South Africa, but also to: erode external support for the liberation movements; secure recognition of South Africa's hegemony in the region; thwart attempts by SADCC countries to lessen their economic dependence on South Africa; and destroy the image of non-racial states in the SADCC region as a model for South Africa (Ostergaard 1990: 52). To counter such efforts, the governing elite in the region's countries that had achieved political freedom from colonial powers – notably Tanzania, Botswana, Zambia, Lesotho and Malawi – established themselves as frontline states (FLS).

This collective show of unity was to later culminate in the establishment of SADC with a strong security dimension. Apart from South Africa's destabilisation agenda, issuing from its 'Total Strategy', there were also Cold War interplays that further moulded a particular security environment in the region, forcing the elite to be singularly concerned with preservation of territorial integrity and staying alert to external threats.

Even after the collapse of the Cold War and apartheid South Africa, hostilities continued to run deep within the region. During the Cold War this situation was made all the more septic by persisting internal conflicts in Angola and Mozambique – both taking more than two decades to abate – with apartheid South Africa playing a major role in fuelling these wars. However, in the post-apartheid and post-Cold War era, the region has, by and large, remained frozen in time. The outbreak of conflict in the Great Lakes in 1998 brought out sharply the complexities of inter-state security and demonstrated quite emphatically that regional integration has a long way to go before creating sustained peace in southern Africa.

As I noted earlier, the conception of security in SADC and in most of Africa is generally informed by the traditional Realist view that regards state survival as supreme, and in which the pursuit of power lies at the core of defining relations between states. By implication, this de-emphasises, if not invalidates, the place of individuals or non-state actors as referent objects for security (Van Schalkwyk and Cilliers 2004: 6–10). The political tensions in Zimbabwe and SADC's inability to play any meaningful role is one example where conflict affecting individuals is trivialised compared to conflict between different states. This is the mindset that still dominates SADC today. SADC countries that participated in the Great Lakes conflict did so ostensibly to defend a fellow SADC country facing external aggression, and using the ambiguously constructed 'Mutual Defence Pact' as a justification.

The notion of 'existential threat' and what Buzan and Weaver characterise as 'the continued prominence of territoriality in the domain of security' (Buzan and Weaver 2003: 11), has been the obsession of political actors in the region for many years, and moving away from this narrow view remains an important challenge in southern Africa. The thinking behind this approach is still reminiscent of the Cold War milieu. State actors expend most of their energies on security cooperation rather than economic integration. The two most critical facets of SADC's work are kept apart both conceptually and institutionally, with little effort to integrate the two or to treat them symmetrically.

The main instrument for dealing with politics, security and defence in the region (the OPSD) was established on the recommendations of an SADC workshop on democracy, peace and security held in Windhoek on 11–16 July 1994. In this workshop SADC's commitment to a greater role in areas of security coordination, conflict mediation and military cooperation became noticeably evident (Malan 1998: 267). It must be emphasised though, as Hammerstad has pointed out, that the OPSD was established rather too hastily, and lacked a solid basis for evolving common values and shared understanding on the future of regional security, as well as the precise meaning of security in the context of new regional relations.

The OPSD, as Van Nieuwkerk pointed out, was 'characterised by inappropriate design, the suffocating arrogant state elites, and lack of resources'.[19] The seeds of its failure were very much sown in its beginnings. Robert Mugabe, the president of Zimbabwe, presided over the newly established body in August 1996, in part as a way of repositioning himself vis-à-vis South Africa's entry into SADC. He insisted on the independence of this structure from the SADC, which was chaired by Nelson Mandela, then president of South Africa. This immediately brought to the surface tensions between Zimbabwe and South Africa.

The existence of two potentially rival summits – both supreme decision-making structures – in the SADC created a situation that was bound to unravel the pretence of post-apartheid regional unity. This tension has also played itself out on a number of occasions in other SADC processes, including trade relations. This counter-tendency is also reflected in the overlapping membership between two competing regional integration schemes – SADC and COMESA.

In its first few years of existence, the OPSD lacked a clear direction, and its work was characterised by acrimony and discord. The first signs of fragility were evident in 1996 when SADC refused to endorse Mandela's criticism of human rights violations in Nigeria (Leysons and Thompson 2001: 58). Given the undemocratic nature of many SADC leaders, this was to be expected. However, Mandela also protested at the manner in which the OPSD functioned and the way Mugabe ran it as his prized power base in SADC, and threatened to resign if it remained structurally de-linked from the SADC body. The mutual acrimony generated by these sets of events continued to shape political relations in the region and emphasised the limits South Africa had in using its political clout to achieve certain outcomes.

Although the instruments of economic integration and political and security cooperation existed separately, developments in one area could feed into the other. However, the lack of institutional and policy coherence in dealing with economic and security challenges render the potentially positive association between the two weak. These are both important initiatives that suffer from poor institutional design.

Although the idea of the OPSD was initially a laudable attempt at creating a security regime, the complexity of regional power politics rapidly undermined its effectiveness. The rivalry between South Africa and Zimbabwe did not help build sustainable foundations for a security framework and, in fact, the OPSD's agenda dominated SADC and over-shadowed other concerns related to human security, collectively referred to as development security: water, food, gender issues and health.

### The OPSD and the Great Lakes conflict

The weaknesses of the OPSD's operating modalities under Mugabe were tested and exposed during the DRC conflict when Laurent Kabila, the DRC's president, faced internal and external threats to his rule. Having joined SADC (something that SADC has since bitterly regretted), the DRC issue soon rose to prominence and would for a considerable amount of time dominate regional relations.

The war in the DRC started in 1998 when Uganda and Rwanda sent their armies to help various rebel movements to topple Kabila's government, which they had helped put in power the previous year. In response to Kabila's call for aid, Angola, Zimbabwe and Namibia (the so-called 'SADC allies') sent troops to the DRC, ostensibly to 'protect' an SADC member against foreign invasion. There is no doubt that Mugabe also saw this as an opportunity to reinforce his regional authority, which was slowly evaporating with South Africa increasingly gaining a leadership foothold in regional affairs.

Yet, the DRC admittance was another South African creation in SADC; its application for membership was sponsored by South Africa when Mandela made a persuasive point about the space SADC would have in influencing political developments in the DRC. This was despite the opposition from the majority of SADC countries who had argued that it would not be viable to accept a new member when meaningful integration amongst existing members had not been achieved. Having accepted the DRC into SADC, there was a sense of obligation amongst some SADC countries to come to its defence.

South Africa was excluded from participating in a meeting hosted by Mugabe at Lake Victoria in August 1998, where the decision to commit troops to the Great Lakes was taken.[20] This again exposed the cracks that lay underneath the surface of unity in the SADC structure, as well as the weaknesses of the security arrangement, especially the fact that there were no enduring common values that bound various actors together. Tensions between the Zimbabwe-led group, including Namibia and Angola on the one hand, and South Africa on the other were all too apparent. The Great Lakes conflict lasted for over two years and was temporarily halted when a diplomatic solution was explored, with Zambia initially assuming the role of a neutral mediator. The process initiated by Zambia led to the signing of a ceasefire agreement in Lusaka in 1999.

The ceasefire did not last for very long. It was followed by South Africa's initiative, supported by Botswana and the United Nations, to broker a lasting peace accord known as the Inter-Congolese Dialogue, in Gaborone, Botswana, in August 2001. As its name suggests, it was aimed at fostering a dialogue and pulling together a framework that would lead into a power-sharing arrangement. The shape of the power-sharing formula first emerged on 30 July 2002 in Sun City, South Africa, with the final peace agreement – effectively ending formal hostilities between the belligerents – signed in April 2003. This did not completely stem the conflict, as intermittent skirmishes along the eastern parts of the DRC continue. It is here that informal trade networks, linked to the looting of resources, including diamonds and other commodities, flourish. Such networks expand on the back of pre-existing informal and illegal trade processes that bypass, and sometimes involve, state officials.

The weakness of regional integration and cooperation in southern Africa is evident on two fronts: first with regards to low levels of formal trade amongst neighbouring countries; and second with respect to the tenuous security foundations in SADC, especially in view of the impending political and economic crisis in Zimbabwe and the fragile situation in the Great Lakes. These have clearly shown how weak the institutional architecture of the regional organisation is and the lack of appropriate and enduring policy instruments to deal with such security crises.

### Institutional restructuring of security relations

On the security front, efforts were made between 2000 and 2004 to restructure the institutional design and processes. The Strategic Indicative Plan for the OPSD (SIPO) was signed in 2001 and this sought to overhaul the previous security arrangement in the region by placing a strong emphasis on peace and security as a linchpin for socio-economic development. One of its key object-ives is to encourage greater interdependence and shared interests in the region. There is recognition that 'the region still faces potential and actual military threats that include *inter-alia* armed conflicts in some Member States, unfinished demobilisation, disarmament, re-integration, monitoring of former military personnel, and the prevalence of terrorism'.[21] SIPO is divided into two related policy instruments: the protocol on politics, security and defence, and a mutual defence pact.

The language used in crafting this policy framework adopts the rhetoric of democratisation, institution-building, human rights, political pluralism and civil society quite liberally – something that is a far cry from observed practices on the ground, especially in countries such as Zimbabwe, Angola, Swaziland and the DRC. The SIPO framework defines security along four sectors: the political sector; the defence sector; the state security sector; and the public security sector. We will only look here at the political sector, which also touches on the other dimensions.

The political sector objectives are structured along the theme of prevent-ing, containing and resolving inter- and intra-state conflict through peaceful means. More specifically this would entail standardisation of conflict indica-tors; developing early warning systems in member countries; enhancing capacity for conflict prevention, management and resolution; and a regular assessment of factors that have a potential to lead to conflict, including imbalances in welfare and poverty.

On the face of it, it would be difficult to contend with these lofty objectives, but the reality sharply diverges from the rhetoric: SADC has limited capacity – both financially and in terms of human capital – to undertake some of these complex processes. The organisation draws much of its financial resources from donor countries, without which it cannot exist as a viable structure.

The key objectives are: promotion of political cooperation among member states; promotion of democratic institutions and practices; observation of universal human rights; and the protection of civilians against instability arising from the breakdown of law and order, intra- and inter-state conflict and aggression. Again the recent practices in Zimbabwe, where the state has trampled human rights with no positive intervention from SADC to help affected citizens makes it difficult to take this formal policy process seriously.

It would be fair to observe that much of the language is framed for the international (including donor) community who have historically played a significant role in shoring up SADC financially. Interestingly, the outlines of SADC's strategic plan for security mirror those of the North Atlantic Treaty Organisation (NATO) charters, with similar wording in some respects. SADC has sought to modernise its institutions when the constituents' state foundations are quite shaky, and with shallow democratic ethos and institutions.

There is little doubt that SADC is obsessed with its international image, as its lifeline derives from international donors. Some of the 'modern' practices that SADC is promoting include those related to peace missions, humanitarian efforts, disaster management and support for civilian authorities. In this respect, it has established a peace-keeping centre in Zimbabwe – a country that has so far shown little respect for human rights and the rule of law. Furthermore, there is also allusion to combating terrorism, exchanging intelligence and confronting challenges related to organised crime, including drug trafficking, money laundering and human trafficking.

A lack of trust and a strong consensual platform of shared interests, based on values that are rooted in democratic practices, will continue to undermine SADC and any processes towards building a sustainable peace and security environment in the region. The institutionalisation of peace and security in the region would derive weightier force from bottom-up processes, and this would be possible when democratic ideals with appropriate institutions have taken root at the domestic level.

## Conclusion: some questions for policy consideration

Given the fact that SADC(C) was established in a climate fuelled by security tensions, it would have been expected that there would be volumes of studies examining the relationship between the security dimension and trade relations in a more specific context. At the policy level, there is an implicit linkage between the two. For example, SADC's OPSD has been an important leg alongside the economic integration agenda, and has in fact dominated much of the SADC's agenda after 1996, notwithstanding its severe limitations, as discussed earlier.

One of the arguments that this chapter has been making is that strong institution building and consolidation, both at the domestic and regional level, is a critical component in building a sustainable security community in the region. This will not simply be a function of increased commercial relations – as such relations already exist in an informal manner straddling both legal and illegal lines – but, most fundamentally, it will be the outcome of a maturing domestic polity.

Deepening democracy would entail, amongst other things, strong commitment to building strong institutions, recasting of state–society nexus in a manner that ensures institutional separation between the state and civil society, and with social movements given space to exist independently, and to participate meaningfully in political processes. Furthermore, rather than dealing with trade integration or developmental cooperation and security separately, it would be far more helpful, for policy coherence, to articulate these in tandem. There is therefore an important policy imperative to examine the intersection between trade and security in regional contexts.

One of the important questions that also needs further exploration deals with the distribution of material gains: where there are asymmetries of power and skewed distribution of gains, how can a 'core' or pivotal state within a region use its position of advantage positively to equalise benefits or off-set losses arising from asymmetrical transactional arrangements? Is there a room for making developmental transfers in order to incentivise greater commitment to regional integration, especially for countries that are likely to lose in the short term?

These questions are linked to questions related to the commitment of the pivotal state in the region to play a greater role and give meaningful leadership in integrating the region. There does not seem to be such a commitment or urge to play a positive leadership role by South Africa, partly due to resource limits imposed by its own domestic social challenges, as well as awareness of hegemonic limits linked to the negative regional role that South Africa has played in the past. Redeeming itself, and thus salvaging the region, will either be a function of time or resource commitment.

In this regard, the SACU, which has a very long history of integration and which is firmly anchored in South Africa's trade and industrial structure, emerges as one important vehicle to drive integration in the region in the future. There is a possibility for SACU to expand in future. This would come on the back of its success in consolidating itself as a trade liberalisation project and an instrument to achieve regulatory reforms and harmonisation in the integrating area.

Furthermore, as SACU grows in its stature as a global actor, first structuring trade and developmental relations with the EU (under South Africa's leadership – a process that is currently underway), and second concluding external trade linkages as a solid trade bloc, the epicentre of regional trade integration will fundamentally shift away from SADC. This would also help in overcoming the problems related to multiple and over-lapping membership in regional integration schemes.

South African policy-makers have hinted that their attention will be turned towards building SACU structures and consolidating its international identity, which could effectively mean SADC would cease to be an instrument of trade integration, while retaining important developmental and security functions. This should then make it less difficult for South Africa to enlarge its developmental assistance to fewer SACU countries as it deepens its hegemony in the immediate sub-region. Much of this assistance can come from the EU itself. While it is not clear how the much-needed relationship would be structured between SACU (as a trade liberalisation instrument) and SADC (as a developmental and security structure), with greater clarity of purpose in both structures defining the future of the region it should be less difficult than it currently is.

## Notes

1    This theme is explored in greater detail in Hirschmann (1977).
2    Ibid.: 80.
3    Ibid.: 79.
4    Ibid.: 219.
5    Ibid.: 692.

6 Ibid.
7 Ibid.: 194.
8 Ibid.
9 Ibid.: 17.
10 Ibid.: 1297.
11 Ibid.
12 See TRALAC (2005).
13 SACU includes South Africa, Botswana, Lesotho, Namibia and Swaziland.
14 See Charalambides (2005).
15 See Flatters (2004).
16 Ibid.: 70.
17 See SADC (2004).
18 Ibid.
19 See Van Nieuwkerk (2001).
20 James Barber (2004: 194).
21 SIPO, 2004.

## References

Ahwireng-Obeng, F. and McGowan, P.J. (1998) 'Partner or hegemon? South Africa in Africa', *Journal of Contemporary African Studies*, 16:1, 5–38.

Anglin, D.G. (1983) 'Economic liberation and regional co-operation in Southern Africa: SADCC and PTA', *International Organisation*, 37:4, Autumn, 681–711.

Asante, S.K.B. (1997) *Regionalism and Africa's Development*, London: Macmillan.

Ayoob, M. (1995) *The Third World Security Predicament: State-making, Regional Conflict, and the International System*, London: Lynne Rienner.

Azam, J.-P. (1995) 'Development policy for Africa: a research agenda', in J. Berthelemy (ed.) *Wither African Economies?* Paris: OECD.

Barber, J. (2004) *Mandela's World*, Oxford: James Currey.

Barbieri, K. and Schneider, G. (1999) 'Globalization and peace: assessing new directions in the study of trade and conflict', *Journal of Peace Research*, 36:4, 387–404.

Buzan, B. (1991) *People, States and Fear: An Agenda for International Security Studies in Post-Cold War era*, 2nd edn, London: Harvester-Wheatsheaf.

Buzan, B. and Weaver, O. (2003) *Regions and Powers: The Structure of International Security*, Cambridge: Cambridge University Press.

Chabal, P. and Daloz, J.-P. (1999) *Africa Works: Disorder as Political Instrument*, Indiana: James Currey.

Charalambides, N. (2005) 'Perspectives, priorities, and role of the private sector in regional integration and implications for regional trade arrangements', ECDPM discussion paper, Maastricht: European Centre for Development Policy Management.

Flatters, F. (2004) 'SADC rules of origin: undermining regional free trade', paper presented at the USAID-funded 'Trade Policy Workshop', Johannesburg.

Hirschmann, A.O. (1977) *The Passions and the Interests: Political Arguments for Capitalism before its Triumph*, Princeton, NJ: Princeton University Press.

Irwin, D. (1991) 'Mercantilism as strategic trade policy: the Anglo-Dutch rivalry for the East India trade', *Journal of Political Economy*, 6, 1296–1314.

Jackson, R.H. (1991) *Quasi-states, Sovereignty and International Relations*, Cambridge: Cambridge University Press.

Khandelwal, P. (2004) 'COMESA and SADC: prospects and challenges for regional trade integration', IMF working paper, WP/04/227, International Monetary Fund, Washington DC.

Lal, D. (1994) *The Case for Unshackling Economic Markets: Against Dirigisme*, San Francisco: International Center for Economic Growth.

Lee, M. (2003) *The Political Economy of Regionalism in Southern Africa*, Boulder, CO: Lynne Rienner.

Leysens, A. and Thompson, L. (2001) 'Emancipating the dead? Revisiting changing notions of human security in Southern Africa', in L. Thompson, N. Poku and C. Thomas (eds) *Development and Security in Southern Africa*, Westport, CT: Greenwood Press.

Malan, M. (1998) 'Prospects for keeping the peace', in R.I. Rothberg and G. Mills (eds) *War and Peace in Southern Africa: Crime, Drugs, Armies and Trade*, Cambridge, MA: Brookings Institution Press.

Mansfield, E.D. and Pevehouse, J.C. (2000) 'Trade blocs, trade flows and international conflict', *International Organization*, 54:4, Autumn, 775–808.

Ostergaard, T. (1990) *SADC: A Political and Economic Survey*, Copenhagen: Ministry of Foreign Affairs.

SADC (2004) *Regional Indicative Strategic Development Plan*, Gaberone: SADC.

TRALAC (2005) 'SADC/COMESA/EAC and EPA negotiations', University of Stellenbosch: TRALAC.

Van Nieuwkerk, A. (2001) 'Sub regional collaborative security: lessons from the OAU and SADC', *South African Journal of International Affairs*, 8:2, Winter, 81–94.

Van Schalkwyk, G. and Cilliers, J. (2004) *Civil Society and the SADC Security Agenda*, draft mimeo, Pretoria: Institute of Security Studies.

World Bank (2005) *Global Economic Prospects 2005*, Washington, DC: World Bank.

# 4 Regional trade agreements in South Asia

## Trade and conflict linkages

*Shaheen Rafi Khan, Moeed Yusuf, Faisal Haq Shaheen and Azka Tanveer*

## Introduction

As the number of regional trade agreements (RTAs) has grown, so has the interest in the impact that RTAs tend to have within and outside the region. Perhaps the most significant aspect is the link between RTAs and political stability. In this chapter, we focus on the South Asian region and examine the economic, political and strategic context in which the sub-continental RTAs are embedded. South Asia is a strategically important region with a history of both integration and conflict. While the Mughals consolidated the Indian sub-continent, it remained internally divided. The British colonial rulers unified India administratively and also integrated it economically through the development of elaborate rail, road and canal networks. The post-1947 colonial era saw India divide into two countries. Subsequently Bangladesh broke away from Pakistan in 1971. These sub-continental divisions weakened the integration process considerably and the region has continued to experience long spells of intra and inter-state tensions.

The region presents itself as an interesting case to examine the trade–conflict linkage. For this study, we look at all three existing RTAs in the region. The South Asian Association for Regional Cooperation (SAARC) is the overarching RTA with an economic and political mandate. Members include Pakistan, India, Sri Lanka, Maldives, Nepal, Bangladesh and Bhutan. Two South Asian agreements aiming at economic integration have been constituted within the SAARC mandate, namely the South Asian Preferential Trade Agreement (SAPTA) and the South Asian Free Trade Agreement (SAFTA). Both agreements are primarily trade focused and were formulated during the course of SAARC negotiations. While other sub-regional and bilateral groupings exist, these are the only truly regional initiatives that can be analysed to shed light on the RTA–conflict linkage in South Asia.

In particular, we look at RTAs as part of a larger regional integration process. We deconstruct the somewhat binary question, 'Does trade promote or mitigate conflict?' In doing so, we attempt to determine whether conflict

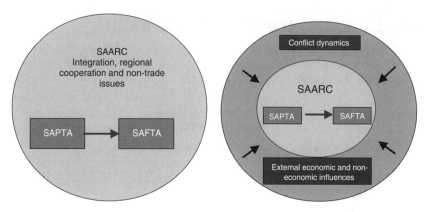

*Figure 4.1* Trade and conflict dynamics.

Source: SDPI in-house compilation

mitigation precedes or follows trade. If the former, then can we view conflict mitigation as an outcome of a broader integration process as represented in Figure 4.1.

The analysis addresses two simple questions:

- Do RTAs promote trade?
- Does trade mitigate conflict?

The chapter has six sections. The second section provides a brief overview of the theory of the trade–conflict linkage. The third section reviews the history of conflict in South Asia and maps the RTAs while the fourth section examines the causal links between trade and conflict. The fifth section analyses conflict mitigation within a broader regional integration process and the sixth section concludes with a look into the future.

## Theoretical underpinnings of the trade–conflict linkage

Literature on the relationship between RTAs and peace principally draws on two theories, the classical theory of trade and international relations (IR) theory. Classical trade theory is premised on the fact that trade is inherently beneficial for countries as it brings efficiency gains for producers, consumers and governments. More recent literature carries this argument forward with regard to regional and preferential trade agreements (PTAs) (Robson 1998). Proponents argue that regional trading blocs (through PTAs or RTAs) bring about political stability by increasing interdependence.[1] By increasing the economic incentive for peace and by providing channels for the non-military resolution of disputes, interdependence may bring amelioration of international or regional conflict, as a welcome political externality. With respect to intra-state conflicts, trade theorists contend that increased trade spurs domestic economic activity, thus generating employment and reducing unrest within domestic populations.

IR theory presents the opposite thesis. It suggests that trade by itself is not sufficient to ensure the absence of conflict. In fact, in certain cases, it can exacerbate conflict. According to IR specialists, the decision to trade or go to war depends on the potential returns from trade and the future expectations of the level of trade. Moreover, a state's choice between conflict and trade is said to be based on relative trade benefits, and not absolute gains as classical trade theory suggests. Hence, if a country perceives its neighbour to gain much more from trading, it would deem it in its interest not to liberalise trade. On the issue of intra-state conflict, IR theory is extended to suggest that the gains from trade are likely to be asymmetrical within the trading countries, given distortions in domestic distribution mechanisms. This increases the likelihood of intra-state strife reflecting the privileged elite's control over the entire resource pie.

The empirical evidence, provided in case studies, supports both views. The liberal approach is substantiated by the cases of Europe and to a lesser extent, Latin America, where economic inter-linkages have led to a significant decline in conflict between states. On the other hand, in South Asia and in less developed regions in Latin America and Africa where RTAs such as the SAPTA and Southern African Development Cooperation (SADC) have been in place for some time, there has been little evidence of political stability. Barbieri (2002) finds a consistent, positive relationship between trade ties and conflict, specifically participation in militarised inter-state disputes. Hegre (2000), on the other hand, demonstrates a clear negative relationship between trade and conflict. Reuveny (2000) documents empirical evidence which points in both directions. Rodrik (2000) demonstrates that the yardstick that matters with respect to internal conflict mitigation is the construction of a high quality institutional environment, rather than trade-openness or consistency with World Trade Organization (WTO) rules. The divergence of views and empirical results illustrates clearly that the scope for innovative research in the trade–conflict linkage remains considerable.

## Mapping RTAs and conflicts

### *Conflict in South Asia*

South Asia is a conflict-prone region that has been subjected to continuous political tensions. India, by far the largest country and centrally located geographically, has developed differences with most of its smaller neighbours. Tensions have tended to recur periodically and have corroded trust between South Asian countries. Reflecting these tensions, a recent European Union (EU) report rates political risk in the context of trade and investment in South Asia – as presented in Figure 4.2. The report indicates that only the two smallest SAARC members, Maldives and Bhutan, are politically stable.

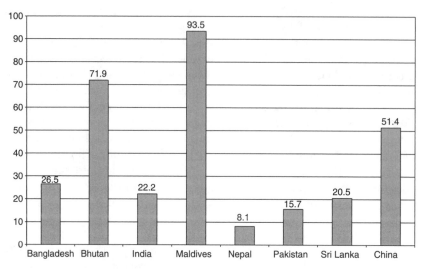

*Figure 4.2* Political stability.

Source: SDPI in-house compilation.

Note: Higher values imply better ratings. Figures shown are in percentage.

All other states are considered fragile, with the average stability values falling well below the global average (European Commission 2005).

### *Chronology of conflict in South Asia since 1980*

A timeline of the region's history of conflict since 1980 indicates a high incidence of inter and intra-state conflict. Internal instability and external tensions and conflict feed off each other to create a cycle of political and economic instability. Relations between India and Pakistan have been particularly volatile, interspersed by short periods of peace. This was historically true in Sri Lanka and India's case, although the violence appears to have developed an internal momentum and has become more sustained. Intrinsically, the nexus of intra and inter-state conflicts between these two dyads has delayed internal economic and political reforms, and stalled regional economic integration and trade. We present an overview of conflict in the region, focusing on the post-SAARC period when South Asian countries were making efforts to institute RTAs. It is important to note that all bilateral conflicts during this period have been Indo-centric reflecting, to a large extent, India's hegemonic aspirations backed by its military supremacy in the region.

### Bilateral conflicts and tensions

#### India and Pakistan

Relations between India and Pakistan, the region's two largest states, are almost permanently unstable. The two states have been perpetually locked in either overt or covert conflict, since they gained independence in 1947, presenting the single largest constraint to regional economic integration. The early part of the 1980s was marked by latent rather than active conflict. Having lost a decisive war to India in 1971, which resulted in the separation of Bangladesh from Pakistan, Pakistan took a more muted and realistic stance on Kashmir, allowing the two countries to address economic and trade issues. Discussions, eventually, led to the creation of SAARC in 1985. However, the underlying intransigence, reflecting historical rifts, the religious divide and military dynamics, led to a significant deterioration in relations by the late 1980s; in particular, the Kashmiri separatist movement gained momentum in Indian Kashmir. Soon after Pakistan started providing political and military support to the insurgents. Such support kept the two sides at loggerheads throughout the 1990s. India continuously blamed Pakistan for the unrest in Kashmir, accusing its neighbour of training and sending cadres to join the insurgency (Bose 2001).[2]

Security concerns between Pakistan and India peaked in 1998, when both sides tested nuclear weapons, introducing a highly unstable dimension to the security paradigm.[3] In 1999, Pakistan and India were embroiled in an armed confrontation in the Kargil region of Kashmir. Although the conflict ended in a stalemate, Kargil marked the first conflict between two nuclear-armed neighbours exposing the region to the danger of a nuclear catastrophe. Tensions reached a new high in 2002 when India blamed Pakistan for having engineered a terrorist attack on the Indian parliament. The two sides found themselves in the midst of a ten-month-long stand-off, with a million troops amassed on the Indo-Pakistan border, making this the largest military mobilisation in the region's history. Fortunately, intense international pressure achieved détente before the conflict could escalate further (Synnott 1999; Khan *et al.* 2007).

Amidst continuing tensions, Pakistan and India made several efforts to initiate a peace process. The two major initiatives preceding the Kargil War in 1999, were the 'Lahore Declaration', and President Pervez Musharraf's unsuccessful peace bid in 2001 (Bose 2001). Currently, a peace initiative is underway aiming to seek rapprochement. While this effort has lasted longer than preceding initiatives, by and large, Indo-Pakistan tensions still remain high. Mutual suspicion remains deep-rooted and major outstanding issues remain unresolved. Even if the current peace initiative were to remain on track, it would take decades before Pakistan and India began to trust each other.

*India and Sri Lanka*

In the 1980s, Sri Lanka slowly slipped into the grip of ethnic conflict as the majority Sinhalese witnessed the rising influence of minority Tamil separatists seeking independence for northern Sri Lanka. With its sizable Tamil population in the south, India had a natural interest in the issue. As early as 1983 it attempted to mediate Sri Lanka's conflict, albeit unsuccessfully.

In time, ethnic violence in Sri Lanka led to Indo-Sri Lankan tensions as the Indian government openly began to sympathise with the Sri Lankan Tamils. The Indian state of Tamil Nadu reportedly funded the militant Liberation Tigers of Tamil Eelam (LTTE), a fact tolerated by the central government in New Delhi (Uyangoda 2003). Moreover, in 1987, India came to the rescue of the Tamils when the Sri Lankan government attempted to regain control of its northern territory through an economic blockade. In July 1987, India decided to send the Indian Peace-Keeping Force (IPKF) to Tamil Nadu under an agreement that sought to disarm the Tamils and achieve peace. The agreement caused further resentment among Sri Lankan Sinhalese who saw this as an Indian attempt to establish its hegemony over Sri Lanka. Relations between India and Sri Lanka reached their nadir in 1989, when the Sri Lankan government demanded the withdrawal of the IPKF (Bhasin 2001; Kumar 2001).

Consequently, India boycotted the 1991 SAARC summit in Colombo, causing its postponement. When the summit eventually took place, it was an abrupt one-day affair, punctuated by the tensions between the hosts and India (Uyangoda 2003).

Since the early 1990s, India has refrained from intervening directly while maintaining its interest in the Tamil movement. It has also started to officially support the Sri Lankan government's position. Moreover, the two sides have looked to enhance cooperation in other sectors leading to a significant improvement in their relationship. While the Tamil separatist movement does create minor irritants from time to time, India seems genuinely interested in a peaceful internal solution to the problem. On the whole, Sri Lankan suspicions of India's hegemonic designs have reduced substantially, allowing relations between the two countries to become more cordial.

*India and Bangladesh*

Despite India's support for East Pakistani separatists, who eventually gained independence for what is now Bangladesh, relations between the two countries have see-sawed. Although the two sides penned economic agreements and an annually renewable treaty on the contentious issue of water sharing, a number of concerns remain unsettled. A general concern, which Bangladesh shares with other SAARC members, pertains to India's efforts to increase its direct influence on its neighbours.

Specifically, in the early 1990s, Indo-Bangladesh relations deteriorated over a dispute concerning the Farakka Barrage, where India has built a feeder canal to divert water to its side of the river (MacGregor 2000). Tensions surface intermittently as no permanent solution to major outstanding issues has been found. In 2001, India and Bangladesh were involved in a minor border confrontation. The conflict centred on the disputed border territory near Pyrdiwah village but remained contained to the border forces on both sides (CNN 2001). The two countries also claim the river island of Muhurichar. However, this issue has remained dormant since 1985. In the late 1980s, India sought to build a fence on the Indo-Bangladesh international border to stop illegal immigrants from pouring into West Bengal. This problem has assumed serious proportions in the recent past as the west-bound influx has increased (Bowring 2003). Lately, India has also accused Bangladesh of being sympathetic towards Pakistan and acting as a conduit for anti-Indian terrorist operations. Bangladesh, on the other hand, blames India for supporting anti-government, Chakma insurgents.

*India and Nepal*

The Indo-Nepal relationship has also been fraught with tension although the two sides have not allowed their overall relationship to be held hostage to their differences. The Indo-Nepal equation is a classic example of big power–small power political manoeuvring with the smaller power, Nepal, trying its utmost to retain an independent posture, despite being economically dependent on India. The majority of the problems between the two sides are grounded in economic concerns.

Indo-Nepal relations were quite strained when SAARC was originally formed. India had denied Nepal's bid to be declared an international security zone (Murthy 1999). Nepal's acquisition of Chinese weaponry elicited a strong official protest from the Indian government, worried about losing its influence in Katmandu. In 1988, Nepal refused to accommodate Indian demands on the long-standing transit treaty between the two countries. Nepal took a hard-line approach, and after the expiration of the treaty in 1989, faced an economic blockade from India, a development that led to further escalation in Indo-Nepal tensions (Murthy 1999).

More recently, a conciliatory strain in bilateral relations has emerged. Although India and Nepal have an outstanding territorial dispute on a 75 square kilometre area, the issue has not impacted Indo-Nepal relations to any significant degree (International Boundary Monitor 1998). Since the early 1990s, Nepal's worsening economic and political situation has forced it to seek rapprochement with India. In 1990, the special security relationship between the two countries was restored and in the mid-1990s, fresh trade and transit treaties were signed along with other economic agreements (Murthy 1999). India has also supported the Nepalese government in its fight against the ongoing Maoist rebellion in the country, a fact that has further improved relations between the two countries.

*Relations between other SAARC members*

By and large, relations between other SAARC members have remained tension free, a direct product of their tension fraught relations with India. By the same token, India has been wary of the designs of smaller states to 'gang up' in order to neutralise its influence. This has added to mutual suspicions between smaller members and India, leading to alliances between non-Indian member states. In 1999, Sri Lanka acquired military assistance from Pakistan to defend itself against possible aggression from the Tamil rebels at a time when New Delhi refused to come forward with such assistance (Uyangoda 2003). India also blamed Bangladesh for allowing Pakistani intelligence to operate from its territory, and for acting as a base for terrorist attacks inside India, an allegation it levies against Pakistan as well. Nepal–Bangladesh relations have been cordial, as Kathmandu has attempted to neutralise some of New Delhi's influence by entering into various agreements with Dhaka.

### Intra-state strife in South Asia

In addition to the inter-state tensions that have plagued South Asia, countries in the region have also experienced extended periods of intra-state strife. As mentioned earlier, the two should be viewed in conjunction, feeding off each other in dampening or expanding cycles of violence. With the exception of the Maldives and Bhutan, intra-state conflict has been almost endemic to SAARC member states. India has long battled the insurgency in Kashmir that was initiated by Kashmiri Muslims opposing New Delhi's rule. In addition, during the 1980s, India experienced the rise of the 'Khalistan' separatist movement, fighting for an independent Indian state of Punjab. Resistance to Delhi's rule also exists in pockets of Nagaland in the country's north-east (Sahadevan 1999). Of these, the Kashmiri struggle is by far the most threatening in the region.

Pakistan has also had its share of internal conflicts. Since SAARC's inception, Pakistan has struggled with sectarian violence. Sunni–Shia violence peaked following the Afghan jihad in the early 1990s;[4] while conditions have improved ever since, sectarian violence continues to erupt periodically. More recently, the inflexible centrist policies of an army-dominated government have reignited the dormant nationalist movement in Balochistan (Hussaini 2005). The 'Talibanisation' of the Federally Administered Tribal Areas (FATA), a large swathe of the North West Frontier Province (NWFP), also reflects converging resentment against central government neglect and its pro-US stance. The most recent evidence of creeping Talibanisation has been the Jamia Hafsa incident. Vigilantes consisting of armed Islamic militants (male and female) terrorised Islamabad and drew widespread media attention by proclaiming their intention to establish *Sharia* (religious) law. Their provocations led to a bloody confrontation with the government. While the militants were wiped out in a subsequent army operation, the country braced for a bloody backlash that was not long in coming. Despite tight security precautions the Al Qaeda/Taliban combination continues to strike at will, at any time and at any place of its own choosing.

The Sri Lankan ethnic conflict between the Sinhalese and Tamil separatists has already been discussed. The conflict continues and despite numerous attempts at peace talks, including third-party mediation, most notably by the Norwegian government, no breakthrough has been achieved. While violence is intermittent, it escalates periodically.

Since 1996, Nepal has been threatened by a well-organised Maoist rebellion that is challenging the country's monarchy (Thapa and Sijapati 2003). The rebellion is one of the major factors responsible for the decline of the Nepalese economy. While initiatives to accommodate Maoist demands have been undertaken, none have satisfied the rebels. Consequently, the rebellion remains active and continues to threaten the centre through constant targeting of state functionaries.

Bangladesh has mobilised counter-insurgency operations against the Chakma insurgents in the Chittagong hill tracts. The area has been quite turbulent in the past, with the insurgents demanding regional autonomy from the centre. Despite intermittent tensions, the government has managed to keep the insurgents under control. In 1999, a peace accord was signed by the Awami League government that promised increased autonomy to the insurgents. However, the accord has not been implemented fuelling resentment among the Chakmas and the goal of finding a permanent solution remains elusive (Chowdhury 2002).

The Maldives government foiled a coup attempt in 1988 with assistance from Indian paratroopers and naval forces. More recently, it has seen constitutional differences emerging among political actors (European Commission 2005). However, neither event was significant enough to destabilise the state.

Bhutan has remained free of internal strife. A chronology of major conflicts in South Asia is presented in Table 4.1.

### Mapping South Asian RTAs

#### Cooperation despite conflict

The idea of regional cooperation in South Asia had come under discussion at three conferences: the Asian Relations Conference in New Delhi in April 1947, the Baguio Conference in the Philippines in May 1950, and the Colombo Powers Conference in April 1954. However, the idea did not take root with the leadership of the region, until President Zia ur-Rehman of Bangladesh shared his 'Working paper on regional cooperation in South Asia' with the heads of states of South Asia in November 1980. A variety of reasons contributed to the success of the president's initiative.

The new regimes in the region displayed more accommodative diplomacy than their predecessors. However, a renewed, more open stance towards

*Table 4.1* Chronology of major conflicts in South Asia

*Inter-state conflict*

| Year | India–Bangladesh | India–Sri Lanka | India–Nepal | India–Pakistan |
|---|---|---|---|---|
| 1985 | Muhurichar Island conflict | | | |
| 1987 | | IKPF sent to Tamil Nadu to disarm the Tamils | | |
| 1988 | | | Tensions over disagreement on transit treaty | |
| 1989 | | Withdrawal of IPKF demanded by Sri Lankan government | | |
| 1991 | | India boycotts SAARC Colombo summit | | |
| 1998 | | | | Both countries test nuclear weapons |
| 1999 | | | | Kargil conflict in Indian-held Kashmir |
| 2001 | Pyrdiwah village border conflict | | | Terrorist attack on Indian parliament blamed on Pakistan, leading to both countries amassing troops along the border |

*Intra-state conflict*

| | Sri Lanka | India | Maldives | Pakistan |
|---|---|---|---|---|
| 1983 | Widespread anti-Tamil rioting following the deaths of soldiers in an LTTE ambush | | | |
| 1984 | | Prime Minister Indira Gandhi killed by Sikh bodyguards after ordering troops to flush out Sikh militants from Amritsar | | |

| | | |
|---|---|---|
| 1988 | | Attempted coup thwarted with the help of Indian commandos |
| 1990 | Kashmiri separatist movement gains momentum | |
| 1992 | Hindu–Muslim riots in Ayodhya following the demolition of Babri Mosque | |
| 1993 | President Premadasa killed in LTTE bomb attack | |
| 1999 | | Prime Minister Nawaz Sharif ousted in military coup led by General Pervez Musharraf |
| 2004 | | On-going Waziristan and Balochistan conflict |

Source: SDPI in-house compilation, August 2006.

foreign relations was not the only impetus for cooperation. The North–South dialogue seemed to be failing, resulting in the North adopting more protectionist attitudes. The 1979 oil crisis put pressure on South Asian economies, which were already suffering from balance of payments difficulties. The 1979 Soviet invasion of Afghanistan put the security of South Asia at risk and provided the leaders with another reason to have closer ties in order to foster understanding of common problems and conflicts before they spun out of control. At this critical juncture, a report by the Committee on Studies for Cooperation in Development in South Asia (CSCD) identified many feasible areas of cooperation between the countries of South Asia (Dash 1996).

Despite these commonalities, the adversarial Indo-Pakistan relations, a fear of Indian hegemony and India's fear of a hostile small-country coalition presented hurdles to integration. In view of this lack of trust, the CSCD proposal showed remarkable foresight in ensuring its acceptability. Avoiding all political and controversial matters, the report identified specific areas of cooperation that were truly regional in nature. Moreover, it adopted an incremental approach to integration. As a result, between 1980 and 1983, four meetings at the foreign secretary levels took place to establish the principles of organisation and narrow down areas of cooperation. Three years of preparatory discussions at the official level culminated in the first South Asian foreign ministers' conference, held in New Delhi in August 1983. The meeting concluded by launching the Integrated Programme of Action (IPA) on mutually agreed areas of cooperation, constituting the first step towards establishing SAARC.[5]

### South Asian Association for Regional Cooperation

SAARC aimed to bring stability to South Asia by enhancing regional cooperation, with a view to improving the welfare and quality of life of its people through economic growth, social progress and cultural development in the region. SAARC also promoted the cooperation of member countries with other developing countries on matters of common interests in international and regional fora and with organisations with similar aims and purposes.[6] While SAARC's charter promotes active collaboration and mutual assistance in the economic, social, cultural, technical and scientific fields, the main thrust of regional efforts has been directed towards economic integration. South Asian leaders recognised that opening their economies to trade and investment, especially with neighbouring countries, could lay the groundwork for peace in their conflict-ridden region.

All activities to be undertaken within the SAARC framework are governed by the overarching principles of 'sovereign *equality, territorial integrity, political independence and non-interference in the internal affairs of other States.*' On the one hand, mutual benefit is a primary consideration; the sovereign equality condition weighs in against powerful countries leveraging their power against weaker countries. On the other hand, member states cannot involve themselves in bilateral conflicts within the region. The clauses on territorial integrity and non-interference in member countries' internal affairs rules out SAARC's role as a peace-keeper. Its charter states explicitly that 'bilateral and contentious issues shall be excluded from the deliberations of SAARC'. This clause effectively keeps inter-state conflict off the table in all member-to-member interactions.

### South Asian Preferential Trade Agreement

The SAPTA signed in 1993 expired on 31 December 2003. The agreement dealt exclusively with trade in goods and constituted the first step in establishing an economic union. Under SAPTA, member countries extended concessions to each other on tariff, para-tariff and non-tariff measures in successive stages. They were free to liberalise trade at their own pace and to decide upon which items to offer on concessional terms. The agreement made provisions for establishing a Committee of Participants (COP), consisting of representatives of all contracting states as the monitoring body of SAPTA. Its objective was to review the progress made by SAPTA and ensure that the gains from trade were shared by all contracting states. The COP also acted as the dispute resolution body for SAPTA.

The agreement also included several provisions extending special treatment to least developed countries (LDCs). Support to LDCs involved the identification, preparation and establishment of industrial and agricultural projects in their territories, with the aim of creating an export base. SAPTA also contained anti-dumping clauses which suspended concessions to member states involved in dumping. The intent behind such measures was to ensure fair trade for all member states, and eliminate the possibility for potential conflicts/tensions between member states as a result of skewed economic power relations. Similarly, SAPTA allowed countries to withdraw from the agreement in the event they faced balance of payments difficulties, with the aim to minimise intra-state economic disruptions. Also, SAPTA deferred to other bilateral, multilateral and plurilateral agreements that contracting countries were signatory to. In doing so it sought to harmonise itself with other agreements.

Despite the inclusion of these measures, SAPTA proved unable to handle trade-related disputes. The more powerful member states were unwilling to accept embedded rules-based institutional and legal mechanisms for dispute settlement. They preferred to resolve such disputes bilaterally. When the matter could not be resolved, it was deferred to the COP, which issued decisions that were neither time-bound nor legally binding. Essentially, the COP developed its own procedures for dealing with contentious issues on a case-by-case basis.

*South Asian Free Trade Agreement*

SAFTA came into force on 1 January 2006 and has proved to be the most comprehensive mechanism to date that strives to achieve intra-regional economic cooperation. Unlike SAPTA, SAFTA has a well-defined approach to trade liberalisation. It specifies time-staggered tariff reductions for each member country. India and Pakistan have committed to reduce tariffs from existing levels to 20 per cent within two years effective from January 2006. Subsequently, they are to come down to 0–5 per cent from 2008 to 2013. For LDC members, a more flexible schedule allows them to reduce their tariffs to 30 per cent in the first two years of the agreement. The time period for the second stage of reductions, at the end of which tariff levels are to be reduced to 0–5 per cent, is eight years i.e. achieved by 2016. SAFTA concedes more than SAPTA on trade-related dispute resolution. It stipulates that the anti-dumping and safeguard provision cannot be invoked against a product originating in a LDC, if its exports do not exceed 5 per cent of its total imports.[7]

The more comprehensive SAFTA also addresses a broader range of trade-related issues, such as the harmonisation of standards and certification, customs clearance procedures and classification, transit and transport facilitation as well as rules for fair competition and foreign exchange liberalisation.

In the light of its fair trade provisions and the broadening of its economic agenda, SAFTA offers better prospects than its predecessor for improving relations between the member countries. Member countries are allowed to maintain higher tariffs for sensitive lists of commodities (industry protection) and pull back from the agreement if they face balance of payments difficulties, underscoring that SAFTA is sensitive to national economic concerns and a country's political stability.

SAFTA's dispute settlement mechanism is substantively similar to SAPTA – if anything there are more tiers of consultations, involving a Committee of Experts (COE) and the SAFTA Ministerial Council (SMC). However, much as in the case of SAPTA, no institutional or legal mechanisms for dispute settlement exist and both the COE and the SMC continue to devise procedures on a case-by-case basis.

In an intra-state security context, the agreement includes a clause on national security where states are not to be forced to take any measures that compromise their national interests. This effort to allay domestic political sensitivities can also assure buy-in to the agreement. In addition, the General Exceptions clause deals with animal and plant life and health, and articles of artistic, historic and archaeological value. Such confidence building clauses demonstrate that SAFTA does not threaten but safeguards quality of life.

Table 4.2 presents the broad scope of trade, conflict and conflict-related (governance) language across the RTAs, bilateral, sub-regional and extra-regional agreements in South Asia.

During SAARC's inception, South Asian leaders realised that introducing political conditions in the incipient regional integration process could stall regional economic cooperation. Consequently, as indicated earlier, bilateral issues were kept out of SAARC's purview. Today, the absence of recourse to deliberate upon bilateral political relations has become a major concern for member states. Realising the negative impact of political tensions on trade arrangements in the region, some analysts have called for a regional institutional mechanism to contain conflict among members. Others have even suggested the need to amend the SAARC charter to allow it to deliberate upon bilateral issues. As early as 1990, Ariyasinghe had proposed a 'strategic regional security framework' designed to ensure regional security in South Asia. No progress has been made on this front, and realistically such a development is not on the cards any time soon. Member states, particularly Pakistan and India, must find means outside the SAARC arrangement to resolve their differences.

Two key points emerge. First, the incidence of inter and intra-state conflict in South Asia is high and shows no signs of abating. Second, RTAs have not been designed explicitly to mitigate inter and intra-state conflicts and tensions. As the mapping shows, these RTAs focus primarily on economic cooperation. Having said that the progressively extended economic mandate of the agreements, the concessions built into the agreements for LDCs, sensitive lists and

Table 4.2 Trade and conflict language in RTAs

Trade and conflict language

| RTAs | Trade | Dispute settlement | | | Conflict mitigation/ resolution within member states | Security clauses | |
|---|---|---|---|---|---|---|---|
| | | Consultation | Arbitration | Decision by established body | | General security exception* | Cooperation on specific security concern |
| SAARC | ○ | | | | — | — | — |
| SAPTA | ● | ● | — | ● | — | ● | — |
| SAFTA | ● | ● | — | ● | — | | — |
| *Bilateral agreements* | | | | | | | |
| India–Sri Lanka | ● | ● | — | ○ | — | ● | — |
| India–Nepal | ○ | ● | — | — | — | ○ | — |
| India–Maldives | ○ | ○ | — | — | — | ○ | |
| India–Bhutan | ● | ● | — | — | — | ○ | — |
| Pakistan–Nepal | ○ | ○ | — | ○ | — | ● | — |
| Sri Lanka–Nepal | ○ | — | — | — | — | — | — |
| Nepal–Bangladesh | ● | ○ | — | — | — | ● | — |
| *Sub/extra-regional agreements* | | | | | | | |
| BIMSTEC | ● | ● | — | ● | | ● | — |
| SAGQ | | | | | ○ | | |

(Continued overleaf)

Table 4.2 continued.

Conflict-related (governance) language

| RTAs | Rule of law | Transparency | Property rights | Democracy | Human rights and gender issues |
|---|---|---|---|---|---|
| SAARC | – | – | – | – | o |
| SAPTA | – | – | – | – | – |
| SAFTA | – | – | – | – | – |
| *Bilateral agreements* | | | | | |
| India–Sri Lanka | o | – | – | – | – |
| India–Nepal | o | – | – | – | – |
| India–Maldives | – | – | – | – | – |
| India–Bhutan | – | – | – | – | – |
| Pakistan–Nepal | – | – | – | – | – |
| Sri Lanka–Nepal | – | – | – | – | – |
| Nepal–Bangladesh | o | – | – | – | – |
| *Sub/extra-regional agreements* | | | | | |
| BIMSTEC | | | | | |
| SAGQ | – | – | – | – | – |

Key
● Mentioned in sufficient detail to be implemented under the agreement
o Mentioned in agreement but with minor detail; no implementation procedure provided
– Not mentioned in agreement
* A general exception security clause allows the contracting parties to violate the agreement in case of threat to national security.

national security clauses, which are at odds with the liberalisation mandate, and dispute settlement mechanisms have both inter and intra-state security implications, even though these are not formally articulated.

In the following section, we explore causal links between the RTAs, trade and conflict looking for answers to the following questions: Have RTAs an economic/trade rationale? Have RTAs fulfilled their mandate in generating intra-regional trade? Conversely, are RTAs a mirror image of regional political developments, and RTA negotiations hostage to what happens on the political front? Alternatively, what has been the role of RTAs in conflict mitigation?

## RTAs, trade and conflict

### *Existence of trade complementarities in South Asia: the basis for trade*

Recent literature (Wickramasinghe 2001; Burki 2004) on South Asian trade indicates significant trade and service sector complementarities across the region. The literature also suggests that increased trade flows are likely to engender technical efficiency, improve resource allocation and allow countries to create niches by specialising in different products within a given industry. A number of studies have predicted gains from regional trade. One estimate projects the long-term trade increase ensuing from SAFTA at US$14 billion (FPCCI 2003). A 1993 World Bank study suggested that a free trade arrangement (FTA) between Pakistan and India could have increased their trade flows ninefold within a ten-year period (Burki 2004).

Mukherji (2002) identified as many as 113 potentially tradable items within the SAARC region. These include tea and coffee, cotton and textiles, garments, rubber, light engineering goods, iron and steel, cement, edibles (dry fruits, spices and vegetables), medical equipment, pharmaceuticals and agro-chemicals, among others. Owing to existing trade barriers a number of these items are currently imported into the region. Specifically, in the Pakistan–India context, Pakistan could import from India pharmaceuticals, textile machinery, light engineering industry items, refrigerators, irons, air-conditioners, washing machines, televisions, sugar, cement, organic and inorganic chemicals, and paper and pulp, which it currently does from elsewhere at much higher cost. Reciprocally, Pakistan could export to India cotton, surgical and sports goods, leather products and dry and fresh fruits.

Zones of comparative advantage embrace countries making trade feasible across these zones. Thus, Sri Lanka, Bangladesh and India all export tea, while Pakistan imports it. India and Bangladesh export jute and jute products to the rest of the SAARC member countries. Pakistan and India produce cotton, which its neighbours require. Similarly, India and, to a lesser degree, Pakistan, export manufactured goods within the region.

Informal trade (smuggling) in South Asia also is a good index of trade complementarity. Under free trade, a substantial proportion of informal trade is likely to switch to formal channels. The major items currently being traded informally in the region include cloth of different varieties, cosmetics, jewelry, bicycles, medicines, cattle, sugar, spices, raw cotton, garments, machinery, cement, aluminum, petroleum products, automobiles, tyres and tubes, electrical goods, unprocessed food, rice and flour.[8]

Bilateral FTAs in South Asia are proof that trade is capturing complementarities between countries. The Indo-Sri Lanka FTA – fears of industry contraction in both countries notwithstanding – has led to a threefold increase in bilateral trade flows (Thakurta 2006).

### Potential investment collaboration

The services sector is potentially a major driver of economic integration. India's dominance in information technology can be a trigger for profitable affiliations with reputed institutions in India. These can be joint ventures or strategic alliances that can utilise skilled professionals from neighbouring countries, especially Pakistan (FPCCI 2003; Taneja 2004a). Mutually beneficial joint ventures between India and Pakistan in the agro sector, especially in processing and packaging, could generate 0.4 million jobs in both countries (FPCCI 2003).

Energy is another area of possible collaboration. India, the most energy deficient country in the region, stands to gain from investment partnerships with countries with hydropower surpluses, such as Pakistan, Nepal and Bhutan. Pakistan is on line as a conduit for Iranian natural gas to India. Bangladesh's considerable gas reserves have yet to be tapped. Ultimately, over a long-term planning horizon, one could envisage connectivity through a network of energy, gas and oil grids to help lower energy costs (Burki 2004).

India's comparative advantage in technical education, the new cornerstone of economic development, can be deployed to the advantage of its South Asian neighbours. Pakistan can mobilise its potential in the areas of irrigation, food preparation and textiles, for a similar purpose (Burki 2004). Other service sectors with promise for regional cooperation are water, tourism and health. In the tourism sector, joint marketing and management strategies could bring collective gains to the region.

### RTAs and trade growth: evidence from South Asia

#### Formal and informal trade trends in South Asia

Despite the indicated complementarities, trade between SAARC countries has remained low. Intra-regional trade in South Asia accounts for a mere 4–5 per cent of the SAARC countries' total exports (FPCCI 2003). In contrast to the global trend, intra-regional trade in South Asia has declined dramatically over the past five decades, and has remained stagnant at approximately

*Table 4.3* Intra-regional export shares: a comparison across southern RTAs

|  | *1990* | *2001* | *Year in force* |
|---|---|---|---|
| *Latin America* | | | |
| CAN | 4.2 | 11.2 | 1988 |
| MERCOSUR | 8.9 | 20.8 | 1991 |
| *Africa* | | | |
| COMESA | 6.3 | 5.2 | 1994 |
| SADC | 3.1 | 10.9 | 1992 |
| UEMOA | 12.1 | 13.5 | 2000 |
| *Asia* | | | |
| ASEAN/AFTA | 19.0 | 22.4 | 1992 |
| SAARC | 2.4 | 4.6 | 1985 |

Source: UNCTAD (2002); WTO (2002).

2 per cent during 1980–2002, a figure lower than most other regional trading blocs, as is evident in Table 4.3.

Formal trade statistics in South Asia, however, do not reflect the true magnitude of intra-regional trade. A substantial volume of trade flows through illegal channels, either smuggled across borders or transiting through third countries. The total value of informal trade in South Asia is estimated at US$1.5 billion. While informal trade volumes are substantial, even the addition of these to formal trade flows does not accurately reflect the true trade potential of the region. It is the persistence of tariff and non-tariff barriers that have both choked intra-regional trade and diverted it into illegal channels. Tables 4.4 and 4.5 present comparative formal and informal intra-regional trade trends.

## RTAs and trade promotion

The explicit linkages between RTAs and trade promotion are to be found through SAPTA and SAFTA which were, as noted, established under the SAARC mandate, but whose primary fiat is trade promotion. The combined value of trade (exports and imports) increased from US$1.24 billion in 1980 to US$6.5 billion in 2001, as shown in Table 4.6. The bulk of this increase occurred during the SAPTA period. As a percentage of total SAARC trade, intra-regional trade increased from 2 to 4.6 per cent over the same period. However, this increase should be seen against the backdrop of extremely low absolutes.

### TARIFF AND NON-TARIFF BARRIERS

South Asian economists argue that for significant trade to ensue, all quantitative restrictions and non-tariff barriers should be removed (Mukherji 2002; Upreti 2000). Second, they point out while many items have been brought

*Table 4.4* SAARC intra-regional trade (US$ millions)

| Year | Intra-SAARC trade | SAARC world trade | Percentage |
|------|------------------|------------------|------------|
| *Pre-SAPTA period* | | | |
| 1986 | 1,055 | 44,042 | 2.4 |
| 1987 | 1,146 | 49,480 | 2.3 |
| 1988 | 1,732 | 52,669 | 3.3 |
| 1989 | 1,723 | 58,595 | 2.9 |
| 1990 | 1,590 | 65,490 | 2.4 |
| 1991 | 1,914 | 63,435 | 3.0 |
| 1992 | 2,488 | 71,149 | 3.5 |
| 1993 | 2,458 | 72,211 | 3.4 |
| *Post-SAPTA period* | | | |
| 1994 | 2,937 | 82,839 | 3.5 |
| 1995 | 4,263 | 103,878 | 4.1 |
| 1996 | 4,928 | 110,962 | 4.4 |
| 1997 | 4,447 | 115,370 | 3.9 |
| 1998 | 6,001 | 123,144 | 4.9 |
| 1999 | 5,511 | 131,152 | 4.2 |
| 2000 | 5,884 | 146,924 | 4.0 |
| 2001 | 6,537 | 143,443 | 4.6 |

Source: International Monetary Fund (1997, 2002).

*Table 4.5* India's informal trade with South Asian countries (US$ millions)

| | Exports | Imports | Total trade |
|------|---------|---------|-------------|
| Bangladesh | 299.0 | 14.0 | 313.0 |
| Sri Lanka | 185.5 | 21.8 | 207.3 |
| Pakistan | 10.3 | 534.5 | 544.8 |
| Nepal | 180.0 | 228.0 | 408.0 |
| Bhutan | 31.3 | 1.2 | 32.6 |
| | | **Total** | **1,505.7** |

Sources: Taneja (2004a) for Sri Lanka and Nepal; Khan *et al.* (2007) for Pakistan.

*Table 4.6* Non-tariff measures–coverage ratio of South Asian countries

| Country | Non tariff measures–coverage (%) | |
|---------|---------|---------------|
| | Primary | Manufactured |
| India | 72 | 59 |
| Pakistan | 7 | 17 |
| Bangladesh | 55 | 47 |
| Sri Lanka | 3 | 4 |
| Nepal | 1 | 1 |

Source: Khan *et al.* (2007).

under preferential trade, only a handful is actively traded items (Mukherji 2000). Third, the fears of economic dominance by more powerful partners should be allayed.

As mentioned, tariff and non-tariff barriers are a key constraint to trade growth in South Asia. In fact, South Asia is debited with the highest inter-state barriers to trade in the world. In the early 1990s, Bangladesh's unweighted average tariff was as high as 79 per cent, followed by Pakistan at 59 per cent and India at 51 per cent (Taneja 2004b). While the averages have come down significantly and currently stand at around 20 per cent, they are still higher than the average in other regional trading blocs. India has consistently had the highest tariffs among all South Asian countries, as indicated in Figure 4.3.

Pursell and Sattar (2004) found India and Bangladesh to be in the top 10 per cent out of the 139 sampled countries on the basis of unweighted tariffs. In another study that researched all types of border barriers, Kee *et al.* (2006) found India to be the most protected economy in the world and Bangladesh the fifth most protected. Moreover, Bangladesh uses 'supplementary duties' that often end up doubling the effective tariff. Bangladesh and Pakistan also maintain a substantial negative list specific to India, thus restricting or banning the import of potentially tradable items.

Non-tariff barriers are equally high among South Asian countries, and continue to pose major hurdles to intra-regional trade. In the early 1990s, India and Bangladesh had the highest non-tariff barrier coverage ratio for primary and manufactured goods, as is evident in Table 4.7. For primary

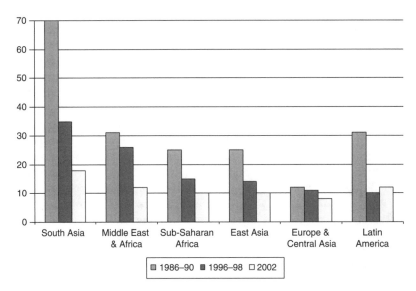

*Figure 4.3* Comparison of South Asian tariffs with other regional trading blocs.

Source: World Bank, WTO, IMF (statistics from various years).

*Table 4.7* Chronology of key bilateral agreements

| Nations | Nature of agreement and date |
| --- | --- |
| India–Pakistan | Peace (Place of Worship) – 1953, 1955<br>Border – 1948, 1952, 1955, 1958, 1959, 1960, Indus Water Treaty (1960), 1965, 1965, 1966, 1972, 1974, 1991, 1999<br>Conflict – 1965, 1966, 1971, 1972, 1973, 1974(2), 1975, 1988<br>Trade – 1947, 1957, 1960, 1961, 1963, 1974, India extending MFN, Pakistan declines |
| India–Bangladesh | Border – 1972(2), 1974, 1976,<br>Resource – Farakka 1977, 1982, 1983, 1984, Ganga Water Sharing (1996)<br>Trade – 1972, 1973, 1974, 1980, 1981, 1982, 1988<br>FTA India interested, Bangladesh wary of protectionism |
| India–Bhutan | Peace – 1949<br>Trade – Trade and Commerce (1995) |
| India–Maldives | Border – 1976(2)<br>Trade – 1975, 1981 |
| India–Nepal | Peace – 1950, 1953, 1954<br>Resource – 1958, 1987, Mahakali Treaty (1996)<br>Trade – 1950, 1954, 1958, 1959, 1960, 1964, 1966, 1971, 1973, 1976, 1978(3), 1985, 1987, 1990, 1991(3), 1996, 1999, 2001 |
| India–Sri Lanka | Peace – 1954, 1986, 1987, 1989<br>Border – 1964, 1974, 1986<br>Trade – FTA (1998), Credit Agreement (2001) |

Source: South Asia Foundation www.southasiafoundation.org; Bilaterals www.bilaterals.org.

products, India's ratio stood at 72 per cent and Bangladesh's at 59 per cent (Taneja 1999). Moreover, India has employed anti-dumping measures most frequently in recent times, even surpassing the US (Khan *et al.* 2007). Pakistan accuses Indian customs authorities of biased treatment towards Pakistani consignments, as a way of neutralising the formal most favoured nation (MFN) status India has granted to Pakistan.[9]

Further, all South Asian countries are lax in implementing trade facilitation measures. A key aspect of trade facilitation is improving the efficiency of customs authorities. Customs clearance procedures are time-consuming. For example, as many as 38 signatures are required to clear a consignment imported into Pakistan (Khan *et al.* 2007). In India, an export consignment needs 258 signatures and key punching can take up to 22 hours (Roy 2004). The average time required to clear Indian and Bangladeshi customs is about three times that found in the customs agencies of the developed world (Khan *et al.* 2007). In short, the high tariff and non-tariff barriers in South Asia have stunted trade growth significantly and have led to trade leakages to extra-regional sources.

While SAPTA has contributed to lowering these barriers, the low trade response suggests that more drastic measures are required. It is hoped that

SAFTA, with its broader trade facilitation mandate will be able to reduce trade barriers substantively. In a dynamic context, trade liberalisation needs to be undertaken in conjunction with investment liberalisation, as it will foster structural changes in industry. For example, allowing regional competitive advantages and specialisation to flourish will build the horizontal and vertical capacities of rising firms, enabling them to compete globally (FPCCI 2003). This will then sustain the thrust towards diversification. Also, joint ventures between firms within the region will present a viable way of circumventing trade barriers. Thus far however, South Asian RTAs have failed to make a lasting impact on intra-regional trade.

A related concern specific to RTAs is whether they actually contribute to the creation of new trade or simply divert extra-regional to relatively high cost intra-regional trade. In the latter case, the cost for the importing country would increase and it would end up foregoing tariff revenues (Khan *et al.* 2007). High existing tariffs pre-SAFTA has implications for trade diversion. A large proportion of South Asian imports from outside the region cost less due to high intra-regional trade barriers (high transport costs notwith-standing). For example, Sri Lanka currently imports railway coaches from Romania foregoing the much cheaper alternative available in southern India. In cement and ship building Sri Lanka trades with South Korea instead of tapping the cheaper options in Pakistan and India (Dash 1996). Pakistan imports iron ore and textile machinery at a higher cost than are available from India. Existing tariff barriers also drive up local input costs, thus making South Asian exports more expensive in relation to sources outside the region. An initial reduction from these high levels would probably lead to such diversion because inefficient local producers would now have a cost advantage (lower transport costs) over exporters to the region. However, over the long run, when tariffs fall to zero and industries become more competitive, trade creation is likely to kick in.

*Global and multilateral institutions: trade leakages outside the region*

The SAARC member countries have continued reforms within the ambit of World Bank and International Monetary Fund (IMF) conditionalities. They have, to various degrees, introduced trade, industrial and investment policy reforms. The reforms include reductions in tariff slabs, tariff rates, quantitative restrictions, establishing export processing zones for foreign direct investment (FDI), joint venture arrangements, fiscal and financial incentives to industry and currency convertibility. These reforms have contributed in large measure to the growth of trade with the North.

Although trade has increased between some member states (growth increases have been dramatic between Bangladesh–India and Sri Lanka–India), trade within the region has been increasingly dwarfed by trade with outside nations. The largest trading partners are North America and the EU followed by East Asia and Australasia (in the case of Bangladesh). As mentioned, only 4–5 per cent of the region's total trade is within the SAARC region.

In order to counter these leakages and restore parity in intra-regional trade, the Research and Information System for the Non-aligned and Other Developing Countries (RISNODEC 2001) proposes equivalent measures within the region, such as pushing regional economic integration more holistically via the creation of a customs union, as envisaged under SAFTA. It also proposes to diversify extra-regional trade to countries such as China in order to obtain better terms of trade for South Asian products.

On balance, while trade volumes have increased in the region, they are low in absolute terms – the lowered trade barriers associated with the global push towards liberalisation are diverting a substantial portion of the trade outside the region and towards the North. This trend, as we mentioned earlier, is exacerbated by the persistence of intra-regional trade barriers.

## Exploring the causality between trade and conflict

### From conflict to trade

Existing literature is reticent in exploring the causal links from conflict to trade. The South Asian paradigm seems to be that conflict hinders trade and economic integration. In common with other developing nations in Latin America, Africa and the Middle East, South Asia illustrates that economic liberalisation cannot serve as the sole driver of peace within the region (Ades and Chua 1997). In fact, political stability is a prerequisite for instituting and locking in economic liberalisation measures, an environment that South Asia has not been able to develop.

Inter-state conflicts in the region have slowed trade growth. While it is more difficult to establish a direct link between intra-state strife and stunted trade growth, there is little disagreement that almost all major intra-state tensions in South Asia have had spill-over effects on inter-state relations. Ethnic violence in Sri Lanka caused disruption of the Indo-Sri Lankan relationship, the Kashmir struggle has put Pakistan and India at odds and the Bangladesh insurgency has strained relations between Bangladesh and India. Intra-state strife has exacerbated inter-state tensions and thus, indirectly, played a role in curtailing trade flows within the region.

An analysis along a timeline explains the link between inter-state conflicts and trade relations within South Asia. SAPTA's sub-par performance can be attributed to the fact that in the early 1990s, intra-regional tensions had escalated. SAPTA only made modest headway, with member countries imposing stringent limitations on the number of potentially tradable items. Political tensions between member states also delayed the finalisation of the SAFTA agreement. The agreement, initially planned to be finalised in 2001, was signed with a three-year lag in 2004 (Bandara 2001). Just as SAARC was formally established when the Pakistan–India conflict was dormant and no other major conflict was active in the region, SAFTA was also finalised utilising the rare window when no SAARC member state was embroiled in conflict.

Further, political tensions and mutual suspicions between SAARC members have prevented the delegation of SAARC's negotiation procedures. In the prevailing mistrust between member states, regional cooperation remains the fiat of foreign affairs ministries, where perceptions of national security normally dominate political decision-making. No country has allowed the institutional framework to be widened to include line ministries, such as finance, labor and transport, which would make SAARC processes more relevant to domestic agendas. Clearly political stability and mutual trust are prerequisites for such delegation.

### Bilateral agreements: a mixed bag

Formal trade agreements have materialised between countries in an effort to bypass the political logjam that has stalled movement on the RTAs. Part of this momentum has been generated by India's desire to leverage its economic size and influence over its neighbours. While smaller countries, such as Bangladesh, Nepal and Sri Lanka, have complied in an effort to circumvent the Indo-Pakistan induced SAARC stalemate, increased trade with their larger neighbour has also contributed to fears of Indian economic and cultural domination. The outcomes are ambiguous. In some cases, there is evidence that the ensuing trade has improved bilateral relations; in other cases, political obstacles continue to hinder both bilateral agreements – and bilateral trade, once these agreements are in force.

India signed an FTA with Sri Lanka in 1998 (European Commission 2005) and a new trade and transit treaty with Nepal in the mid-1990s. India also entered into an FTA with Bhutan, one of the only two SAARC members which have not had any substantial disputes with India (European Commission 2005). The only two major SAARC members that have not concluded any trade pact with India are Pakistan and Bangladesh. While the ongoing peace process has engendered improved trade ties between the two countries, Pakistan is still reluctant to grant India MFN status. Pakistan continues to view trade relations as secondary to settlement of outstanding disputes, specifically Kashmir.[10] The Indo-Pakistan case is a clear illustration of bilateral trade being held hostage to conflict. Also, despite India and Bangladesh having signed an MFN trade arrangement as early as 1980, political tensions have limited trade flows. Bangladesh continues to maintain a restrictive trade regime vis-à-vis India and, in defiance of trade logic, has refused to trade even in commodities in which it possesses a comparative advantage (Bowring 2003). Even in the Indo-Sri Lankan and Indo-Nepalese cases the enhanced trade ties have not led to a permanent settlement of historical political disputes. In fact, trade has hardly impacted political relations. Even today, the long-standing points of contention cause temporary disruption in trade relations from time to time.

## Regional integration processes

As RTAs have been unable to develop momentum due to persisting regional tensions, their ability to proactively mitigate conflict has also been limited. However, concurrent processes are in evidence that aim to promote political stability. These processes encompass intra-regional non-trade, non-economic arrangements. Alternatively, they reflect pressure by external powers with political stakes in the region. In particular, informal political dialogue and processes from beyond the region are playing an increasing role in conflict mitigation. These processes can impact intra-state conditions and, in turn, be impacted by them.

### *Internal/regional processes*

India has signed a series of agreements over the years with its neighbours, with whom it shares a history of conflict and tension, shown in Table 4.7. A characteristic of the more successful bilateral agreements is that they cover a range of issues that are independent of one another. In the case of Bangladesh and Sri Lanka, addressing 'foundational' issues of peace building and border issues early on has been key to relationship building. While earlier agreements cover border treaty, water sharing, religious harmony and peace building issues, more recent agreements involve credit, and economic development (commitments to research and infrastructure cooperation followed by credit agreements and tariff reductions). The Indus Water Treaty between Pakistan and India is an example of one of the intra-regional agreements (Iyer 1999) that exemplifies successful conflict resolution between two countries bedevilled by tensions and unresolved issues (Iyer 2002).

### *External processes*

Interestingly, most of the processes that have achieved some success in mitigating conflict in South Asia have been externally driven. While intra-regional dialogues are part of normal diplomacy, there have been few internally generated movements geared towards sustained mitigation efforts. We indicated earlier that bilateral political issues have been kept out of SAARC's purview to accommodate the sensitivities of member countries. In view of the negative fallout of political tensions on trade arrangements in the region, some analysts have called for a regional institutional mechanism to address conflict among members; Ariyasinghe (1990) proposed a 'strategic regional security framework' designed to ensure regional security in South Asia. Others have suggested amending the SAARC charter to allow it to deliberate upon bilateral issues.

SAARC's ineptness has allowed extra-regional forces to step into the political vacuum in South Asia. Norway initiated the peace process between the Tamil and the Sinhalese factions in Sri Lanka. The World Bank and the Asian

Development Bank (ADB) among other financial institutions backed its efforts (Uyangoda 2003). Scandinavian countries have played a significant role in moving the Sri Lankan–LTTE peace process forward, through, for instance, the 2002 Memorandum of Understanding. Also international pressure from the US, consequent upon the LTTE being listed as a terrorist organisation, has led to a clamp down on financial flows from the Tamil diaspora. In the case of India and Pakistan, US pressure has impelled the peace process towards settling and resolving bilateral disputes between the two countries. With two nuclear states and a conflict-prone geo-political situation, the international community has every interest in diffusing violent conflict in South Asia. At the same time however, Western involvement can create contradictions. The recent US–India rapprochement has alienated Pakistan and threatened a fragile peace, which the US wished to engineer in the first place. Similarly, the Iran–Pakistan–India gas pipeline is a classic example of a promising regional initiative being undermined by external pressure. While all regional parties are interested in the project, which analysts believe could provide the much-needed framework for energy cooperation in South Asia, US influence on India has forced it to remain non-committal on the issue. That said however, third party mediation by Western countries has, for the most part, mediated violent inter-state conflict in the region.

China, along with Association of South East Asian Nations (ASEAN) countries is likely to be a key player in future South Asian geo-politics. Beijing maintains a military interest in the region due to Sino-Indian territorial disputes and has hosted regular visits by leaders from Nepal, Bangladesh and Sri Lanka to ensure that improved Sino-Indian relations would not be to their detriment. Beijing remains critical of India's coercive diplomacy and maintains diplomatic and military relations with Pakistan. As an SAARC observer, China may become a more formal player in terms of maintaining peace in the region (Malik 2001).

*Impact on intra-state conflict*

The impact of external political processes on intra-state conflict in South Asia has been negative. Such influences, particularly in the case of Pakistan, illustrate how external involvement can increase divisive tendencies within a country. On the one hand, the secular elite have welcomed US intervention, while those within the lower classes sway towards more conservative rhetoric from religious quarters. As a result, an already weakened state risks further destabilisation due to an increase in intra-state extremist activities. Similarly, United Nations (UN) involvement in the Nepalese crisis has driven a wedge between the government of Nepal, the mainstream political parties and the Nepali citizens (Pradhan 2005). Electing for arbitration from a third party rather than looking inwards for a solution prevents the region from evolving into a politically mature and self-sufficient political entity. In this manner, SAARC countries settle for short-term conflict mitigation rather than developing a lasting internal solution that eliminates the cause of the conflict. The efficacy of external processes has its limits, as dispute resolution through mediation or under third-party pressure can only prevent conflict, not resolve it. For conflict to be resolved permanently, and for long-term peace to be achieved, dispute resolution measures have to be built and institutionalised by the SAARC countries themselves.

## Looking to the future

In looking forward, it is difficult to prescribe a set of proven remedies that will cure the region's myriad problems that constrain peace, stability and sustainable development. Peace remains an elusive goal despite SAARC's emergence as a regional entity in the international political system. Antagonistic relations between countries with outstanding political issues, low levels of intra-SAARC trade and joint economic ventures and inadequate communication and infrastructure links present a bleak future. However, the fact that formal cooperation has survived recurrent setbacks is testimony to the resilience of the organisation. On the other hand, militarisation, elitism and fundamentalism as competing forms of governance, present a worrisome political paradigm that will continue to challenge SAARC.

International players can contribute to peaceful relations within the region by mitigating the impacts that economic globalisation and market failures are having on the region's marginalised communities. More important, they should engage with all stakeholders in South Asia in a manner that elevates development to include not just economic needs but also social, cultural and religious values intrinsic to the region.

While lessons from the EU and ASEAN prove the benefits of regional integration, there is still a need to shape institutions that, as commentators indicate, are asked to compete and yet cooperate in a neo-liberal political economy (Mukherjee-Reed 1997). Economic integration will depend on how individual nations deal with contentious issues and remain committed to regional cooperation. Durable peace must therefore include the resolution of domestic and long-standing differences, including of the Kashmir issue, border disputes, inequitable distribution of natural resources, and of the corrosive politics that divides Hindu, Muslim, Sikh and Buddhist communities.

Political analysts have proposed the creation of an SAARC parliament as a new interactive mechanism to increase transactions, linkages and coalitions beyond the divisive politics that exacerbate antagonism. This might go beyond the bureaucratic-technical parameters of SAARC and introduce political, religious, moral, cultural and civilisational dimensions of regionalism. Such a parliament could address conflict in the region, take advantage of civil society, incorporate the principal of 'unity in diversity' and incorporate a two-stage development process, where government has high influence, to a level where popular participation begins to weigh in. Conflict could be managed through three stages, input (source, latent and manifestation of identified conflict) to management (understanding, containing and negotiating problems) and finally to output (consequences defined and outputs generated and drafted) (Paranjpe 2002).

Shared management of renewable resources such as water can leverage peace building efforts within the region (India–Pakistan and India–Nepal–Bhutan), especially as there is a precedence for doing so. There are clear linkages between environmental factors and security, namely trans-boundary water issues in conflict settings. The environment in the context of conflict can be most effectively defined as resources at risk of depletion, as well as damage that can result from human impact. Such was the case between India and Pakistan during partition with the separation of the Indus river tributaries which Pakistan relied upon heavily (Carius *et al.* 2004). The World Bank mediated agreement can inform a sub-regional grouping to address the water and energy dependency between Nepal, Bhutan and India, and between India and Bangladesh. SAARC could and should serve as a regional vehicle for extending resource management across the region. Other threats to South Asia's environmental security include acid precipitation, deforestation, degradation of agricultural land, over use and pollution of water supplies and depletion of fish stocks (Homer-Dixon 2001). As international cooperation within Asia is required to address such issues, relevant negotiation must extend beyond South Asia. Cross-boundary conservation efforts to jointly manage resources and conserve natural ecosystems that benefit the South Asian biome are feasible. For example, the South Asian Seas Action Plan has been developed and, following adoption in March 1995, has been agreed to by the governments of Bangladesh, Maldives, Sri Lanka, Pakistan and India. Data collection between India and Pakistan also exists through the Global Environment Measurement System (GEMS) and the Global Resource Information database (Rajen 2003). While such agreements do enhance people-to-people contact, they have not been capable in and of themselves, in mitigating conflict and easing tensions.

Beneath the political colourations of South Asia, reside the socio-economic aspirations of its middle class. Some argue that in order for the region to prosper, a new idea of South Asia will have to emerge and the primary driver will have to be the aspirations of the middle class for something more than private affluence in the midst of public squalor. Hence, social capital building that challenges all of the region's societies and effective collective action within and then across will be the test of whether or not this society emerges (Singh 2005). Other informal political dialogues need to include citizen-to-citizen contact, which addresses displaced persons following partition (East Bangladesh and West Bengal, the two Punjabs) and the social and religious values of being able to visit one's homeland, place of birth and ancestral grave sites. Education and cultural exchange should allow students, writers, intellectuals and artists to be able to mix and exchange ideas on a new South Asia (Ahmed 2003).

Summing up, SAARC security discourses must be expanded to include political, social and environmental perspectives in order to achieve sustainability (Thakur and Newman 2004). Joint law enforcement, intelligence and linkages with international organisations could suppress violence if linked with broader development objectives that take into account the root causes of violence and the injustices that fan the flames of conflict.

The international community can take measures through bilateral agreements and trade by encouraging equitable development within agreements, fair trade and better understanding of the socio-economic and political reality of poorer segments of society. While their current understanding is framed within an economic paradigm that seeks to modernise South Asia at the expense of sustainable and pro-poor development, a shift towards all encompassing development would address concerns and issues within the marginalised classes, which is where intra-state conflict manifests itself.

## Notes

1  For a discussion on PTAs, see C. Parr Rosson *et al.* 'Preferential trading arrangements: gainers and losers from regional trading blocs', http://www.ces.ncsu.edu/depts/agecon/trade/eight.html (accessed 26 March 2007).
2  Bose provides a detailed account of the problem in Kashmir.
3  Some, albeit pro-establishment analysts, argue differently claiming that nuclear capability creates a deterrent.
4  In the province of Punjab, official figures indicate 776 deaths from 1990–2001. *The News*, 18 May 2002.
5  The areas of cooperation were agriculture, rural development, telecommunications, meteorology, health and population control, transport, sports, arts and culture, postal services and scientific and technical cooperation.
6  SAARC Secretariat.
7  See http://www.saarc-sec.org/main.php?id=12&t=2.1 (accessed 26 March 2007).
8  This list has been compiled from Taneja (1999) and Khan *et al.* (2007).
9  We found this during primary research for Khan *et al.* (2007).
10 Trade between the two countries went up sixfold in the current fiscal year, compared to the previous year.

## References

Ades, A. and Chua, H.B. (1997) 'Thy neighbor's curse: regional instability and economic growth', *Journal of Economic Growth*, 2:3, September, 279–304, Netherlands: Springer.

Ahmed, I. (2003) 'Contours of regional cooperation: peoples to peoples contacts and parliamentary initiatives in searching for common ground in South Asia', a report of a CPAS-SIPSIR workshop 'New Initiatives for Risk Reduction on Unsettled Asian Borders', Stockholm: Center for Pacific Asia Studies, Stockholm University.

Ariyasinghe, P.R. (1990) *South Asian Association for Regional Co-operation (SAARC), The Potential for Regional Security*, Colombo: Bandaranaike Centre for International Studies.

Bandara, J.S. and Yu, W. (2001) *How Desirable is the South Asian Free Trade Area?* Frederiksberg: Danish Institute of Agricultural and Fisheries Economies.

Barbieri, K. (2002) *The Liberal Illusion: Does Trade Promote Peace?* Ann Arbor: University of Michigan Press.

Bhasin, A.S. (2001) *India–Sri Lanka relations and Sri Lanka's ethnic conflict documents: 1947–2000*, New Delhi: India Research Press.

Bose, T.K. (2001) 'Resumption of India–Pakistan official dialogue and the prospects of peace', paper presented at the Second International South Asia Forum Conference.

Bowring, P. (2003) 'India is causing trouble for Bangladesh', *International Herald Tribune – Opinion*, Wednesday 22 January 2003.

Burki, S.J. (2004) *Prospects of Peace, Stability and Prosperity in South Asia: An Economic Perspective*, Islamabad.

Carius, A., Dabelko, G. and Wolf, A.T. (2004) 'Water, conflict and cooperation', *Policy Brief Series*, Washington DC: United States Aid Office of Conflict Management and Mitigation.

Chowdhury, B.H. (2002) 'Building lasting peace: issues of the implementation of the Chittagong Hill Tracts Accord', ACDIS occasional paper, University of Illinois at Urbana-Champaign.

CNN (2001) 'Truce on India–Bangladesh border', Associated Press and Reuters. Available from CNN.com. Accessed 11 June 2008.

Dash, K.C. (1996) 'The political economy of regional cooperation in South Asia', *Pacific Affairs*, 69:2, 185–209.

European Commission (2005) 'Business opportunities through the liberalization of SAARC', Luxembourg: European Commission.

FPCCI (Federation of Pakistan Chambers of Commerce and Industry) (2003) *Statistics on Trade, Pakistan and SAARC*. Available from www.fpcci.com.pk. Accessed 5 February 2006.

Hegre, H. (2000) 'Development and the liberal peace: what does it take to be a trading state?', *Journal of Peace Research*, 37:1, 5–30.

Homer-Dixon, T. (2001) 'On the threshold: environmental changes as causes of acute conflict', *International Security*, 16:2, 76–116.

Hussaini, A. (2005) 'Balochistan, crisis and conflict', Pakistan Link News Network. Available from www.pakistanlink.com. Accessed 19 February 2006.

International Boundary Monitor (1998) 'India's boundary disputes with China, Nepal and Pakistan', International Boundary Monitor. Available from www.boundaries.comernational. Accessed 19 February 2006.

International Monetary Fund (1997, 2002) *Direction of Trade Statistics Yearbook*, Washington, DC: International Monetary Fund.

Iyer, R. (1999) 'Conflict resolution: three river treaties', *Economic and Political Weekly* special articles. Available from www.epw.org. Accessed 13 March 2006.

Iyer, R. (2002) 'Was the Indus Waters Treaty in trouble?' *Economic and Political Weekly* commentary. Available from www.epw.org. Accessed 13 March 2006.

Kee, H.L., Nicita, A. and Olarreaga, M. (2006) 'Estimating trade restrictiveness indices', World Bank policy research working paper, 3840, Washington, D.C.

Khan, S.R., Yusuf, M., Bokhari, S. and Aziz, S. (2007) 'Quantifying informal trade between India and Pakistan', in Z.F. Naqvi and P. Schuler (eds) *The Challenges and Potential of Pakistan–India Trade*, Washington, DC: World Bank.

Kumar, R. (2001) 'Sovereignty and intervention: opinions in South Asia, *Pugwash Online*, 2:1. Available from http://www.Pugwash.org/reports/rc/como_india.htm. Accessed 13 March 2006.

MacGregor, J. (2000) 'The internalization of disputes over Water: The Case of Bangladesh and India', paper presented at Australasian Political Studies Association Conference, Canberra: ANU.

Malik, J.M. (2001) 'South Asia in China's foreign relations', *Pacifica Review*, 13:1, February, 73–90.

Mukherjee-Reed, A. (1997) 'Rationalization in South Asia: theory and praxis', *Pacific Affairs*, 70:2, Summer, 235.

Mukerji, I.N. (2000) 'Towards a free trade area in South Asia: instruments and modalities', in B.C. Upreti (ed.) *SAARC – Dynamics of Regional Cooperation in South Asia*, New Delhi: Kalinga Publications.

Mukherji, I.N. (2002) 'Charting a free trade area in South Asia: instruments and modalities', in T.N. Srinivasan (ed.) *Trade, Finance and Investment in South Asia*, New Delhi: Social Science Press, SANEI, pp. 79–108.

Murthy, P. (1999) 'India and Nepal: security and economic dimensions, strategic analysis', *Journal of the IDSA*, XXIII:9, December.

Paranjpe, S. (2002) 'Development order in South Asia: towards a South Asian association for regional cooperation parliament', *Contemporary South Asia*, II, 345–356.

Pradhan, S. (2005) 'South Asia intelligence review', *Weekly Assessments and Briefings*, 4:2. Available from www.satp.org. Accessed 25 July 2006.

Pursell, G. and Sattar, Z. (2004) 'Trade policies in South Asian countries', World Bank report no. 2 949, 7 September, Poverty Reduction and Economic Management Sector Unit. Available from http://www-wds.worldbank.org/servlet/WDS ContentServer/WDSP/IB/2004/09/30/000160016_20040930094505/Rendered/PDF/299490vol.2.pdf. Accessed 11 June 2008.

Rajen, G. (2003) 'Strengthening regional security in South Asia: cooperative monitoring in coastal regions', *Faultlines*, 14, Institute for Conflict Management, New Delhi, India. Available from www.satp.org. Accessed 13 April 2007.

Reuveny, R. (2000) 'Bilateral import, export and political conflict simultaneity', *International Studies Quarterly*, 45, 131–158.

RISNODEC (2001) 'Economic impact of trade and investment facilitation and liberalization in South Asia (BBIN): a developmental perspective', paper in the Asian Development Bank Identification and Prioritization of Sub-regional Projects in South Asia.

Robson, P. (1998) *The Economics of International Integration*, London: Routledge.

Rodrik, D. (2000) 'Can integration into the world economy substitute for a development strategy?', unpublished paper, Cambridge, MA: Harvard University.

Roy, J. (2004) 'Trade facilitation in India: Current situation and the road ahead', presented at the EU–World Bank Asia Workshop on Trade Facilitation in East Asia, China, 3–5 November.

Sahadevan, P. (1999) 'Ethnic conflict in South Asia', occasional paper #16:OP4, University of Notre Dame, IN: Joan B. Kroc Institute for International Peace Studies.

Singh, N. (2005) 'The idea of South Asia and the role of the middle class', New Dehli: National Institute of Public Finance and Policy.

Synnott, H. (1999) 'The causes and consequences of South Asia's nuclear tests', *Adelphi Papers*, London: International Institute for Strategic Studies.

Taneja, N. (1999) 'Informal trade in the SAARC region', working paper, 47, New Dehli: Indian Council for Research on International Economic Relations, March.

Taneja, N. (2004a) 'Trade facilitation in the WTO: implications for India', working paper, 128, New Dehli: Indian Council for Research on International Economic Relations.

Taneja, N. (2004b) 'Informal and free trade arrangements', *South Asian Journal*, 4, April–June. Available from www.southasianmedia.net. Accessed 11 June 2008.

Thakur, R. and Newman, E. (2004) *Broadening Asia's Security Discourse and Agenda: Political, Social and Environmental Perspectives*, Tokyo: United Nations University Press.

Thakurta, P.G. (2006) *South Asia: Burying Quarrels for Regional Free Trade*, Bangkok IPS Inter Press Service. Available from www.ipsnews.net. Accessed 11 June 2008.

Thapa, D. and Sijapati, B. (2003) *A Kingdom Under Siege: Nepal's Maoist Insurgency, 1996 to 2003*, Kathmandu: The Printhouse.

UNCTAD (2002) *Handbook of Statistics*, Geneva: UNCTAD.

Upreti, B.C. (2000) 'Nepal's role in SAARC', in B.C. Upreti (ed.) *SAARC – Dynamics of Regional Cooperation in South Asia Vol. 1: Nature, Scope and Perceptions*, New Delhi: Kalinga Publications.

Uyangoda, J. (2003) 'Sri Lankan conflict and SAARC', *South Asian Journal*, 1, August–September.

Wickramasinghe, U. (2001) 'How can South Asia turn the new emphasis on IT provisions to their advantage?', Kathmandu: South Asia Watch on Trade, Economics and Environment (SAWTEE).

WTO (2002) *International Trade Statistics*, Geneva: WTO.

# 5 Regional trade agreements and conflict

## The case of Southeast Asia

*Hank Lim*

## Introduction

Southeast Asia has witnessed a relative subsidence in conventional security threats such as territorial disputes, arms races and inter-state warfare over the last decade or so.[1] Instead, non-traditional security threats and intra-state conflict have taken greater precedence in recent years.[2] These non-traditional security threats in the region have manifested themselves as social unrest (including forced displacement) and political instability associated with environmental crises, energy shortfalls, terrorist attacks, pandemic diseases, religious differences and economic recession. Such threats have risen sharply since the Asian financial crisis in 1997.

The region is one of the most ecologically and ethnically diverse in the world with divergent development paths and non-inclusive economic strategies that some Southeast Asian nations adopted, particularly before 1997. The strategies generated rapid growth in income and output but they also engendered widespread unemployment and poverty. Differentiated benefits along the lines of religion, ethnicity and resource use have precipitated intra-state conflicts, such as in Myanmar (with the Karen group over issues of regional autonomy, land rights and discrimination), Laos and Cambodia (instigated by remnants of the Khmer Rouge until 1997), Indonesia (the secession of East Timor and Aceh), Thailand (over its southern provinces) and the Philippines (over discrimination of the Muslims Moros, in the south).

The following sub-sections provide an overview of inter and intra-state conflicts in the region.

### Overview of inter-state conflicts in Southeast Asia

Sovereignty-related disputes remain a flashpoint in the region with different colonial histories. Indonesia annexed East Timor in 1975 after the latter declared independence from the Portuguese. Initially, the invasion and the subsequent violation of human rights by the occupying military forces were tolerated. In 1999, following a referendum, East Timor secured its independence as the Democratic Republic of Timor Leste. This victory for independence triggered a massive and violent response from disaffected groups in East Timor (and Indonesia), who did not want independence from Indonesia. The ensuing violence resulted in extensive damage to infrastructure and loss of human lives.

The Philippines and Malaysia have competing claims over Sabah. The Philippines claim eastern Sabah as part of its territory. This claim is based upon the Sultanate of Brunei's cession of its north-east territories to the Sultanate of Sulu in 1703, as recompense for military assistance by the latter. Malaysia, on the other hand, has claimed sovereign rights over Sabah on the basis of the leasing agreements secured by Baron von Overbeck and Alfred Dent with the Brunei Sultanate on 29 December 1877, and the Sulu Sultanate on 22 January 1878. The British Crown renewed the lease on 15 July 1946, but finally ceded Sabah to Malaysia on 16 September 1963. Currently, Malaysia continues to reject Philippine calls to bring the matter of Sabah's jurisdiction to the International Court of Justice.

On 24 July 2003, Malaysia and Singapore jointly approached the International Court of Justice regarding a dispute concerning sovereignty over the island of Pedra Branca (Pulau Batu Puteh), Middle Rocks and South Ledge. Malaysia first claimed the island in 1979 after publishing new official maps. Singapore, on the other hand, states that it has managed Horsburgh Lighthouse and exercised full sovereignty over the island since the 1840s without any protest from Malaysia. However, Malaysia insists that when Johor ceded Singapore to the British in 1824, the island was not part of the secession and that the Sultan of Johor only allowed the British to construct a lighthouse on the island in 1844. The International Court of Justice in The Hague has ruled on 23 May 2008 that Pedra Branca belongs to Singapore and Middle Rocks to Malaysia. It cannot make a decision on South Ledge because it does not have the mandate to do so. It further stated that South Ledge should belong to a country that has jurisdiction over it.

Elsewhere, Indonesia and Malaysia also went to the International Court of Justice with competing claims over the islands of Ligitan and Sepadan. Indonesia's claim to sovereignty over the islands is based primarily on a conventional title, the 1891 Convention between Great Britain and the Netherlands. However, the Court found that the Convention, when read in context and in the light of its object and purpose, cannot be interpreted as establishing an allocation line determining sovereignty over the islands. The Court ruled in favour of Malaysia on 17 December 2002 on the basis of 'effectivities', that is, 'based on activities evidencing an actual, continued exercise of authority over the islands, i.e., the intention and will to act as sovereign'.[3]

Sovereignty-related disputes are also sourced in energy security concerns. The South China Sea is a disputed site; specifically, some of the islands on the key shipping routes are oil and natural gas repositories. The resource-rich islands have evoked competing claims from claimants such as Brunei, China, Indonesia, Malaysia, the Philippines, Taiwan and Vietnam. On several occasions armed open conflict has erupted, involving naval vessels. Chinese and Vietnamese vessels clashed 1974, 1988 and 2002. In 1996, China and the Philippines faced off against each other. In 2002, the country claimants agreed to resolve the issue of the islands peacefully and signed the 'Declaration on the Conduct of Parties in the South China Sea'.[4] There now appears to be a greater commitment to negotiate rather than resorting to force, and a recent interest in cooperation via joint exploration initiatives. In March 2005, Chinese, Vietnamese and Philippine oil companies signed an agreement to conduct a joint marine seismic survey of oil potential in the South China Sea, signifying 'a historic contribution to peace, stability and development in the region'.[5]

Elsewhere, refugee inflows due to political unrest in the country of origin have threatened state security. Relations between Thailand and Malaysia became strained in 2005, when 130 Muslim Thais sought refuge in Malaysia. Subsequently, the Thai interior minister, Kongsak Wantana, insinuated that the bombs that exploded in southern Thailand were made in Malaysia. Thai security and intelligence officials claimed that the insurgent and separatist leaders were based in northern Malaysia and that Kuala Lumpur adamantly refused to hand them over to the Thai government. During the military coup launched in Thailand on 19 September 2006, Malaysia tightened its border security to prevent refugee movements and smuggling activities from Thailand.[6]

### Overview of intra-state conflicts in Southeast Asia

With the exception of Singapore, Brunei and Malaysia, separatist and other forms of intra-state violent conflict are prevalent in Southeast Asia. The shift of Myanmar's administrative capital from colonial Rangoon to remote Pyinmana in April 2006 signifies a new wave of political insularism, inviting sharp criticism from the international community. The move represents an attempt to consolidate power, and to use repressive tactics to wipe out the opposition. The military junta has announced new plans to step up the pressure on Aung San Suu Kyi's National League for Democracy, and to launch an offensive against the Karen National Union (KNU) which is agitating over issues of regional autonomy, land rights and discrimination. An attempt to diffuse criticism by organising a local and foreign press trip to a remote part of the Karen area (in eastern Burma) affected by the fighting backfired. It only aggravated the international outcry over alleged reports of murder, rape and mutilation, marking the junta's most brutal offensive since 1997.

Laos gained its independence from the French in 1954. The US bombed the country in retaliation for its support to the Vietcong during the war, which extended through the 1960s and 1970s. In 1975 the Communist Pathet Lao, backed by the Soviet Union and Vietnam, overthrew the royalist government. Presently, minority groups such as the Hmong and disaffected military personnel continue to mount sporadic resistance against the Communist regime. The US trained the ethnic Hmongs to fight against the Communists during the Vietnam War; after the US withdrew, the Communist Laotian government drove the Hmongs out of Cambodia and massacred those who remained. Amnesty International is active in highlighting the human rights abuses against them.[7]

Cambodia has only recently emerged from extended inter- and intra-state conflict. The country invited retaliatory bombing from the US in 1969, after it supported the Vietcong. In 1970, General Lon Nol deposed King Sihanouk, who had ruled the country since independence in 1953. In turn, the Khmer Rouge removed General Lon Nol in 1975. Although the Vietnamese drove the Khmer Rouge out of Phnom Penh in 1979, it continued to resist the government in the provinces until 1996, when a large number of soldiers left the organisation.

Indonesia faced domestic insurgency by the separatist Free Aceh Movement (or Gerakan Aceh Merdeka (GAM)), and sectarian violence between Christians and Muslims in Central Sulawesi. GAM has sought independence for the Aceh region of Sumatra from Indonesia since 1976, particularly during Suharto's reign. The main flashpoints were a dilution of Acehnese religion and culture, especially with the influx of Javanese migrants and the uneven income allocation from Aceh's rich oil reserves. Initial GAM guerrilla resistance was put down by government forces in the late 1970s. But renewed efforts by the group, sponsored by Libya and Iran during the 1980s, led to more violent repression and human rights abuses. GAM declared a cease-fire during the December 2004 tsunami, and the government temporarily removed restrictions for aid relief. A peace deal was forged on 16 July 2005 to end the 30-year insurgency through the negotiation efforts, brokered in part by the Swedish government. On 27 December 2005, the GAM leaders disbanded their military wing.

Indonesia experienced one of the bloodiest religious conflicts between Christians and Muslims in Central Sulawesi from 1998 to 2002, where more than 1,000 antagonists from both communities were killed and tens of thousands rendered homeless. Fresh violence broke out in a May 2000 attack on the Muslims in Poso district. As the world's most populous Muslim state practising a moderate form of Islam, its porous maritime borders and a weak central government have made Indonesia victim to the Al Qaeda-linked terror group, Jemaah Islamiya (JI). The October 2002 Bali bombing took 202 lives (including 88 Australians). Subsequent years witnessed the Marriott Hotel blast and Australian Embassy attack in Jakarta. The most recent attack took place in October last year in Bali, which was bombed for the second time.

The Philippines has seen a long ongoing struggle by secessionist Muslim groups in Mindanao to break free from Manila. These movements include the Abu Sayyaf, JI and the more nationalistic Moro Islamic Liberation Front (MILF). A truce between the Philippines government and the MILF has been sustained since 2003. This has allowed the military to concentrate its fighting with Abu Sayyaf rebels on the remote southern island of Jolo. Fresh violence broke out in September 2006 between security forces and Muslim militants, and some 6,000 Marine and Army troops sealed off Jolo Island.[8]

In the case of Thailand, separatist movements are concentrated in its southern provinces. These provinces are predominantly Muslim, unlike the rest of Thailand which has a Buddhist majority. The ongoing violence since January 2004 has resulted in the deaths of more than 1,400 people.

### *Non-traditional threats to peace*

As related in the sections above, threats and opportunities abound when building trade links and formalising trading relationships between states previously at war, or at risk of war. Such relationships become especially difficult in the presence of development gaps and uneven resource allocation. Economic development has assigned priority to non-inclusive growth over income distribution and employment creation in some Association of South East Asian Nations (ASEAN) countries. This has resulted in income disparities and poverty existing side by side with economic prosperity. Priorities such as social welfare and reducing the poverty gap have also been neglected as Southeast Asia marches towards economic development and integration into the global economy. Many fault lines define relations between the state and non-governmental stakeholders, including religion, ethnicity, resource use, pandemic outbreaks and environmental degradation.

Growing interdependence between states in the region has exposed unprecedented vulnerabilities. At the tenth ASEAN Regional Forum (ARF) meeting, held in Kuala Lumpur on 5 September 2006, Malaysia Deputy Prime Minister Datuk Seri Najib noted that 'the Asia-Pacific is not free from conflicts . . . There are on-going sensitive security issues around us such as overlapping claims on the Spratlys, nuclear proliferation and transnational security issues.'

Najib's caution points in part towards the conflation of energy resource conflicts in the region, spurred to a large degree by China and India's rapidly expanding economies, with their corresponding energy demands. The development presages a threat to the region with politically charged bilateral energy trading and new interest in developing nuclear energy.

Environmental woes also plague Southeast Asia, as a result of short-term economic goals. The region continues to be gripped by trans-boundary haze pollution annually from July to September since 1997. Indonesia's problem with unchecked slash-and-burn practices is further exacerbated with recent news of the country's fast vanishing mangrove trees, with 6.6 million hectares destroyed over the past seven years, constituting around 70 per cent of mangrove areas damaged. The problem has similarly afflicted several other Southeast Asian countries such as Myanmar, Thailand, Malaysia, Vietnam, Brunei Darussalam and the Philippines. Indonesia has just experienced another tsunami, albeit on a smaller scale than the one in 2004. Earlier in

May 2005, an earthquake in Central Java killed more than 57,000 people and left tens of thousands homeless. Almost exactly one year later, the Yogyakarta quake took over 3,000 lives.[9]

Southeast Asia also holds the unenviable record of avian flu fatalities, especially in Indonesia, Vietnam and Thailand. May 2005 saw the world's first lab-confirmed human-to-human transmission of bird flu in Indonesia, raising the spectre of a flu pandemic. The country has recorded 49 deaths as of 13 September 2006, the highest in the world.

One of the greatest threats facing the region is terrorism, as demonstrated by the Bali bombing in 2002. While greater cooperation and more concerted efforts to address the dangers of terrorism have been undertaken, the record remains mixed. The Southeast Asian strategy has been to tackle poverty and social ostracism from mainstream secular society. However, a sustainable long-term solution is needed which addresses the genesis of terrorism – namely, what triggered the movement in the first place in Southeast Asia. The Israel–Hizbollah war has further deepened the Islam–West chasm in Southeast Asia, home to an estimated 230 million Muslims and which may spark a new wave of Islamic radicalisation in the region.[10]

On the upside, efforts by Malaysia, Indonesia and Singapore to combat piracy and terrorism in the Strait of Malacca have paid off. In August 2006 London's insurance market, Lloyd's Market Association (LMA), dropped the war-risk rating on the strategic waterway, which links Asia with the Middle East and Europe and carries some 50,000 vessels a year (or some 40 per cent of the world's trade and 80 per cent of the energy supplies of Japan and China). LMA had classed the Malacca Strait a 'war risk' zone earlier and added it to a list of 21 other areas deemed high risk and vulnerable to war, strikes and terrorism.

While the security threats are very real and remain a concern for Southeast Asia's future political and economic fate, the opportunities that exist through forging RTAs outweigh the threats. By creating regional stability through the ASEAN process and mechanism, Southeast Asia has been able to attract foreign direct investment (FDI) and to create a policy environment for good and effective macroeconomic management through regional demonstration effects. In turn, rapid economic development, especially before the Asian economic crisis in 1997, contributed to reducing inter-state conflicts in Southeast Asia. For one thing, regional resources were directed to productive economic activities rather than destructive inter-state conflicts.

### Problem statement and aims

The regions representative groupings have considerably mitigated the risk of intra-state conflicts from developing into inter-state strife. These groupings include ASEAN and its associated RTAs, namely, the ASEAN Free Trade Area (AFTA) and the ASEAN Community. The groupings act as political and economic security buffers to promote peace and prosperity in the region.

Southeast Asia's experience with regional integration is closer to Latin America and South Asia than to the European Union (EU), whose genesis lay in demonstrated economic synergies. Thus, in ASEAN's case, it was only when conflicts and tensions in the region abated that the RTAs were conceived and formulated. Subsequently, these RTAs have played a key role in maintaining peace and security in Southeast Asia. The RTAs were forged to promote economic cooperation and intra-regional growth, and to direct the region's resources towards productive economic activities. The AFTA pushed towards lower tariffs under the Common Effective Preferential Tariff (CEPT) scheme. This raised the level of intra-regional trade, creating more interdependence and linkages and cementing ties within ASEAN. With closer economic integration, the cost of conflict becomes higher. Further, AFTA's non-enforcing nature is geared to diffusing tension between partner countries. Finally, AFTA's non-trade provisions, such as the rule of law and respect for human rights and socio-cultural values could potentially yield additional peace dividends. Admittedly, while there are many intervening variables, a convincing case can be made for AFTA's impact in terms of increased intra-regional trade, better economic coordination and improved regional ties.

In the following section, we describe how the formation of ASEAN created the impetus for regional economic and political integration. We follow with a review of AFTA, which ASEAN established in 1992 and which represents an attempt to give more formal shape to its objectives. Subsequently we examine intra-ASEAN trade trends and assess the impact of trade on regional peace and security. We then look at the evolution of ASEAN from an association into an institution-building community, comprising the ASEAN Economic Community (AEC), ASEAN Security Community (ASC), and ASEAN Socio-Cultural Community (ASCC), which strengthened ASEAN's peace-building role in the wider Asia-Pacific region. We focus on AFTA's role and functional expansion into the AEC, ASC and ASCC. We then conclude with a recap.

## Association of South East Asian Nations

The part of the Southeast Asian region that ASEAN embraces occupies a total area of 4.5 million square kilometres with a population of about 500 million, a combined gross domestic product (GDP) of almost US$700 billion and total trade amounting to about US$850 billion. ASEAN was the outcome of a politically motivated agenda. Inspired by the EU and North American Free Trade Agreement (NAFTA), its initial objective was to promote regional political harmony, especially as the region was gripped by a critical security threat. In subsequent years, when the security threat had subsided, primacy was given to efforts to achieve regional economic integration. ASEAN's transition from political to economic status can be classified into four distinct periods. These periods fall between the years 1967 to 1982, 1983 to 1990, 1991 to 1993 and 1994 to 1999.

*ASEAN's development phases*

*1967–1982*

Southeast Asian countries came together in Bangkok on 8 August 1967, in an attempt to meet the diverse challenges confronting a region recognised as one of the most ecologically and ethnically diverse in the world. The Bangkok Declaration to establish ASEAN was signed by Indonesia, Malaysia, Philippines, Singapore and Thailand.[11] The initial impulse came out of strategic and security concerns, even though the stated aims and purposes of the Declaration were comparatively more eclectic, namely: (1) to accelerate economic growth, social progress and cultural development in the region; and (2) to promote regional peace and stability through abiding respect for justice and the rule of law in the relationship among countries in the region and adherence to the principles of the United Nations (UN) Charter.

The political orientation of ASEAN has its roots in Malaysia's confrontation with Indonesia, which had ended a year earlier. In addition, non-Communist countries felt the need to develop a more concerted response to the Vietnam War. This need became more pressing with the withdrawal of the US following the end of the war in April 1975, and the corresponding spread of Communism in the region. In order to stem the Communist tide, ASEAN's five founding nations established the Zone of Peace, Freedom and Neutrality (ZOPFAN) – signing the declaration in November 1971, with the aim of securing international recognition for its political stance. The declaration built upon the principles of peace, freedom, sovereignty, territorial integrity and the non-use of force advocated in the Bangkok Declaration and by the UN. The emphasis on peaceful dispute settlements and abstinence from threats of force sets the framework for subsequent ASEAN approaches towards the maintenance of regional and international security. ZOPFAN's significance also lies in strengthening the political will of ASEAN to reduce external influences in the region; to avoid becoming a proxy war theatre for superpower rivalries. Subsequently, US and Russian bases in the region were closed (Ruland 2005).[12]

Until 1976, a loose and highly decentralised structure dominated by state-to-state cooperation and involving mostly foreign ministers characterised ASEAN. Consequently, member countries felt the need to ratchet up ASEAN as the defining regional community. The first ASEAN summit in Bali in February 1976 formalised the Treaty of Amity and Cooperation (TAC). The treaty specifically and legally binds all its ASEAN signatories to peaceful co-existence and respect for the principles of sovereignty, territorial integrity, non-interference in internal affairs and non-use of force (the ASEAN way), that have been enshrined in the Bangkok Declaration.[13] Its amity clause emphasises increased contact and interaction among ASEAN's peoples to ensure closer understanding. Its cooperation clauses oblige active efforts at consultation on international and regional matters with a view to coordinating policy and action. The clauses also restrict individual signatory states from participating in activities that constitute a threat to the political and economic stability, sovereignty and territorial integrity of another signatory state.

In its operations, the TAC attempts to balance the principles of sovereignty and non-interference, with the regulatory provisions for transnational action and coordination towards peaceful dispute settlement. The High Council, also established in 1976, is entrusted with recommending appropriate modes of settlement. The Council consists of a representative (at ministerial level) from each of the ASEAN members as well as dialogue partners involved in a particular dispute. The TAC is accompanied by two amending protocols which: (1) permit its extension to non-Southeast Asian states with qualifying clauses and; (2) acknowledge the inclusion of new members, namely, Brunei, Cambodia, Laos, Myanmar and Vietnam.

The inaugural Bali summit also issued the Declaration of ASEAN Concord I (Bali Concord I), with the collective objectives of regional resilience, promoting social justice and national development, peaceful settlement of disputes and the creation of an ASEAN community and identity. The Bali Concord I adopted a framework of cooperation in six areas: political, economic, social, cultural and information, security and the improvement of ASEAN machinery.

In time, member states also began to see the role of economic cooperation in helping ASEAN to develop into a stronger political entity. The foreseen cooperation entailed both market-sharing and resource-pooling strategies. Member states experimented with preferential trading arrangements (PTAs) to allow access to ASEAN markets, and embarked upon large-scale projects such as the ASEAN Industrial Projects and the ASEAN Industrial Joint Ventures to benefit from economies of scale. In reality, reflecting the mutual distrust among member states, businesses in the region continue to adopt protectionist strategies in both tariff and non-tariff forms.[14]

### *1983–1990*

This period is marked by the fallout from the second oil crisis of 1979–1980, which led to a dramatic drop in commodity prices and a weakened global economy. ASEAN leaders created a task force to formulate a regional response aimed at reviving their economies; the crisis spurred member countries to use economic cooperation as a revival tool. However, the recovery was fast as a result of the Plaza Accord of September 1985, which led to the depreciation of the US dollar vis-à-vis other major currencies, particularly the Japanese yen. Exchange rates turned in favour of ASEAN as most of the currencies in the region were linked to the US dollar. Consequently, interest in regional economic integration flagged.

*1991–1993*

Trade liberalisation emerged as the new mantra, with the imminent conclusion of the General Agreement on Tariffs and Trade (GATT) Uruguay Round leading to the formation of the World Trade Organization (WTO). As a result, ASEAN member states began to seriously consider the need for an economic safeguard. The CEPT and the AFTA were mooted in 1992 with a view towards regional economic integration. ASEAN also joined the Asia-Pacific Economic Cooperation (APEC) forum to promote trade, investment and economic and technical cooperation among the member states.

*1994–1999*

In 1994, Indochina and Myanmar began to express interest in joining ASEAN. By 1999, the ASEAN-10 vision was a reality with membership extending to all Southeast Asian countries. However ASEAN continued to grapple with the political uncertainties of Cambodia, and the comparatively lower economic status of the state-led economies of the ASEAN-4 (Cambodia, Laos, Myanmar and Vietnam).

Member states launched the ARF in 1994 as a regional security forum which included the ASEAN member states, the observers and consultative and dialogue partners of ASEAN.[15] The ARF is responsible for the analysis and identification of key regional challenges, and for resolving differences and diffusing tensions among stakeholders. The approach is incremental, as reflected in its three-stage development plan: Promotion of Confidence-Building Measures (Stage I); Development of Preventive Diplomacy Mechanisms (Stage II); and Development of Conflict Resolution Mechanisms (Stage III). The ten ASEAN member states also signed the Treaty of the Southeast Asia Nuclear Weapon-Free Zone in December 1995. Three years later, at the third ASEAN informal summit in Manila in 1998, the ASEAN heads of government agreed to the Thai prime minister, Chuan Leekpai's proposal for an ASEAN Troika to be constituted as an ad-hoc body at the ministerial level for the leaders to cooperate more closely and mitigate conflict.

The Asian financial crisis of 1997 was a watershed moment that undermined the structural integrity of ASEAN. Massive domestic imbalances destabilised the region's economies, reversing the growth trends of the 1980s. Many ASEAN countries abandoned economic liberalisation (the outward, export-oriented newly industrialised economy (NIE) model) and reverted to protectionist and insular economic policies. For instance, Malaysia began experimenting with controls over capital flows and currency rates. The timing of ASEAN's expansion during the financial crisis was regarded by many as inopportune. The crisis drove a wedge in the integration process; among other things, it widened the gap between the ASEAN-4 and ASEAN-6 countries. The upside is that it increased perceptions of the need to accelerate economic integration if ASEAN was to enhance itself.[16] In the ASEAN

Vision 2020 issued in December 1997, ASEAN leaders resolved to: (1) maintain regional macroeconomic and financial stability by promoting closer consultations on macroeconomic and financial policies; and (2) continue to liberalise the financial services sector and closely cooperate in money and capital market, tax, insurance and customs matters.

To carry out the mandate, officials have drawn up an ASEAN Finance Work Programme, outlining measures to establish sound international financial practices and standards, deepen capital markets and improve corporate governance. ASEAN countries also worked towards the proper sequencing of the liberalisation of capital accounts to allow freer capital flows, while cushioning the impact of sudden shifts in these flows. In October 1998, the ASEAN finance ministers formalised the ASEAN Surveillance Process (ASP), which served as a framework for closer consultations on economic policies. The first element of the ASP involves monitoring of global as well as regional and national economic and financial developments as an 'early warning system': to keep track of the recovery process and to detect any sign of recurring vulnerability in the ASEAN financial systems and economies. The second element of the ASP takes the form of a peer review where ASEAN finance ministers exchange views and information on developments in their domestic economies, including policy measures carried out and the progress of structural reforms. The review also provides an opportunity for the consideration of jointly unilateral or collective action to counter potential threats to any member economy. The foundation of the ASP process later led to the adoption of the Chiang Mai Initiative (CMI) in May 2000, as the ASEAN+3 (China, Japan and the Republic of Korea) finance ministers came together to establish a regional financing arrangement. The CMI consists of two components: an expanded ASEAN Swap Arrangement and a network of bilateral swap arrangements among ASEAN+3 members.

## ASEAN Free Trade Area

As we indicated earlier, ASEAN established AFTA in 1992 to bolster itself as both a credible political and economic entity. Subsequently AFTA evolved into the AEC. This section addresses the following questions:

- the constraining environment for RTAs;
- the significance of the recent development of RTAs for global and intra-regional competitiveness;
- the contribution of RTAs to trade promotion;
- the role of RTAs in conflict mitigation.

### Impetus for AFTA

A move towards economic cooperation became evident after the end of the Cold War and with the resolution of the Cambodian conflict. In 1991, the

Thai prime minister, Anand Panyarachun, proposed the formation of a free trade agreement (FTA) within ASEAN in 1991, a suggestion that Singapore and then Malaysia endorsed enthusiastically. The European Economic Union and negotiations towards a North American Free Trade Area (NAFTA) had engendered fears of a possible loss of markets to other regions, due to regional protectionism. In particular, the ASEAN was concerned about Mexico gaining free access to US markets (the largest consumer of its exports) through NAFTA. Second, the 'socialist economies of China and Vietnam, with their low-cost labour and land, [had] become attractive, both as production locations for export and for the domestic market' (Lee 2003: 195). ASEAN felt threatened by the potential diversion of investments away from the region.

To maintain its economic competitiveness and its US, European and Japanese markets, ASEAN adopted the CEPT under the umbrella of AFTA. The non-binding and non-punitive nature of these tariffs ensured they were implemented swiftly. The understanding was that existing tariffs on inclusion list (IL) goods would be reduced to 5 per cent within 15 years.[17] Subsequently, some of the ASEAN-6 countries added an amendment to the CEPT in 1995 to shorten the timeline by five years to 2002. By 2002, the target had been largely met: tariffs on IL goods had been lowered among the ASEAN-6 countries from an average 12.76 per cent in 1993, to 1.96 per cent in 2003. Almost all the lines on the IL (98.62 per cent) are below the 5 per cent CEPT target. The ASEAN-6 countries also shifted more products from their temporary exclusion lists (TEL) and general exception lists (GEL) to the IL. The GEL, which makes an exception for products on the basis of national security, health or cultural reasons, contains 292 lines, or about 0.65 per cent of all tariff lines in ASEAN. The TEL, which makes a temporary exception for products at the request of member states, contains 218 lines, or about 0.49 per cent of all tariff lines.

The ASEAN-4 countries, on the other hand, had agreed to the following timelines to reduce tariffs on their IL goods to 5 per cent or less: Vietnam by 2006, Myanmar and Laos by 2008 and Cambodia by 2010. They have put 60.89 per cent of their total tariff lines on the IL. Their TEL lines account for 25.09 per cent of their total lines. The success of ASEAN's member states in reducing their tariffs lends credibility to the zero-tariff goal. In the 2003 CEPT package, ASEAN-6 countries agreed to have zero tariffs on 60 per cent of their IL goods by 2003, a target they slightly surpassed (60.89 per cent). By 2010, all goods on their IL lists will have zero tariffs. Cambodia, Myanmar, Laos and Vietnam (CMLV) are to follow suit in 2015.

### The constraining environment: threats to AFTA

The linkage of RTAs and conflict assumes a complex and unique relationship in Southeast Asia. AFTA's initial implementation in the early 1990s was not a smooth one; inter and intra-state conflict threats almost derailed the entire agenda. At the time, the region's rapid economic success was threatened by the global economic transition that saw the emergence of trading blocs and protectionist sentiments.

Domestic turmoil in the form of leadership change also occurred during the year AFTA was mooted.[18] Thailand was shaken by a series of elections and public revolt that year. Chuan Leekpai took office after ousting Anand Panyarachun, who had initiated AFTA a year before. The Leekpai administration's postponed the scheduled AFTA Ministerial Council meeting. Economic nationalism also fuelled the reversal with the pro-business government responding to the demands of local business. Thailand's petrochemical industry sought exclusion from AFTA, accusing Singapore of unfair competition. Other sectors, namely, electronics and plastics products – both on the 'fast track' – soon followed suit.

Similarly, in Malaysia, the bureaucracy–business nexus stalled liberalisation efforts. According to then Malaysian minister for international trade and industry, Rafidah Aziz, the bureaucracy (with more than 45,000 different tariff lines at their disposal) had plenty of room to manoeuvre and obstruct the AFTA implementation process. Malaysia was also protective over its car, the Proton Saga, and pushed for its automobile industry to be exempted from AFTA. The government also sought a similar dispensation for its petrochemical industry.

With only 23.4 per cent of popular vote, Fidel Ramos' election victory over Aquino in 1992, raised concerns that the weak political leadership would not commit to AFTA. In the Philippines, the business community, represented by the textiles, apparel, footwear, and iron and steel industries, protested the implementation of AFTA. It went into dispute with Singapore, by refusing to reduce tariffs on 11 petrochemical products. While the Philippines had formerly undertaken to lower tariffs under CEPT, the government subsequently gave its petrochemical industry special interest status to defer its earlier CEPT commitments.

Similarly, the Indonesian government continued to protect its powerful indigenous corporations.

### AFTA's impact on intra-ASEAN trade trends

Many ASEAN countries have opted for export-led growth. These countries share similar resource inputs and are engaged in producing high-tech and labour-intensive exports. Thus, the intra-regional competition for developed country markets is high. For instance, electronics and computer products account for 50 per cent of all ASEAN trade, but are ranked fortieth in terms of intra-ASEAN trade. In addition, the total lines on the IL account for as little as 5 per cent of ASEAN's total trade by some estimates, despite having drastically lower tariffs. Intra-regional competition in commonly produced goods has slowed integration, as member countries fear losing out to each other if they cooperate too closely. Generically, the export-oriented regimes

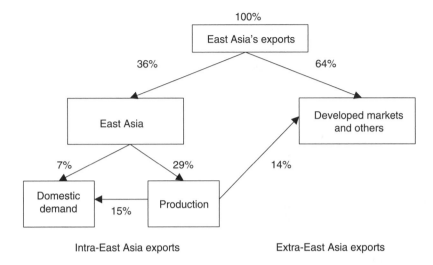

*Figure 5.1* East Asia's export shares using input–output table calculations, 2003.

Source: Economic Policy Department (2003: 64).

Note: Export shares are the Export Promotion Department's internal estimates based on the 1995 Asian input–output tables. Adjustments have also been made using 2001 data for East Asia's exports within and without the region; domestic demand refers to private consumption, government consumption, gross and domestic fixed capital formation and increase in stock.

are limited in terms of the intra-regional trade they can generate. Figure 5.1 refers to East Asia's export shares in 2003 based on input–output table calculations. The figure indicates that there is a limit to the amount of intra-regional trade that can take place in East Asia (and similarly in ASEAN).

Despite such competition, intra-regional trade among ASEAN members does exist, in complimentary items, taking the form of intra-industry trade in electrical items. Tables 5.1 and 5.2 show the dominant share of trade in these items.

In addition, Table 5.3 shows that intra-ASEAN trade exceeds trade with other individual countries by a substantial margin. From the data in these tables we can infer that a large proportion of intra-regional trade comprises intra-industry trade.

As a first step in economic integration, AFTA achieved a moderate degree of success. Total intra-ASEAN trade increased from US$44.2 billion in 1993 to US$174.39 billion in 2003. Figure 5.1 shows a steady increase in intra-ASEAN exports every year post-AFTA with a temporary dip in 1998 due to the financial crisis.

Forging consensus is particularly important given that ASEAN does not operate on a voting system. Instead, it has traditionally worked on the principle of consensus. As reported by former Indonesian president, Megawati Soekarnoputri, at the AFTA 2002 Symposium – ten years after the

*Table 5.1* ASEAN-6 top ten export commodities by two-digit HS codes in 2004

| HS | Commodities | Value (US$ millions) | Share (%) |
|----|-------------|----------------------|-----------|
| 85 | Electrical machinery, equipment parts, sound equipment, TV equipment | 163,220.3 | 31.4 |
| 84 | Nuclear reactors, broilers, machinery and mechanical appliances, parts | 88,665.9 | 17.1 |
| 27 | Mineral fuels, mineral oils and products of their distillation, bituminous substances, mineral waxes | 58,987.9 | 11.4 |
| 29 | Organic chemicals | 16,877.1 | 3.3 |
| 39 | Plastics and articles thereof | 14,498.5 | 2.8 |
| 40 | Rubber and articles thereof | 12,417.3 | 2.4 |
| 15 | Animal or vegetable fats and oils and their cleavage products, prepared edible fats, animal or vegetable waxes | 12,095.5 | 2.3 |
| 90 | Optical, photographic, cinematographic, measuring, checking, precision, medical or surgical instruments and apparatus, and parts and accessories thereof | 10,946.2 | 2.1 |
| 87 | Vehicles others than railway or tramway rolling-stock, and parts and accessories thereof | 10,820.2 | 2.1 |
| 44 | Vehicles others than railway or tramway rolling-stock, and parts and accessories thereof | 8,283.1 | 1.6 |
| | Ten major commodities | 396,812.0 | 76.4 |
| | Others | 122,413.0 | 23.6 |
| | Total | 519,225.0 | 100.0 |

Source: ASEAN (2005: 83, Table V13).

Note: HS refers to Harmonized System of Tariffs any slight discrepancies in numbers are due to rounding.

implementation of AFTA – intra-regional trade had increased approximately 11.6 per cent per annum, and appeared promising for AFTA's eventual materialisation. Through AFTA, President Megawati argued, 'there will also be an improvement of income of its members individually or collectively . . . regional demanding and bargaining powers would increase which, in turn, [would] also increase the intra-ASEAN trading volumes'.

However, the results look less promising. We observe that intra-ASEAN trade as a percentage of total trade rose less than 1 per cent, from 21.7 percent in 1993 to 22.08 per cent in 2003. Stronger economies from ASEAN-6 countries such as Singapore and Malaysia represented a disproportionately

*Table 5.2* ASEAN-6 top ten import commodities by two-digit HS codes in 2004

| HS | Commodities | Value ( US$ millions ) | Share (%) |
|----|-------------|------------------------|-----------|
| 85 | Electrical machinery and equipment and parts thereof, sound recorders and reproducers, television image and sound recorders and reproducers, and parts and accessories of such articles | 140,991.1 | 30.9 |
| 84 | Nuclear reactors, boilers, machinery and mechanical appliances, and parts thereof | 73,372.3 | 16.1 |
| 27 | Mineral fuels, mineral oils and products of their distillation, bituminous substances, mineral waxes | 60,995.2 | 13.4 |
| 72 | Iron and steel | 15,765.0 | 3.5 |
| 87 | Vehicles others than railway or tramway rolling-stock, and parts and accessories thereof | 13,615.9 | 3.0 |
| 39 | Plastics and articles thereof | 12,756.3 | 2.8 |
| 90 | Optical, photographic, cinematographic, measuring, checking, precision, medical or surgical instruments and apparatus, and parts and accessories thereof | 12,454.5 | 2.7 |
| 29 | Organic chemicals | 12,258.0 | 2.7 |
| 71 | Natural or cultured pearls, precious or semi-precious stones, precious metals, metals clad with precious metal and articles thereof, imitation jewellery, coins | 6,905.0 | 1.5 |
| 73 | Articles of iron or steel | 6,769.0 | 1.5 |
|    | Ten major commodities | 355,882.3 | 78.1 |
|    | Others | 100,124.8 | 22.0 |
|    | Total | 456,007.1 | 100.0 |

Source: ASEAN (2005: 83, Table V14).

Note: HS refers to Harmonized System of Tariffs; any slight discrepancies in numbers are due to rounding.

large share most of total intra-regional trade. Yet, this situation might have been different today had it not been for the 1997 Asian financial crisis. Nonetheless, intra-regional trade is heavily concentrated on bilateral trade relations between Singapore–Malaysia and Singapore–Indonesia.

### Dispute settlement mechanisms

According to a study conducted by Nesadurai (2003), there has been a 'progressive institutionalisation of AFTA since 1992 as far as the nature of constitutional documents is concerned'. Nesadurai observes that with AFTA's

*Table 5.3* ASEAN-6 top ten major import and export markets in 2001–2004 (US$ thousands)

| Exports Country | 2001 Value | Share | 2002 Value | Share | 2003 Value | Share | 2004 Value | Share |
|---|---|---|---|---|---|---|---|---|
| ASEAN | 81,302.1 | 22.2 | 85,0774.4 | 22.4 | 97,157.1 | 22.9 | 117,090.1 | 22.6 |
| US | 61,594.4 | 16.8 | 60,317.4 | 15.9 | 60,146.6 | 14.2 | 73,960.5 | 14.2 |
| EU | 56,148.0 | 15.3 | 53,828.9 | 14.2 | 56,381.9 | 13.3 | 68,666.0 | 13.2 |
| Japan | 48,152.7 | 13.1 | 44,411.0 | 11.7 | 50,086.5 | 11.8 | 63,613.2 | 12.3 |
| Hong Kong | 20,061.8 | 5.5 | 21,861.4 | 5.8 | 28,583.7 | 6.7 | 29,668.9 | 5.7 |
| South Korea | 14,710.6 | 4.0 | 15,676.9 | 4.1 | 16,890.6 | 4.0 | 19,770.6 | 3.8 |
| China | 14,454.9 | 3.9 | 19,486.1 | 5.1 | 26,974.6 | 6.4 | 38,554.1 | 7.4 |
| Taiwan | 8,693.5 | 2.4 | 18,556.1 | 4.9 | 13,823.0 | 3.3 | 17,537.5 | 3.4 |
| Australia | 8,495.5 | 2.3 | 9,567.4 | 2.5 | 11,531.8 | 2.7 | 16,170.9 | 3.1 |
| India | 5,861.3 | 1.6 | 8,099.0 | 2.1 | 7,773.0 | 1.8 | 10,609.6 | 2.0 |
| Top ten countries | 319,474.8 | 87.1 | 336,881.5 | 88.8 | 369,348.8 | 87.0 | 455,641.4 | 87.8 |
| Others | 47,167.5 | 12.9 | 42,604.3 | 11.2 | 55,105.1 | 13.0 | 63,583.6 | 12.2 |
| Total | 366,642.3 | 100.0 | 379,485.9 | 100.0 | 424,453.9 | 100.0 | 519,255.0 | 100.0 |

Source: ASEAN (2005: 78–79, Table V.11).

| Imports Country | 2001 Value | Share | 2002 Value | Share | 2003 Value | Share | 2004 Value | Share |
|---|---|---|---|---|---|---|---|---|
| ASEAN | 64,423.0 | 20.6 | 70,534.8 | 21.7 | 73,216.0 | 20.6 | 100,172.0 | 22.0 |
| Japan | 52,861.4 | 16.9 | 52,789.5 | 16.3 | 57,788.9 | 16.3 | 72,192.2 | 15.8 |
| US | 45,565.8 | 14.6 | 49,814.8 | 14.0 | 49,814.8 | 14.0 | 54,526.3 | 12.0 |
| EU | 39,561.2 | 12.6 | 39,903.2 | 12.3 | 42,711.4 | 12.0 | 51,674.3 | 11.3 |
| China | 17,009.7 | 5.4 | 22,803.2 | 7.0 | 27,783.7 | 7.8 | 42,522.0 | 9.3 |
| South Korea | 13,057.1 | 4.2 | 14,586.8 | 4.5 | 14,857.2 | 4.2 | 20,530.2 | 4.5 |
| Australia | 9,481.0 | 3.0 | 7,215.1 | 2.2 | 7,555.2 | 2.1 | 9,116.4 | 2.0 |
| Hong Kong | 7,049.5 | 2.3 | 7,804.6 | 2.4 | 7,532.9 | 2.1 | 8,576.2 | 1.9 |
| Taiwan | 6,792.9 | 2.2 | 12,477.6 | 3.8 | 15,589.5 | 4.4 | 19,509.4 | 4.3 |
| India | 3,589.9 | 1.1 | N/A | N/A | N/A | N/A | N/A | N/A |
| Saudi Arabia | N/A | N/A | 6,252.1 | 1.9 | 7,095.1 | 2.0 | 9,757.4 | 2.1 |
| Top ten countries | 259,391.5 | 82.9 | 277,721.9 | 85.6 | 303,944.6 | 85.6 | 388,576.6 | 85.2 |
| Others | 53,423.8 | 17.1 | 46,607.9 | 14.4 | 51,195.8 | 14.4 | 67,430.6 | 14.8 |
| Total | 312,815.2 | 100.0 | 324,329.8 | 100.0 | 355,140.4 | 100.0 | 456,007.1 | 100.0 |

Source: ASEAN (2005: 78–79, Table V.12).

Note: The table above only shows the share of the top ten markets. India was not among the top ten import markets for ASEAN in 2002–2004, hence its figures are not reflected in the table. Saudi Arabia was not one of the top ten import markets of ASEAN in 2001, hence its figures are not reflected in the table; any slight discrepancies in numbers are due to rounding.

inception, progressive improvements were made on the initial general guidelines such as implementation details for the CEPT (Operational Procedures for CEPT, Rules of Origin for CEPT and Interpretative Notes to the Agreement on the CEPT Scheme for AFTA). After 1995 in particular, 'the constitutional documents pertaining to AFTA [also] became formal and binding on signatories'.

While the 1992 CEPT agreement did not include any dispute settlement mechanisms (DSM), with the exception of Article 8 stating that member states should try to amicably settle any disputes arising from implementation of AFTA through consultations, ASEAN member states adopted a protocol on DSM in November 1996. Five stages in the dispute settlement process were detailed for guiding governments in the event of a dispute: consultation, elevation of dispute to the senior economic officials meeting (SEOM), appeal of SEOM ruling to the ASEAN economic ministers (AEM), implementation of decision of the SEOM or AEM, and compensation or suspension of concessions.

There is also a DSM in place to address private sector complaints on non-tariff barrier (NTB) issues, which are to be channelled directly to member countries and to the ASEAN Secretariat. The complaints will undergo a process of clarification and verification by the member countries concerned, and if found to be valid, efforts will be made to remove them.

Thus far, ASEAN member countries have yet to invoke the DSM process, even as disputes have arisen in the course of implementing AFTA, in the areas of agriculture, automobiles and petrochemicals. Affected countries such as Thailand, Malaysia, Singapore and the Philippines have preferred to settle their disputes via diplomatic consultations and bargaining. Nesadurai's (2003) interviews with senior officials from Indonesia, Singapore, Thailand and Malaysia revealed that invoking the DSM could jeopardise political relationships in ASEAN.

With the inter-governmental mechanisms in place, AFTA's implementation could be pursued against an institutionalised backdrop, which helps to advance the AFTA process. While Nesadurai (2003) noted that 'these institutionalised mechanisms have served as the arena in which compromises resulting in a lower level of compliance were worked out . . . it is [nevertheless] unlikely that AFTA could have advanced as far as it has done without these compromises'. AFTA is generally recognised as an initial step in pushing ASEAN towards realising Vision 2020's goal of 'a concert of Southeast Asian Nations, outward-looking, living in peace, stability and prosperity, bonded together in partnership in dynamic development and in a community of caring societies'. The new AEC will build upon AFTA by increasing economic integration, bridging the divide between the ASEAN-6 and CMLV, and bringing greater economic benefits to the region as a whole.

*Potential impact of AFTA on regional peace and security*

ASEAN's political economy is characterised by entrenched interests and economic nationalism, especially during its early founding years. AFTA's structure attempts to neutralise these insular tendencies by allowing for exceptions without penalty. Also, CEPT is based on the lowest common denominator to harmonise effective tariffs, and is designed to diffuse tensions if the reductions progress too quickly.

AFTA is not restricted to tariff reductions. The CEPT Agreement for AFTA also provides for the immediate elimination of quantitative restrictions for products included in the CEPT Scheme. The scheme also eliminates other NTBs within a period of five years upon enjoyment of the CEPT concession, through efforts such as the harmonisation of product standards and mutual recognition of conformity assessment requirements, simplification of customs clearance procedures and harmonisation of sanitary and phytosanitary standards.

AFTA's non-binding and non-punitive nature arguably promotes the mitigation of potential conflict, while at the same time pushing towards lower tariffs to raise the level of intra-regional trade, thereby creating more interdependence and linkages as a way to cement better ties within ASEAN. With closer economic integration, the cost of conflict becomes higher. While there are many intervening variables, a case can be made for AFTA's impact – especially with its expansion in scope and function in ensuing years – on increased intra-regional trade and better economic coordination and regional ties.

## Towards an ASEAN Community

Since its inception in 1967, ASEAN is seen to be moving from an association into an institution-building community. Apart from promoting peace and security in Southeast Asia, ASEAN also seeks to strengthen its peace-building role in the wider Asia-Pacific region.

The Declaration of ASEAN Concord II, forged in October 2003, addresses new challenges that accompany both ASEAN's evolving place in the international context, as well as ASEAN's expansion to ten countries in Southeast Asia. Through this Declaration, ASEAN affirms its political will to forge a sustainable future for the region, based on political solidarity, economic cooperation and mutually derived benefits, as embodied by the adoption of 'Prosper Thy Neighbour' policies. These aims, which give a coherent structure and organisation to the ASEAN Vision 2020, are to be attained through the realisation of the proposed ASEAN Community – comprising the ASC, the AEC and the ASCC.

This section will attempt to address the following questions:

- What range of non-trade provisions such as the rule of law and respect for human rights are included in RTAs?

- How effective are these provisions at improving domestic governance and reducing the risk of future conflict?

### Expanding the role and functions of AFTA

The extension of AFTA membership to CMLV has diversified the ASEAN grouping in terms of political regimes and economic priorities. This has also made the decision-making process more time-consuming, which has in turn slowed down the progress of economic integration. Another obstacle for AFTA is the proliferation of bilateral FTAs, which could minimise its effectiveness as a PTA.

ASEAN's weakness in not having a mechanism for redistributing resources, and the lack of an independent regional authority to ensure compliance with the ASEAN agreement, limits its ability to move new members in lock-step with the agreement. It also makes them unable to reap the full benefits of regional integration which, potentially, could reduce their interest in ASEAN.

This is particularly true of Myanmar, which seems to be tilting towards a strategy of playing India and China against each other, instead of relying on ASEAN for its diplomatic support.

ASEAN therefore needs to move rapidly and boldly in creating competitive production clusters and greater regional domestic demand to increase growth within the region. The expansion of AFTA's role and functions also recognises the close link between economics and security, and the openness to non-trade provisions, such as the rule of law and respect for human rights and socio-cultural values.

### From AFTA to AEC: consolidating economic integration

ASEAN leaders finalised the details of the AEC at the tenth ASEAN summit in Vientiane in November 2004. The new AEC will build upon AFTA by increasing economic integration, bridging the divide between the ASEAN-6 countries and CMLV, and bringing greater economic benefits to the region as a whole.

The AEC vision, proposed during the Bali Concord II, envisages a free flow of goods, investment and services, and a freer flow of capital and labour by 2020. Unlike a common market, the AEC restricts the flow of labour to skilled labourers and business persons, and does not plan to impose a uniform tariff rate on non-members. For this reason, some proponents of the AEC have called it an 'AFTA-plus'. Others, who would like to see a fully economically integrated ASEAN, have suggested that ASEAN adopts a 'common market-minus' framework. This would act like an FTA-plus at the beginning, but would delay the deep integration measures needed for a common market until after 2020. It might be more agreeable to newer members, as it would grant them greater flexibility as they begin reforming their economies and integrating them into ASEAN.

The purpose of the AEC, as explained in the Bali Concord II, is to make ASEAN into a single market and production base that would be more economically competitive and attractive to investors. It would incorporate all the existing trade and investment agreements, fast-track the integration of priority sectors and make the AEC into a rules-bound body. While the Bali Concord II does not provide much detail, the declaration reveals that ASEAN would adopt the recommendations of the High Level Task Force on ASEAN Economic Integration; its report identifies 11 priority sectors slated for trade and investment liberalisation.

The Task Force's report provides a comprehensive strategy to accelerate economic integration, and also recommends several new features, including an independent panel to solve trade disputes. It names 11 sectors as priority sectors for integration, assigning responsibility for each to various ASEAN members: wood, automotives, rubber, textiles, agriculture, fisheries, electronics, e-ASEAN, healthcare, air transport and tourism. The integration clause would be advanced by moving quickly on these sectors. The report recommends the following steps:

- zero tariffs;
- the immediate elimination of trade barriers;
- faster and simplified customs;
- faster harmonisation of mutually recognised agreements;
- standards and regulations.

Services relating to these sectors should be liberalised by 2010. For tourism, the report recommends an intra-ASEAN travel visa by 2005, and urges members to draw up an agreement on skilled labour mobility by the same year. These steps should be combined with an outreach and promotional programme to establish pan-ASEAN companies, with divisions located according to the comparative advantages of countries. This includes outsourcing, more intra-ASEAN investing and an eventual 'ASEAN brand' for goods and services.

At the thirty-sixth ASEAN economic ministers meeting in September 2004, ministers endorsed the framework agreement for the integration of the 11 priority sectors and the roadmaps for integration of the priority sectors. Both were ratified at the tenth ASEAN summit in Vientiane in November 2004.

During the thirty-ninth ASEAN ministerial meeting on 24–25 July 2006, ASEAN officials revealed plans to craft a charter by 2007 (ASEAN's fortieth founding anniversary), to substantively complete the integration process by 2015, instead of 2020, albeit without a single currency system.[19] The rise of India and China prompted the move to accelerate the process. Singapore, Thailand and Brunei strongly supported the move, with the rest of the member states 'not averse' to the initiative, according to Singaporean Foreign Minister George Yeo.

### From AFTA to ASCC: social development

The ASCC, in consonance with the goal set by ASEAN Vision 2020, envisages a Southeast Asia bonded together in partnership as a community of caring societies and founded on a common regional identity. Members of the ASCC are committed to cooperation in social development, aimed at raising the standard of living of disadvantaged groups and the rural population, and to seek the active involvement of all sectors of society, in particular women, youth and local communities. Additionally, ASEAN member states are to ensure that their individual work forces are prepared for and benefit from economic integration, by investing more resources for basic and higher education, training, science and technology development, job creation and social protection. The area of public health, including the prevention and control of infectious and communicable diseases, will also see intensified cooperation. Human resource development takes precedence and represents a key strategy for employment generation, alleviating poverty and socio-economic disparities, and ensuring economic growth with equity.

### Addressing non-traditional security threats

In order to address development gaps and uneven resource allocation within ASEAN, there also exist alternative RTAs which take the shape of market-oriented sub-regionalism, also known as the Greater Mekong Sub-region (GMS). The difference between the GMS project and other formal economic regional integration is that the former is a sub-regional grouping that is more concerned about environmental security, infrastructural networking and sustainable development than trade or economic issues per se. This focus on infrastructure includes not only physical infrastructure (e.g. roads, rail and water transportation) but also complementary 'software' issues, such as improving procedures for customs clearance and enhancing skills for regulatory systems. Most notably, there has not been an official trade liberalisation programme under the GMS project (Than 2005: 94).

The GMS is currently focusing on constructing, upgrading and rehabilitating critical sections of road and the East–West, North–South and Southern economic corridors (see Table 5.4 for other projects). The East–West economic corridor is the most advanced and will link the India Ocean to the South China Sea via a 1,500-km road network. By 2007, this will allow all-weather travel between Da Nang port in Vietnam and the Mawlamyine port in Myanmar, via Laos and Thailand. By 2012, all three economic corridors should be established.

In November 2001, the six members agreed to a Ten-Year Strategic Framework that consists of 11 flagship programmes to physically and commercially link the GMS countries. The members have also agreed to focus on five strategic developmental thrusts:

- strengthen infrastructure linkages through a multi-sectoral approach;
- facilitate cross-border trade and investment;
- enhance private sector participation in development and improve its competitiveness;
- develop human resources and skill competencies; and
- protect the environment and promote sustainable use of the sub-region's shared natural resources.[20]

*Table 5.4* Other projects in the Mekong sub-region

| Projects | Year started | Members | Remarks |
| --- | --- | --- | --- |
| Mekong Committee or Committee for Coordination of Investigations of the Lower Mekong Basin – the Mekong Committee* or Mekong River Commission | 1957 | Cambodia, Laos, Thailand, Vietnam | Sponsored by the UN. In 1995, it was changed to an intergovernmental body and renamed the Mekong River Commission. |
| Golden Quadrangle Economic Cooperation (GQEC) | 1993 | Thailand, Laos, Myanmar, China | Loose forum |
| ASEAN-Mekong Basin Development Cooperation (ASEAN-MBDC) | 1995 | All ten ASEAN members | |
| Ayeyawady-Chao Phya-Mekong Economic Cooperation Strategy (ACM-ECS) | 1995 | Cambodia, Laos, Myanmar, Thailand | Started in 1995 but was effectively abandoned during the Asian crisis. Revived by Prime Minister Thaksin. Essentially this is a vehicle for Thailand to provide export credits and aid to its neighbours. First summit held in Bagan, Myanmar in 2003; second summit in Bangkok, Thailand in 2005; third summit is scheduled to be held in Vietnam in 2007. |
| Forum for Comprehensive Development in Indochina | 1993 | | Proposed by Japanese Prime Minister Kiichi Miyazawa. |
| Cambodia–Laos–Vietnam Development Triangle | 1999 | Cambodia, Laos, Vietnam | Proposed by Cambodian Prime Minister Hun Sen. |

Sources: Compiled from various sources.

Note: *http://www.mrcmekong.org/.

The success of the GMS project would enable both Myanmar and Laos to benefit much more quickly than from AFTA and ASEAN's external FTAs. This is because the improved infrastructure would make the transportation of goods more efficient, facilitating trade along the Mekong sub-region. Facilitating border movement will also help to reduce the costs of transaction and increase trade. In a study done by the Asian Development Bank, Menon (2005) found that the GMS would help its members be more 'effective members of ASEAN' and that the 'GMS program is assisting its members to integrate more closely with the ASEAN region and through this, with the rest of the world'.

## ASC: consolidating the institutional environment for conflict mitigation

The ASC builds on efforts made by ASEAN to prevent major inter-state conflict over the past four decades or so. The ASC's aim is to ensure that countries in the region live at peace with one another and with the world in a just, democratic and harmonious environment. ASC members are committed to relying exclusively on peaceful processes for the settlement of intra-regional differences, and regard their security as fundamentally linked to one another and bound by geographic location, common vision and objectives.

The ASC comprises the following components: political development; shaping and sharing of norms; conflict prevention; conflict resolution; post-conflict peace building; and implementing mechanisms. It will be built on the strong foundation of ASEAN processes, principles, agreements and structures, which evolved over the years and are contained in the following major political agreements:

- ASEAN Declaration, Bangkok, 8 August 1967;
- ZOPFAN Declaration, Kuala Lumpur, 27 November 1971;
- Declaration of ASEAN Concord I, Bali, 24 February 1976;
- Treaty of Amity and Cooperation in Southeast Asia, Bali, 24 February 1976;
- ASEAN Declaration on the South China Sea, Manila, 22 July 1992;
- Treaty on the Southeast Asia Nuclear Weapon-Free Zone, Bangkok, 15 December 1995;
- ASEAN Vision 2020, Kuala Lumpur, 15 December 1997; and
- Declaration of ASEAN Concord II, Bali, 7 October 2003.

The essence of the ASC in particular, is the principle of comprehensive security, in line with the strong interconnections among contemporary political, economic and social realities. It does not connote a defence pact, military alliance or joint foreign policy. The High Council of the TAC and the ASEAN-steered ARF are also singled out as important pillars of the ASC.

The procedures for the High Council were further clarified in 2001. However, members tend to ignore the High Council, preferring international arbitration over intra-regional intermediation.

ASEAN established the ARF in 1994. Its agenda will unfold in three stages, namely: the promotion of confidence building; development of preventive diplomacy; and the elaboration of approaches to conflicts for major regional security issues in the region, such as non-proliferation, counter-terrorism, transnational crime.

Critics have pointed out the ARF's slow progress in developing its confidence-building and preventive diplomacy agenda, overall institutional growth and problem-solving mechanisms to engage the US and other key members. China in particular, resisted the development of preventive diplomacy measures within the ARF, as compared to confidence-building measures. There is also the concern that ASEAN may dominate the ARF core, which prevents the resolution of more intractable security problems in Northeast Asia.[21]

The ARF has also posted achievements. At its tenth meeting on 18 June 2003, it provided a venue for multilateral and bilateral dialogue, and established effective principles of dialogue and cooperation amongst its 26 members. The meeting also included the networking and exchange of information relating to defence policy and the publication of defence white papers.[22] The ARF also recently attempted to play a role in addressing the North Korean missile crisis via an appeal to a return to the six-party talks but North Korea rejected the move.[23]

The ARF has recently developed some modest structures and capacities towards preventive diplomacy. It has also focused on non-traditional security threats such as terrorism, maritime security and disaster management. The forum has also taken institutional measures, such as strengthening the ARF chair, developing a Register of Eminent and Expert Persons and establishing an ARF unit within the ASEAN Secretariat.

The last ARF meeting on 28 July 2006 ended on a positive note with ASEAN seemingly regaining its previous prominence in regional affairs, especially with the renewed US focus on the region, to counter China's increasing influence. In a promising development, France agreed to be signatory to the TAC with the EU indicating interest as well.[24]

The Declaration of ASEAN Concord II reveals how ASEAN has matured since its inception. It has demonstrated a new-found receptiveness and assurance with regard to the establishment and implementation of rules, institutional mechanisms and planned strategic initiatives. Part of this confidence stems from the international endorsement given to ASEAN-driven mechanisms, such as the TAC and the ARF. ASEAN is also coming to terms with its capacity to shape its own future, with constructive initiatives taking precedence over response and reaction.

Other security measures include the Treaty of the Southeast Asia Nuclear Weapon-Free Zone and the ASEAN Troika. Established in December 1995, the Treaty of the Southeast Asia Nuclear Weapon-Free Zone plans progressive, concrete action by ASEAN towards general and complete disarmament, and upholds the international non-proliferation system. The treaty also promotes the use of nuclear energy for peaceful purposes – particularly economic development and social progress while conforming to International Atomic Energy Agency (IAEA) guidelines and standards. These measures underscore the emphasis placed on shared norms among ASEAN states, not merely common action. A number of mechanisms have been put in place to enforce the implementation of the treaty, including information exchange, clarification and fact-finding missions, as well as a system of controls and safeguards. Cooperation with international organisations is encouraged to facilitate the enforcement of the treaty. The treaty is to remain in force indefinitely, and any breach of it will give other states the right to withdraw.

All ten ASEAN countries have signed the Convention on the Prohibition of the Development, Production and Stockpiling of Bacteriological (Biological) and Toxic Weapons and their Destruction, as well as the Convention on Chemical Weapons.

On 25 August 2006, the Cambodian parliament launched the 'The Cambodia Parliamentary Caucus on Myanmar' in Phnom Penh, which represented an unprecedented move to condemn Myanmar's military junta for its lack of reform and flagrant rights abuses. Other initiatives include the draft charter circulated by the ASEAN Institute of Strategic and International Studies (ASEAN-ISIS) at the Track Two diplomacy level in April 2006, aimed at mitigating potential conflict within ASEAN. An ASEAN Court of Justice was mooted to address the emerging trend of agreements that involve legally binding rules, beyond political commitments. Its draft charter proposes to establish an ASEAN Peace and Reconciliation Council to play a stronger role in conflict prevention and resolution.

Such proposals have the potential to ameliorate inter and intra-state conflicts, upholding the principle of non-intervention embodied in the 'ASEAN Way', and building more confidence in the ASEAN mechanism. Issues that have regional implications, such as maritime security, terrorism, transboundary haze pollution and pandemic diseases can be better dealt with through more open consultation and communication between member states.

## Conclusion

ASEAN as a regional grouping has been successful in reducing and minimising regional conflicts, particularly inter-state conflicts among ASEAN members. This chapter has argued further that AFTA's non-binding and non-punitive nature arguably promotes the mitigation of potential conflict, while at the same time pushing towards lower tariffs to raise the level of intra-regional trade, thereby creating more interdependence and linkages as a way to cement better ties within ASEAN.

With closer economic integration, the cost of conflict becomes higher, as AFTA serves as a 'passive' indirect link between trade/investments and conflict/peace building, with non-pure tariff reductions under the CEPT scheme playing the role of enhancing security.

While there are many intervening variables, this chapter has put forward the case that AFTA – with its expansion in scope and function in ensuing years into an ASEAN Community vision – has increased intra-regional trade and better economic coordination and regional ties. AFTA's development into an ASEAN Community is indicative of the realisation amongst the ASEAN member states of the close nexus between economics and security, and openness to non-trade provisions such as the rule of law and respect for human rights and socio-cultural values as a necessary adjunct to the RTA's economic impetus.

The viability of RTAs to promote the region's economy and security is not in question. Yet, the relationship between RTAs and conflict in the future remains tied to the political will of the ASEAN member states to set up the requisite regional institutions and mechanisms to implement economics, security, social-cultural agreements towards fulfilling the vision of enhanced regionalism under the ASEAN Community framework.

## Notes

1  See Ruland (2005).
2  See Yeo *et al.* (2005).
3  See   http://www.icj-cij.org/icjwww/ipresscom/ipress2002/ipresscom200239_inma_20021217.htm (accessed 13 September 2006).
4  The agreement is available from http://www.aseansec.org/13163.htm (accessed 28 March 2006).
5  See 'South China Sea cooperation hailed: FM', *Xinhua*, 16 March 2005.
6  See 'Malaysia increases border security', *Bangkok Post*, 23 September 2006.
7  Annual reports available from Amnesty International website http://www.amnesty.org (accessed 11 June 2008).
8  See 'New violence in south Philippines', BBC News, 4 September 2006.
9  This one was 6.2 on the Richter scale.
10  Constituting 20 per cent of the world's total.
11  Brunei Darussalam joined on 8 January 1984, Vietnam on 28 July 1995, Lao People's Democratic Republic and Myanmar on 23 July 1997, and Cambodia on 30 April 1999.
12  However, the ensuing years of financial crisis and international terrorism renewed the need for external influence to achieve regional security.
13  The ASEAN Way emphasises the norm of non-interference in other states' affairs, prefers consensus and non-binding plans to treaties and legalistic rules, and relies on national institutions and actions, rather than creating a strong central bureaucracy.
14  Singapore was the exception.
15  They are: Australia, Bangladesh, Brunei Darussalam, Cambodia, Canada, China, EU, India, Indonesia, Japan, Democratic People's Republic of Korea, Republic of Korea, Laos, Malaysia, Myanmar, Mongolia, New Zealand, Pakistan, Papua New Guinea, Philippines, Russian Federation, Singapore, Thailand, Timor Leste, United States and Vietnam.

16 See http://www.aseansec.org/7660.htm (accessed 11 June 2008).
17 Lim and Walls (2005).
18 See Stubbs (2003).
19 See 'Officials discuss timeline to realize ASEAN Economic Community', Bernama, 16 August 2006.
20 See http://www.adb.org/GMS/Projects/default.asp (accessed 11 June 2008).
21 See Choi (2004).
22 See https://www.aseanregionalforum.org/Default.aspx?tabid=49 (accessed 10 September 2006).
23 See 'Asean forum to condemn N. Korea missile tests', *Chosun Ilbo*, 20 July 2006.
24 See 'EU likely to accede to ASEAN Treaty of Amity', *Business Times*, 29 July 2006.

## References

ASEAN (2005) ASEAN *Statistical Yearbook 2005*, Jakarta: ASEAN Secretariat.
Choi, S.-Y. (2004) 'Regionalism and open regionalism in the APEC region', *Trends in Southeast Asia Series, Institute of Southeast Asian Studies*, 12.
Economic Policy Department (2003) 'Assessing the support from regional domestic demand', *Macroeconomic Review*, II: 1, 60–70. Singapore: Monetary Authority of Singapore.
Lee, T.Y. (2003) 'The ASEAN free trade area: the search for a common prosperity', in S. Siddique and S. Kumar (eds) *The 2nd ASEAN Reader*, Singapore: Institute of Southeast Asian Studies, pp. 194–197.
Lim, H. and Wallace, M. (2005) 'ASEAN after AFTA: what's next?' *Dialogue + Cooperation*, occasional papers, Southeast Asia–Europe, 10, 91–103.
Menon J. (2005) 'Building blocks or stumbling blocks? Regional cooperation arrangements in Southeast Asia', *Asian Development Bank Institute Discussion Paper Number 41*, Tokyo: ADB Institute.
Nesadurai, H. (2003) 'Cooperation and institutional transformation in ASEAN: insights from the AFTA project', in S. Siddique and S. Kumar (eds) *The 2nd ASEAN Reader*, Singapore: Institute of Southeast Asian Studies, pp. 198–204.
Ruland, J. (2005) 'The nature of Southeast Asian security challenges', *Security Dialogue*, 36:4, 545–563.
Stubbs, R. (2003) 'AFTA and the politics of regional economic cooperation', in S. Siddique and S. Kumar (eds) *The 2nd ASEAN Reader*, Singapore: Institute of Southeast Asian Studies, pp. 205–210.
Than, M. (2005) 'Trade liberalisation in the GMS nations', in J. Dosch, C. Durkop and N.X. Thang (eds) *Economic and Non-traditional Security Cooperation in the Greater Mekong Sub region (GMS)*, Singapore: Konrad Adenauer Foundation.
Yeo, L.H., Zaur, I. and Ekeroth, M. (2005) 'Conflict map of Southeast Asia', *Dialogue + Cooperation*, occasional papers, Southeast Asia–Europe, 13, 5–17.

# 6 Managing conflict through trade

## The case of Pakistan and India

*Shaheen Rafi Khan, Faisal Haq Shaheen and Moeed Yusuf*

### Introduction

Histories of recurrent inter and intra-state tensions have constrained progress on regional trade agreements (RTAs) within South Asia. While India tends to see itself as an omnipresent Lord Buddha, with surrounding smaller states taking on the persona of clinging acolytes, this is not a shared vision. Relations between India and its neighbours have been historically volatile, epitomised in particular by India and Pakistan. In fact, bilateral differences between the two have spilled over and stalled the South Asian regional integration process. While both countries share common historical, ethnic, linguistic, cultural and religious roots, their potential to synergise constructive bilateral relations have been subverted by a number of 'push factors', most importantly the collapse of democracy in Pakistan, and growing sectarian and religious militancy in both countries. Inter and intra-state conflict have fuelled each other, stifling trade and economic relations and, in the extreme, evoking the spectre of a nuclear conflict.

The share of regional trade and foreign investment between both nations has historically hovered around 1 per cent of their total global trade. Open conflict and latent tensions between the two states have restricted trade volumes to levels that are low in relation to their gross national product (GNP), population, proximity and cultural ties. The high level of unofficial trade between the two countries further demonstrates this trade potential. Conflict induces economic protectionism. Pakistan maintains a narrowly defined positive list of products that may be legally imported from India. In turn, despite granting of most favoured nation (MFN) status to Pakistan, India maintains a ban on most imports. South Asian Free Trade Agreement (SAFTA) efforts towards tariff reductions, originally seen as promising, are being deflected by the emphasis on composite dialogue, which links trade concessions to resolving the impasse on Kashmir, along with lesser bilateral issues. Consequently, India has begun to build on a 'look East' policy, which entails an economic interface between eastern South Asian Association for Regional Cooperation (SAARC) nations, a surging China and Association of South East Asian Nations (ASEAN).

Since 1947, both nations have fought three wars and engaged in several localised skirmishes. Conflict has institutionalised an accelerating arms race and growing nuclear capability. Kashmir is the most prominent and enduring flashpoint between the two countries – the source of two wars and several skirmishes. Differences also linger over Siachen, Sir Creek and, more recently, the threat of freshwater retention by India has invited international arbitration. Politicians invoke cross-border issues to divert attention from domestic misgovernance. The concentration of wealth, urban–rural and inter-provincial disparities, deficient social services and infrastructure and the loss of livelihoods contribute to economic and social insecurity. Impoverished and disenfranchised groups and ethnic minorities find refuge in militancy, which feeds internal discord and cross-border provocations, to which the state is often privy.

The geo-strategic importance of the region sustains western involvement in Pakistan and India, and has produced an assortment of alliances with both religious zealots and modernists. Despite the pendulum swing, the military remains the common denominator attesting to the reactive nature of the engagement. Economic and military support to Afghanistan and Pakistan emanates from security concerns; it has been historically unsustainable and has come at great cost to Pakistan's political development. In contrast, western involvement in India is premised on political and economic synergies; even the defence relationship focuses as much on building India's military capabilities as on arms deliveries.

This chapter seeks to understand the trade conflict links in a bilateral context. It addresses the question whether economic interdependence between Pakistan and India is possible, and if such interdependence is likely to engender peaceful coexistence between the two. The second section outlines the history and causes of conflict between India and Pakistan. The third section compares existing levels of bilateral trade with the assessed potential and identifies the barriers that constrain this trade. The fourth section argues that these barriers have a political genesis and that, in fact, trade is being held hostage to conflict between the two countries. The fifth section is the concluding section.

## The politics of conflict

### *A chronology of conflict*

The adversarial relations between Pakistan and India have embroiled them in several crises and three full-scale conventional wars in the past. The first active conflict was initiated in Kashmir just a year after the two countries gained independence. In 1965, they clashed again, and in 1971 yet another conventional war led to the dismemberment of Pakistan and to the creation of the new state of Bangladesh.

Apart from overt conflict, there have been four major crises, which have brought India and Pakistan perilously close to war. The first of these crises occurred in 1987 when India conducted an aggressive military exercise on the Pakistani border. Three years later, in 1990, Pakistan responded with *Zarb-e-Momin*, another military exercise. Tensions escalated as India linked the exercise to surging violence in Kashmir. In 1999, Pakistan and India were involved in a limited conflict in the Kargil sector of Indian Kashmir, where Pakistan's Northern Light Infantry, infiltrating across the line of control (LOC), captured Indian posts. Subsequently, India retaliated militarily. In 2001–2002, the two sides were on the brink of war again as Indian mobilised its forces on the international border, provoking a Pakistani response and leading to a ten-month-long eyeball-to-eyeball confrontation.

Internal instability can lead to cross-border spillovers and exacerbate threats of conflict. Both India and Pakistan have suffered separatist movements in the brief span since they became independent states – Khalistan, Assam, Kashmir, Balochistan, Sindh and the North West Frontier Province (NWFP) tribal areas, to name but a few. Intelligence agencies in both countries have interfered across borders, seeking to exploit these movements to their own advantage (see Table 6.1). India's Research and Intelligence Wing (RAW) has supported insurrections in the former East Pakistan and, more recently, in Balochistan. Pakistan's Inter-Services Intelligence (ISI) has used the diffuse but more explosive force of religion to fight a proxy war in Kashmir. In general, sectarian and ethnic divides have become increasingly pronounced over time, generating a nexus of internal and external instability, and fuelling insecurity between two nuclear-armed states.

*Table 6.1* Chronology of India–Pakistan conflicts

| Open conflict | Crises | Cross-border subversion | |
|---|---|---|---|
| | | Pakistan | India |
| Kashmir (1948–1949) | Operation Brass Tacks (1987) | East Pakistan (1971) | Northeast insurgency (1950s) |
| Kashmir (1965) | Operation *Zarb-e-Momin* (1990) | Sindh violence (1990s) | Khalistan movement (1980s) |
| East Pakistan (1971) | Kargil (1999) | Balochistan insurgency (2004–present) | Kashmir insurgency (1989–present) |
| | Terrorist attack on Indian parliament (2001–2002) | | |

Source: SDPI in-house compilation.

### *Open conflict*

Pakistan and India have gone to war three times over the course of their 58-year history. The two triggers for these conflicts were the territorial dispute over Kashmir, which continues to fester, and the unrest in Pakistan's exploited eastern wing, which invited Indian intervention.

The first armed conflict between the two sides occurred over Kashmir. Following the partition of Pakistan from British India in 1947, the reigning Hindu Maharaja requested military assistance from the Indian government and as a pre-condition acceded the state to India.[1] In a reflex response, Muslim rebels supported by Pakistani infiltrators, captured Muzaffarabad, now the capital of the Pakistan-affiliated Azad Kashmir. The conflict ended with both sides agreeing to a United Nations (UN) brokered ceasefire on 1 January 1949, and to the establishment of an LOC to serve as the common border. Over time the LOC came to be recognised as the de facto border, which separates Pakistani and Indian Kashmir today.

Tensions remained high between the two sides despite a number of UN proposals to resolve the Kashmir issue. In September 1965, both countries went to war; Kashmir, again, was the *casus belli*. The '17-day War' ended in a stalemate and subsequently the Soviet Union effected a face-saving ceasefire. While India opened the war on the international border, the aggression was preceded by Pakistan's 'Operation Gibraltar' through which the mujahedeen launched a limited offensive in Indian Kashmir (Mohan *et al.* 2005).

Six years later the two countries were locked in conflict again. This was the most shameful event in Pakistan's history, marked by the atrocities the army committed in its eastern wing. An extended period of economic and political excesses culminated in open rebellion in 1970, when the West Pakistan establishment denied the Awami League office after its electoral victory (Sisson and Rose 1990). The Indian military, allied with Bengali insurgents, launched a full-scale attack on Dhaka. The offensive lasted 12 days. Dhaka fell on 16 December 1971, to the allied forces, which annihilated the Pakistani army in East Pakistan and established complete supremacy.

### *Crises*

Four crises, as opposed to open conflict, are of note. In 1986–1987, India conducted 'Operation Brass Tacks', and Pakistan counter-mobilised, both sides amassing a quarter of a million troops along the border. Opinions vary as to the motives. Some researchers are of the view that it was an attempt to discourage Pakistan's support to Sikh separatists (*Khalistanis*) in eastern Punjab. Others contend that the Indian mobilisation aimed at a war designed to split Pakistani territory (Cheema 2004; Chengappa 2000).

Tensions between the two countries mounted again in 1990, following an upsurge in violence in Indian Kashmir and subsequent Indian allegations of Pakistani support to the insurgents. Pakistan conducted Operation

*Zarb-e-Momin*, a large-scale military exercise to which India retaliated with its own 'precautionary' reinforcements (Chari 2003). Both armies were placed on high alert and the crisis seemed set to escalate into open conflict. Some reports indicated movement of nuclear arsenals during the crisis.

The third crisis, in effect a localised conflict, occurred in the spring of 1999, a year after both countries had conducted nuclear tests. A large contingent of Pakistani soldiers from the Northern Light Infantry crossed the LOC and captured Indian army posts in the Kargil–Drass area of Kashmir (Synnott 1990). Indian forces counter-attacked in an attempt to regain the posts and made slow headway. The conflict remained confined as the Indian forces were under strict orders not to retaliate across the LOC (Chari 2003). In July 1999, Pakistan withdrew its troops under US pressure.[2]

The latest crisis was spurred by a terrorist attack on the Indian parliament on 13 December 2001. New Delhi blamed the terrorist attack on two Pakistan-based militant outfits (Thies and Hellmuth 2004). On 14 May 2002, Islamic extremists struck again in Indian Kashmir, attacking a passenger bus and then an Indian army camp in Kaluchak, just outside Jammu in Indian Kashmir. The attack reignited tensions between the two countries. Shortly, thereafter, a million soldiers amassed on the international border, making it the largest mobilisation in the two countries' history (Chaudhury 2004). Tensions remained high for a while but then cooled off, and the troops demobilised in late 2002. Although war was averted, the standoff is considered the worst 'nuclear' crisis in South Asian history.

### Intra-state conflict

Internal tensions within both countries fuelled by sectarian and ethnic strife and growing religious militancy have created space for covert operations, which further inflame these tensions. They have also brought both countries to the brink of war several times, as indicated above. While the two mistrusting neighbours tend to see a 'foreign hand' in every episode, there are instances where such intervention has been clearly established.

### Indian intra-state conflict

Perhaps the most serious intrusion in what India considers an internal affair is the ongoing insurgency in Indian Kashmir. The insurgency is sourced in a local uprising by disgruntled Kashmiri Muslim youth.[3] India alleges active Pakistani involvement in training and arming the insurgents. Pakistan, on the other hand, denies the accusation, attributing it to indigenous unrest and focusing on human rights abuses by the Indian security forces (Suri 2003).[4] While such abuses are clearly in evidence, Pakistan has exploited the situation to its advantage.[5] The evidence is out that the ISI was training, funding and infiltrating freedom fighters (mujahedeen) into Indian Kashmir, as a low-cost option aimed at 'bleeding India to death' (Cohen 2003). Regardless, the insurgency has proved to be extremely costly for India to manage. More than 600,000 troops have been committed by New Delhi to quash the insurgency, which has led to a loss of over 60,000 lives since 1989.

India also alleges Pakistani ISI involvement in the Khalistan movement, a Sikh drive for independence in the East Punjab province during the 1980s (Kozicki 2002).[6] In fact, the alleged link tracks back to support for its precursor, the 'Sikh Home Rule Movement', being run out of London in the late 1960s, and later transformed into the Khalistan movement.

Finally, Pakistan has always been vocal about the plight of Indian Muslims victimised by communal violence. Perhaps the two most traumatic instances of communal violence were the demolition of the Babri Mosque, and the 2002 Gujarat massacre. In the numerous Babri-related riots that took place from 1986–1992, thousands of Muslim deaths were recorded (Allen 1992). The Gujarat massacre in 2002 was even more violent. Communal violence radiated from an attack by a Muslim mob on a passenger train in Godhra, Gujarat, in February 2002. The state-sponsored retaliation led to the death of over 2,000 people, the majority of whom were Muslims. The violence was allegedly authorised from the highest tiers of the government. During 2002, communal riots also took place in Harayana, Kerala, Rajasthan and a number of other states (Engineer 2003). Pakistan wasted no opportunity to point to the Gujarat incident as a proof of India's maltreatment of Indian Muslims. Both incidents have tarnished India's international image considerably.

*Pakistani intra-state conflict*

Pakistan too has had its share of intra-state strife and, reciprocally, has blamed India for inciting and fanning it. Indian involvement was central to the dismemberment of East Pakistan in 1971. As indicated, this was a direct outcome of extended political and economic excesses committed by West Pakistan. The Indian role in accelerating what, perhaps, was inevitable has left a permanent scar on Indo-Pak relations.

Pakistan also blamed India for supporting acts of sectarian and ethnic violence across the country in the 1990s, especially in the troubled city of Karachi. Islamabad alleged Indian support to Altaf Hussein, leader of the *Muhajir Qaumi Mahaz* (Mutahidda Qaumi Movement, MQM) who was aiming to destabilise Karachi in a bid to acquire greater powers for Urdu-speaking Muhajirs (Mazari 1999). The Indian role in Karachi's sectarian violence was even officially hinted at when Pakistan ordered the closing down of the Indian consulate in Karachi, although the act was portrayed as retaliation to the Babri Mosque incident in 1992. The Supreme Court of Pakistan recently handed the death sentence to an RAW agent for having engineered bombings in various Pakistan cities in 1990, a crime he confessed to have masterminded.

Pakistan also accuses India of supporting Baloch insurgents involved in anti-state violence. Recently, India was alleged to have trained as well as funded insurgents in the volatile and impoverished Pakistani province. While India continues to deny any involvement, India's increasing clout in Kabul and its access to Balochistan via Afghanistan has provided it with an opportunity to destabilise Balochistan, an option confidential Pakistani intelligence reports suggest it has opted to embrace.

## Drivers of conflict

### The democracy deficit

A paradigm presents itself, based on a chronological interpretation of events. The period from 1958 to 1971 exposed Pakistan to its first cycle of military rule. The pattern repeated itself three times, with martial law in the early stages, followed by a semblance of democratic governance, in an effort to impart legitimacy to army rule. It was during this first cycle that two major conflicts occurred, namely, the 1965 war with India over Kashmir and, following another war in 1971, the creation of independent Bangladesh. Subsequently, to date, no major wars have occurred although, as observed above, both countries have come close to the brink.

The clue to this may lie in the two alternating systems of governance, post-1971. Thus, the democratically elected governments of Zulfiqar Ali Bhutto (1971–1977) and of Benazir Bhutto and Nawaz Sharif (1988–1999) preceded two cycles of military rule, namely, 1977–1988, and 1999 to the present. One possible conjecture is that elected governments imparted stability in bilateral relations. In other words, negotiators were able to talk on the same wavelength; the formal and informal channels of dialogue and communication established were able to diffuse tensions before they reached the point of no return. It goes to the credit of these governments – and to various civil society initiatives – that, despite their subservience to the army and the intelligence agencies on strategic issues, they found enough wriggle room to improve political relations with India.[7] Subsequently, when they were dislodged, the communication modalities they established, and the residual goodwill they garnered continued to dampen bilateral hostilities.

Admittedly, there is a linear dimension to this hypothesis, which ignores the other influences affecting the ebb and flow of relations between the two countries. However, an assessment of their antecedents and impacts appears to support our thesis. Thus, pre-1971, the key source of internal strife was the tensions between the two wings of the country, which eventually led to Pakistan splitting up. With respect to external relations, the army central command opted for the western-dominated defence pacts, namely the Central Treaty Organisation (CENTO) and South East Asia Treaty Organisation (SEATO). In turn, external economic and military support extended the army's hold on power. The army overestimated its leverage with the United States to launch an incursion into 'occupied' Kashmir in 1965, agreeing to a negotiated peace in short order. Six years later, the growing tensions generated by army misrule instigated the Indian strike in East Pakistan. The point we make is that internal strife had its roots in army rule; the army directed the course of external relations and its subsequent miscalculations became a basis for cross-border adventurism.

The internal political situation, post-1971, was comparatively far more unstable – in fact, by many factors. Balochistan haemorrhaged steadily, reflecting dissatisfaction with central government policies; the 'Talibanisation' of northern Balochistan and the NWFP tribal areas is threatening to fan south; the tribal areas are also host to the Al Qaeda influx; inter-ethnic discord has intensified with the creation of the MQM and the Sindhi card; and sectarian strife (Shia–Sunni) has scaled new heights of violence across the country. Adding to this explosive mix, Pakistan and India detonated nuclear devices in 1998. Internal developments also fuelled cross-border incursions by both countries as mentioned above. In particular, the ISI linked up with *jihadi* groups to foment unrest in Indian Kashmir.

Yet, outright conflict was averted despite the repeated provocations. We can attribute this partly to the periods of democratic governance, which alternated with stints of army rule and hence, moderated its influence. Equally important, the volatile mix of political instability, nuclear-armed status and extremism invited forceful US restraint. Both countries remain under tremendous pressure to ensure détente. However, a worrisome aspect is that US intervention is becoming increasingly reactive, as opposed to the more proactive relations it is developing with India; the US strategic relationship with India is multi-pronged, while the relationship with Pakistan remains narrowly focused on the 'War on Terror'. Fissures may develop in Pak–US relations with a continuance of the status quo – as long as the army's stranglehold on power remains and it continues to maintain uneasy alliances with extremist elements.

The prognosis for sustained democratic rule (not the official version) is bleak. The military, with its outright predominance in the strategic enclave and heavy clout in the political sphere has stifled any voices that question the logic of a highly conservative strategic outlook. With the entire discourse set within the confines of the narrow-minded national security paradigm, and the virtual subservience of political governments (in addition to periods of direct military rule), the military has managed to implement its agenda unopposed. Perhaps the more damaging affect of such a lopsided balance of power has been on institution building within the country. In order to maintain its institutional supremacy the military has, over the years, severely undermined the civilian institutions of governance. While it argues that it is the only organised institution in the country that does not suffer from capacity constraints, this clouds the fact that it has suborned civilian political institutions, stifled their growth and kept them from evolving into robust functional units.

India has not lagged in leveraging the 'democracy deficit', using it as a convenient excuse for lack of progress on the peace front. Whenever New

Delhi raises this concern, the international community is quick to support its contention, pointing fingers towards Pakistan for not having allowed democracy to flourish. In essence, the 'democracy deficit' in Pakistan has exacerbated the state of the other conflict drivers. It is within this paradigm that the various drivers of conflict need to be assessed. Several leading Pakistani analysts hold little hope for the future of Indo-Pakistan relations.

> There are enormous stakes for vested interests on both sides to maintain bilateral tensions; these are people who depend on the tense atmosphere for their livelihoods.
>
> (Zafar Nawaz Jaspal, Professor of International Relations, Quaid-I-Azam University)

> Securing and protecting economic, political and other benefits by sustaining the 'enemy images' seem to play well in the two countries because of illiteracy, ignorance, poverty and religious intolerance.
>
> (Moonis Ahmar, Professor of International Relations, Karachi University)

> Normalization in terms of absence of conflict suits the military's interests but beyond mere normalization the military's institutional interests and institutional memory impedes rapprochement. This implies that friendly ties between Pakistan and India are likely to remain an elusive goal.
>
> (Ayesha Siddiqa Agha, Defense Analyst)

*Bilateral disputes*

Outstanding bilateral issues between Pakistan and India are arguably the most important factors behind conflicts, crises, as well as the overall high level of tensions between the two sides. Kashmir is undoubtedly the most serious issue and more than just an international dispute. For Pakistan, Kashmir has become a central pillar of national pride, national aspiration and national identity. It is considered the litmus test of Pakistani nationalism and even patriotism. It is thus political suicidal for any politician in Pakistan to be seen to waffle on or be seen as weak on the Kashmir question (Yusuf and Najam 2005). For India, the rhetoric of Kashmir being an '*atoot ang*' (inseparable part) of India has been promulgated by all Indian governments.[8] The highly intractable positions of both sides on the issue have not allowed any substantial movement towards reconciliation. The issue has been the major cause of at least two conflicts and three crises.

While idealism, whether of the secular or religious sort has its *locus standi*, not atypically, it mingles with murkier motives. Thus Kashmir is integral to India's perception of itself as a global superpower (Siddiqa Agha 2004). In Pakistan's case, Kashmir represents a large part of the army's *raison d'être*, justifying its size, its large defence appropriations, its political excesses and its compromises with obscurantist elements. Without such motives, it becomes difficult to reconcile the passion felt over Kashmir with the atrocities committed against fellow Muslims in former East Pakistan. These motives also make it possible to understand the mindless nature of the Siachen dispute – a fracas over a large chunk of ice with little strategic value but at great cost to human lives. Similarly, the dispute over Sir Creek in the Rann of Kutch seems facile. Hence, while the two countries differ over which of the three imaginary lines in the 60-mile-long estuary defines the international boundary, all of which are difficult to patrol, the reality is that the boundaries themselves are not as much the issue as the need to affirm either side's stature relative to its adversary.

Conversely, attributing the Indian threat to a construction of the Pakistani establishment is also erroneous. India continues to exercise a policy of economic dominance and interference in the internal affairs of other South Asian countries (Khan and Haider 2004). Moreover, much of India's defence policies remain Pakistan specific. A large chunk of India's military formations, certain political doctrines and its recent war doctrines maintain an outright focus on Pakistan.[9] Hindu nationalist parties and activist factions use the anti-Pakistan rhetoric for political gains much as the army does in Pakistan.

The cumulative environment of mistrust diminishes the leverage to be gained from historical and cultural affinities and natural trade ties. It also imparts unpredictability to the peace initiatives. As Zaidi (2004) puts it:

> Discussing India–Pakistan relations is like walking on shifting sand: one moment you are sure of your position, ready to make proclamations to change the world, and the next the whole landscape has changed, become unrecognizable, presenting a completely different scenario. . . . The nature of India–Pakistan relations has become extremely variable and fluctuating, often touching extremes at both ends, with great euphoria of the prospects of peace followed within weeks by war.

*The religious divide*

A treasured belief is that Pakistan emerged as a separate homeland for the Muslims of India who believed they would be targeted in a Hindu majority in India – the much cited 'two-nation theory'. The Pakistani state is quick to exploit this religious divide. It continues to portray India as the 'evil empire' – aiming to undermine the interests of the 'Muslim' Pakistan (Nizamani 2000).[10] Often enough, hardcore inter-state problems are immersed in such religious discourse, one which religious factions are quick to pick up and perpetuate.

The story is not much different in India. India has seen a tremendous increase in Hindu militancy over the past two decades. Although the government cannot afford to cast inter-state tensions in religious terms given its substantial Muslim population, it has not hesitated to do so through party politics and rhetoric. The Hindu Nationalist Bharatiya Janata Party (BJP) and other activist factions such as the Rashtriya Swayamsevak Sangh (RSS) and the Vishva Hindu Parishad (VHP) have openly appealed to domestic constituencies. Often internal problems, especially those communal in nature, have been blamed on Pakistan, thus automatically tying these with the ideological discourse (Siddiqa Agha 2004).

In essence, while the divergent ideological perceptions are a reality and may impact relations at some level, it is the political compulsions that have led leaders on both sides to play up this divide. No Pakistan–India conflict or crisis has ever been initiated on ideological grounds. The issues that spur conflict have always been relevant to realpolitik, although ideology features regularly in raising political temperatures during periods of high tension. Stakeholders in both countries are quick to grasp such opportunities. Communal tensions in Kashmir have given an impetus to the military–*jihadi* nexus in Kashmir and have brought the two countries to the brink of war on several occasions. The sectarian and ethnic strife in Pakistan has provided similar opportunities to India, as evident in its support to Balochi insurgents and Sindhi separatists in the 1990s. Analysts have been quick to see through the ploy:

> I don't think ideology matters in Indo-Pak relations any more. It is purely parochial interests held by the ruling establishments of the two sides to maintain some sort of insecurity, tension and hostility in their relations in order to secure their vested interests.
>
> (Moonis Ahmar, Professor of International Relations,
> Karachi University)

> Under the current circumstances ideology is a barrier. Both countries have systematically and deliberately redefined their national ideology, with India pushing for the secular agenda and Pakistan considering itself an Islamic state under siege.
>
> (Ayesha Siddiqa Agha, Defense Analyst)

*External actors*

External actors have played a dual role in conflict. In hindsight, it is difficult to tell whether the ill effects outweighed the good. Throughout the Cold War years, Pakistan and India opted for opposite camps, with Pakistan electing to become a western ally and India – while keeping an official non-aligned stance – tilting towards the Soviet bloc.[11] The Cold War rivals contributed significantly to the military build up of their South Asian allies. Pakistan received considerable military support from the US over the years. As Sino–Indian tensions continued, Pakistan sought to establish a close relationship with China as well. Much of Pakistan's military capability has been built up on US and Chinese assistance. The Soviet Union assisted India, which was adamant on finding a counter to the US–Pakistan and Pakistan–China relationship. While India claims its military arsenal is indigenous, much of it is based on Soviet military hardware and technology.

Externally assisted military build ups have both deterred and promoted conflicts. As weapons capable states, India and Pakistan have gone to war on three separate occasions and both the US and Russia have interceded to effect a ceasefire. As nuclear capable states, the US stepped in on two occasions before war broke out, first in 1999 and then again in 2002. An indictment of US policy is that it has stalled democratic evolution in Pakistan by support-ing military governments to further its own strategic interests – even when they knowingly aligned with or condoned extremism – thus perpetuating a state of tension between two heavily armed states. Another negative by-product was the spill over effect of the millions of dollars worth of arms that poured into Pakistan during the Afghan *Jihad* (Burki and Baxter 1991). Elements supporting Pakistani policy as well as insurgents aiming to destabilise the Pakistani state subsequently used much of the weaponry (Yusuf 2003).

*Economic drivers*

Pakistan and India remain poor countries with unenviable human develop-ment indicators. Persisting with a macroeconomic model that has maintained an outright focus on growth rates has excluded the poor from the benefits of development. In the past seven years of the Musharraf regime, Pakistan's gross domestic product (GDP) growth rates have been impressive. Yet poverty and income inequality has increased in tandem, leaving many of the underprivileged disgruntled and creating a climate of social unrest (see Table 6.2). Further, the increasing disparity in terms of development and economic

*Table 6.2* Gini coefficient and consumption shares by quintiles in Pakistan

|  | 2000–2001 | | | 2004–2005 | | |
| --- | --- | --- | --- | --- | --- | --- |
|  | *Urban* | *Rural* | *Pakistan* | *Urban* | *Rural* | *Pakistan* |
| Gini coefficient | 0.3227 | 0.2367 | 0.2752 | 0.3388 | 0.2519 | 0.2976 |
| *Consumption share by quintile* | | | | | | |
| Quintile 1 | 5.3 | 12.8 | 10.1 | 4.8 | 12.6 | 9.5 |
| Quintile 2 | 8.1 | 16.9 | 13.7 | 7.6 | 17.1 | 13.2 |
| Quintile 3 | 12.1 | 19.5 | 16.8 | 11.6 | 19.7 | 16.4 |
| Quintile 4 | 19.4 | 22.4 | 21.3 | 18.3 | 23.0 | 21.4 |
| Quintile 5 | 55.1 | 28.4 | 38.0 | 57.7 | 27.6 | 39.4 |
| *Ratio of highest to lowest* | 10.40 | 2.22 | 3.76 | 12.02 | 2.19 | 4.15 |

Source: Pakistan Economic Survey 2005–2006

growth between Punjab and the three 'lesser' provinces is exacerbating the fault lines between those already disillusioned by the 'Punjabi military'.

Rising inequality has been exploited by radical madrassahs to further their agendas. Findings of an ISI survey undertaken in the mid-1990s suggest that as many as 70–80 per cent of madrassah students come from the impoverished rural areas (Bokhari 2003). Finding little or no opportunities for social and economic advancement, they embrace martyrdom. As mentioned, extremist elements have contributed to both cross-border subversion and crises. The 2001–2002 crisis was triggered by the attack on the Indian parliament, an episode India blamed on Pakistani militant outfits. In India, extreme poverty levels have also led to growing militarism. However, there is a caveat here; the centrality of economics to extremism and militarism is not clearly established. There is enough evidence to the contrary that economic deprivation does not necessarily lead to violent recourse.

The above discussion highlights the various factors that drive conflict between the two countries. While each of these remains important in its own right, the military presence is overarching. An ever-widening civil–military divide has also meant that the national security paradigm continues to be defined by the military. Apart from the impact on other 'drivers' of conflict, one major negative spin-off of the fixation with security has been lack of any real impetus to open economic ties between the two sides. Interestingly, while India seems interested in moving along the economic front, its economic posturing has been no less restrictive than Pakistan's. This is despite that fact that existing estimates suggest the presence of significant trade potential between the two countries. We examine this aspect in the next section.

## The rationale for trade

Improved economic and political relations in a globally interdependent market place can further peace-building efforts between countries. The assumption is that synergies from economic cooperation clearly exist and can be leveraged to the benefit of domestic enterprises, reducing more costly dependence on countries outside the region. This section attempts to estimate the static and dynamic potential for trade.

### Current state of bilateral trade

Since the mid-1990s, Pakistan's exports to India have remained between 0.4 per cent and 2.5 per cent of its total exports while, in India's case, the proportion is less than 0.5 per cent. This does not say much for trade between the two countries – barring last year's increase, total annual trade over the past seven years has never exceeded US$250 million. This is less than 1 per cent of the combined value of total trade of the two countries averaged over the past four years. Moreover, the balance of trade has remained consistently in India's favour (see Table 6.3).

*Table 6.3* Pakistan trade with India (US$ millions)

| Year | Exports | Imports | Trade balance | Percentage of total exports for Pakistan | Percentage of total exports for India |
|------|---------|---------|---------------|------------------------------------------|---------------------------------------|
| 1996–1997 | 36.23 | 204.70 | (168.47) | 0.43 | 0.61 |
| 1997–1998 | 90.57 | 154.53 | (63.98) | 1.04 | 0.44 |
| 1998–1999 | 173.66 | 145.85 | 28.81 | 2.39 | 0.43 |
| 1999–2000 | 53.84 | 127.38 | (73.74) | 0.62 | 0.34 |
| 2000–2001 | 55.41 | 238.33 | (182.92) | 0.60 | 0.53 |
| 2001–2002 | 49.37 | 186.80 | (137.44) | 0.54 | 0.42 |
| 2002–2003 | 70.66 | 166.57 | (95.91) | 0.63 | 0.31 |
| 2004–2005 | 288.13 | 491.66 | (205.53) | 1.99 | 2.71 |
| 2005–2006 | 293.31 | 634.91 | (341.60) | 1.77 | 2.49 |

Source: Export Promotion Bureau, Pakistan; Federal Bureau of Statistics, Pakistan; Karachi Chamber of Commerce and Industry, Pakistan; Directorate General of Foreign Trade, India.

The major items of export from Pakistan include petroleum products, yarn, organic chemicals and cotton. Major imports from India include organic chemicals, rubber (and articles thereof), animal fodder, waste from food industries, plastics, iron and steel, among others.[12]

### *Trade switching – the static potential for trade*

The static potential for trade between India and Pakistan is quite considerable, reflecting production complementarities and geographical proximity. Concrete evidence of this appeared immediately after 1947, when political relations between the two countries were benign and, resultantly, trade flows were significant. In the period 1948–1949, exports to India accounted for 56 per cent of Pakistan's total exports while 32 per cent of its imports also came from India (Nabi and Nasim 2001). However, in 1949, with the intent of protecting import levels, Pakistan refused to devalue its currency as a reciprocal gesture to India's devaluation, causing trade between the two countries to plummet sharply. Trade volumes remained low and trade ties were suspended completely in 1971. Although economic relations were resumed, subsequently, they continue to remain severely depressed.

One could argue that, prior to 1949, the situation can be viewed as a variant of trade diversion, in that inter-regional trade channels had not opened up, and the two countries were compelled to trade with each other. Therefore, the present situation could, conceivably, be viewed as a more normal and competitive one. However, the counter to this argument is that informal trade, which is quite substantial, is the real index of the static trade potential that currently exists between the two countries in the presence of existing trade barriers.

A recent study by Khan *et al.* (2007) estimates the value of informal trade between India and Pakistan at over US$0.5 billion. Informal trade is defined as illicit and quasi-legal trade. While illicit trade is outright smuggling, quasi-legal trade shows in official trade statistics as trade between Pakistan and a country other than India – even though it is actually sourced in India. The source, destination and value of informal trade for the two countries are shown in Tables 6.4, 6.5 and 6.6.

Two aspects are of note: (1) informal trade is tilted greatly in India's favour, replicating formal trade between the two countries; and (2) informal trade exceeds formal trade by over US$150 million. The combined value of trade is close to US$1 billion. Clearly, trade-related barriers (tariffs and transactions costs) have restricted formal trade and have forced a significant volume of trade to switch to informal channels.

The process is driven by traditional connections with ethnicity playing a major role. Particular tribes dominate the trade in each major location. Consequently, communication and access to information is virtually uninterrupted. The financial arrangement is driven by trust, without any formal guarantees and yet default in payments has never been recorded. Moreover, informal trade sustains communities. It becomes the only viable recourse, a source of enormous profit for the favoured few, and meagre livelihoods for a multitude of dependent carriers and transporters working under brutally harsh conditions.

In the static sense, if tariff barriers were to be removed completely, there would be an immediate and significant re-routing from informal to formal trade. In a comparative static sense, additional trade would be induced over and above the amount switched. However, induced trade also depends on a number of other enabling factors, which give it a dynamic aspect. The next sub-section provides an overview of the barriers that constrain trade and of the enabling factors that can give trade an additional boost if instituted in tandem with trade liberalisation measures.

### Trade barriers between Pakistan and India

Eliminating quota and tariff restrictions and trade facilitation are an integral part of the World Trade Organization's (WTO) global mandate. Notwithstanding, trade barriers between India and Pakistan take the form of both formal and informal barriers.

Formal trade barriers are comprised of:

- tariff barriers;
- non-tariff barriers. These consist of:

    – quota restrictions;
    – trade bans, such as the denial of MFN status.

Table 6.4 Source, destination and value of informal imports (US$ thousands)

| Items | Dubai–Bandar Abbas–Bara | Dubai–Bandar Abbas–Chaman | Dubai–Karachi (informal) | Dubai–Karachi (third country) | Sindh cross-border | Delhi–Lahore | Singapore–Karachi | Total value by item |
|---|---|---|---|---|---|---|---|---|
| Cloth | 128,000 | 1,066 | 45,350 | 2,500 | 7,800 | 1,280 | | 185,996 |
| Livestock | | | | | 33,340 | | | 33,340 |
| Medicines | 1,600 | 18,250 | | | 10,400 | 500 | 2,000 | 32,750 |
| Pharmaceutical and textile machinery | | | | 75,000 | | | | 75,000 |
| Electroplating chemicals | | | | 15,000 | | | | 15,000 |
| Cosmetics and jewellery | 20,000 | | 40,280 | | 2,600 | 960 | | 63,840 |
| Herbs and spices | 6,250 | | | | 1,300 | 800 | | 8,350 |
| Ispaghol (husk) | | 1,350 | | | | | | 1,350 |
| Big elachi | | 8,500 | | | | | | 8,500 |
| Black hareer | | 3,825 | | | | | | 3,825 |
| Betel | | | | | | 2,880 | | 2,880 |
| Blankets | | | 5,000 | | | | | 5,000 |
| Rickshaw/motorbike parts | | | | 5,000 | | 250 | | 5,250 |
| Tyres | 1,000 | 72,282 | | | | | | 73,282 |
| Paan ghutka, Paan parag | | 3,306 | | | | | | 3,306 |
| Indian razor blades | | 2,225 | | | | | | 2,225 |
| Biri (cigarettes) | | 8,572 | | | | | | 8,572 |
| Others | | | 5,070 | | | 480 | 500 | 6,050 |
| Total value | 156,850 | 119,376 | 95,700 | 97,500 | 55,440 | 7,150 | 2,500 | |
| Sigma total | | | | | | | | 534,516 |

Source: SDPI survey, January–May, 2005.

*Table 6.5* Source, destination and value of informal exports (US$ thousands)

| Items | Dubai–Karachi (third country) | Sindh cross-border | Delhi–Lahore | Total by item |
|---|---|---|---|---|
| Cloth | 6,800 | 1,775 | 520 | 9,095 |
| Cigarettes | | | 100 | 100 |
| Dry fruit | | 375 | 52 | 427 |
| Video games, CDs | | | 100 | 100 |
| Footwear | | | 52 | 52 |
| Prayer mats | | | 52 | 52 |
| Bed sheets | | | 135 | 135 |
| Other items | | 375 | 30 | 405 |
| Total value | 6,800 | 2,525 | 1,041 | |
| Sigma total | | | | 10,366 |

Source: SDPI Survey, January–May, 2005.

Note: 'Other items' include surma, hardware used in drills (TIPS/VITS), Rexene and cigarettes. Edible oil and wheat were once considered 'hot ticket' export items. However, the price differentials for edible oil suggest that this should be entering Pakistan rather than the other way around. Also, India has become self-sufficient in wheat. Furthermore, there are large outflows via the African transit trade to Afghanistan under various aid/relief programmes.

*Table 6.6* Combined trade, 2005 (US$ millions)

| Total formal trade | Total informal trade | Combined trade |
|---|---|---|
| 384,6567 | 544,882 | 929,54 |

Source: Khan *et al.* (2007).

Note: The formal trade figure is an average for nine years, as there is no discernible trend over time.

Informal barriers are defined as transaction costs and they fall into three categories namely:

- procedural costs;
- transport costs;
- rent seeking – a euphemism for bribes.

*Formal barriers*

In terms of their global trade, both India and Pakistan have abolished quota restrictions and reduced tariff rates steadily in conformance with their obligations under the WTO mandate. Bilaterally, tariffs in India remain much higher, on average, than in Pakistan. Similarly, Pakistan has not given India reciprocal MFN status.[13] It maintains a positive list of over 800 importable items from India. One would expect this one-sided arrangement to lead to a positive trade balance for Pakistan. The reality is that relatively higher tariffs in India and an array of hidden barriers leave little wriggle room for Pakistani exports to India. By and large, moves to facilitate trade by India have remained cosmetic. The perception is that, despite the MFN status, official tariff rates and transaction costs (especially hidden costs) remain higher in India.[14] Such perceptions are supported by multilateral studies – according to an International Monetary Fund (IMF) study, India's trade restrictiveness measures eight (on a scale from one to ten), while Pakistan's index stands at six (IMF 2005).[15]

Social, environmental and quality standards are other forms of non-tariff barriers. These will not be considered in our study as their impact relates mostly to inter- rather than intra-regional trade (see Khan and Haider 2004).

### Informal barriers

In the same way that formal barriers have restricted trade, informal barriers in the shape of high transactions costs have forced much of the trade, even in commodities that are legally tradable, to flow through informal channels. These informal barriers, in effect, become a key factor in determining whether informal trade is likely to flow through formal/legal channels. In other words, if the formal sector's transaction costs of importing exceed those in the informal sector, and this difference is greater than the tariff rate, then informal trade is unlikely to revert to formal trade channels.

In the broadest sense, transaction costs have three aspects: (1) procedural costs; (2) transport related costs; and (3) rent seeking. Examples of transaction costs include: port clearance times for cargo; extent of cargo movement required in the port; sanitary standards; bribes; documentation requirements for trade transactions (as well as the average amount of time spent in fulfilling these requirements); procedural delays (such as absence of staff, administrative inefficiencies, excessive department clearances and signatures); limited vehicle access; inefficient rail links and transport through third ports. The cost of trading is increased significantly by the existence of transaction costs, not only financially but also in terms of added time spent in completing trade transactions (Khan *et al.* 2007).

### Enabling factors

Trade flows are induced not just by removing trade-related barriers. For example, certain institutional pre-conditions at the regional level need to be met; communication and transport links established and policy and regulatory frameworks for supporting investments need to be created before trade between two countries can reach its full potential. Whether the push factors are strong enough gets into a debate of the linkage between trade and the broader notion of peace, a subject we will address in the next section. Here, we simply discuss the various factors that could potentially push trade.

Perhaps the most important pre-condition is that of the RTAs, which provide an overarching framework for a broad spectrum of trade enabling activities. We have dwelt upon the SAARC, SAFTA and SAPTA at some length elsewhere in this book (see Chapter 4).

Logistics are another key trade driver. Currently, there are very few examples by both sides that indicate efforts to develop these arrangements. However, one welcome development in the shipping sector is the recent agreement to sign a revised shipping protocol. This agreement will permit India's use of Karachi's Port Qasim to facilitate transit trade to Afghanistan, as well as Pakistan's access to Indian ports. The key benefit of utilising nearby ports is the substantial mutual reductions in freight bills. Currently, Pakistan's freight bill stands at US$1.3 billion a year and India's is at least four times as high (Ansar and Vohra 2003). Similarly, despite having inherited an integrated rail network from the British colonial era, neither side has maintained active communication channels. There has been some progress on opening previously abandoned rail routes, although road connectivity between the two nations still does not exist (Burki 2004).

Business people on both sides suffer from a dearth of information and restrictions in their mobility and interaction. They find it difficult to obtain timely, reliable and inexpensive information on trade-related matters, such as product specifications, technologies, prices, exportable surpluses, manufacturers and distributors of goods, domestic production and consumption patterns, market structures, industrial trends, changes to tariffs and non-tariff barriers, trade regulations, list of banned items and various other technical requirements. Stringent travel restrictions between India and Pakistan have prevented the development of business contacts and have hindered the exchange of information among the business communities in the region (Jain 1999). Khan *et al.* (2007) found that business people often meet in a mutually agreeable third country location, most frequently Dubai, to finalise deals. The only existing institutions for trade are the near perfect market-based instruments used to conduct informal trade. Deals are financed through '*hundi*' or '*hawala*', basically a chit system based on trust and relationships involving no cash transfers, uninterrupted communication flows and boasting a very low incidence of disputes and defaults (Khan *et al.* 2007).

A welcome sign has been the willingness by the two sides to discuss the potential for joint ventures and investment projects across borders. Many experts have begun to argue that it is joint investment projects that actually hold the key to Pakistan–India trade growth, as trade by itself would not be able to provide the necessary integration in the way that manageable, long-term investment projects could. The India–Pakistan–Iran (IPI) gas pipeline project is one example of such potential interdependence:

> The attraction of mutual trading between the two sides is linked to low freight costs that translate into cheaper prices, given the contiguous borders between these two countries. The other conducive conditions

are cultural affinity, common language, similar economic and social systems that provide an ideal foundation for broader India–Pakistan trade ties.

(Benazir Bhutto, Former Prime Minister of Pakistan)

Joint projects, whether joint investment ventures on mega-projects are key to enhancing trade ties and interdependence. The IPI gas pipeline could become a major driver of such interdependence between the two sides.

(Akbar Zaidi, Economic Consultant)

### *Inducing trade: the dynamic trade potential*

In this sub-section we try and quantify the trade potential between the two countries, assuming some give in the variables that restrict trade. We use two approaches as the figures are conjectural, and for such purposes a range of estimates is more useful than a single point estimate. In the first approach, we denote Pakistan's and India's trade with the rest of the world (ROW) as the outer limit for intra-country trade. The second approach draws on Baroncelli's (2005) use of a gravity model – essentially an econometric approach to estimating the potential for trade between the two countries.

### *A global comparison approach*

This first approach is simple and compiles both Pakistan and India's global trade with the ROW in identical commodities traded between the two countries. It must be noted, however, that these are outer limits as they considerably overstate the trade absorption potential in both countries.

The potential outer limits for both countries' exports are calculated by taking the maximum traded volumes for each commodity. For instance, if the commodity exported by Pakistan to the ROW is less than the value imported by India from the ROW, the latter value represents Pakistan's export potential to India in that commodity. If it exceeds it, the former value represents the outer limit for export. The potential outer limits for Indian exports to Pakistan are calculated similarly. Tables 6.7 and 6.8 present both estimates by commodities.

The combined potential outer limit of trade is valued at almost US$12 billion. Not surprisingly, the balance of potential trade continues to remain in India's favour (by a factor of almost three).

### *An econometric approach*

Baroncelli uses a gravity model to generate hypothetical estimates of trade flows. These estimates are based on certain macro variables, such as GDP, population and geographic distance as well as cultural variables. The technique introduces three variables attributing the gap between real and hypothetical trade to them. The impact of two of these variables is positive,

*Table 6.7* Export potential from Pakistan

| Items | Current trade | Total Pakistani exports to ROW | Total Indian imports from ROW | Total exportable value from Pakistan |
|---|---|---|---|---|
| 1 | 2 | 3 | 4 | 5 |
| *Formal trade* | | | | |
| Petroleum products | 96.87 | 825.65 | 20,500 | 825.65 |
| Yarn | 80.53 | 1,382.87 | 438.09 | 438.09 |
| Organic chemicals | 36.48 | 432.83 | 5,144.21 | 432.83 |
| Cotton | 28.12 | 2,108.48 | 438.09 | 438.09 |
| Edible fruits, nuts | 27.88 | 229.41 | 787.09 | 229.41 |
| Leather and articles thereof | 20.22 | 945.63 | 332.73 | 332.73 |
| Synthetic textiles | 13.83 | 200.30 | 127.33 | 127.33 |
| Edible vegetables and roots | 11.78 | 42.79 | 637.64 | 42.79 |
| Fish and fish preparations | 0.43 | 194.15 | 24.20 | 24.20 |
| Informal trade | | | | |
| Footwear | 0.07 | 142.22 | 92.61 | 92.61 |
| Bed linen, sheets | 1.67 | 2,038.06 | 107.06 | 107.06 |
| Total | 317.88 | 8,542.39 | 28,629.05 | 3,090.79 |

Sources: Federal Bureau of Statistics, Pakistan; Directorate General of Foreign Trade, India; Export Promotion Bureau, Pakistan; State Bank of Pakistan.

namely: (1) granting of MFN status to India by Pakistan and mutual tariff relaxations and; (2) the institution of RTAs (using a dummy). The third variable, conflict (again introduced via a dummy) captures the trade reducing impact. Baroncelli tests her model on a larger aggregate panel dataset, covering the period from post-Second World War up to 2003. The model also shows in real time an inverse correlation between trade and conflict, demonstrating that conflict does stifle trade.

Based on annual data for the period 1987–2003, the hypothetical trade flows for the year 2002 are estimated to be US$2.62 billion. This number is composed of US$1.24 billion in exports from India to Pakistan and US$1.38 billion in exports from Pakistan to India. Counter intuitively, the hypothetical trade balance is in Pakistan's favour. Thus, the estimates for overall trade generated by the two approaches range from US$2.62 billion to almost US$12 billion. Despite the wide range, the trade potential is considerable.

Baroncelli selects a few product groups and demonstrates trade gains in these groups consequent upon tariff reductions. She does a similar exercise for institutional arrangements (RTAs) over a longer time span and demonstrates that the hypothetical benefits are completely offset by hypothetical losses thanks to conflict. We introduce this in more detail in the next section as a quantitative lead-in to the discussion that follows.

*Table 6.8* Export potential from India (US$ millions)

| Items | Current volume | Total Indian exports to ROW | Total Pakistani imports from ROW | Total importable value to Pakistan |
|---|---|---|---|---|
| 1 | 2 | 3 | 4 | 5 |
| *Formal trade* | | | | |
| Organic chemicals | 205.66 | 4,857.09 | 1,224.97 | 1,224.97 |
| Rubber and articles thereof | 115.89 | 1,034.96 | 219.00 | 219.00 |
| Animal fodder, waste from food industries | 54.01 | 1,122.88 | 49.65 | 49.65 |
| Plastics and articles | 44.89 | 2,160.51 | 1,792.90 | 1,792.90 |
| Iron and steel | 32.63 | 3,813.47 | 320.06 | 320.06 |
| Sugars | 30.48 | 168.53 | 87.87 | 87.87 |
| Edible vegetables, roots | 30.47 | 567.87 | 142.57 | 142.57 |
| Tanning and dyeing extracts | 20.55 | 846.94 | 187.05 | 187.05 |
| Ores, slag, ash | 19.90 | 4,452.61 | 50.46 | 50.46 |
| Oil seeds, fruits, grains, medicinal plants | 13.63 | 421.35 | 1091.14 | 421.35 |
| Tea, coffee mate, spices | 12.01 | 905.11 | 222.55 | 222.55 |
| *Informal trade* | | | | |
| Light engineering, machinery | 75.00 | 2000.55 | 2601.00 | 2000.55 |
| Cosmetics and jewellery | 63.84 | 764.93 | 123.98 | 123.98 |
| Buffaloes | 33.34 | 6.00 | – | 6.00 |
| Pharmaceuticals | 32.75 | 2444.18 | 292.15 | 292.15 |
| Chemicals (apart from organic) | 15.00 | 1079.06 | 1365.80 | 1079.06 |
| Auto parts | 5.25 | 252.92 | N/A | 252.92 |
| Blankets | 5.00 | 87.56 | N/A | 87.56 |
| Value-added textiles, silk | – | 11,399.75 | 320.79 | 320.79 |
| Total: | 810.3 | 38,386.27 | 10,091.94 | 8,881.44 |

Sources: Federal Bureau of Statistics, Pakistan; Directorate General of Foreign Trade, India; Export Promotion Bureau, Pakistan; State Bank of Pakistan.

## Trade and conflict linkages

### *The peace dividend: estimating the trade potential*

Considerable potential for trade between Pakistan and India does exist, as demonstrated in the previous section. Similarly, the scope for cross-border investment in manufacturing, energy, information technology and other ventures is considerable. Further, infrastructure links (transport and communication) have increased over time to catalyse economic and trade activities. There is also potentially a vast market for each other's products; one tangible manifestation being a large and growing middle class in both growing countries. Finally, the enabling institutional frameworks, in the shape of regional trade and economic agreements are in place, and both countries have entered into bilateral trade agreements with other countries in the region.

While all the indicators underscore the scope for meaningful economic and trade integration, the reality is very different. Trade between the two countries is infinitesimal, thanks to tariff and non-tariff barriers. Unlike other bilateral economic initiatives within the region (see Chapter 4), cross-border investment ventures between the two countries virtually do not exist. Similarly, while transport and communication links have improved, they suffer frequent disruption. This brings us to our central thesis, derived from the first section of the chapter, namely, that conflict deters trade specifically, and economic integration in a broader sense. Baroncelli (2005) estimates this peace dividend in the two graphs presented (Figure 6.1).

The dividend, presented in nominal and real terms, is denoted by the conflict variable in the econometric analysis. It reduces the divergence between potential and real trade, with the points of convergence coinciding with periods of conflict. In fact, as mentioned, the dividend almost exactly offsets the trade creating impact of RTAs. As we indicated, Baroncelli's estimate is derived from a lower base of potential trade of US$2.62 billion. The upper base, encompassing a more dynamic scenario, is in the region of US$12 billion, implying an even higher peace dividend.

### Why has this dividend stalled?

Sustained conflict between the two countries has transformed Pakistan into a war economy and stalled its democratic evolution. India's defence expenditures have escalated to higher than normal levels. The benign links between internal growth and expanding trade have given way to a malign nexus, where defence appropriations and arms procurement feed off each other through the budgetary decisions and funding allocations. The consequence is social sector neglect.

Indian social sector indicators are not much better than the ones presented for Pakistan. Such neglect fuels internal discord, which obscurantist elements prey upon. In turn, this feeds xenophobia and encourages cross-border adventurism. The global superpower agenda, originally anti-communist, but driven now by the terrorist threat has, ironically, nurtured military governments in Pakistan that remain locked in conflict with India. Recently, these governments have been prone to develop murky relations with terrorist elements, and strategic alliances with global powers are increasingly underpinned by mercenary considerations.

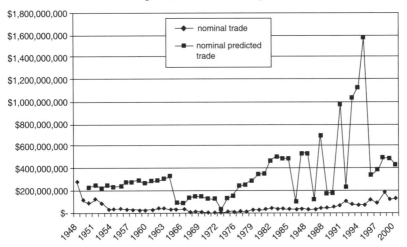

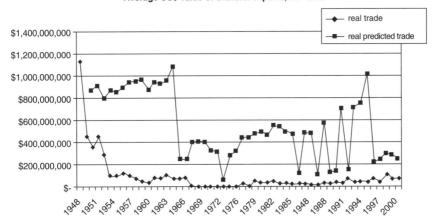

*Figure 6.1* The peace dividend.

Source: Baroncelli (2005).

Conflict entrenched relations have hampered the sanction of transit rights and pipeline projects; more fundamentally, they have arrested economic diversification and given way to large investments in military hardware. The costs of the Siachen Glacier conflict (Table 6.9) and annual defence expenditures (Table 6.10) illustrate the strain that military investment and costs place on both nations in economic and social terms. Figures 6.2 and 6.3 present some comparative numbers.

*Table 6.9* Costing conflict: Siachen

|  |  | *Criteria* |  |  |
| --- | --- | --- | --- | --- |
| *India* | 8,733 | *Total casualties from four wars* | 13,896 | *Pakistan* |
|  | $1.8 billion | *2002 Siachen conflict* | $1.2 billion |  |
|  | 0.38 percent of GDP | *Mobilisation cost* | 1.79 percent of GDP |  |
|  |  | *Costs of continuation* |  |  |
|  | 100,000 people | *Internal displacement* | 50,000 people |  |
|  | $1.6 billion | *Localised costs of Siachen* | $0.3 billion |  |
|  | 900 lives | *Conflict over five years* | 450 lives |  |
|  | 40 million Rs. per day | *Cost of Siachen conflict* | 10 million Rs. per day |  |
|  | 14.6 billion Rs. per year |  | 3.7 billion Rs. per year |  |
|  | 73 billion Rs. | *2003–2007 economic costs* | 18 billion Rs. |  |
|  | 0.07 | *Annual % of GDP* | 0.09 |  |

Sources: Table compiled from Sahni (2001); Rao (1999).

*Table 6.10* Pakistan and India defence expenditures

| *Year* | *India ($ millions)* | *Pakistan ($ millions)* |
| --- | --- | --- |
| 1988 | 7,941 | 2,500 |
| 1989 | 8,161 | 2,499 |
| 1990 | 8,051 | 2,636 |
| 1991 | 7,532 | 2,823 |
| 1992 | 7,209 | 2,997 |
| 1993 | 8,137 | 2,993 |
| 1994 | 8,109 | 2,917 |
| 1995 | 8,340 | 2,965 |
| 1996 | 8,565 | 2,961 |
| 1997 | 9,307 | 2,837 |
| 1998 | 9,387 | 2,833 |
| 1999 | 10,482 | 2,858 |
| 2000 | 10,900 | 2,867 |
| 2001 | 11,397 | 3,071 |
| 2002 | 11,426 | 3,304 |
| 2003 | 12,394 | 3,350 |

Source: Compiled from various SIPRI Year Books.

The high military expenditures are the financial counterpart to the confrontations between the two countries, and are the minimum considered by both countries to keep them in a state of war readiness. The magnitude of these expenditures, both for a single event and sustained over time, underscore the fragility of trade initiatives by subsuming them.

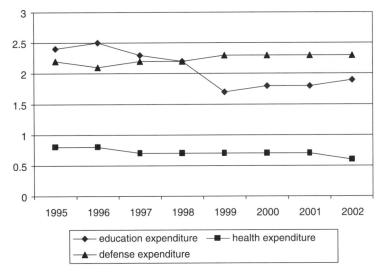

*Figure 6.2* Pakistan's defence, education and health expenditures.

Source: Compiled from various budget documents from Pakistan and India

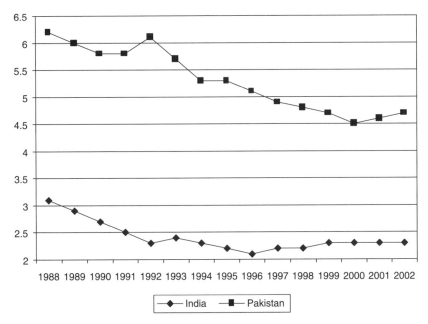

*Figure 6.3* Defence expenditures as a percentage of GDP (Pakistan and India).

Source: Compiled from various budget documents from Pakistan and India

Zaidi (2004) points out that: 'The constraints to better regional cooperation and free trade are more political than economic, and there are no real economic arguments for not trading with each other.' He claims less convincingly: 'Moreover the gains that can accrue to both countries are disproportionately tilted in Pakistan's favor.'

## Trade hostage to conflict

We demonstrate this relationship chronologically, highlighting the large number of trade/economic agreements and investments/communications protocols that the two countries have signed. However, as noted, such agreements and protocols have not made much headway in terms of increased trade and investment flows and transit rights. While political rapprochement has paved the way for such agreements and protocols, recurring political tensions have undermined their implementation; as a result, both countries have 'returned to square one'.

### AGREEMENT FOR THE AVOIDANCE OF DOUBLE TAXATION OF INCOME BETWEEN THE GOVERNMENT OF THE DOMINION OF INDIA AND PAKISTAN (DECEMBER 1947)

Pakistan and India were major trading partners at the time of independence in 1947. A conciliatory spirit prompted the agreement to avoid double taxation. However, just months after independence, the two countries found themselves embroiled in conflict over Kashmir. Political tensions stalled trade when, in 1949, Pakistan's refusal to devalue reciprocally led to trade ties being curtailed.

### INDO-PAKISTAN TRADE AGREEMENT (JANUARY 1957)

The 1957 trade agreement was the first, following a decade of silence between the two countries. A thaw in relations made the agreement possible. However, the agreement was limited in scope and only valid for a period of three years, reflecting a cautious 'wait-and-see' approach on both sides. Failing any major breakthroughs on Kashmir, the 1957 agreement was extended but only for another three years. Following yet another three-year extension, Pakistan and India went to war in 1965. The result was a virtual stalling of trade ties and the de facto expiry of the agreement.

### AGREEMENT ON BILATERAL RELATIONS BETWEEN INDIA AND PAKISTAN SIGNED AT SIMLA (JULY 1972)

Relations between Pakistan and India reached their nadir after the 1971 Indo-Pak war and the dismemberment of East Pakistan. All trade relations, that is the little that continued in the wake of the 1965 war, ceased. Left with little choice but to accept the final outcome as permanent, Pakistan and India signed the 1972 Simla Agreement. The agreement was holistic in nature; while it stressed the need to reinitiate trade ties a number of political qualifiers were attached as well. However, as political relations remained cold, the two neighbours did not make much headway in terms of trade. Following the Simla Agreement, Pakistan and India signed an accord on Kashmir in 1975.

PROTOCOL ON THE RESUMPTION OF TRADE BETWEEN INDIA AND PAKISTAN (NOVEMBER 1974); PROTOCOL ON THE RESUMPTION OF SHIPPING SERVICES BETWEEN INDIA AND PAKISTAN (JANUARY 1975); TRADE AGREEMENT WITH PAKISTAN (JANUARY 1975)

Pakistan and India officially signed a new trade protocol in 1974, and a shipping protocol and a fresh trade agreement a year later. Both sides agreed to reinitiate trade ties, and by virtue of these protocols were able to generate increased trade flows. Existing political tensions were pushed to the back-burner. Surprisingly, the increase in economic activity was not affected by a 1977 military coup in Pakistan.

CREATION OF THE SAARC (1985)

The potential loss of staying out of a South Asian regional forum led to both countries agreeing to be included in SAARC, which was created in 1985. However, the two sides found themselves in the midst of a crisis in 1987, which led to relations cooling again. Towards the end of the military rule in 1987, and especially with the return of democracy to Pakistan in 1988, the two countries began to negotiate again on linked political and economic concessions.

AGREEMENT BETWEEN INDIA AND PAKISTAN FOR THE AVOIDANCE OF DOUBLE TAXATION OF INCOME DERIVED FROM INTERNATIONAL AIR TRANSPORT (DECEMBER 1988)

The agreement celebrated the return of democracy to Pakistan in 1988 and was the result of rapprochement efforts by Prime Ministers Benazir Bhutto and Rajiv Gandhi.

THE LAHORE DECLARATION (FEBRUARY 1999)

During the 1990s, when Indo-Pak relations remained tense, not a single trade agreement was signed. Although elected governments were in power throughout the 1990s, frequent military interventions behind the scenes and persistent political turmoil did not allow progress on the trade/economic front. The Lahore Declaration signed in 1999 was largely the result of efforts to resolve political differences and suggested that cooperation in all spheres would be achieved. For the first time in a decade, the region was euphoric about the possibility of open relations. However, the effort was stymied before it could generate momentum by the 1999 crisis in Indian Kashmir and the resultant mini-war between Pakistan and India. Another crisis followed two years later when the military staged yet another *coup d'état*.

THE COMPOSITE DIALOGUE

Indian Prime Minister Atal Behari Vajpayee's 'Hand of Friendship' speech in April 2003 led to the initiation of a fresh peace bid.[16] Trade ties formed an important pillar of the resulting dialogue. The dialogue has for the first time taken a parallel approach to discussing all issues of mutual interest. Pakistan has finally agreed to move away from its 'Kashmir first' stance and discuss issues such as commercial ties concurrently. This has come to be defined in official jargon as 'composite dialogue'. As part of the dialogue, Pakistan and India now regularly exchange commissions and hold meetings on various aspects of trade and trade facilitation. Some of the important exchanges are listed below:

- A meeting of foreign ministers of both countries at the ASEAN Regional Forum (ARF) where Pakistan is formally accepted as a member of the ARF after India drops its objections (June–July 2004).
- A meeting of commerce secretaries in Islamabad to discuss economic and commercial cooperation (August 2004).
- Pakistan accepts 25 tons of food, medicine, tents, blankets, plastic sheets from India after the earthquake (October–November 2005).
- Pakistan–India resume train services after 40 years (February 2006).
- An agreement to revive trade in Kashmir (May 2006). This represented an attempt to redress the ravages of the recent earthquake. Subsequent to this agreement the two sides agreed to trade food and raw materials between divided regions of Jammu and Kashmir. No manufactured (value added) items, which would signal confidence in trade building efforts, have been allowed thus far.
- Both countries agreed to sign a Revised Shipping Protocol (October 2006). The accord, when signed, will be the first revision of the original protocol signed in 1975.

However, while encouraging in intent, the progression of events clearly suggests that the dialogue has reverted to more historical patterns, as detailed in Box 6.1.

---

**Box 6.1  The composite dialogue: old wine in new bottles?**

The composite dialogue represents a breakthrough in that it has allowed both sides to interact more freely than was possible previously. As mentioned, regular commissions are being exchanged. Moreover, such developments are not restricted to trade. However, the optimism that the dialogue has generated has tended to obscure a key structural deficiency in the dialogue framework; in other words, parallel movement on political and trade issues without removing the linkages between the two. While Pakistan has agreed to experiment with a parallel approach, it has been categorical in maintaining that the progress on Kashmir must be linked with progress in other spheres for the process to continue. India on the other hand, is more interested in using the parallel approach to move forward on 'non-contentious' issues while leaving the contentious ones on the backburner. The linkage represents a 'spanner in the works', as it is virtually impossible to move simultaneously in the political and non-political spheres.

Such an approach is likely to yield dividends in the initial stages, when both sides are willing – albeit cautiously – to push the envelope. Indeed, bilateral trade volumes have increased substantially. However, the more important structural impediments and institutional barriers to trade have not been addressed at all. In that sense, the gains have deliberately been kept narrow. Moreover, there is little movement on the political front, as was to be expected given the virtually irreconcilable positions on Kashmir (despite some flexibility shown by Pakistan). Increasingly then, one is beginning to witness tensions resurface and experts have observed that the process might be dying a natural death. Certainly, if progress is not made on political issues, which in all likelihood seems to be the case, progress on trade might also be reversed. This reaffirms our point that unless political differences are resolved, it is unrealistic to expect permanent and meaningful trade ties between India and Pakistan.

---

SAFTA SIGNED (JANUARY 2004)

A positive spin-off of the composite dialogue was that SAFTA was finally signed in January 2004. The agreement, which had been agreed in principal a decade ago and was supposed to be implemented by 2001, continued to be delayed in the wake of Indo-Pak tensions. The thaw in relations finally gave the opportunity to the regional members to ink the deal. The timing of the SAFTA accord, in relation to the state of Indo-Pak relations, also underscores the geo-political weight the two countries carry in the region.

However, progress on SAFTA remains limited. Pakistan continues to refuse MFN status to India and the concessions it has allowed are in the South Asian Preferential Trade Agreement (SAPTA) mode, namely enhancing the positive list, which contravenes SAFTA's free trade spirit. A combination of factors inhibit substantive economic and trade breakthroughs. First, militant voices within Pakistan's government, fearing the Kashmir issue would be skirted should trade volumes and reliance upon India increase, have lobbied the government to refuse to grant India MFN status. Second, a strong sense of nationalism coloured by religious discourse has created an inward-looking mindset vis-à-vis India. Both sentiments drive national policy on trade. Third, the Pakistani business community rightly points out that invisible barriers have diluted the MFN concession and that, in fact, India is no less protectionist. Fourth, there is evidence to support the concern that Indian products would flood local markets and destroy local industry or, conversely, their supply cannot be assured. Thus, Pakistan was heavily dependent on Indian coal and iron steel in the mid-1960s, until the 1965 war disrupted shipments. Similarly, cotton exports to India (constituting 30 per cent of Pakistan's global export) risked disruption following the hijacking of an Indian Airlines passenger jet in 1999. Shortly thereafter, India banned Pakistani cotton, finding it contaminated. However, as indicated, trade complementarities do exist, as does informal trade between the two countries. This suggests that a thaw on the political front could dampen concerns about market domination and supply unpredictability. The political complexity associated with each trade agreement has forced both India and Pakistan to turn to markets and suppliers elsewhere. As mentioned, India is increasingly favouring a 'look East' trade policy and is pursuing regional energy projects with Nepal, Sri Lanka and Bangladesh.

The discussion presents a clear trend in the linkage between political and trade-related events between the two sides. Without exception, each trade agreement between Pakistan and India can be traced back to positive movements on the political front. In fact, the scope of trade agreements in part has been a gauge of the temperature of the political climate prevailing at the time. This was clear from the narrow scope and periodic short-term extensions of the 1957 trade agreement. By the same token, the Indo-Pak history shows that political tensions emanating at a time when a trade arrangement was in place invariably ended up stalling trade and commercial exchanges. Such a cyclical relationship has continued unabated. While the composite dialogue attempts to break the cycle by pursuing a parallel approach, it is unlikely to deliver lasting results, unless progress on political tensions is substantial and precedes complete liberalisation of trade.

## Conclusion: is there hope for the future?

Both India and Pakistan confront political challenges in moving forward. In recent years, experts have pointed to a realisation among Indian policy makers that concessions on Kashmir are a confidence building measure, which will legitimise its global power status and appease its Muslim electorate. Similarly, Pakistan's recent moves towards rapprochement – albeit under a military regime – are indicative of a need for respite, after years of conflict and deterioration in its own security environment, thanks to growing militancy. There is also a perception that the Pakistan economy may plummet irreversibly, if defence allocations are not curbed. Further, the rattled nerves of international players during the 1998 nuclear tests and the confrontation of 2001–2002 have provided a spur to international mediation.

In the aftermath of September 11, a potential for bilateral collaboration has emerged in the global fight against terrorism. Both India and Pakistan need to reorient their external policies to address this threat. The large amounts of economic and military aid being invested in countries that are key to the new security order are likely to energise mutual collaboration. Almost certainly the United States will continue to engage India and Pakistan in the foreseeable future with a view to developing peaceful relations between them.[17] Although hedged in with the usual caveats about a history of prolonged conflict and turmoil, it is in the mutual interest of both countries to look beyond Kashmir. The bilateral issues need to be faced squarely. As the last election in Kashmir has shown, the populace has emphatically opted for democratic rule, which, to an extent, has delegitimised the conflict between the Indian and the Pakistani governments.

If India and Pakistan were able to agree on a resolution to the conflict, tensions in the South Asian region would decrease significantly, and the resulting political and economic rewards for both countries would be considerable. Aside from the obvious reduction in military tensions, a resolution of the India–Pakistan rivalry would translate into decreases in military spending, increased trade and economic benefits and increased spending on infrastructure, social and educational programmes. Furthermore, it could allow for increased trade, investment, energy cooperation, tourism benefits and a likely increase in the standard of living in both countries.

Finally, SAARC must be reactivated. SAARC's most important collective role must lie in resisting the 'Columbus' model of export-led growth being advocated by multilateral institutions, such as the IMF, the World Bank and the WTO. Enamoured with the theory of comparative advantage, these international institutions are encouraging trade in natural products and keeping developing countries from engaging in the trade of value added products.[18] A holistic, cooperative trading relationship between India and Pakistan that benefits all socio-economic segments of their societies will be a cornerstone to anchoring such a vision of SAARC. In that sense, it is probably more useful to draw lessons from the European Commission or North American Free Trade Agreement, regional arrangements that have grown 'organically' out of the changed context.

## Notes

1 Pakistan argued that the Maharaja's decision to accede to India was against the spirit of independence according to which geographically contiguous Muslim majority areas should have acceded to Pakistan. For a detailed discussion of the rebellion and its role in the Maharaja's decision to accede, see Victoria Schofield (2003: 41–60).

2 Pakistani Prime Minister Nawaz Sharif flew to Washington to secure an agreement with US President Bill Clinton. Troop withdrawal took place shortly afterwards. See 'U.S.-Pakistan deal calls for withdrawal of Kashmir fighters', CNN, 5 July 1999, http://www.cnn.com/WORLD/asiapcf/9907/05/kashmir.01/ (accessed 16 March 2007).

3 Although India officially contends that the insurgency was spurred by Pakistan to begin with, neutral observers and even Indian experts confess that the reasons for the insurgency were domestic. George Fernandez, former Indian minister for Kashmir, has aptly summarised the major causes: (1) excessive corruption; (2) failure of the government to address economic problems; and (3) an engineered election process. See Fernandez (1992: 288).

4 Both sides have maintained this stance throughout the insurgency. India has raised the issue of cross-border support for the insurgency countless number of times in international fora.

5 Amnesty International has also regularly documented human rights abuses in Indian Kashmir. See for example, Amnesty International Report on India, 2001, www.amnesty.org (accessed 16 March 2007).

6 Also see Bhatt (2002).

7 The 'Two Track Diplomacy Initiative', and the 'Indo-Pak Forum for Peace and Democracy'.

8 In recent times, the BJP has rallied the cry of Kashmir as *'atoot ang'*. India's unequivocal right over the entire Jammu and Kashmir is even stated in the party's official manifesto.

9 India latest war doctrine, 'Cold Start' is highly Pakistan specific. Moreover, much of India's western active missile deployment is also directed towards Pakistan.

10 This argument was most often used to defend Pakistan's nuclear programme pre-overt nuclearisation.

11 Pakistan signed a defence pact with the US in 1954. The Indo-Soviet 'Treaty of Peace, Friendship and Cooperation' was concluded in 1971.

12 Source: Directorate General of Foreign Trade (2006), India, http://dgft.delhi. nic.in (accessed 16 March 2007); Export Promotion Bureau, Pakistan (2006).

13 India granted MFN status to Pakistan in 1995.

14 A detailed analysis of these hidden costs is in Pakistan–India CEO's Business Forum (2005), www.statpak.gov.pk/depts/index.html (accessed 16 March 2007).

15 The non-tariff barriers generally quoted by exporters in Pakistan include requirement of political/security clearance, sampling/customs inspection, requirement of technical/standard certification, labeling and marking rules and packaging specifications. In addition, India maintains tariff rate quotas in the agricultural sector and the efficiency of customs operations also act as a de facto barrier to trade.

16 The speech delivered from the capital of the state of Jammu and Kashmir was well received in Pakistan as a genuine effort by India to come to terms with its nuclear-armed neighbour.

17 See Lloyd and Nankivell (2002).

18 See Mukherjee-Reed (1997: 235–251).

# References

Allen, D. (1992) *Religion and Political Conflict in South Asia: India, Pakistan and Sri Lanka*, Westport, CT: Greenwood Press.

Ansara, H. and Vohra, R. (2003) 'Confidence building measures at sea: opportunities for India and Pakistan', Cooperative Monitoring Center occasional paper, 33, Albuquerque, NM: SANDIA.

Baroncelli, E. (2005) 'Pakistan–India trade study: economic gains and the "peace dividend" from SAFTA', Washington, DC: World Bank.

Bhatt, S. (2002) 'Chronicle of terrorism now told', Rediff Special, Rediff Online, 8 October. Available from http://www.rediff.com/news/2002/oct/08spec.htm. Accessed 19 June 2008.

Bokhari, F. (2003) 'The rise and long-term outlook for the MMA in Pakistan', Working Group Meeting on Pakistan's Future and US Policy Options Project, Washington, DC: Center for Strategic and International Studies.

Burki, S.J. (2004) *Prospects of Peace, Stability and Prosperity in South Asia: An Economic Perspective*, Islamabad.

Burki, S.J. and Baxter, C. (1991) *Pakistan Under the Military: Eleven Years of Zia-ul-Haq*, Boulder, CO: Westview Press.

Chari, P.R. (2003) 'Nuclear crisis, escalation control, and deterrence in South Asia', working paper version 1.0, Washington, DC: The Henry L. Stimson Center.

Chaudhury, R.R. (2004) 'Nuclear doctrine, declaratory policy, and escalation control', South Asian Regional Security Project, Washington, DC: The Henry L. Stimson Center.

Cheema, P.I. and Nuri, M.H. (2005) *The Kashmir Imbroglio: Looking Towards the Future*, Islamabad: Islamabad Policy Research Institute.

Cheema, Z.I. (2004) 'Conflict, crisis and nuclear stability in South Asia', paper presented at the workshop titled, 'New Challenges to Strategic Stability in South Asia', Bradford: University of Bradford.

Chengappa, R. (2000) *Weapons of Peace: The Secret Story of India's Quest to be a Nuclear Power*, New Delhi: HarperCollins.

Cohen, S.P. (2003) 'The *Jihadist* threat to Pakistan', *The Washington Quarterly*, 26:3, Summer, 7–25.

Engineer, A.A. (2003) 'Communal riots: 2002', South Asia Citizens Web. Available from http://www.sacw.net/2002/EngineerJan03.html. Accessed 14 June 2006.

Fernandez, G. (1992) 'India's policies in Kashmir: an assessment and discourse', in G.C. Thomas (ed.) *Perspectives on Kashmir: The Roots of Conflict in South Asia*, Boulder, CO: Westview Press, p. 288.

IMF (2005) 'Study on the implications of the 2005 trade liberalization in the textile and clothing sector', consolidated report, Part 1, Paris: IMF.

Jain, S. (1999) 'Prospects for a South Asian free trade agreement: problems and challenges', *International Business Review*, 8, 399–419.

Khan, S.R. and Haider, S. (2004) 'Regional initiatives (institutional, human, organizational) required to implement the Agreements on Technical Barriers to Trade (TBT), and on the application of Sanitary and Phytosanitary Measures (SPS) and their provisions', Working paper, Islamabad: Sustainable Development Policy Institute.

Khan, S.R., Yusuf, M., Bokhari, S. and Aziz, S. (2007) 'Quantifying informal trade between India and Pakistan', in Z.F. Naqvi and P. Schuler (eds) *The Challenges and Potential of Pakistan–India Trade*, Washington, DC: World Bank.

Kozicki, R.J. (2002) 'The changed world of South Asia: Afghanistan, Pakistan and India after September 11', *Asia Pacific Perspectives*, 2:2, 1–10, San Francisco: Center for the Pacific Rim, University of San Francisco.

Lloyd, J. and Nankivell, N. (2002) 'India, Pakistan and the legacy of September 11', *Cambridge Review of International Affairs*, 15:2, 269–287.

Mazari, S.M. (1999) 'Subversion and its linkage to low intensity conflicts, ethnic movements and violence', *Defense Journal*, 3:4.

Mohan, P.V., Jagan, S. and Chopra, S. (2005) *The India–Pakistan Air War of 1965*, New Delhi: Manohar.

Mukherjee-Reed, A. (1997) 'Regionalization in South Asia: theory and praxis', *Pacific Affairs*, 70:2, 235–251.

Nabi, I. and Nasim, A. (2001) 'Trading with the enemy: a case for liberalizing Pakistan–India trade', in S. Lahiri (ed.) *Regionalism and Globalization: Theory and Practice*, London: Routledge, pp. 170–198.

Nizamani, H. (2000) *The Roots of Rhetoric: Politics of Nuclear Weapons in India and Pakistan*, Westport, CT: Praeger.

Pakistan–India CEO's Business forum (2005) 'Barriers to trade in India', Presented to the World Bank, Islamabad, 11 July.

Rao, S. (1999) 'The Price of War', *Sunday Mid Day*, 4 July.

Sahni, V. (2001) 'Monitoring the borders', *The Hindu*, 15 December.

Salim, A. and Zaffarullah, K. (2004) 'Messing up the past: evolution of history textbooks in Pakistan, 1947–2000', Islamabad: Sustainable Development Policy Institute.

Schofield, V. (2003) *Kashmir in Conflict: India, Pakistan and the Unending War*, London: I. B. Tauris.

Siddiqa Agha, A. (2004) *India–Pakistan Relations: Confrontation to Conciliation*, Islamabad: Centre for Democratic Governance and the Network for Consumer Protection.

Sisson, R. and Rose, L.E. (1990) *War and Secession: Pakistan, India and the Creation of Bangladesh*, Berkeley, CA and Los Angeles: University of California Press.

Suri, A. (2003) 'NGOs in Kashmir – Agents of peace and development?', *IPCS Research Paper*, 2, New Delhi: Institute of Peace and Conflict Studies.

Synnott, H. (1990) *The Causes and Consequences of South Asia's Nuclear Tests*, Adelphi paper, 332, Oxford: The International Institute for Strategic Studies, Oxford University Press.

Thies, W.J. and Hellmuth, D. (2004) 'Critical risk and the 2002 Kashmir crisis', *The Nonproliferation Review*, 11:3, Fall–Winter.

Yusuf, M. (2003) 'Rise of Islamic militancy in Pakistan: causes and the threat of "*Talibanization*"', unpublished paper.

Yusuf, M. and Najam, A. (2005) 'Kashmir: identifying the components of a sustainable solution', in SDPI (ed.) *Troubled Times: Sustainable Development and Governance in the Age of Extremes*, Islamabad: SAMA Books.

Zaidi, A. (2004) *Issues in Pakistan's Economy*, Oxford: Oxford University Press.

# 7 Outlines of intra-state conflict in Zimbabwe and regional challenges

*Mzukisi Qobo*

## Introduction

The political and economic contours of present-day Zimbabwe present a country at war with itself. The political elite are arrayed against its people, civil–military relations are at a nadir, and militarism, intimidation, paranoia and fear engulf Zimbabwean society. The political leadership has lost legitimacy and lacks the confidence to govern. The prevailing crisis has raised questions about the effectiveness and relevance of regional institutions such as the Southern African Development Community (SADC) in defending human rights abuses and ensuring the rule of law among member countries.

In other words, the 'intra-state' crisis in Zimbabwe has reduced the ability of regional integration processes to guarantee peace and security, both within states and between neighbouring states. Internal instability in Zimbabwe has generated regional insecurities, although not in a strictly militaristic sense. Contrast this with the 1980s, when Zimbabwe was a pivotal actor against apartheid and Mugabe earned international respect as a chair of the Non-Aligned Movement (NAM) in 1989, and for his role as part of the front-line states (FLS) in Southern Africa.[1] The volte-face, therefore, is all the more worrying. The genesis of Zimbabwe's crisis is multifaceted. Much has been written about some of its aspects, especially the land redistribution process and the narrowing of democratic space.

I posit that the crisis in Zimbabwe is a limited form of 'intra-state conflict' in the making, and that the deepening crisis in that country has revealed the ineffectiveness of regional structures, such as the SADC to mitigate this conflict. Underscoring its flawed design, the regional integration mechanism has also failed to achieve trade integration.

I contend that only when a pact is founded on shared values can regional institutions play a role as agents of restraint and promoters of regional peace and stability. Zimbabwe's case clearly demonstrates that the absence of deeply ingrained and shared political values such as accountability, democracy and human rights have rendered regional integration processes ineffectual and limited their ability to curb intra-state conflict. Despite the existence of regional trade integration mechanisms – the Common Market for Eastern and Southern African countries (COMESA) and the SADC Protocol on Trade – Zimbabwe's social and economic regression continues to deepen. This is a testament to the inadequacy of formal trade structures in creating conditions for peace and stability in sub-Saharan Africa.

This chapter adds a new dimension to the perspective introduced by the other studies in that I examine trade–conflict linkages in an intra-state rather than an inter-state context.

## An anatomy of the political and economic crisis in Zimbabwe: an overview

Zimbabwe attained its liberation from the administration of Ian Smith in 1979, following protracted hostilities between Smith's Rhodesian Front and the Zimbabwe liberation movements – comprising mainly the Zimbabwe African National Union (ZANU) and the Zimbabwean African People's Union (ZAPU). Previous attempts at a détente, brokered mainly by Zambia, proved fruitless reflecting the mistrust between the liberation movements and the Rhodesian Front. The history of the liberation struggle in Zimbabwe is covered extensively in the literature and I will not repeat here. I focus primarily on the potential for intra-state conflict in Zimbabwe, and the challenges that this presents for the SADC region. The backdrop is the SADC trade and security cooperation and integration process.

The post-independence settlement in Zimbabwe was negotiated through the Lancaster House Agreement. The liberation movements, Ian Smith's Rhodesian Front, Muzorewa's United African National Congress (UANC), Britain and, to a lesser extent, South Africa were all represented in these deliberations and became party to the agreement.[2] The manner in which Zimbabwe's political transition was managed contained some of the seeds that led to the contemporary crisis in the country.

The pre-independence Rhodesian state was in essence a security state, which the post-independence settlement failed to transform. The nationalistic tendencies of the new political elite combined with a strong element of militarism defined the security edifice of the new state. The militarisation of the state that began with Ian Smith's unilateral declaration of independence in 1965 permeated every societal institution. The Zimbabwean African National Union-Patriotic Front (ZANU-PF) simply continued on a path that was already charted, and sought to militarise the nascent post-liberation society in Zimbabwe.[3] Parallels – and indeed continuities – between the Smith era and the emergence of ZANU-PF in government are striking. Various state agencies, including marketing boards and parastatals set up at independence were regarded as strategic sectors in which the military was to play a central role in future.

## Early signs of militarism in the ZANU-PF: Matabeleland purges

The political repression evident in Zimbabwe today has its roots in the period between 1982 to 1985. On Mugabe's instructions, the Zimbabwean army's Fifth Brigade (trained by the North Koreans) massacred or tortured thousands of civilians in Matabeleland – mostly believed to be Ndebele and Zimbabwean African People's Union-Patriotic Front (ZAPU-PF) supporters. Supporting the Fifth Brigade were ZANU-PF youth who, like today's youth militias in Zimbabwe, were also trained in military tactics. The acts of violence carried out by ZAPU dissidents against ZANU-PF officials and innocent civilians provoked the purging (Kriger 2005: 1–34). Although ignored by the international community, the systematic massacre bordered on ethnic cleansing of the Ndebeles. The Fifth Brigade army units, as Meredith observed, were 'drawn almost entirely from Shona-speaking ex-Zanla forces loyal to Mugabe' (Meredith 2002: 65).

The dissidents in the entire Matabeleland were said to number no more than 400, comprising ex-Zimbabwe People's Revolutionary Army (ZIPRA) soldiers and ordinary criminals. The reprisal did not warrant the level of ferocity that Mugabe unleashed. Troops were deployed in 1983 and began systematic attacks against civilians, which included beatings, arson and mass murder. The blood-letting in Matabeleland – dubbed Gukurahundi[4] – represents a grim period whose scars still lie buried in the nation's psyche. I argue that the army's recourse to violence sowed the seeds of a latent 'intra-state' conflict waiting to surface. The deep-rooted hatred between the Ndebeles and the ZANU-PF go way beyond the healthy disagreements found in democracies.

## Emerging signs of crisis

The 1990s represented a difficult period for Zimbabwe, characterised by economic duress in the form of drought, unsustainable fiscal deficits, declining productivity and falling tax revenues (Bracking 2005: 341–357). The government's interventionist measures to halt structural decline did not work. Rising unemployment reached the unprecedented mark of one million – almost half the total number of workers employed in the formal economy at the time. From 10 per cent in 1980, unemployment surged to 40 per cent in 1990 (Hawkins 2004: 63).

The state came under pressure to undertake structural reforms in order to reverse the downward spiral. Introduced as the Economic Structural Adjustment Programme (ESAP) the reforms aimed to stimulate economic growth, cut the budget deficit, encourage private sector and foreign direct investment and embark on trade liberalisation. The reform objectives never materialised (Bond and Manyanya 2002: 31–32). The crisis did not abate; rather it was exacerbated by wage cuts, reduced subsidies and curbed social spending (Chattopadhyay 2000: 307–316). Health and education – Zimbabwe's flagship developmental projects – became casualties of these retrenchment programs. Critics are divided between those who blame the stabilisation programme itself for imposing economic hardship, and those who feel poor management and misgovernance by the elite did more harm.

Adding to Zimbabwe's economic difficulties, South Africa refused to renew the preferential trade agreement that had existed since 1964. According to Bond and Manyanya, the refusal to renew was in response to pressure by South Africa's domestic textile interests.[5] The reasons for Zimbabwe's economic decline in the period leading to the reforms of the early 1990s are varied.

The droughts of 1992 and 1995 further aggravated the situation.[6] Also, despite the economic security guarantees offered to whites at independence, there continued to be outflows of critical white skills, leaving the country with insufficient human capital. Even five years before independence, Zimbabwe's economy had begun to experience a significant loss of critical professional and technological skills as a result of emigration (Giliomee 1980: 8–9).

The crisis in the early 1990s triggered popular discontent, which the liberation war veterans were quick to seize for their parochial financial interests. These veterans had a close association with the former Zimbabwean African National Liberation Army (ZANLA) commander, Josiah Tongogara, and considered themselves the midwives of Zimbabwe's independence.[7] They publicly challenged Mugabe, demanding massive pension pay outs. The issue of these pensions was a sore point. The veterans felt short-changed by the negotiated settlement that had entrenched rights and privileges for former Rhodesian forces and the white minority and leaving nothing materially substantive for them (Alexander *et al.* 2000: 182–183). In an attempt to stave-off a potential revolt that could damage the little legitimacy that the ZANU-PF had, Mugabe, in 1997, authorised an upfront payment of Z\$50,000 each (then about US\$6,000), with an additional Z\$2,000 every month.[8] The payment, not backed by budgetary resources, would have far-reaching macroeconomic implications, especially with the economy going through turbulent times.

### Zimbabwe and regional conflict: regionalising a domestic crisis in the Great Lakes

The two incidents that forced Zimbabwe's economy to the brink of collapse were the pension payments to the war veterans and Mugabe's involvement in what became a regional conflict – the Great Lakes conflict. Both actions were misguided and reduced the confidence of international financial institutions in Zimbabwe. The involvement of SADC countries, especially Zimbabwe (as chair of the SADC Organ for Politics, Security and Defence (OPSD)) in the conflict, did much to damage intra-regional political relations. In turn, this engendered adverse trade relations.

Under Zimbabwe's influence, two other countries in the region, namely

Angola and Namibia (dubbed 'SADC Allies') also entered the Great Lakes conflict. Having come under military shelling from Rwanda and Uganda in 1998, the Democratic Republic of Congo (DRC) sought help from the SADC OPSD. Zimbabwe took the lead in involving SADC and, as would later be evident, material considerations were a driving factor. First, in the distressed economic environment, Mugabe saw the war as a means to enhance economic dividends for the elite, including top military personnel. Second, Ngoma notes the material interests underlying the Great Lakes intervention. Zimbabwe had invested US$200 million in the country and, together with Angola and Namibia, was part owner of a commercial bank in the country. Firms in these countries also held a number of mineral contracts in the DRC.

The Great Lakes conflict proved to be one of the testing points for SADC, as agreement could not be reached on the deployment of troops to the DRC. A fundamental weakness in the SADC was exposed when Mugabe flouted all proper decision-making channels to use the cover of SADC in engaging in the conflict. He excluded South Africa, a strong opponent of military involvement, from the meeting he hosted at Lake Victoria in August 1998, where the decision to commit troops to the Great Lakes was taken (Barber 2004: 194). This sheds light on the cracks that lay underneath the surface of unity in the SADC; in fact, there were no enduring common values that bound various actors together.

Zimbabwe committed an initial contingent of 6,000 soldiers to the war, the number increasing eventually to about 13,000, approximately one-third of Zimbabwe's army (Taylor and Williams 2002: 551). The war casualties were not without consequence at home. Zimbabwe lost over 600 soldiers and the war proved to be a financial drain. Rene Lemarchand points out that 'political and economic costs of military involvement (estimated at US$1 million dollars a day) have come home to roost, causing violent anti-war protests in the capital city' (Lemarchand 2000: 346–347).

## Economic effects of Zimbabwe's collapse on neighbouring countries: trade linkages and the informal economy

### Zimbabwe and regional relations

As one of the founding members of the Southern African Development Coordinating Community (SADCC) – a precursor to SADC – Zimbabwe has always enjoyed a special status. Mugabe, the region's eldest statesman in the region wields considerable influence. This was apparent in the muted response of other neighbouring countries during the land seizures in early 2000. In general, SADC members have never been forthright in condemning Zimbabwe's human rights excesses, even though this has had a deleterious impact on the process of regional integration. Going a step further, SADC has been complicit in Zimbabwe's political collapse. Its members continue to overlook the economic meltdown in the country. Pivotal countries such as

South Africa have also demonstrated indifference to Zimbabwe's political and economic plight, electing to characterise the situation as an internal crisis that Zimbabweans should themselves deal with.

Internal contradictions, in turn, have generated adverse political and economic impacts on neighbouring counties. Although Zimbabwe is meant to implement the SADC Protocol on Trade, it has also signed a number of bilateral trade deals with other SADC members (see Table 7.1).

Admittedly, other countries in the region have also entered into bilateral agreements. The multiplicity of trade arrangements, regional and bilateral, has led to problems related to rules of origin that continue to fester as there is no dispute settlement mechanism. Confusion prevails on which agreement takes pre-eminence, bilateral or regional. Essentially the bilateral trade deals outside the regional trade integration framework have compounded implementation challenges in the SADC Protocol on Trade. Indeed, tensions arising between countries at the bilateral level strain relations at the regional level and act to inhibit progress. Since early 2000, Zimbabwe substantially delayed its trade protocol implementation schedule. It is unlikely that it will meet the deadline of 2008. Economists Daniel Ndlela and Moses Tekere noted that Zimbabwe would complete 75 per cent of its tariff phase-down schedule by

*Table 7.1* A chronology of bilateral trade agreements

| Country | Nature of the agreement | Year |
| --- | --- | --- |
| Botswana | Reciprocal duty-free trade agreement on wholly produced products subject to 25 per cent local content | 1988 |
| Namibia | Reciprocal duty-free agreement Has rules of origin requiring 25 per cent domestic value added for manufactured | 1992 |
| Malawi | Reciprocal duty-free trade agreement subject to 25 per cent domestic value added Rules of origin problems exist | 1995 |
| South Africa | Duty-free regime on preferential tariff quota: dairy products, potatoes, birds and eggs Woven fabric is subject to concessional tariff rates when meeting 75 per cent local (Zimbabwean) content | Initially signed in 1964; the recent version was signed in 1996 |
| Mozambique | Aimed at eliminating tariff and non-tariff barriers Customs admin cooperation and trade promotion Rules of origin specifying 25 per cent of domestic value Excludes sensitive products | 2004 |

Source: SAIIA in-house compilation.

2008.[9] There are 26 per cent of lines that Zimbabwe still needs to remove tariffs on. The combination of domestic crises and weak regional enforcement has reduced Zimbabwe's commitment to trade integration. Given its centrality in the process, the adverse ripple effects have radiated rapidly within the region.

### Informalisation of the economy

The economy has not only shrunk, but large segments have receded into an informal mode. At the outset, the informal economy was always a feature of the country since colonial times and Smith's era. For instance, temporary migration from Zimbabwe to South Africa was triggered by pull factors such as employment. As Ndlela notes, 'men flocked to South Africa in search of employment and returned home with bicycles, watches, clothing and other goods' (Ndlela 2006: 7). Post-independence, informalisation of the economy has also been driven by internal migration from rural to urban centres.

However, the present rapid growth of Zimbabwe's informal economy coincides with its economic slide and internal political conflict. The effects manifested themselves as a shrinking of the formal productive sector of the economy, a rise in unemployment and the growth of informal economic activities. The urban informal sector includes micro-enterprises (largely survivalists and predominantly women), and cross-border traders.[10] Nyatanga, Mpofu and Tekere, note in their study that much of this trade passes through unofficial routes and is therefore unrecorded (Nyatanga *et al.* 2000: 1).

The sector derives no significant resource or policy benefits from the government. Informal cross-border trade is not documented. In his study, which focuses on product markets, Ndlela plots cross-border trade between Mozambique, South Africa and Zambia. Interviews that I conducted in Harare reveal informal to formal linkages in the services sector, especially in the auto services in South Africa. These linkages are characterised by the procurement of services by taxi operators in Zimbabwe from informal auto parts and spares businesses in South Africa.[11] Indeed, the emerging lines of integration in SADC are along informal trade (see Tables 7.2 and 7.3).

Despite the inherent risks in informal cross-border trade, traders prefer to work through parallel exchange markets for foreign currency as they are perceived to be more reliable than banks.[12] For traders the most important factor is the availability of foreign exchange and obtaining this from the bank requires complicated bureaucratic procedures, as the country has exchange controls owing to insufficient foreign currency. Traders cite harassment by corrupt customs officials at border posts, including extraction of bribes for travel documents.[13]

The informal economy and the black market have become the de facto institutions that people, including the elite, trust and through which almost all economic transactions take place. This includes, *inter alia*, transactions in currency, fuels and other basic commodities.[14] The size of the informal sector is symptomatic of the underlying economic, political and administrative

*Table 7.2* Estimated Zimbabwean informal imports from SADC countries

| Country | Goods |
| --- | --- |
| South Africa | Electrical household items, motor vehicles and parts, industrial equipment and machinery spares, printers, industrial chemicals, cosmetics, pharmaceuticals, clothing, shoes, furniture, tyres, bicycles, eggs and cooking oil |
| Zambia | African design clothing materials, cosmetics, toilet soaps, sandals and footwear, second-hand clothing, masks and wooden/stone curios, suitcases, jackets and bags |
| Botswana | Electrical household items, cosmetics, pharmaceuticals, kitchen utensils |
| Mozambique | Prawns, fish, kapentra, coconuts, soap, second-hand clothing, sandals and footwear |
| Malawi | African design clothing materials, wooden carvings, rice, sandals and footwear, second-hand clothing |

Source: Nyatanga *et al.* (2000); Ndlela (2006); and author's own observations.

*Table 7.3* Estimated informal Zimbabwean exports to SADC countries

| Country | Goods |
| --- | --- |
| South Africa | Crafts, cane furniture, baskets, clothing, tie dye, bed and seat covers, reed mats, brooms, mops, agricultural goods, whole and ground nuts |
| Zambia | Clothing, bed and seat covers, jerseys, crochet, artefacts, wooden curios |
| Botswana | Crafts, crochet, tie dye, bed and seat covers, agricultural goods, sugar cane, fruits, greeneries, dried vegetables, millet, whole and ground nuts |
| Mozambique | Plastic utensils, seat and bed covers, tie dye, plastic grain bags, wines and spirits |
| Malawi | Clothing, dresses, jerseys, bed and seat covers, crochet, plastic utensils, cups, buckets, dishes, plastic grain bags |

Source: Ndlela (2006).

collapse of the country. The social costs are yet to be quantified. However, it is apparent that the informal sector drives the economy and this creates an unenviable climate for administrative malpractice, tax evasion, corruption and flouting of health and safety standards. While the government ignores the scale of informal sector activities, non-state actors such as trade unions have acknowledged the pivotal economic role of this sector. The Zimbabwean Congress of Trade Unions (ZCTU) – an influential civil society organ – has investigated the circumstances and scale of the informal economy. This has led to the formation of the Zimbabwe Chamber of Informal Economy Association (ZCIA).[15]

By the same token, the SADC Protocol on Trade also does not acknowledge informal cross-border trade, even though it affects the entire region. Ndlela notes in his study that the items traded across the border are quite significant. In Zimbabwe's case they comprise wooden carvings, curios and other artefacts, which are an important mainstay of South Africa's tourism industry.[16] Possibly such trade is not only limited to South Africa, but extends to other neighbouring countries, such as Zambia. Given the salience of such trade, one would expect that inter-governmental structures such as SADC and related protocols would give due recognition to this phenomenon and allow representation by informal cross-border traders' associations in its meetings. As Ndlela notes: 'The SADC Trade Protocol is silent on the development and facilitation of SMEs [small and medium enterprises] in general, and the informal sector and cross-border trade in particular.'[17]

Recapping, regionalism in countries in sub-Saharan Africa, with collapsing economies and weak institutions, is driven largely by non-state actors and in its economic expression is highly informalised. This fact should not be ignored in region-level governance and economic policy-making. It is no longer sufficient to merely study formal-level processes; informal processes driven by non-state actors are powerful drivers of regionalism. This reality will need to be factored in when conceptualising solutions for conflict and building mechanisms for sustainable peace.

## The security dimension for spill-over effects

On the face of it, Zimbabwe is not an obvious candidate for studying intra-state conflict. There is no evidence of overt militarised tensions between groups in society, and neither are there visible signs of emergent counter-insurgency or civil war along ethnic lines – a classical expression of intra-state conflicts in sub-Saharan Africa. Therefore, to suggest that Zimbabwe is staring at an intra-state conflict in the classical sense does not reflect reality. However, often-times reality is not what it appears to be.

This chapter has elected to frame the current crisis in Zimbabwe as an intra-state conflict, albeit a subtly militarised one. The ruling elite regard the country as in a 'state of war', a war with the Western world and its proxy – the opposition Movement for Democratic Change (MDC). This mindset echoes Smith's Rhodesian Front's siege mentality when it saw itself as 'beleaguered, attacked by the international community led by the British government, and by all African countries led by the Organisation of African Unity' (Chung 2006: 62). A closer look at the civil–military relations suggests that the real tension is between the political elite, using the army and other security forces as its instruments, and the citizens. Zimbabwe is engulfed in a cloud of tension, fear and anxiety. Trust between the political elite – and by indirect implication the military – and the citizens has been severed. Various pronouncements by senior security officers point to the symbiotic linkages between the political and the military elite. Threats to elite power (i.e. ZANU-PF rule) are increasingly equated with threats to the security of the country, and this is where the military sees itself playing a role as the guardian of independence for which ZANU-PF is seen as the sole proprietor.

Consequently, the potential for intra-state conflict cannot be ignored in the ongoing crisis, especially in view of the fact that post-2000 the military has been significantly politicised and society militarised.[18] When ZANU-PF's authority began to ebb away during parliamentary elections in June 2000, the government created more space for the military in civilian affairs. Tendai Biti suggests, however, that this practice goes back to the 1980s (and continues from Smith's era) when the ZANU was intent on using the military to project its authority.[19] However, done more subtly in the past, militarisation has now become overt. The military overshadows the cabinet as 'the country's primary policy-making body, with the National Security Council, which Mugabe chairs, effectively managing macro-economic policy' (International Crisis Group 2006: 10). Reminiscent of the Smith era's 'youth conscription service', ZANU-PF is also using young people as pawns in its securitisation of the state. The National Youth Service (NYS), ostensibly designed to impart economic skills among young people, has been perversely used to indoctrinate the youth in militia tactics. These young people are often deployed to deal with the 'enemies of the state' – a designation applied to the MDC opposition and anyone who criticises ZANU-PF policies.[20]

ZANU-PF has taken to brazenly invoking metaphors of war and views itself as under siege. The state has become 'commandist', reflecting the interests of the elite, with its writ extended large over every sphere of society: production, food distribution, judiciary and the media. Indeed, it resembles a Stalinist 'plan-ideological state'. Parastals are used as a means to dispense patronage, often to retired army generals who still wield huge influence in the army. For example, critical economic agencies such as the Grain Marketing Board and electricity supply parastatals are headed by retired military officers. The state of the economy alone resembles a war zone; Zimbabwe is the only country in the world outside a war zone to have inflation that runs up to 100,000 per cent, and an extremely weak currency.[21]

### Spill-over to South Africa

The situation has not been without ramifications for neighbouring countries, especially South Africa. South African intelligence claims that a number of armed robberies in South Africa since 2002 'could be traced to former Zimbabwean soldiers'.[22] A steady flow of immigrants continues to pour into South Africa as the political and economic situation worsens daily in Zimbabwe. While most of these are economic immigrants, a number of them get caught in the web of criminal networks in South Africa. In 2002 an airport heist led to the theft of more than R115 million with four of the culprits being apprehended in a hotel in Bulawayo, Zimbabwe. In March

2006, gunmen stole more than R70 million in cash from a South African Airways flight and suspects were arrested en route to Zimbabwe. In 2004, police arrested six members of a notorious gang that was said to be responsible for robbing several banks and foreign exchange agencies – four of these were Zimbabwean. The criminal gangs involved in various crimes, including cash-in-transit heists, that have been apprehended by police have exhibited military skills believed to be honed in the Zimbabwean army, and are working with South African locals in their criminal activities.[23] In July 2006, a military-style shoot-out took place in Johannesburg between the South African police force and a criminal gang that included former security personnel from the Zimbabwe Defence Force.

## Regional institutions

SADC has been wholly ineffectual in stemming the crisis in Zimbabwe. The organisation seems to have split into various alliances and lacks common values that bind member states together. Similarly, the African Union (AU) has prevaricated in dealing with the situation in Zimbabwe, despite the fact that it has a commission dedicated to the protection of human rights – the AU Commission on Human and People's Rights (ACPHR). A resolution moved by the commission in December 2005 to condemn excessive use of force in Zimbabwe was defeated at the January 2006 AU meeting.

International organisations such as the European Union (EU) and the Commonwealth and countries such as the United States and Britain have not shied away from criticising Mugabe's policies and imposing economic sanctions. However, the sanctions have not deflected the government from its errant path; if anything, Mugabe has become more defiant. The crucial point is that efforts by African countries could have produced more tangible results, but these countries elected to confine themselves to hollow statements about solidarity. Good governance and human rights have been sacrificed at the altar of political expedience and regional solidarity. It could thus be argued that to a certain degree Zimbabwe's failure is a collective failure of regional institutions since Zimbabwe is a member of these regional structures and their failure to intervene have tacitly encouraged political mismanagement. Mugabe is a member of the supposed 'concert of Africa', and it is his peers in regional bodies who should have demanded greater political accountability and economic stewardship from him.

These organisations, including the regional power-house, South Africa, have also failed to show 'enlightened leadership' despite the fact that the crisis in Zimbabwe has had spill-over effects in neighbouring countries. One is then left to ask: What is the purpose of regional institutions when they cannot act where it matters? And why have they set lofty goals for themselves? The need to gain international credibility, play the aid game with the West and cultivate a deeper understanding of what it means to be part of a collective regional regime lies at the heart of the explanation. The conclusion that I can draw from the failure of these institutions is that they have lost their sense of conviction resulting in a loss of credibility. In the following sub-section, I look at the specific role that South Africa has played in the crisis.

### South Africa's involvement in Zimbabwe

Relationships between South Africa and Zimbabwe go back a long way. Apartheid South Africa and Smith's Rhodesian Front shared broadly similar racist ideologies and repressive practices, even though there were intermittent tensions between the two. With both countries facing security threats from liberation movements and hostility from FLS, they became natural, although uneasy, allies.

South Africa has always had some involvement in Zimbabwe's political affairs, including its role in détente attempts by FSL, facilitated mainly by Zambia, in the early 1970s. Again, South Africa was part of the processes leading to independence in 1979, and witnessed the signing of the ceasefire agreement under the Lancaster House negotiations.[24]

Although regional perceptions about South Africa changed somewhat in the post-apartheid dispensation, there has always been wariness of the country's big brother image in regional affairs. This has acted to constrain any decisive leadership role the country could play in the future. To use Joseph Nye's phraseology, South Africa has been unable to ensure 'power conversion'[25] that would be essential in influencing events in its neighbourhood (Nye 2004: 54). For example, South Africa cannot simply threaten Zimbabwe with military strikes, nor can it impose economic sanctions or cut sources of electricity supply, without risking isolation by other leaders in the region, or serious damage to its own business interests in Zimbabwe.

The political elite is more worried about South Africa's image with its neighbours, and cultivating good relations is seen as of supreme importance. As such South Africa has defined its role in the region as that of a 'developmental partner' however ambiguous such a designation may be. Nye argues that 'if a state can make its power legitimate in the eyes of others, it will encounter less resistance to its wishes. If its culture and ideology are attractive, others will more willingly follow.'[26]

Because of its perceived gravitas, Western countries expect South Africa to play a role of a stabiliser or hegemon in its immediate region. This is partly because South Africa's normative orientation broadly conforms to the West and the country could be a perfect conduit for such values in its regional 'backyard'. However, while South Africa's hard-power dimension is unquestioned, the country faces severe strictures in exporting its (democratic and human rights) values or creating stability in its neighbouring region. Its soft-power image is not readily received by its neighbours, despite its projection through instruments such as the New Economic Partnership for Africa's Development (NEPAD) – Africa's economic development framework initiated by South Africa.

This scepticism towards South Africa's soft-power leadership is partly due to diverging political values and cultures. The majority of African states are steeped in neo-patrimonial practices. In contrast South Africa portrays itself as a modern democratic state in Africa, with an economy that is globally integrated. Moreover, there is a sense of grievance harboured by a number of African countries regarding South Africa's destabilising role in these countries in the past. South Africa is well aware of these perceptions and has been reluctant to condemn Mugabe's excesses in Zimbabwe.

There are other explanations for South Africa's 'soft' diplomatic approach towards Zimbabwe. The International Crisis Group (ICG) report on Zimbabwe highlighted three. First, Mbeki does not wish to be seen to be acting in concert with external Western powers. As the ICG suggests, 'the more President Mbeki is perceived to be carrying an external agenda, the more isolated he will become in a regional context, making South Africa's leadership all the more difficult' (International Crisis Group 2002: 12). In this respect, working closely with other African leaders could prove to be a more credible strategy. Second, the African National Congress (ANC) is more concerned with weaning ZANU-PF away from its socialist past, and is providing silent support for a more technocratic leader in the mould of Simba Makoni, the former finance minister and head of SADC Secretariat. Third, the ANC and, indeed, ex-liberation movements in the region fear challenges by labour-based movements, such as the MDC, to entrenched leadership in sub-Saharan African countries.[27]

## Conclusion and recommendations

With a view to a synthesis, it is important to restate a number of observations on Zimbabwe's crisis and the role of regional agencies. I argue that the crisis in Zimbabwe represents militarised conflict at an early stage of development. Since it is difficult to predict the future, any sign of the deepening politicisation of the military and its extension to civilian arenas should be a great cause for concern. The risk that such politicisation may mutate into a classical security state is very real. Zimbabwe's crisis and the relationship between the political elite and the military, especially reflected in the management of various parastatals and in the succession tussle within the ZANU-PF, have the markings of intra-state conflict.

To understand the crisis one needs to follow the history of the country. First the ZANU-PF has acquired a distinct militaristic culture and shown a strong inclination towards one-party rule. This inclination has its roots in the past. Quite clearly, there was never a meaningful attempt at transforming the fundamental architecture of the state from its strong militaristic orientation towards democratisation. There was simply a change of elite – a process facilitated through the Lancaster House Agreement.

Rather than obsessing with the defence of sovereignty – since there is no likely external threat to Zimbabwe – regional institutions such as SADC need to focus on human rights and the promotion of democratisation in member states. A new contract established on common normative assumptions about governance and economic management is required in regional institutions. Furthermore, given the ubiquity of cross-border informal trade processes and region-wide linkages driven by non-state actors it would make sense that informal regionalism be given more attention in academic and policy research. This reflects empirical realities in most of sub-Saharan Africa and, as this chapter illustrated, countries going through political and economic crisis such as Zimbabwe are drifting towards such informalisation.

## Notes

1  The FLS organisation was an inter-governmental initiative amongst post-colonial states in southern Africa that sought to buffer South Africa's military encroachment in the sub-region and oppose South Africa's apartheid government. At its beginning in the early 1970s countries that were active included Botswana under Seretse Khama, Zambia under Kenneth Kaunda, Mozambique under Samora Machel and Tanzania under Julius Nyerere. After the independence of Zimbabwe Mugabe also played an important role in this structure.
2  Abel Muzorewa, a Methodist bishop, was accorded the position of prime minister by Ian Smith in May 1979, in response to international pressure for change. Substantially, power remained in the hands of Smith's party and Muzorewa became a token leader of the country until independence in 1980.
3  This section draws on an interview with Tendai Biti, secretary-general of the MDC-Tsvingarai, 16 August 2006, Harare, Zimbabwe.
4  In Shona language this refers to the rain that washes away the chaff before the spring rains. Gurukundani was the name given to the Fifth Brigade that was trained by North Koreans after an agreement signed in October 1980 between Mugabe and Kim Il Sung of North Korea. This brigade completed its training around September 1982 and it was answerable to Mugabe. See Catholic Commission for Justice and Peace in Zimbabwe (n.d.).
5  Bond and Manyanya (2002: 33).
6  Ibid.: 27.
7  Tongogara was an ambitious and popular top ZANLA commander during the liberation struggle and Mugabe's nemesis. His mysterious car accident in 1979 is widely believed to have been engineered by Mugabe's close associates. This draws from various interviews in Zimbabwe, 13–22 August 2006. See also Fay Chung (2006: 124–139).
8  Bond and Manyanya (2002: 39).
9  See Tekere and Ndlela (2003).
10  Ndlela (2006: 7).
11  This draws on informal interviews the author conducted with taxi drivers and individuals in Zimbabwe, 13–22 August 2006.
12  Ndlela (2006: 32).
13  Ibid.: 33.
14  This draws on the field-research the author undertook and from various (confidential) interviews in Zimbabwe, 14–22 August 2006.
15  Nyatanga *et al.* (2000: 22).
16  Ibid.: 33.
17  Ibid.: 37.
18  See a detailed analysis of the politicisation of the military by Rupiya (2004).

Rupiya is a retired lieutenant colonel from the Zimbabwe Defence Force. He notes that prior to 2000 civil–military relations were stable.

19  Interview with Tendai Biti, secretary-general of the MDC-Tsvingarai, 16 August 2006.

20  This section mainly draws from an interview with the MDC-Youth National Executive Committee members, 17 August 2006, Harare. Accounts by non-partisan youth in Zimbabwe as well as various media reports confirm that the NYS is used as a partisan instrument by ZANU-PF.

21  See Muleya (2006).

22  See *Sunday Times* (2006).

23  Ibid.

24  Campbell (2003: 23–24).

25  Joseph Nye (2004: 54) defines power conversion as 'the capacity to convert potential power, as measured by resources, to realised power, as measured by the changed behaviour of others'.

26  Ibid.: 57.

27  International Crisis Group (2002: 5).

## References

Alexander, J., McGregor, J. and Ranger, T. (2000) *One Hundred Years in the Dark Forests of Matabeleland*, Oxford: James Currey.

Barber, J. (2004) *Mandela's World*, Oxford: James Currey.

Bond, P. and Manyanya, M. (2002) *Zimbabwe's Plunge: Exhausted Nationalism, Neoliberalism and the Search for Social Justice*, Scottsville: University of Natal Press.

Bracking, S. (2005) 'Development denied: autocratic militarism in post-election Zimbabwe', *Review of African Political Economy*, 32:104/105, 341–357.

Campbell, H. (2003) *Reclaiming Zimbabwe: The Exhaustion of the Patriarchal Model of Liberation*, Cape Town: David Philip.

Catholic Commission for Justice and Peace in Zimbabwe (n.d.) 'Breaking the silence: building true peace – a report into the disturbances in Matabeleland and the Midlands, 1980–1988'. Available from www.zwnews.com/BTS/BTS.html (accessed 11 June 2008).

Chattopadhyay, R. (2000) 'Zimbabwe: structural adjustment programme, distribution and food insecurity', *Review of African Political Economy*, 27:84, 307–316.

Chung, F. (2006) *Re-living the Second Chimurenga: Memories from Zimbabwe's Liberation Struggle*, Harare: Weaver Press.

Giliomee, H. (1980) 'The short and long-term socio-political prospects of a new state', Stellenbosch: *Bureau for Economic Research*, University of Stellenbosch.

Hawkins, T. (2004) 'The Zimbabwe economy: domestic and regional implications', in M. Houghs and A. Du Plessis (eds) *State Failure: The Case of Zimbabwe*, Pretoria: Institute for Strategic Studies (ISS).

International Crisis Group (2002) 'Zimbabwe at the crossroads: transition or conflict?' *ICG Africa Report No. 41*, Harare/Brussels: International Crisis Group. Available from www.crisisgroup.org/home/index.cfm?l=1&id=1481 (accessed 11 June 2008).

International Crisis Group (2006) 'Zimbabwe's continuing self-destruction', *Africa Briefing No. 38*, Harare/Brussels: International Crisis Group.

Kriger, N. (2005) 'Zanu (PF) strategies in general elections 1980–2000: discourse and coercion', *African Affairs*, 104:414, 1–34.

Lemarchand, R. (2000) 'Crisis in the Great Lakes', in John W. Haberson and Donald Rothchild (eds) *Africa in World Politics*, Oxford: Westview Press.

Meredith, M. (2002) *Robert Mugabe: Power, Plunder and Tyranny in Zimbabwe*, Jeppestown: Jonathan Ball.

Muleya, D. (2006) 'Economic ruin, not MDC, will bring Mugabe down', *Business Day*, 6 April.

Ndlela, D. (2006) 'Informal cross-border trade: the case of Zimbabwe', occasional paper, 51, Johannesburg: Institute for Global Dialogue.

Nyatanga, P., Mpofu, S. and Tekere, M. (2000) 'Informal cross-border trade: salient features and impact on welfare – case studies of Beitbridge and Chirundu border posts and selected households in Chitungwiza', Harare: Trade and Development Studies Centre – Trust.

Nye, J.J. (2004) *Power in the Global Information Age: From Realism to Globalization*, London: Routledge.

Rupiya, M.R. (2004) 'Contextualising the military in Zimbabwe between 1980 and 2004 and beyond', in Brian Raftopoulos and Tyrone Savage (eds) *Zimbabwe: Injustice and Political Reconciliation*, Cape Town: Institute for Justice and Reconciliation.

*Sunday Times* (2006) 'Zimbabwe soldiers behind wave of heists', *Sunday Times*, South Africa, 2 July.

Taylor, I. and Williams, P. (2002) 'The limits of engagement: British foreign policy and the crisis in Zimbabwe', *International Affairs*, 78, 547–565.

Tekere, M. and Ndlela, D. (2003) *Study of the Compatibility of Trade Policies in the Context of Current Regional Economic Integration Processes: The Case of SADC*, Gaberone: SADC.

# 8 Peru and Ecuador

## A case study of Latin American integration and conflict

*Alejandra Ruiz-Dana*

### Introduction

Both economic and political variables affect trade. In economic terms, trade partners seek material gains associated with the exchange of goods. Politics may impede such transactions, depending on the tradeoffs or costs. If the economic gains are significant, bilateral conflicts or tensions tend to be overlooked. For example, Venezuela and Colombia continue to trade despite the existing tension between the two countries.[1] Conversely, trade can be conflict inducing. The outcome of the World Trade Organization's (WTO) Doha ministerial meeting produced more discord than cooperation. Perceptions that the terms favoured one party over the other fuelled this discord. The offending article was the European Union (EU) and United States refusal to give up farm subsidies and provide fairer terms of trade for developing country farmers.

Security threats, transaction costs and concerns about relative gains make free trade less likely among adversaries (Gowa 1989). Any or all of these factors can kick in when a dispute becomes active, its presumed effects exaggerated by negative propaganda. In particular, close proximity between two countries throws the trade–conflict dynamic into sharp relief. This is particularly true when the borders separating them are porous and not well defined. The situation can give way to disagreements over jurisdictional rights and responsibilities. Also, tensions at the border might affect the flow of goods. 'But the broader reason for stagnant trade will have to do with the general uncertainty surrounding property rights (broadly conceived) when two countries' governments dispute territorial jurisdiction' (Simmons 2005). This uncertainty raises the cost of doing business in the area. It is, therefore, not surprising to find that border zones lag behind the rest of the country in terms of development.

Bilateral trade flows do take place in the presence of conflict, although they are potentially lower than would be expected in a conflict-free scenario. A trade freeze normally occurs when a dispute provokes armed hostilities. Even if a boundary dispute does not escalate into an armed conflict, its irresolution fuels nationalistic sentiment and generates bilateral mistrust. This mistrust tends to feed fears of an eventual attack and, consequently, leads to an arms race. Hence countries in a state of outright or incipient conflict end up vying with each other militarily while more pressing problems such as poverty go unattended. Overcoming this vicious cycle is essential for trade and integration to flourish.

In Latin America, open armed conflict has often been associated with territorial disputes. Having said that their incidence has been infrequent, characterising the region as relatively peaceful and stable. This does not, however, prevent attempts to identify links between conflict and trade. For this purpose, I have elected to study Ecuador and Peru, two countries engaged in the longest-running territorial dispute in the region. I examine the potential for trade to mitigate conflict, as well as the implications that such conflict has on trade.

The chapter is divided into three further sections. The second section details the chronology and consequences of bilateral conflict. The third section analyses trade patterns between the two countries over the duration of the conflict, and predicts future trends in its aftermath. It also attempts to determine whether regional integration schemes emerge spontaneously or are the outcome of cause and effect relations. The fourth section presents my vision of how future relations will be shaped by past and present events, and assesses the feasibility of using trade concessions to mediate or resolve future conflicts.

## History of conflicts

### *Origin and evolution*

The conflict between Peru and Ecuador can be traced to the independence era. It is the only territorial dispute in the region that has resulted in armed clashes since World War II (Simmons 1999). The principle of *uti possidetis* was applied at the time Peru and Ecuador attained their independence, which granted each country sovereignty over the territory it occupied during the colonial period. Both countries interpreted the concessions differently. Peru defined its limits according to those established by the Royal Seal of 1802, which gave it administrative control over an area once part of the Viceroyalty of New Granada. Other sources indicate that this decree granted military jurisdiction to the Viceroyalty of Lima and administrative control to the Audiencia of Quito[2] (Ruiz 2006). Ecuador, on the other hand, defined its boundaries according to those demarcated by the Audiencia of Quito (Sethi 2000).

The colonial administrators did not attempt to define precise borders since all the lands they governed belonged to the Crown. Land divisions were carried out primarily for administrative convenience. In the same vein, several factors negated the need to define borders, post-independence. These were *uti possidetis* (as mentioned); the borders were isolated[3] and did not bisect populated areas; nor were they considered valuable in economic terms; finally, the focus was on post-independence consolidation. Only the territorial water-ways constituted a valuable asset. Since Peru and Lima were the colonial capitals furthest from Spain, the Amazon River becomes strategically important as it allows quicker access to the Atlantic Ocean. The alternative is for commercial fleets to round the Cape of Horn to reach Europe.

Differences over riparian claims on the Amazon drove the two countries to war. The first wars took place in the nineteenth century, in 1829[4] and 1859. By 1936, 13 attempts to settle the border had failed (Palmer 1997), including one by the king of Spain. To avoid a potential confrontation at an inter-American conference in Buenos Aires,[5] Peru agreed to discuss the boundary issue with Ecuador, with the United States acting as arbitrator. Both parties agreed to maintain the status quo line[6] pending a final resolution. Good will did not move forward beyond this point, though. After a series of tense negotiations, Peru withdrew from the talks in 1938.

Nearly two years later, Peru invaded Ecuador, supposedly in response to Ecuadorian incursions into Peruvian territory. The 1941 war, known as the Zarumilla War, resulted in more than 500 combatant casualties. Peru's army of 13,000 soldiers quickly overwhelmed Ecuador's 1,800 troops.[7] Its weaponry and aircraft were far superior. Indeed, Peru was one of the best equipped military forces in the region at the time. Ecuador, on the other hand, had no warplanes. Because of its military superiority, Peru quickly secured its hold over 40 per cent of the territory in dispute, as well as undisputed Ecuadorian territory (Mares 2001: 34). This was Peru's first military victory since its independence in 1821.

Upon cessation of hostilities, a final attempt to resolve the dispute was made with the signing of the Rio Protocol of Peace, Friendship and Boundaries in 1942. The Rio Protocol granted Ecuador unsovereign access to the Amazon and established a new boundary, closely based on the status quo line, dividing the disputed area in half (see Figure 8.1, the map of the disputed area). Out of 15 existing arguments, ten were resolved in favour of Ecuador and the remaining five in favour of Peru (Leonard 2006). The solution was defective in that the demarcation skipped difficult terrain (Economist 1995). In doing so, it overlooked 78 kilometres of mountain range, in an area known as *Cordillera del Cóndor* (the Condor Range), east of the Andes Mountains.

The boundary commission was put to work almost immediately after the signing of the Protocol. Ecuador questioned its work when an aerial survey by the US Air Force in 1946 revealed the existence of a river where a watershed was believed to exist. Indeed, Article VIII of the Rio Protocol stipulates that, in this particular area, the boundary line is to arise 'from the Quebrada de San Francisco, the watershed between the Zamora and Santiago Rivers, to the confluence of the Santiago River with the Yaupi'.[8] The discovery of 'a 120 mile (190 km) fluvial system' (St John *et al.* 1999: 23), the Cenepa River, put a dent in the Protocol's validity and prompted Ecuador to halt the demarcation process in 1948.[9]

The unmarked territory became the depository of Ecuador's dream of

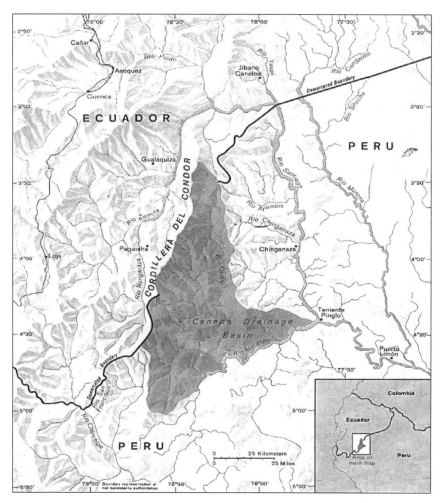

*Figure 8.1* Peru–Ecuador: area of boundary dispute.

Source: http://www.lib.utexas.edu/maps/americas/peru_ecuador_81.jpg

sovereign access to the Amazon River. That dream could easily be achieved by extending the border line into the Marañón River, the river the Cenepa flows into. According to some sources, Ecuador knew of the existence of the Cenepa River before its 'discovery' by the US Air Force. Its officials delayed the work of the commission on purpose, playing for time in order to find a way to improve Ecuador's prospects of gaining access to the Amazon River (St John *et al.* 1999: 26; Palmer 1997). By halting the demarcation, Ecuador hoped to coerce a border renegotiation.

Geographic discrepancies were not the sole basis of Ecuador's argument against the Protocol's validity. It also claimed signing under duress, in deference to the US wish to resolve the dispute before the Second World War began. Peruvian occupation of Ecuadorian territory at the time also made the Protocol contrary to international law, since conquest was no longer considered an accepted form of territorial acquisition.[10]

The Protocol's four guarantors (Argentina, Brazil, Chile and the United States) attempted to resolve the outstanding issues through arbitration. The Protocol was, after all, a legally binding agreement. Notwithstanding, Ecuador withdrew its commitment to the Protocol entirely, in refusal of any solution that did not recognise it as an Amazon country. One of its presidents, Jose Maria Velasco, went so far as to declare it null in 1960. This action suspended the Protocol's application for 35 years, during which further militarisation of the border zone and sporadic encounters between both forces took place, usually around the anniversary of the Protocol.

Meanwhile, Ecuador proposed other solutions. Peru remained inflexible; it was unwilling to give up any of the rights conceded by the Protocol. Both countries did attempt to establish 'cooperative agreements on the use of bi-national river basins, and the passage of individuals and vehicles in the 1960s and 1970s' (Simmons 1999). However, the efforts did little to allay the existing tension, which finally flared in 1981, at Paquisha. Peru repulsed the Ecuadorian army infiltrators in less than a week (Bonilla 1996: 4). Ecuador requested mediation from the Organization of American States (OAS), whereas Peru sought the intervention of the Protocol guarantors (Palmer 1997). Both helped the conflicting parties reach a settlement.

In early 1991, hostilities broke out once again. The provocation this time was the presence of Peruvian troops in the disputed zone. Ecuadorian authorities became aware of their presence in 1987, but did not request their withdrawal until January 1991, when the threat could no longer be ignored (Bonilla 1996: 11). The subsequent conflict ended with a 'gentlemen's agreement' negotiated by the presidents of both countries (Palmer 1997). Besides putting an end to the tension, the agreement established a military protocol for a designated common security zone. Although the security zone never materialised, other events did much to calm the atmosphere, including President Alberto Fujimori's visit to Ecuador in 1992 – the first ever by a Peruvian president.

A few skirmishes between soldiers stationed on both sides of the disputed border erupted into a localised war in early 1995. Conflicting accounts make it hard to identify the perpetrator. More likely, both sides played an important part in the unfolding events. The conflict lasted five weeks and involved more than 3,000 Ecuadorian troops and 2,000 Peruvian troops (Marcella 1995; Homza 2004). Ecuador quickly established air and ground superiority through a combination of efficient military planning, commanding positioning and advanced equipment, such global positioning systems (GPSs) and satellites to locate targets. The encounter, the most serious since 1941, marked the first Peruvian setback since the Battle of Tarqui in 1829 and resulted in hundreds of casualties. The Ecuadorian president, Sixto Durán Ballén, attributed this victory to 14 years of arduous preparation (Marcella 1995). Peru lost nine warplanes and sought retribution, even after President Fujimori declared a victory and ordered a unilateral ceasefire on 16 February 1995 (Cooper 2003). Ecuador lost no aircraft.[11]

The four guarantors of the Rio Protocol negotiated a second ceasefire and a peace agreement, the Itamaraty Peace Accord, on February 17. It marked the first time in almost 50 years that Ecuador submitted to the Protocol (although it still disputed its validity).[12] In addition to setting the stage for bilateral negotiations, the Peace Accord assigned a military observer mission to Ecuador–Peru (MOMEP) to oversee the separation of forces and the demilitarisation of the disputed area. This mission, made up of military personnel from the guarantor countries, was financed by Ecuador and Peru. MOMEP managed to evacuate most soldiers within five weeks (Weidner 1996). This is noteworthy given the original programme's six-week duration. This was complemented with aerial surveillance.[13] Once the conflict zone was cleared, MOMEP was able to propose a 528 square kilometre demilitar-ised zone (DMZ),[14] which was accepted by the Peruvian and Ecuadorian representatives on 24–25 July 1995.[15]

Confrontations continued at the border, forcing MOMEP to extend the DMZ by 10 kilometres on either side. Tension heightened in August 1998,[16] and it was necessary to reaffirm the parties' commitment to a common solution. Many apparently intractable issues needed to be discussed while each country dealt with problems of their own. Ecuador was in the midst of a political crisis soon after President Abdalá Bucaram's impeachment in February 1997,[17] and Peru had to deal with the Shining Path (the infamous guerrilla group), as well as its severe economic problems.

The Peru–Ecuador territorial dispute officially came to an end on 26 October 1998. Both countries signed a peace treaty, the Presidential Act of Brasilia, which not only settled the remaining border issues, but also paved the way for further trade and development. The treaty favoured Peru by mandating the Rio Protocol's demarcation. Further, the disputed zone was to be demilitarised and converted into an ecological park. Thus, Ecuador did not get free and sovereign access to the Amazon River (the main concession it sought). As compensation, it received a block of private property in the area where it could fly its flag and erect a monument to its fallen soldiers. The area measures 1 square kilometre at Tiwinza, the site of the most violent confrontation between Ecuadorian and Peruvian troops. The conflict timeline is summarised in the list below (Palmer 2007):

1822    Independence of Ecuador
1824    Independence of Peru
1829    Battle of Tarqui (over Guayaquil). Gran Colombia[18] defeats Peru
1830    Ecuador separates from Gran Colombia
1859    War leads to Peru's temporary occupation of Guayaquil
1941    Peru–Ecuador war (July–September). Peru defeats Ecuador

1981  Border clashes end with intervention of OAS and the guarantors
1991  Tension flares in the disputed area and leads presidents to formu-
      late a 'gentlemen's agreement'
1995  Renewed hostilities quickly escalate, leading President Fujimori
      to unilaterally call for a ceasefire

## Main actors involved

The duration and intensity of the dispute between Ecuador and Peru involved many actors. The international scope of the dispute brought in foreign entities and individuals. Understanding their motivation is key to unlocking the succession of events.

### National actors

Since the post-colonial era, the governments of Peru and Ecuador maintained 'contrary historical claims on many chunks of their common border, according to different interpretations of treaties and agreements that they had entered into over the last two centuries' (COHA 1998). Schoolbooks articulated these claims, fuelling popular sentiment against any territorial concession. Both countries, for example, still bicker over whether a Spanish expedition in 1542 that 'discovered the Amazon River, set out from Cuzco, Peru, merely stopping in Quito for supplies (the Peruvian version), or whether the expedition was in fact organized and led from Quito' (COHA 1998).

While the waterway was a genuine concern, nationalistic politics also fuelled the disagreement over the border's real location. They led each state to refuse to make any related concession. Historical discourse not only made it difficult to pinpoint facts, but it also tied the disputed territory to national identity. Ecuadorian textbooks, for instance, portrayed this discovery as a transcendental event in the nation's history (Carreras 2007: 6). The slogan 'Ecuador has been, is, and will be an Amazonian country' had a special resonance after the Protocol was declared null (Carreras 2007: 7). Hence, national pride got in the way of negotiations, often to the detriment of the national interests.

According to Dominguez *et al.* (2003):

> [P]olitical leaders are likely to have a strong base of domestic political support for continuing to pursue territorial claims by a combination of confrontational diplomatic or military policies whenever there is a long-term history of past conflict (the Venezuela – Guyana case). All these findings point to a key insight: disputes are path dependent.

Politicians often resort to nationalistic rhetoric and militarise a dispute in order to exploit the issue for their own political benefit. Spatial control becomes a means to attain political control.

As indicated in the previous section, Ecuador judged the Rio Protocol unfair and non-executable. This stance contravened international law since Ecuador had signed *and* ratified the treaty; it could not 'unilaterally withdraw from being subject to its provisions' (Palmer 1997). Peru claimed that Ecuador had already gained an unfair land concession through the Protocol. A revision would thus be unacceptable; Peru wanted the Protocol to be upheld. Both countries did not waver in their positions, which became more intractable with the passage of time as they were further ingrained into each country's collective consciousness.

The military's prominent role in the dispute as well as in the internal affairs of both countries[19] also made it difficult to retract. The military had resources to continue the conflict largely due to the substantial budget allocations.[20] Table 8.1 shows Ecuador and Peru's military spending as a percentage of their respective annual budgets and time trends for these expenditures. For developing countries, the expenditures are extremely high and represent some important tradeoffs. For instance, in 1990, Peru had an inflation rate of

*Table 8.1* Military spending as percentage of federal budget

| Year | Ecuador | Peru |
| --- | --- | --- |
| 1973 | 15.7 | 20.3 |
| 1974 | 16.4 | 20.3 |
| 1975 | 19.5 | 23.9 |
| 1976 | 18.7 | 26.3 |
| 1977 | 16.7 | 39.3 |
| 1978 | 24.7 | 32.0 |
| 1979 | 21.6 | 21.4 |
| 1980 | 15.0 | 27.0 |
| 1981 | 13.2 | 23.7 |
| 1982 | 12.1 | 24.3 |
| 1983 | 11.0 | 26.2 |
| 1984 | 18.1 | 30.5 |
| 1985 | 16.9 | 36.3 |
| 1986 | 16.7 | 39.8 |
| 1987 | 16.2 | 33.2 |
| 1988 | 18.5 | N/A |
| 1989 | 16.4 | N/A |
| 1990 | 20.4 | 10.7 |
| 1991 | 22.3 | 9.9 |
| 1992 | 20.6 | 11.1 |
| 1993 | 19.0 | 11.0 |
| 1994 | 21.1 | 12.5 |
| 1995 | 18.5 | 10.2 |
| 1996 | 11.7 | 11.7 |
| 1997 | 12.9 | 12.9 |
| 1998 | 12.6 | 12.6 |
| 1999 | 12.3 | 12.3 |

Source: Ruiz (2006: 66–67).

2 million per cent, US$10 billion in damages caused by the ongoing guerrilla war, and a bankrupt government (Palmer 1997). Diverting scarce funds to the military in this context certainly seemed reckless.

Overall, Ecuador's military spending was half that of Peru's in the 1970s and 1980s. Peru actually engaged in an arms race in the 1980s. It became the region's largest importer of arms, spending US$1 billion a year until 1998 (Sethi 2000). The Peruvian air force is one of the most powerful in the region, possessing a significant inventory of high-tech warplanes (Cooper 2003).

Ecuador's military spending was reactive. Perceived threats, such as Peru's arms race, would prompt its increase. To keep Peru from consolidating its military position during the negotiations after the 1995 war, Ecuador increased its military spending from US$447 million in 1995 to US$640 million in 1998 (Ruiz 2006: 67). It purchased four refurbished Kfir fighter-bombers from Israel right in the midst of the negotiations (Economist 1996; Sims 1996). Figure 8.2 shows defence spending trends over 1973 to 1999.

In absolute terms Peru spent substantially larger amounts on defence (US$2.3 billion in 1986, compared to Uruguay's US$244.4 million 1981). However, in relation to the total budget, the percentage amounts converged; after 1996 these amounts were almost the same (see Table 8.1). Peru's armed forces are two times larger than Ecuador's, but the latter's army is proportional to the country's size and its population (Ruiz 2006: 68). Additionally, Table 8.1 shows peaks in military spending in the aftermath of armed conflicts. Clearly, as the threat increased, military spending rose in order to achieve higher levels of deterrence.

The outcome of the 1995 border war helped pave the way to a resolution of the conflict. As Simmons (1999) correctly observes, Ecuador's military victory allowed it to make a dignified submission to the Protocol. Peru, on the other hand, was in the midst of a serious economic crisis and, therefore, could no longer sustain its military expenditures. The Peace Accord allowed funds to be redirected for development purposes and also permitted each country to focus on regional trade and integration efforts.

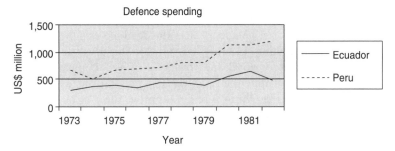

*Figure 8.2* Defence spending.
Source: Ruiz (2006: 66–67).

Consolidation of democracy in the region also heralded the demise of military regimes. The peace process itself was indicative of an increase in civilian leverage; popular opinion was in favour of a resolution. The results of a 1995 poll indicated that 58 per cent of Peru's and 71 per cent of the Ecuador's population were keen on seeing the dispute reach a final resolution (Simmons 1999).

### External actors

There have been 22 cases of legally binding third-party rulings on contested territorial sovereignty in Latin America, the largest number for any geographic region in the world (Simmons 1999). Given the military balance in the region, resolving border disputes through a third party is the preferred method. The Ecuador–Peru border dispute itself was resolved through extensive third-party involvement, made possible by the Rio Protocol.

The Rio Protocol is a unique third-party dispute settlement mechanism that exemplifies the power of international law through the mediators' observance of treaty obligations. These obligations were meant to assure the engagement of the guarantor states (Argentina, Brazil, Chile and the United States). They were legally mandated to oversee the treaty's provisions, including the mediation and arbitration of the dispute. Further, the guarantors were obligated, under Article 5, to mediate the conflict until it reached its final resolution.

Since an ongoing dispute meant continuous engagement, the guarantors reacted immediately to flare-ups for fear that an escalation could potentially complicate their attempts to find a resolution. By 1995, the protracted nature of the conflict allowed the guarantors to build strong intra-group relations, as well as good rapport with the disputing parties. These diplomatic dynamics allowed greater agility in the guarantors' efforts when the antagonists, Ecuador in particular, expressed willingness to settle the border dispute for good.

After the 1995 ceasefire, Ecuador and Peru initiated a series of encounters that paved the way for the conclusion of negotiations in 1998. These negotiations included an agreement to resolve pending matters through four commissions.[21] A deadline for the submission of all proposals was set for 30 May 1998. The only commission unable to meet the deadline was the one responsible for border demarcation. In order to overcome this drawback and put an end to military tensions for good, the presidents of both countries requested that the guarantors determine the boundary. The guarantors' condition was that Peru and Ecuador's legislatures had to approve the proposal in advance to avoid interminable negotiations. This made a 'fast track peace agreement possible, and was an elegant way for [Presidents] Mahuad and Fujimori to politically survive the consequences of this potentially explosive issue in their own countries' (COHA 1998).

Reliance on an observer mission, MOMEP, was essential to lend continuum to the negotiations. Although it was not required to enforce the peace, MOMEP gradually became a confidence building measure (CBM) as it increased the scope of its operations from observation and demilitarisation, to actual prevention of conflict.[22] The then US Secretary of State Madeleine Albright observed that, 'what was truly unique about this observer mission was that its expenses were paid for by the two antagonists, who realized it was cheaper to pay the price of peace than the costs of war'.[23] MOMEP was successful because it operated on the principle of shared responsibility,[24] with participating nations providing units that, due to their small size,[25] were easier to manage and did not pose a threat to the antagonists' sovereignty. With time, Peruvian and Ecuadorian officers were integrated into MOMEP to give each country a stake in the process, rather than keeping them on the sideline altogether.

The international context also favoured the guarantors' efforts. Both countries' leaders were quite aware that this border dispute was the last 'active' dispute in the region, which not only affected the risk perception associated with the antagonist countries, but precluded them from enjoying the benefits of regional integration (Carreras 2007: 10).

All in all, the Rio Protocol kept the guarantors engaged for more than 55 years – until the last boundary marker was set in place in May 1999.

*Consequences*

The outcome of the negotiations was well accepted in Ecuador. Ecuadorians were eager to settle the dispute and move on. Not so in Peru, where the settlement sparked riots and protests. The difference in public reaction was, in part, due to the way in which each government approached the negotiations. The government of Ecuador kept the public informed and allowed some input into the process, whereas the Peruvian government did not (Palmer 1997). Also, Ecuador's military was stronger and more unified than Peru's; they were consulted throughout the process and were, therefore, content with the result.

The Ecuador–Peru dispute illustrates how conflict can provoke a costly arms race. Each country has spent over US$500 million (Palmer 1997). In real terms, this exceeds 1 per cent and 3 per cent, respectively, of Peru and Ecuador's gross domestic product (GDP) at the time (Ryser 1995). Now that the dispute is settled, much-needed development projects can get underway. Due to the continued conflict, the border area remained the least developed in both countries. In Peru, the area's per capita income is US$1,301 compared to the national average of US$2,182 (López 2004).

As both countries have expressed their desire to work together in order uplift the border zone, foreign assistance has started to flow in, in support of such an effort. The post-conflict assistance offered by the United States Agency for International Development (USAID), aims to foster development in the region and economic integration at the border. This entails the improvement of infrastructure to improve producers' access to markets, and of overall conditions to foster the stability necessary for business to flourish. Projected contribution is set at US$20 million, to be invested over the course of two phases.[26]

The Bilateral Development Plan of the Ecuador–Peru Border Region, which is expected to be in operation through 2000 to 2014,[27] has provided additional development assistance. The plan objective is to improve the lives of the residents of the border area and to foster integration and cooperation efforts between both countries.[28] Over the course of its duration, the Bilateral Fund will receive a total of US$3 billion from each government, donor countries and participating international organisations.

In addition to rampant poverty in the border zone, Peru and Ecuador face other challenges that could be potentially divisive. One of these is the presence of uncleared land mines in the former conflict zone. Increased cross-border migration could result in the accidental detonation of these mines. In order to diffuse such threats, the Andean Community's (CAN) member countries established the Andean Charter for Peace and Security and for the Limitation and Control of Foreign Defense Spending (Lima Commitment) in 17 June 2002.[29] The CAN members reaffirmed their obligation to peace and security by establishing a peace zone that covered the territory of all member countries, including airspace and waters. The threat or use of force was prohibited, defence spending cutbacks were encouraged, as well as openness and exchange of information regarding the purchase of arms. The Lima Commitment also undertook to clear the land mines.

However, neither Peru nor Ecuador made significant strides in terms of reduced defence spending. The motivation, ostensibly, no longer remained inter-state rivalry. Peru's current Minister of Defense Allan Wagner announced a US$650 million investment to revamp the country's inefficient and corrupt armed forces (Brousek 2006). Although he acknowledged that there were no security threats from neighbouring countries, the armed forces needed to be fully capable of tackling international organised crime, especially smuggling. As justification for its military spending, Ecuador cited guerrilla incursions from Colombia as its main security concern. Still, Ecuador's current military spending is considered excessive by some observers. More than 20 per cent of the federal budget, amounting to US$1.2 billion, goes to the armed forces.[30]

Notwithstanding these defence allocations, both countries remain on good terms and have not lost sight of the bigger goal, which is to proceed with integration efforts. In a recent meeting, the ministers of foreign relations signed a joint declaration, stating their intention to uphold bilateral integration commitments and push ahead with common border projects (*La Oferta* 2005). Ecuador also demonstrated willingness to regularise illegal Peruvian immigrants who had been lured by the dollar-based Ecuadorian economy (*El Universo* 2006). Most importantly, both countries showed interest in consolidating the Andean integration process (*El Vigía* 2006).

## Trade relations

### *Historical trade conditions*

Despite the border dispute, Peru and Ecuador remained trade partners. While commercial channels remained open, the low levels of bilateral trade during the conflict did not suggest mutual interdependence. Peruvian exports to Ecuador in 1992 constituted only 1 per cent of its total exports (Bonilla 1996: 13). Neither country had qualms about closing their common border after war broke out in the Condor Range in 1995 (Bonilla 1996: 12). Given the low level of bilateral trade, the losses associated with closing the common border were not significant relative to overall trade flows. Ecuador achieved an increase of US$0.64 million in its overall trade in 1995 compared to the previous year.

A study by Simmons measured border effects on trade using a gravity model. The study had an institutional focus the premise being that institutions are responsible for reducing transactions and uncertainty at the border. It also focused on the negative externalities associated with reactive institutional measures. The final assessment confirmed that bilateral trade was negatively affected by border disputes. The model 'estimated an average loss of about $35 million in bilateral trade for every year the two countries continued to dispute their borders' (Simmons 2005: 25). Although low, there were costs associated with maintaining the dispute. Overall, the study estimated a cumulative loss of over a billion dollars for both countries. The list at the foot of this page summarises the study's findings with regard to the estimated effects of territorial disputes on trade, 1967–2000 (Simmons 2005).

### *Trade agreements*

Prior to joining the CAN in 1969, Peru and Ecuador had no formal trade agreements between them. Pending a border settlement, there was no serious political will to move forward with a bilateral agenda, which also affected the CAN's effort to achieve full integration. Specifically, the ambiguity surrounding cross-border transactions impaired this integration. Related gains from this integration, including 'involvement with the trading group, MERCOSUR, as well as some $1.5 billion in international loans for future development of the two countries', finally served as an incentive to settle disputes (Henrikson 2005: 366). Once conflict was resolved trade grew.

Estimated average yearly trade:

- with dispute US$59.21 million;
- with no dispute US$92.86 million.

Estimated cumulative impact of disputing:

- US$1043.15 million.

Actual average yearly trade:

- with dispute US$74.94 million;
- with no dispute US$182.67 million.

Figure 8.3 records the flow of bilateral trade. It is evident that trade ebbed when the two countries were at war, particularly in 1981. That year, as well as 1994 and 1995, marked the few instances when Peru's exports to Ecuador were lower than its exports to Bolivia (CAN).[31] Trade took off once the two countries resolved their differences and it has increased continuously since then. Peru is now the primary destination for Ecuadorian exports, constituting 59 per cent of its CAN exports in 2005 and 8.7 per cent of its global exports (CNN 2006). Historically, Colombia was Ecuador's most important CAN market, until 1999.

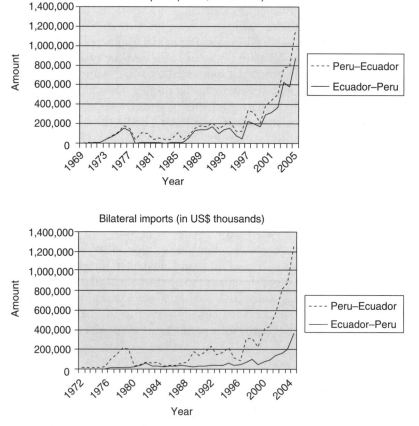

*Figure 8.3* Bilateral trade trends.

Source: Andean Community (2006).

For Peru, Ecuador is now its second most important CAN market, after Colombia, displacing Venezuela in 2002 (CNN 2006). Peru's exports to Ecuador comprise 27 per cent of its intra-community trade and 1.8 per cent of its global trade. While this seems very small in comparison to Ecuador's exports to Peru, signalling an actual trade deficit, it is important to take into account that Peru is a larger market relative to Ecuador's.[32] Overall, the above numbers indicate an upward trend in commercial exchange. What is not so clear is whether Peru can reduce its trade deficit.

### Current trade between Peru and Ecuador

A 2004 report by the Economist Intelligence Unit states:

> Since the demarcation of the border was completed in May 1999, both governments have worked towards strengthening the treaty by deepening trade links. The peace accord includes projects for investment and trade liberalization, such as the planned interconnection of the oil pipelines between the two countries, the improvement of facilities for the cross border transit of tourists from Lambayeque department in Peru to Azuay province in Ecuador, and improved transport links between the Ecuadorian south and the Peruvian north to facilitate cross border transit.
>
> (Economist Intelligence Unit 2004)

The citation confirms Simmons' assertion that 'borders as institutions for organizing understandings about jurisdiction over territory are increasingly important as the potential for economic interdependence increases' (Simmons 2005: 5). To stimulate inter-state trade, the border integration agreement considered suspending the existing tariff barriers and instituting a free trade zone by 2003. The agreement also envisaged the movement of people and vehicles. Towards this end both countries have jointly planned to construct cross-border roads (*La Oferta* 2005).

The trade and navigation treaty signed by both countries, has enabled Ecuadorian vessels to navigate the Amazon River; they receive the same treatment as Peruvian vessels.[33] Ecuador is allowed to set up trading centres along the river to store, transform and commercialise merchandise in transit.[34] Most important, the treaty signals the signatories' commitment to grant each other most favoured nation (MFN) treatment.[35]

These measures yielded concrete results. In the early 1990s, trade between Ecuador and Peru did not exceed US$165 million. In 1999, it stood at US$310 million dollars, increasing to US$873 million in 2004 (*La Oferta* 2005). Table 8.2 indicates the level of commercial exchange in relation to that with other partner countries. The numbers attest the increasing importance of bilateral trade between the two countries. Table 8.3 illustrates the significance of this trade in a global context.

*Table 8.2* Bilateral trade

| Reporter country: Ecuador | | Reporter country: Peru | |
| --- | --- | --- | --- |
| Value of exports to Peru, in US$ thousands | Year, partner ranking | Value of exports to Ecuador, in US$ thousands | Year, partner ranking |
| 238,584 | 1997, 5 | 101,716 | 1998, 19 |
| 199,127 | 1998, 4 | 50,554 | 1999, 21 |
| 180,146 | 1999, 7 | 96,730 | 2000, 18 |
| 293, 822 | 2000, 4 | 124,553 | 2001, 15 |
| 253, 033 | 2001, 2 | | |
| 373,698 | 2002, 2 | | |

Source: Inter-American Development Bank (2003).

*Table 8.3* Global trade partners

| Ecuador's trade partners | Percentage | Peru's trade partners | Percentage |
| --- | --- | --- | --- |
| World | 100.0 | World | 100.0 |
| NAFTA | 54.0 | NAFTA | 23.5 |
| Latin America | 18.6 (Peru, 8.3) | Latin America | 42.0 (Ecuador, 1.7) |
| EU | 17.9 | EU | 11.5 |
| EU candidates | 0.5 | ASEAN | 2.2 |
| EFTA | 0.5 | EFTA | 1.0 |
| Mediterranean countries* | 0.3 | EU candidates | 0.4 |
| ASEAN | 0.1 | Mediterranean countries* | 0.3 |

Source: European Union (2006a, 2006b).

Note: * Excepting Turkey, these include the following: Algeria, Cisjordanie, Egypt, Israel, Jordan, Lebanon, Morocco, Syria and Tunisia.

### Relation to regional integration schemes

I have already discussed the CAN's contribution towards promoting economic and political cooperation between Peru and Ecuador. Figure 8.4 tracks their commercial flows to the CAN. Clearly, the resolution of the conflict has led to enhanced trade flows to the region. Figure 8.5 tracks their trade with the world.

Free trade agreements (FTAs) with the United States, if approved, would constitute another important trade milestone. The US is the top destination for exports originating from both Peru and Ecuador. Securing permanent access to that market would ensure that, at the very least, trade flows remain intact in the aftermath of the Andean Trade Preferences Act (ATPA), which expired in December 2006.[36] Otherwise, a loss of market access would affect the countries' economic stability and, as explained below, elicit illegal trader.

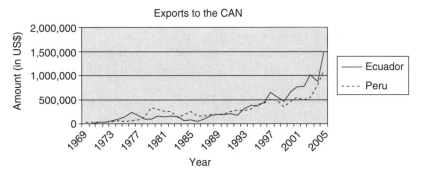

*Figure 8.4* Regional trade.

Source: CAN General Secretariat (2006).

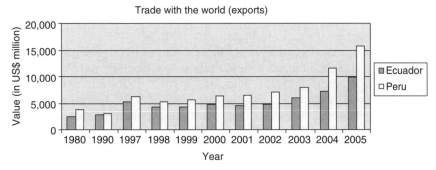

*Figure 8.5* Global trade.

Source: CAN General Secretariat (2006).

The FTA negotiations with the US have not gone smoothly. These negotiations began in May 2004 and have yet to be approved. The US tried to get its Andean counterparts, except Bolivia, to sign an agreement before the 2006 presidential elections in those countries (anticipating fears of populist takeovers).[37] Peru and Ecuador hoped to negotiate a deal before the ATPA's expiration in December 2006. This Act allowed participating countries to export nearly 6,300 products to the US without having to pay tariffs (US International Trade Commission 2005). Losing this edge could be disastrous since Ecuador and Peru, along with other countries in the region, are lagging behind in terms of competitiveness and investment attraction (Bussey 2006).

Peru managed to secure a bilateral deal (Trade Promotion Agreement) with the US in December 2005. Amid popular protests, the Peruvian congress ratified the trade deal in June 2006, by 79–14 votes with six abstentions (CNN 2006). President Alan Garcia, who was sworn in on 28 July 2006, wanted to 'propose an accord for the impoverished majority and not in its elitist conception' (Bloomberg 2006). To do so, he appointed Hernando de Soto, the renowned Peruvian economist, as chief negotiator. Long, drawn-out negotiations ended with the US Congress' approval on 4 December 2007[38] and President Bush's signature on 14 December. While the resulting agreement might not be wholly socialist or favourable to the impoverished majority in Peru, it is the first one requiring compliance with environmental and labour standards.

Ecuador's situation differed greatly. The US pulled out of negotiations in May 2006, after Ecuador annulled a contract with Occidental Petroleum, a US-based oil firm. The discovery of unapproved transfer of assets to a Canadian oil company and excessive oil extraction by Occidental Petroleum motivated the action (Hidalgo 2006). The US labelled it a breach of the US–Ecuador bilateral investment agreement. Prior to this incident, the US had criticised Ecuador's new hydrocarbons law, which had already jeopardised the negotiations.[39] In response to criticism from the business community, particularly the US negotiators, Ecuador's president said that accepting an imposition from an oil company in order to secure an FTA was unacceptable (Hidalgo 2006).

Be that as it may, Ecuador would be at a serious disadvantage if the US manages to negotiate bilateral trade deals with Colombia and Peru. Trade exclusion from the US, given Ecuador's higher production costs, would encourage illicit trade to and from its better-off neighbours. Ecuador's exports to the US constitute 2 per cent of its GDP. As an alternative to the agreement, President Rafael Correa expects to obtain an extension of benefits under the ATPA. In his view, these benefits 'should last as long as the anti-drug fights lasts' (Josephs 2006).

Although the FTAs with the US have inherent benefits, they also have drawbacks. As is the case with other FTAs, eliminating tariffs means foregoing government revenue. Tariffs also provide industry protection, without which there are market losses in the short term, possibly long term as well if the affected industries are not able to become more competitive. The most serious threat is the potential of the FTAs to break down the Andean Pact (Hidalgo 2006). To illustrate, the CAN currently outlaw the patenting of plants, as required under the US FTA stipulations (Montenegro 2006). In general, the FTAs negotiated by the US tend to be more stringent than the WTO law. For this reason, Hugo Chavez decided to pull Venezuela out of the CAN; claiming that 'North American imperialism killed the CAN' (Lucas 2006).

So, recapping, trade with the US is a double-edged sword. It has sparked deep political rifts and it is threatening the integrity of the CAN. But neither Peru nor Ecuador is prepared to terminate trade relations with the US; it would be a devastating blow to their economies and to regional stability, particularly if trade is diverted to neighbouring countries. Next to the massive discontent the situation would breed, an illegal exodus of goods and people appears a minor complication.

*Future trends*

Trade trends, along with the recent declarations by the ministers of foreign relations, suggest that both countries will continue to work together to expand their bilateral trade. They are currently negotiating a deal that will allow Peru to directly import crude oil from Ecuador, the fifth largest oil producer[40] in South America (Palomino 2007). Improved bilateral relations facilitate such exchanges, which could not be expected ten years earlier. On the downside, the flow of illegal Peruvian immigrants to Ecuador could mar trade relations, putting pressure on an already fragile economy. The consequent cessation of border development and integration programmes would constitute a serious economic drawback for both countries. More critically, failing to consolidate the Andean integration process, as a knee-jerk reaction to the potentially disruptive effects of implementing FTAs with the US, will likely cause the greatest harm.

## Conclusion: potential implications for future relations

Diplomatic and trade relations between Peru and Ecuador have normalised since the dispute ended in 1998. Indeed, trade grew rapidly in subsequent years, despite internal economic and political problems. The deposition of Ecuador's President Jamil Mahuad in January 2000 was triggered by the country's worst economic crisis in 70 years.[41] Two specific events brought on the crisis: the banking collapse and El Niño, which devastated crops. Further, since President Bucaram's ousting in 1997, Ecuador has gone through seven presidents (four over the course of the peace negotiations).[42] Overcoming this political instability is necessary for needed reforms to take place.

Defence concerns for Ecuador now lie at the border it shares with Colombia, primarily due to guerrilla incursions. US assistance through Plan Colombia has induced a hike in Ecuador's defence spending. This year's budget allocation alone was almost US$800 million. Eighty per cent of this amount was funnelled into salaries for approximately 55,000 defence personnel.[43]

Peru, on the other hand, fared better in the aftermath of the conflict due to strict fiscal policies put in place to control high inflation rates and other symptoms of economic instability. President Fujimori's austere economic reforms aimed to make Peru an active player in the global economy and succeeded in leading Peru out of its debt crisis.

However, in spite of his economic successes, Fujimori was not immune to public criticism provoked by his authoritarian regime. The public also accused him of human rights abuses.[44] Evidence of corruption among high-ranking officials in his administration triggered his downfall in his third term of office; a salient case was that of the director of Peru's National Intelligence Service, Vladimiro Montesinos. Renewed economic difficulties also fuelled public discontent. 'After the collapse of the Fujimori regime, the government removed army officers accused of involvement with Mr. Montesinos, and scaled down expenditure on the armed forces' (Economist Intelligence Unit 2004). A recent government initiative seeks to revamp Peru's armed forces so that they can be better prepared to address non-traditional security threats.

In terms of future prospects, the evidence presented in this chapter leads us to believe that diplomatic and trade relations between Ecuador and Peru will follow a steady course. Regional integration was key to peace, and considering the absence of conflicts and the upward trend in commercial exchange, including trade with the world as a whole (as seen in Figure 8.5), it is fair to say that trade has supported peace. However, this does not immediately translate into enhanced governance to prevent or mitigate conflicts. While efforts to foster border integration and economic development appear to stabilise political relations, I was unable to identify concrete action plans aimed at improving the crisis-management capacity of related institutions.

External actors have had a significant influence on peace-building efforts. Without their participation, the conflict would have continued. However, future interventions are not guaranteed as the mediators have been relieved of their obligations under the Rio Protocol. This begs the question whether Peru and Ecuador would pursue bilateral negotiations, or would they revert to the CAN for assistance in resolving disputes. Perhaps the CAN should consider establishing independent mediators with obligations similar to those stipulated in the Rio Protocol. In view of the Protocol's success, a similar mechanism would constitute a powerful confidence-building mechanism.

Be that as it may, if the level of interdependency continues to increase, then a swift resolution through diplomatic engagement will tend to be the response to a dispute. This is because putting an immediate end to the conflict or disagreement is clearly a win–win solution. In the case of Ecuador and Peru, if conflict were to arise now or in the future, the outcome would depend on several factors, including the level of interdependency and external actors' involvement. At present, Peru has better prospects at stabilising its economy and internal political climate than Ecuador. Since internal conditions do, to a certain extent, affect the level of engagement and consequently interdependency, Ecuador seems to be in a more vulnerable position. Yet, the fact that it was Ecuador's reluctance to settle the border that perpetuated the dispute allows observers to rest easy knowing that economic interests, along with diplomatic controls and safeguards, will be enough to protect the peace for now.

## Notes

1 Venezuela's president, Hugo Chavez, has expressed sympathy towards Colombian guerrillas and his country is known to harbour them. This frustrates Colombia's efforts to eradicate guerrilla activity, to the point that it has actually been accused of violating Venezuela's territorial sovereignty by going after them across the Venezuelan side of the border.

2 An administrative appendage set up by the Spanish Crown in 1563.

3  The area's high attitude and jungle climate made it difficult to settle homesteads. See US Department of State (1980), as well as Band (2000) and Parodi (2002).

4  At the time, Ecuador was part of Gran Colombia, a federation of newly independent countries led by Simon Bolivar, leader of the independence movement of South America. The federation was comprised primarily by Venezuela, Colombia, Panama and Ecuador. Plagued by factional disagreement, the federation was dissolved in 1830. Although a map outlining the border between Gran Colombia and Peru was drawn after the 1829 war (won by Gran Colombia), Peru never accepted it and used the federation's dissolution as a reason for its invalidation.

5  The Buenos Aires Conference for the Maintenance of Peace, held on 1–23 December 1936. See boundary report by the US Department of State.

6  The 1936 Lima Accord defined this line according to disputants' actual occupation of boundary territory; Ecuadorian groups were settled in the upper jungle, whereas Peruvians occupied larger tracts of land in the lower jungle. For more, see Leonard (2006) and Yepes (1998).

7  Estimates vary among consulted sources. Some, like Cooper, put the number at 15,000 for Peru's troops and 3,000 for Ecuador's. A detailed account of the mobilisation effort can be found in Mundo Andino's website (www.mundoandino.com/Peru/Ecuadorian-Peruvian-war, accessed 11 June 2008), under Territorial Dispute, as well as Mares' (2001) book.

8  See point B-1 of Rio Protocol (1946).

9  By then, the boundary commission had completed 95 per cent of the demarcation.

10  For an overview of the causes and consequences of the demise of the right to conquest in the twentieth century see Korman (1996).

11  According to Homza, only one of Ecuador's A37 was slightly harmed. Cooper offers a different account: two A37Bs and – possibly – a Kfir were damaged.

12  Ecuador actually asked for the guarantor's assistance in resolving the dispute on 24 January 2005.

13  Given the area's land mine infestation and the still latent conflict, most patrolling was done by air.

14  As a precondition to MOMEP operations, the conflicting parties were required to accept a four-phase programme that ended with the establishment of a DMZ. Homza (2004), Marcella (1995) and, in particular, Weidner (1996) discuss MOMEP's peacekeeping efforts.

15  The road to settlement was marred with disagreements over Ecuador's right to retain hold of a minor logistics base, Banderas. Ecuador argued that the base was located in an undisputed area on its side of the border and its inclusion in the DMZ would endanger its efforts to aid indigenous people living there. In the end, Ecuador was granted this concession.

16  In spite of the peace negotiations, both countries engaged in an arms race, most likely fuelled by Peru's irritation at having lost the war. At the height of the negotiations, Peru's navy and army were on call. See Homza's (2004) overview and *Mundo Andino* (n.d.).

17  President Duran Ballen's successor, Bucaram took office on 10 August 1996. He was impeached on corruption charges.

18  Territorial entity comprised of the former colonial territories of the Viceroyalty of New Granada and the General Captaincy of Venezuela.

19  Peru's military had almost half of the population living under a state of emergency, ostensibly in an effort to combat the terrorism that had infested the country. It was also Fujimori's main source of support; the military supported his coup in 1992 by closing the Congress and the courts. On the other side, Ecuador's military has continually intervened in government affairs due to the weakness of the latter's institutions. The socialist policies implemented during the military-led government

in the 1970s earned it high marks among the civilian populace. By 1995, it had control of 60–70 per cent of the Ecuadorian economy. For further details, see Ruiz (2006).

20  At the onset of the 1995 war, some Peruvians speculated that the Ecuadorian military, whose control of the economy was apparently slipping, struck a deal with President Sixto Duran Ballen; the military was to strike against Peru's forces to detract the public's attention from the increasingly unpopular president in exchange for restored rights to royalties in oil production. See Ryser (1995).

21  One commission was assigned the task of preparing a treaty of commerce and navigation to facilitate Ecuador's access to the Amazon River, another was to come up with a comprehensive agreement on border integration to stimulate the disputed area's development, a third was in charge of demarcating the border, and the remaining one was to develop mutual confidence measures aimed at preventing future conflicts.

22  Mainly by obstructing access to strategic areas and preventing military buildup. Homza (2004) evaluates MOMEP's role as a CBM.

23  See Albright (1998).

24  All guarantor contingents had coequal status; their efforts were coordinated by a Brazilian general.

25  Each guarantor was allowed to provide up to ten observers, with the exception the US, which also provided support personnel and equipment.

26  Phase I took place between 2001 and 2004. It focused on community development and, particularly, the consolidation of peace. Phase II began in 2005 and is expected to end in 2009. Its goal is to achieve economic development in the border region. See USAID brief (2005) for further programme details.

27  Originally set to last until 2009, but was recently extended to 2014.

28  For further details see *Plan Binacional* (1999).

29  At the time, Venezuela was one of the five member countries comprising the CAN (the other four are Bolivia, Colombia, Ecuador and Peru). It withdrew from the CAN in June 2006.

30  Some of this money is derived from the assistance received from the government of the United States through Plan Colombia (a plan to combat drug trafficking originating from Colombia). After Colombia, Ecuador is the country that receives the most support under this plan. See *La Hora* (2006) for more details.

31  Bolivia ranked third in terms of intra-community market orientation for exports from both Ecuador and Peru.

32  The population of Peru and Ecuador is, respectively, 28.4 million and 13.2 million.

33  See Article 6 of the treaty.

34  See Article 22 of the treaty.

35  See Article 35 of the treaty.

36  The purpose of this Act, effective since 1991, is to combat drug production and trafficking in four Andean countries (Bolivia, Colombia, Ecuador and Peru) by offering trade benefits to help these countries develop and strengthen alternative, legitimate industries.

37  The US started simultaneous negotiations with Colombia, Ecuador and Peru, with different results to date.

38  Strong anti-trade sentiment delayed the negotiations. The fact that two-way trade between Peru and US is not significant (at US$8.8 billion, it accounts for less than half a per cent of the US's total world trade) assuaged these; the deal is merely a symbolic gesture. The Senate's 77–18 approval was preceded by the House of Representatives' 285–135 vote in November 2007. See related articles by Weisman (2007) and Associated Press (2007).

39  Approved on April 2006, the law aims to distribute benefits equally between the state and oil companies.

40 Interestingly, Ecuador's rich oil fields are adjacent to Peru's border.
41 The economy registered a growth of –7.5 per cent and an inflation rate of over 60 per cent. This dire situation led Ecuador to default on half of its foreign debt of US$13 billion. See Rohter (2000).
42 Officially, a presidential term in Ecuador lasts four years.
43 *La Hora* (2006) details Ecuador's current defence spending behaviour and deems it excessive.
44 Some observers note that the state of emergency and the anti-terrorist legislation were maintained longer than was necessary, thus encouraging human rights violations on the part of the armed forces and the police, which enjoyed significant leeway during the struggle to eradicate leftist rebel violence.

## References

Albright, M. (1998) 'Ecuador and Peru', op-ed, *Diario Las Americas*, 31 October. Available from http://secretary.state.gov/www/statements/1998/981031.html. Accessed 22 October 2007.

Associated Press (2007) 'Bush signs US-Peru free trade pact', 19 December. Available from http://www.usatoday.com. Accessed 19 December 2007.

Baud, M. (2000) 'State-building and borderlands', in P. van Dijck, A. Ouweneel and A. Zoomers (eds) *Fronteras: Towards a Borderless Latin America*, Amsterdam: Centre for Latin American Research and Documentation (CEDLA), pp. 41–82.

Bloomberg (2006) 'Peru seeks to renegotiate free-trade pact with US'. Available from http://www.bilaterals.org. Accessed 13 September 2006.

Bonilla, A. (1996) 'Proceso político e intereses nacionales en el conflicto Ecuador–Perú', *Nueva Sociedad*, 143. Available from http://www.nuso.org/upload/articulos/2499_1.pdf. Accessed 15 June 2006.

Brousek, D. (2006) 'Perú recarga baterías para una guerra distinta: Hombre prevenido vale por dos', *Tiempos del Mundo*.

Bussey, J. (2006) 'Nations rush to make trade pacts', *Miami Herald*. Available from http://www.bilaterals.org. Accessed 13 September 2006.

CAN General Secretariat (2006) '37 Años de integración comercial, 1969–2005', statistical document, SG de 144. Available from http://www.comunidadandina.org/estadisticas/SGde144.pdf. Accessed 2 August 2006.

Carreras, M. (2007) 'La paz trae progreso – La résolution du conflit entre l'equateur et le pérou des négociations "forward-looking" réussies (1995–1998)', Centro Argentino de Estudios Internacionales (CAEI), working paper, 14. Available from http://www.caei.com.ar/es/programas/latam/working.htm. Accessed 22 October 2007.

CNN (2006) 'Peru approves free-trade pact with U.S', June. Available from http://www.bilaterals.org. Accessed 13 September 2006.

Cooper, T. (2003) 'Peru vs. Ecuador; Alto-Cenepa war: 1995', Central and Latin American Database. Available from http://www.acig.org/artman/publish/article_164.shtml. Accessed 13 March 2006.

COHA (Council on Hemispheric Affairs) (1998) 'Peru–Ecuador peace agreement: Hemisphere's last armed territorial dispute finally settled', memorandum to the president 98.29. Available from http://www.coha.org. Accessed 9 July 2006.

Dominguez, J.I. *et al.* (2003) 'Boundary disputes in Latin America', *United States Institute of Peace*, Available from http://www.usip.org. Accessed on 20 November 2005.

Economist (1995) 'A warning from the Andes', 334:7949, 42. Available from http://proquest.umi.com/. Accessed 12 September 2006.

Economist (1996) 'National pride and national frontiers', 338:7949, 42. Available from http://proquest.umi.com/. Accessed 12 September 2006.

Economist Intelligence Unit (2004) 'Peru: international relations and defense', *EIU Views Wire*, London: Economist Intelligence Unit.

*El Universo* (2006) 'Perú y Ecuador analizan migración y limites marítimos', *El Universo*, 6 September. Available from http://www.eluniverso.com. Accessed 10 September 2006.

*El Vigía* (2006) 'Ecuador y Perú estrechan relaciones', *El Vigía*. Available from http://www.elvigia.net. Accessed 10 September 2006.

European Union (2006a) 'Ecuador: trade statistics-economic fiche'. Available from http://trade.ec.europa.eu/doclib/docs/2006/september/tradoc_113378.pdf. Accessed 9 October 2006.

European Union (2006b) 'Peru: trade statistics-economic fiche'. Available from http://trade.ec.europa.eu/doclib/docs/2006/september/tradoc_113435.pdf. Accessed 9 October 2006.

Gowa, J. (1989) 'Bipolarity, multipolarity, and free trade', *American Political Science Review*, 83:4, 1245–1256.

Henrikson, A.H. (2005) 'Good neighbor diplomacy revisited', in I.T. Gault and H. Nicol (eds) *Holding the Line: Borders in a Global World*, Vancouver: UBC Press, pp. 348–378.

Hidalgo, F. (2006) 'Por qué estados unidos abortó el TLC con Ecuador?' Available from http://www.alasru.org/textos/hidalgotlc.htm. Accessed 12 September 2006.

Homza, J.L. (2004) 'Special operators: a key ingredient for successful peacekeeping operations management', *Landpower Essay – Institute of Land Warfare*, 04–6W.

Inter-American Development Bank (2003) *Hemispheric Trade and Tariff Database*. Available from http://alca-ftaa.iadb.org/eng/ngmadb_e.htm. Accessed 21 June 2008.

Josephs, L. (2006) 'New Ecuador leader nixes U.S. trade pact', The Associated Press. Available from http://www.washingtonpost.com. Accessed 22 October 2007.

Korman, S. (1996) *The Right of Conquest: The Acquisition of Territory by force in International Law and Practice*, Oxford: Oxford University Press.

*La Hora* (2006) 'Ecuador: Abusivo gasto militar', 6 September. Available from http://www.iidh.ed.cr/comunidades/segurida/noticia_despliegue.aspx?Codigo=2644. Accessed 13 September 2006.

*La Oferta* (2005) 'Ecuador y Perú impulsan proyectos fronterizos comunes'. Available from http://www.laoferta.com. Accessed 15 June 2006.

Leonard, T.M. (2006) *Encyclopedia of the Developing World*, London: Taylor & Francis.

Lima Commitment: Andean Charter for Peace and Security and for the Limitation and Control of Foreign Defence Spending. Adopted on 17 June 2002. Available from http://projects.sipri.se/cbw/docs/cbw-hist-andean.pdf. Accessed on 20 January 2006.

López, M. (2004) 'Desarrollo en integración fronteriza Perú–Ecuador'. Available from http://planbinancional.rree.gob.pe. Accessed 6 July 2006.

Lucas, K. (2006) 'Community: grasping at unity straws', Inter Press Service News Agency. Available from http://www.bilaterals.org. Accessed 12 September 2006.

Marcella, G. (1995) 'Guerra y paz en el Amazonas: implicancias politicias del conflicto Ecuador–Peru para los estados unidos y America Latina', *Revista Ser en el 2000*, 8. Available from http://www.ser2000.org.ar/articulos-revista-ser/revista-8/marcella.htm. Accessed 11 October 2007.

Mares, D.R. (2001) *Violent Peace: Militarized Interstate Bargaining in Latin America*, New York: Columbia University Press.

Montenegro, I. (2006) 'FTA means deeper poverty in Peru: GMOs arrive. Democracy doesn't', Available from http://www.bilaterals.org. Accessed 12 September 2006.

*Mundo Andino* (n.d.) 'History of the Ecuadorian–Peruvian territorial dispute'. Available from www.mundoandino.com/Peru/History-of-the-Ecuadorian-Peruvian-territorial-dispute. Accessed 10 October 2007.

Palmer, D.S. (1997) 'Peru–Ecuador border conflict: missed opportunities, misplaced nationalism, and multilateral peacekeeping', *Journal of Inter-American Studies and World Affairs*, 39, Fall. Available from http://www.findarticles.com. Accessed 1 August 2006.

*Plan Binacional de Desarrollo de la Región Fronteriza Ecuador–Perú* (1999) Available from http://www.planbinacional.gov.ec and http://www.planbinacional.org.pe. Accessed 22 September 2006.

Palomino, M.L. (2007) 'Peru, Ecuador say they are now best of friends', 1 June, Reuters. Available from www.reuters.com. Accessed 12 October 2007.

Rio Protocol (1946) Adopted 26 February. Available from http://www.usip.org/pubs/peaceworks/pwks27/appndx1_27.html. Accessed 10 October 2007.

Rohter, L. (2000) 'Ecuador coup shifts control to no. 2 man', *New York Times*, 23 January. Available from http://www.nytimes.com. Accessed 22 October 2007.

Ruiz, J.C. (2006) 'Seguridad y defensa de Ecuador: Espejismos y arenas movedizas', Available from http://www.ndu.edu/chds/Journal/PDF/2006/Vasquez-article-edited.pdf. Accessed 5 July 2006.

Ryser, J. (1995) 'The Ecuador thorn', *Global Finance*, May, 95.

St John, Ronald B. *et al.* (1999) *The Ecuador–Peru Boundary Dispute: The Road to Settlement*, Durham: Durham University – International Boundaries Research Unit (IBRU).

Sethi, M. (2000) 'Novel ways of settling border disputes: the Peru–Ecuador case', *IDSA Strategic Analysis Journal*, XXIII:10. Available from http://www.ciaonet.org/olj/sa(sa_00sem01.html. Accessed 5 July 2006.

Simmons, B.A. (1999) 'Territorial disputes and their resolution: the case of Ecuador and Peru', Washington, DC: United States Institute of Peace. Available from http://www.usip.org/pubs/peaceworks/pwks27/pwks27.html. Accessed 23 July 2006.

Simmons, B.A. (2005) 'Trade and territorial conflict: international borders as institutions'. Available from http://iicas.ucsd.edu/papers/GTCconf/Simmons_Territory_and_Trade_UCS.pdf. Accessed 23 July 2006.

Sims, C. (1996) 'Peru protests Israeli jets sale to Ecuador', *New York Times*, 7 January. Available from http://www.nytimes.com. Accessed 22 October 2007.

USAID (United States Agency for International Development) (2005) 'Peru–Ecuador Border Region Development', data sheet. Available from http://www.usaid.gov/budget/cbj2005/lac/pdf/527-008.pdf. Accessed 28 July 2006.

US Department of State, Office of the Geographer (1980) 'Ecuador–Peru boundary', *International Boundary Study*, 172, 19 May.

US International Trade Commission (2005) 'The impact of the Andean Trade Preferences Act', twelfth report, publication no. 3888.

Weidner, G.R. (1996) 'Operation safe border: the Ecuador–Peru crisis', *JFQ Forum*, 52–58.

Weisman, S.R. (2007) 'House panel approves a trade pact with Peru', *New York Times*, 26 September. Available from http://www.nytimes.com. Accessed 11 October 2007.

Yepes, E. (1998) *Perú–Ecuador, 1941–1942: Tres Dias de Guerra, Ciento Ochenta Dias de Negociaciones*, Lima: Universidad Nacional Agraria La Molina and Universidad del Pacifico.

# 9 Trading across the Straits

## Will a free trade agreement between China and Taiwan promote peace?

*Hank Lim*

### Introduction[1]

The relationship of China and Taiwan is a complicated one. It is necessary to provide some context to the current state of affairs since both sides increasingly appeal to different aspects of history to argue their case. It can also be quite daunting at times to understand why either side sometimes gets upset or provoked by the slightest change of terms.

The tension is seen by the government in Beijing as a legacy of an unfinished civil war. The fall of the Qing dynasty saw the declaration of the Republic of China (ROC) on 1 January 1912. However, for the next two decades, China fell into a period of internal chaos and disorder. The country was divided into provinces ruled by warlords by virtue of their command over private armies. By 1927, the Kuomintang (KMT) under Chiang Kai-Shek had more or less unified China and a capital was established in Nanjing from 1927 to 1937.[2] However the Chinese Communist Party (CCP) led by Mao Zedong continued to provide some resistance to the Nanjing government. Both sides continued their civil war, although the Nanjing government was recognised officially as representing the ROC.

In 1937, the Japanese launched a full-scale invasion of China that led to a temporary – if uneasy and often not observed – truce between the CCP led by Mao Zedong and the KMT. With the defeat of the Japanese in 1945, open civil war broke out between the KMT and the CCP.

In 1949, the KMT fled mainland China for Taiwan after it lost the civil war against the CCP. On 1 October 1949, Mao formally declared the establishment of the People's Republic of China (PRC). Both sides continued to claim that they represented 'China'. The importance of this claim is seen in the representation at the United Nations (UN). The ROC held the seat at the UN until 1971, when it was replaced by the PRC.

Many Taiwanese have challenged this version of the story as incomplete and being too 'mainland-centric'. For instance, the *Taiwan Yearbook 2005* published by the Taiwan Government Information Office (GIO) pointed out that Taiwan had 'been a neglected island before the 17th century'.[3] They argued that Taiwan had always been independent of China. In 1662, Jheng

Cheng-gong defeated the Dutch and established a government in opposition to the Qing dynasty. Taiwan only came under the Qing control in 1683. In 1895, it was ceded 'in perpetuity' to the Japanese under the terms of the Treaty of Shimonoseki in April 1895. This treaty was the peace treaty concluded between the Qing and Japanese after the former lost the first Sino-Japanese war in 1894–1895. Some of these Taiwanese historians argue that since Taiwan only came under the brief control of the Qing, it should not be seen as part of mainland China.

The terms of the return of Taiwan to the ROC is another point of contestation, with some Taiwanese arguing that General MacArthur only 'gifted' Taiwan to ROC after the Second World War with the legal status of Taiwan kept ambiguous.[4] An unfortunate episode in 1947 further tested the uneasy relationship between the 'mainlanders' and the 'Taiwanese', when the KMT governor of Taiwan, Chen Yi, put down unrest in Taiwan, killing thousands of people in the process. This episode has since been a symbol of the tension between the two protagonists.[5]

Since martial law was lifted in 1987, some forms of contact between China and Taiwan were allowed. However, the tension between the two remains palpable.

For the purposes of this chapter, the terms 'ROC' and Taiwan are used interchangeably. This is a simplifying definition since it is possible to imagine, though probably not politically feasible at the moment, a Taiwan not being the ROC but a new political entity. The term 'China' refers primarily to mainland China governed by the PRC. However, it could also be used to refer to the territory that both the PRC and ROC leaders, specifically Mao Zedong and Chiang Kai-Shek, had in mind when they talked about 'reunification'.[6]

## A free trade agreement as a means to promote peace

The purpose of this chapter is to investigate the extent to which a formalised agreement, specifically a free trade agreement (FTA), would help to mitigate tensions between the two entities. The term 'free trade agreement' was conventionally understood to refer to a preferential trade agreement (PTA) 'with tariffs eliminated entirely on goods produced in member countries'.[7] However, in the popular media, the term FTA is increasingly used to simply refer to the assortments of economic agreements such as 'closer economic partnership agreements' or 'comprehensive economic partnership agreements' or 'economic partnerships'. Although this chapter uses the term FTA to describe these economic agreements for simplicity, it is important to keep in mind that the coverage, length of implementation and details of these agreements differ widely.

The example of the European Union (EU) has often been cited as an exemplar of how closer economic cooperation and subsequently a security community could be formed through the formation of a customs union. This chapter examines the extent to which an FTA could play a part in mitigating tensions and promoting stability.

### Promoting interdependence

That FTAs might be used to increase interdependence should not be taken for granted. By itself, an FTA simply describes a kind of economic agreement. The actual efficacy of the agreement will depend on other factors such as the trade links between the two partners and complexity of the rules of origin (RO).[8]

The general conception that the likelihood of violent conflict decreases with greater interdependence (which raises the opportunity cost of conflict) is a popular notion. However, this conception depends on other factors. It is entirely plausible that there will be a greater likelihood of war, especially if one state is dependent on another for vital resources such as supply of fuel or raw materials. This dependence could also be in the form of relying on a particular trade partner for national development. One of the immediate causes of the war between Japan and the United States in 1941 was the imposition of an oil embargo on Japan by the US.

A refinement of the theory is the 'trade-expectation argument' by Copeland (1996). Copeland argues that peace will only be promoted when a state has a positive expectation of future trade. Hence, for a state that is dependent on another state, the possibility of war will increase if the state expects disruption to this trading relation.

FTAs also signal the importance of the political relationship between two states, representing a commitment to engage each other.[9] Such integration can be either economic or political. The EU is often cited as an example of how regional integration could take place through economic integration or a gradual 'spill over' of issues to finally encompass some form of political integration.[10]

### Limitations of FTAs

#### Every FTA is different

Ultimately, every FTA differs and is unique in its own right. These differences could relate to:

- the coverage of the trade in goods and services (i.e. how many goods and services actually receive a reduction of tariffs);
- the duration over which concessions are phased in;
- the RO (what conditions are needed for the goods to qualify for the preferential arrangement);
- the dispute settlement mechanism (DSM);
- differences between what has been agreed upon at the multilateral forum

and the bilateral agreement and the reality of what is taking place within the market (often the FTAs that are signed do not promise much more than whatever has been agreed under World Trade Organization (WTO) or other international agreement's obligations);

- the extent of trade facilitation and technical barriers to trade;
- the extent of inclusion determined by 'behind-borders' agreement such as competition policy and mutually recognised standards;
- the scope of coverage as well as exclusion of sensitive products.

*Political will to use institutions in the FTA*

Ultimately, even after an FTA is signed, it does not necessarily mean that the partners will use the institutional tools available under the FTA. Given the proliferation of forums and organisations (both regional and international), states could choose between resolution by political negotiation or by the WTO DSM or through the institutions agreed upon in the bilateral agreement. In the same line, many trade and investment agreements have been signed by the Association of South East Asian Nations (ASEAN) governments but many of them were not implemented.

One should not overstate the importance of formal economic agreements or even admission to the WTO (or its predecessor, General Agreements on Tariffs and Trade (GATT)).[11] Both China and Taiwan have developed rapidly without membership in GATT and the WTO (until 2001). Nor do FTAs guarantee increased economic interactions among partners. For instance, a number of the FTAs recently concluded among trading partners with small volumes of trade, such as Singapore and Bahrain or Singapore and Jordan, are unlikely to generate significant economic integration. Ultimately, an FTA should be seen as a step towards possible closer cooperation but not a panacea. It is possible that countries that are more open and globally integrated are more likely to promote bilateral or regional integration.

# China's policy towards Taiwan

## *Political relations*

Both sides set up quasi-official organisations to deal with some of the bilateral issues. In 1991, Taiwan established the Strait Exchange Foundation (SEF) while China set up the Association for Relations Across the Taiwan Strait (ARATS). In 1992, officials from both organisations held informal talks in Hong Kong that resulted in the '1992 consensus'. The consensus was an informal agreement reached orally between ARATS and SEF stipulating that both sides of the Straits adhere to the one-China principle but with different interpretations.[12]

In 1993, Wang Daohan, the president of ARATS, and the late Koo Chen-Fu, chairman of SEF, held formal talks in Singapore. The talks left difficult economic issues unresolved. In particular, Beijing wanted to institute direct air and sea links, which Taiwan refused. In retaliation, China rejected Taiwan's request for protection of its mainland investments. However, both sides agreed on ways to verify and compensate for lost mail, establish a framework for authenticating legal documents and facilitate follow-up meetings between the two organisations.

The second round of Wang–Koo talks was scheduled for May 1995 but it was postponed indefinitely after Taiwan's then president, Lee Teng Hui, made a visit to Cornell University (in the United States) in June. The relations between both sides also deteriorated with the Chinese conducting missile tests near Taiwan in July and August 1995 and in March in 1996.

In 1998, another round of talks was held in Shanghai. Significantly, the PRC had quietly dropped some conditions it had earlier demanded after the 1995–1996 cross-Straits missile crisis.[13] While the outcome was not substantial, it represented a return to the negotiating table by both sides.

There have been a number of shifts in China's strategy in handling the Taiwan issue. One of the first proposals was by Chinese Deng Xiaoping who introduced the concept of 'one country, two systems' in his 1984 'Guidelines on actions towards Taiwan'. While the terms have changed over the years, the idea that two different political systems could co-exist in a country has not intrinsically been accepted by the PRC. Its objective remains to reunify Taiwan. However, China's leaders seem to have gradually relaxed on the timeframe of the unification. It seems that Beijing is increasingly satisfied as long as Taiwan does not declare independence because China considers that time is more likely on its side.

### *Economic relations*

The evolution of the political relationship between the two should also be seen in the context of the deepening economic relationship between the two. There are two caveats to some of the figures used in this article. First, it is important to note that the trade and investment figures between China and Taiwan are complicated by the role of Hong Kong as a transit between the two countries. Many Taiwanese companies set up shell companies elsewhere in Asia, usually Hong Kong before investing in China. Hong Kong also plays a transshipment role in re-exporting some of the imports to other countries.

Second, the investment figures for China are complicated by the presence of 'round-tripping' in Hong Kong, whereby some of the Chinese firms set up shell companies in Hong Kong to invest in China. This is usually done in order for the Chinese firms to gain more favourable investment terms especially in terms of taxation. China also provides favourable land use rights and better administrative support for foreign investors than local ones.[14]

For most of the statistical information, we have used the figures from the Mainland Affairs Council (MAC), which is based in Taiwan. The reason for using the MAC figures is that they have provided estimates on both PRC and ROC figures.

*Trade patterns*

Since indirect trade was allowed between the two countries in 1987, trade between the two has increased dramatically.[15] In 1987, it was estimated by the MAC that the value of the total trade between China and Taiwan was US$1.5 billion. By 2004, this figure had gone up to US$6.6 billion. This is a 306 per cent increase. Trade between the two grew 33 per cent in 2004 from US$4.6 billion in 2003.

Taiwan was China's fifth largest trading partner in 2004. Taiwan was China's sixth largest exporter but second largest importer (after Japan) in 2004. This also shows the role played by China as the final stop of assembly for many of the East Asian states (see Table 9.1)

Based on the MAC estimate,[16] the share of Taiwanese imports as a portion of China's total imports has increased from 2.8 per cent in 1987 to 8 percent in 2004. The share of Chinese exports to Taiwan as a percentage of Chinese total exports has increased from 0.7 per cent in 1987 to 2.8 per cent in 2004. The percentage of Chinese trade with Taiwan, as a portion of total Chinese trade has increased from 2.1 per cent in 1987 to 5.3 per cent in 2004. From China's perspective, Taiwan is an important but not significant trading partner. It is difficult to get accurate statistics of China's trade with Taiwan because quite a lot of bilateral trade relations went through Hong Kong. Generally, Taiwan exports capital goods and higher end machinery and electronic products to China.

*Table 9.1* Mainland China foreign trade by country (area) (US$ hundred millions)

| Period | 2002 | | 2003 | | 2004 | | January–October 2005 | |
|---|---|---|---|---|---|---|---|---|
| | Exports | Imports | Exports | Imports | Exports | Imports | Exports | Imports |
| Japan | 484.4 | 534.7 | 594.2 | 741.5 | 735.1 | 943.7 | 686.9 | 811.8 |
| USA | 699.5 | 272.3 | 924.7 | 338.6 | 1,249.5 | 446.8 | 1,325.3 | 397.8 |
| Hong Kong | 584.7 | 107.4 | 762.9 | 111.2 | 1,008.8 | 118.0 | 969.9 | 101.1 |
| South Korea | 155.0 | 285.7 | 29.7 | 51.0 | 38.4 | 44.3 | 31.0 | 23.0 |
| Taiwan | 65.9 | 380.6 | 90.0 | 493.6 | 135.5 | 647.8 | 133.5 | 597.7 |
| Germany | 113.7 | 164.3 | 175.4 | 243.4 | 237.6 | 303.7 | 259.9 | 252.1 |
| Singapore | 69.7 | 70.5 | 88.7 | 104.8 | 126.9 | 140.0 | 132.0 | 133.7 |
| UK | 80.6 | 33.4 | 108.2 | 35.7 | 149.7 | 47.6 | 154.0 | 44.4 |
| France | 40.7 | 42.5 | 72.9 | 61.0 | 99.2 | 76.6 | 94.6 | 71.9 |
| Australia | 45.9 | 58.5 | 62.6 | 73.0 | 88.4 | 115.5 | 89.5 | 131.6 |
| Russia | 35.2 | 84.1 | 60.3 | 97.3 | 91.0 | 121.3 | 105.3 | 131.3 |

Source: China Foreign Economic Statistical Yearbook and China's Customs Statistics compiled by MAC. Available from http://www.mac.gov.tw/big5/statistic/em/156/27.pdf.

*Investment*

Again, we should bear the caveat in mind when looking at the figures for investments to China. In particular, it is difficult to determine how much of the high amount of investment of Hong Kong actually originates from Hong Kong due to the phenomenon of 'round-tripping'. It is also difficult to know how much of the investment from Hong Kong is from Taiwanese companies based there.[17]

From Table 9.2, we can see that 11.1 per cent of the total realised foreign direct investment (FDI) in China came from the British Virgin Islands in 2004. The source of investments is difficult to trace since the Virgin Islands is a tax haven and many companies operate investment holding companies or shell companies in order to qualify for preferential tax benefits.

Taiwan was China's sixth largest source of FDI in 2004, accounting for 5.1 per cent for the total realised Chinese investment. This is a slight decline of 7.7 per cent over the figures in 2003. Nevertheless, it is difficult to conclude that there is actually a decline in Taiwanese investment in China since we are uncertain as to the extent to which Taiwanese investment in China has been funnelled through Hong Kong or the British Virgin Islands.

Nevertheless, what is evident from the figures is that Taiwanese investment is an important source of capital for the Chinese economy. It is uncertain whether there is dependence of China on Taiwanese capital or vice versa. However, as the Taiwanese commercial stake in China increases, the PRC government has gained a stronger bargaining position vis-à-vis the ROC. The PRC can use the Taiwanese businesses to exert pressure on the ROC government. (Examples are discussed below.)

*Table 9.2* Sources of realised FDI in China (US$ millions)

| Country/Area | 2002 | | 2003 | | 2004 | |
|---|---|---|---|---|---|---|
| | *Amount* | *%* | *Amount* | *%* | *Amount* | *%* |
| Hong Kong, Macao | 18,329.31 | 34.75 | 18,116.70 | 33.86 | 19,546.60 | 32.24 |
| British Virgin Islands | 6,117.39 | 11.60 | 5,776.96 | 10.80 | 6,730.30 | 11.10 |
| Korea | 2,720.73 | 5.16 | 4,488.54 | 8.39 | 6,247.86 | 10.31 |
| Japan | 4,190.09 | 7.94 | 5,054.19 | 9.45 | 5,451.57 | 8.99 |
| US | 5,423.92 | 10.28 | 4,198.51 | 7.85 | 3,940.95 | 6.50 |
| Taiwan | 3,970.64 | 7.53 | 3,377.24 | 6.31 | 3,117.49 | 5.14 |
| Singapore | 2,337.20 | 4.43 | 2,058.40 | 3.85 | 2,008.14 | 3.31 |
| Germany | 927.96 | 1.76 | 856.97 | 1.60 | 1,058.48 | 1.75 |
| Others | 8,725.62 | 16.55 | 9,577.16 | 17.90 | 12,526.26 | 20.66 |
| Total | 52,742.86 | 100.00 | 53,504.67 | 100.00 | 60,627.65 | 100.00 |

Source: China Statistical Yearbook, *China Foreign Economic Statistical Yearbook and Intertrade*, published on MAC website, http://www.mac.gov.tw/big5/statistic/em/156/31.pdf.

Note: Any slight discrepancies in numbers are due to rounding.

*Tourism*

There has been a steady increase in the number of Taiwanese tourists to China since the two established some links in 1987, despite the absence of direct transport links between the two countries – except during the lunar New Year period. About 3.7 million Taiwanese tourists visited the mainland in 2004, which was a 35 per cent increase over 2003 (see Table 9.3). While the rate of increase was exaggerated by the low base in 2003 (it was low because of the outbreak of severe acute respiratory syndrome (SARS) in the region), it represented a 311 per cent increase over the figures in 1990. This represents an average annual growth rate of approximately 10.7 per cent over 14 years. Taiwanese tourists constitute the third largest source of tourists after Hong Kong (66.6 million) and Macao (21.9 million).[18]

The increase in visits also shows a trend towards broadening of the economic relationship between the two territories. Tourism did not seem to be affected by the ups and downs of the political relationship. Nevertheless, the increase in exchanges or more accurately interactions of the people on both sides do not seem to have diluted the Taiwanese sense of a separate identity. On the other hand, visitors from China are far fewer because of bureaucratic controls imposed by Taiwan's authorities.

*Table 9.3* Number of Taiwanese visitors to mainland China

|  | *Persons* | *Year on year growth* |
| --- | --- | --- |
| 1987–1989 | 1,044,479 | N/A |
| 1990 | 890,500 | 61.38 |
| 1991 | 946,632 | 6.30 |
| 1992 | 1,317,770 | 39.21 |
| 1993 | 1,526,969 | 15.88 |
| 1994 | 1,390,215 | −8.96 |
| 1995 | 1,532,309 | 10.22 |
| 1996 | 1,733,897 | 13.16 |
| 1997 | 2,117,576 | 22.13 |
| 1998 | 2,174,602 | 2.69 |
| 1999 | 2,584,648 | 18.86 |
| 2000 | 3,108,643 | 20.27 |
| 2001 | 3,440,306 | 10.67 |
| 2002 | 3,660,565 | 6.40 |
| 2003 | 2,730,891 | −25.40 |
| 2004 | 3,685,250 | 34.95 |
| *January–October 2005* | 3,513,900 | 13.82 |

Source: China Monthly Statistics and *China Travel Yearbook* produced by MAC, http://www.mac.gov.tw/big5/statistic/em/156/19.pdf.

Note: Taiwanese residents have been allowed to visit mainland China since November 1987.

*Use of FTAs by China*

China seems to have started to use FTA or the 'closer economic partnership agreement' (CEPA) to integrate Hong Kong and Macao with the mainland economy. In January 2004, the CEPA between China and Hong Kong came into effect. It was signed on 29 June 2003 and was notified to the WTO on 12 January 2004.[19] However, since then, there have been two other 'updates' or additions to the original agreement to expand the coverage and refine the rules.

Under the agreement, China agreed to eliminate all tariffs for a list of goods specified in Annex 1 of the agreement. The RO for the CEPA were also quite liberal with goods only needing 30 per cent value-added in Hong Kong to qualify for the preferential treatment.

The CEPA between China and Macao is almost identical to the Hong Kong CEPA. The only minor differences are the difference in agencies and regulations applicable in Hong Kong and Macao as well as the coverage of goods. However, other major components for instance, the main text, RO and requirements for entities operating in the Mainland are the same.[20]

*Lessons from these FTAs for Taiwan*

It is important to note that China is concerned that reunification be seen as beneficial for Hong Kong and Macao. Even though the gains from these CEPAs are limited and will not slow down the deindustrialisation of Hong Kong,[21] the terms are reasonably generous and liberal. It is likely that these CEPAs served as a signal to Taiwan that reunification would be rewarded economically. These CEPAs are also a means through which China could encourage greater dependence by Hong Kong and Macao on the Chinese economy. The CEPA with Hong Kong also acts as a signal to Hong Kong that China is determined to help revive the territory's economy after the SARS outbreak in 2003.[22]

## Taiwan's policy towards the mainland

*Political relations*

In 1949, the KMT lost the Chinese civil war in mainland China and fled to Taiwan. Members of the National Assembly moved to Taiwan and, in effect, the ROC continued to govern.[23] In all, about two million mainland Chinese fled to Taiwan. These mainlanders occupied key positions of authority. Martial law was declared in 1949, which was only lifted in 1987.

The unfortunate '228 Incident' occurred in 1947, when several thousands people were killed after the KMT governor Chen Yi put down unrest in Taiwan. This incident is controversial and was only allowed to be discussed after 1987. It has now become a common example used by many Taiwan nationalists as an example of how the mainlanders have oppressed the Taiwanese.[24] Such negative historical antecedents have helped to strengthen independent movement in Taiwan, especially in southern Taiwan.

After the death of Chiang Kai-Shek in 1975, Yen Chia-Kan briefly became the president. Chiang Kai-Shek's son, Chiang Ching-Kuo, then became the president of the ROC in 1978. Chiang Ching-Kuo introduced the policy of the 'three nos' in 1978, which signified 'no official contact, no official talks and no compromise'.

When Chiang Ching-Kuo passed away in 1988, Lee Teng Hui became the first Taiwanese-born leader of the KMT and correspondingly, for that time, president of Taiwan. Lee established the National Unification Council (NUC) in 1990 to convince the mainland government that Taiwan was committed to reunification.[25] However, the 'three nos' policy had gradually been put aside.[26] The meeting in Singapore between the heads of ARATS and SEF provided one of the most visible breaks in this policy.

The NUC established the National Unification Guidelines which consisted of four principles towards the goal of eventual unification. They included acceptance that the mainland and Taiwan are both Chinese territory and that unification was the 'common responsibility of all Chinese people'.

It was, however, Lee Teng Hui's visit to his Alma Mater, Cornell University, in June 1995 that caused possibly the most serious setback in the cross-Strait relations. The PRC saw it as a betrayal of the US' previous agreement of 'one China', as well as a broken promise by Secretary of State Warren Christopher not to grant a visa to Lee.[27] The People's Liberation Army (PLA) conducted military exercises in the Taiwan Strait between July and November 1995, including two rounds of missile testing.[28] By March 1996, with the PLA carrying out more military exercises, the US President Bill Clinton sent two aircraft carriers to the Straits as a show of US commitment to Taiwan.[29]

Another diplomatic tension in the Straits, though not as serious as in 1995–1996, occurred when President Lee publicly declared in an interview in July 1999 that the relations between Taiwan and the mainland was one of 'state-to-state relations', or at least 'special state-to-state relations'.[30] Lee's statement was seen as a clear desire to seek relations with the PRC on possibly an equal basis.[31] This time, the PRC did not adopt as strong a response as in 1996.[32] In fact, the Clinton administration also responded very differently from 1996. It criticised Lee for being a troublemaker and supported the PRC's view.[33] All along, at an official level, the US maintained a 'one China policy'.

### Economic relations

#### Lee Teng Hui's 'no haste, be patient' (NHBP) policy

The 1996 cross-Strait tension made Lee Teng-Hui realise the importance of not being overly dependent on China. In October 1996, President Lee addressed the eleventh meeting of the National Reunification Committee saying:

> To ensure the security and welfare of the 21 million fellowmen in Taiwan area is the bottom line of our survival and development. Therefore the starting point of our mainland policy must be to keep out roots in Taiwan, enhance construction, and strengthen our national power. We must show no haste, be patient, move steadily, and then go far.[34]

This NHBP policy was effectively a call for a review of Taiwan's then strategy of 'Taiwan–China development nexus'.[35] Under this, Taiwanese companies were barred from investing in infrastructure building and some high-tech industries in the mainland. They were not allowed to invest in any project exceeding US$50 million and were not allowed to put more than 20 per cent of their total assets into the mainland projects. Taiwanese investment in the mainland fell by 43 per cent and some companies such as the Formosa Plastic Group and President Enterprises postponed or cancelled some of their projects in the mainland.[36]

Even when the Taiwanese government allowed 'mini-three-links' (MTL) (transportation, postal and trade links) between China and Taiwan, beginning 1 January 2001, it only allowed these links to apply to the offshore islands of Kinmen and Matsu, rather than the entire Taiwan. Two of the main aims for the establishment of the MTL were to decriminalise activities such as smuggling and trespassing. The Taiwanese government hoped to boost the economy especially in terms of tourism in Kinmen and Matsu. Nevertheless, even such a small move was criticised by some Taiwanese as detrimental to Taiwan's security.[37]

### Proactive Liberalisation with Effective Management (PLEM)

With the slowdown in the global economy (due to 9/11 attacks on the US), as well as deteriorating domestic economic conditions, President Chen relaxed some of the restrictions on Taiwanese investment in the mainland. On 7 November 2001, the Taiwanese Executive Yuan changed its policy of NHBP to the 'proactive liberalisation with effective management (PLEM)'.[38]

The new policy would allow Taiwanese investors to invest in the mainland in more than 7,000 product categories. However, investment in 195 production categories, including upstream petrochemical industries and 12-inch silicon chip foundries, remained banned. The investment ceiling was also raised. For instance, only investment over US$20 million in the mainland needed to be screened on a case-by-case basis whereas investment below that amount would be approved after a 'simple screening process'.[39]

Nevertheless, Chen Shui-Bian has remained wary of being overly dependent on the Chinese economy.[40] In January 2006, he reiterated the need to tighten regulations on Taiwanese firms investing in mainland China, possibly in response to Chinese President Hu Jintao's call for direct transport links between the two countries.

### Existing trade relations

Regardless of the hesitation from the government, the figures show that the economic relations between Taiwan and China are deepening rapidly. If we use estimated figures from the MAC (or 'Mainland 2' in Table 9.4), we can see that China was Taiwan's largest trading partner in 2004, accounting for a total of US$61.6 billion, followed by Japan at US$56.9 billion and the US at US$50.5 billion.

In terms of exports, China is Taiwan's largest export market, absorbing an estimated US$45.0 billion in 2004. Hong Kong is Taiwan's second largest export market at US$29.9 billion.[41] The US is Taiwan's third largest export market at US$28.1 billion.

In terms of imports, Taiwan imported US$43.6 billion worth of products from Japan, its largest import partner in 2004. The second largest import partner is the US with about US$22.4 billion, followed by mainland China at US$16.7 billion.

Based on the estimates from MAC, Taiwan's trade dependence on China was 18.0 per cent in 2004.[42] If the composition of trade is broken down, China accounted for 9.9 per cent of Taiwan's imports and 25.8 per cent of its exports. This dependence seems to be increasing – in 1990, Taiwan's trade dependence on China was only 4.2 per cent. This increase in dependence on trade with China has been noted with alarm by the Taiwanese government.[43]

*Table 9.4* Taiwan's major trade partners (US$ hundred millions)

|  | 2002 | | 2003 | | 2004 | | January–October 2005 | |
| --- | --- | --- | --- | --- | --- | --- | --- | --- |
|  | *Exports* | *Imports* | *Exports* | *Imports* | *Exports* | *Imports* | *Exports* | *Imports* |
| US | 267.6 | 180.9 | 259.5 | 168.2 | 281.3 | 223.9 | 234.8 | 176.8 |
| Japan | 119.7 | 272.8 | 119.4 | 326.4 | 132.3 | 436.5 | 119.1 | 388.9 |
| Hong Kong | 308.5 | 17.4 | 283.7 | 17.3 | 298.8 | 20.9 | 251.4 | 15.8 |
| South Korea | 38.7 | 77.1 | 45.7 | 86.9 | 53.5 | 116.3 | 45.3 | 108.0 |
| Germany | 38.4 | 44.2 | 42.1 | 49.7 | 45.1 | 58.3 | 35.4 | 51.6 |
| Singapore | 43.8 | 35.4 | 49.8 | 38.7 | 63.4 | 42.9 | 61.7 | 40.2 |
| Malaysia | 31.3 | 41.5 | 30.5 | 47.5 | 40.7 | 54.1 | 34.8 | 42.9 |
| Holland | 37.7 | 14.4 | 41.3 | 12.9 | 54.2 | 21.8 | 35.6 | 17.2 |
| UK | 29.1 | 13.6 | 28.8 | 14.2 | 33.8 | 17.3 | 26.5 | 14.2 |
| Mainland (1) | 103.1 | 17.1 | 117.9 | 21.6 | 147.6 | 24.9 | 140.3 | 21.6 |
| Mainland (2) | 294.7 | 79.5 | 353.6 | 109.6 | 449.6 | 166.8 | 422.9 | 162.8 |

Source: MAC website, http://www.mac.gov.tw/big5/statistic/em/156/35.pdf.

Notes: Data for all countries except for the mainland figures are from the Monthly Statistics of Exports and Imports Taiwan Area, ROC; Mainland China (1) data comes from Hong Kong Customs Statistics; Mainland China (2) data are based on estimation from ROC MAC.

*Existing investment relations*

This dependence on China can also be seen in the investment figures. In Table 9.5, we can see that there is a divergence in figures between the approved figures by the ROC and the realised figures (based on the mainland Chinese government data). The amount of realised Taiwanese investment (based on mainland China data) has remained fairly constant since 1993 at around US$2.6 billion–US$4.0 billion. From the ROC perspective, it has also gradually increased the approved amount.

It seems that the Yangtze River Delta region is one of Taiwanese investors' favourite destinations in China. The Yangtze River Delta consists of the Jiangsu, Zhejiang provinces and the Shanghai municipality. It has been estimated that the region attracted 55 per cent of the total Taiwanese investment in China in 2004 (in 1993, the figure was only about 26 per cent). In contrast, both the share of Taiwanese investment in China received by Guangdong and Fujian provinces in the Pearl River fell from 48 per cent in 1993 to 28 per cent in 2004.[44] Regardless of the locality of the investments, there is recognition of a move of Taiwanese business interests towards the mainland.[45] Apparently, the Yangtze River Delta has more cultural affinity to most non-native Taiwanese businessmen as many of them came from this region. In addition, the Yangtze River Delta has better investment opportunities for Taiwan

*Table 9.5* Taiwan's investment in mainland China (US$ millions)

| Year | Approved by Ministry of Economic Affairs, ROC | | Official data from mainland China | | |
|------|-------|--------|----------|-----------------|----------|
| | Cases | Amount | Projects | Contracted amount | Realised amount |
| 1991 | 237 | 174.16 | 3,815 | 3,310.30 | 861.64 |
| 1992 | 264 | 246.99 | 6,430 | 5,543.35 | 1,050.50 |
| 1993 | 1,262 | 1,140.37 | 10,948 | 9,964.87 | 3,138.59 |
| 1994 | 934 | 962.21 | 6,247 | 5,394.88 | 3,391.04 |
| 1995 | 490 | 1,092.71 | 4,847 | 5,849.07 | 3,161.55 |
| 1996 | 383 | 1,229.24 | 3,184 | 5,141.00 | 3,474.84 |
| 1997 | 728 | 1,614.54 | 3,014 | 2,814.49 | 3,289.39 |
| 1998 | 641 | 1,519.21 | 2,970 | 2,981.68 | 2,915.21 |
| 1999 | 488 | 1,252.78 | 2,499 | 3,374.44 | 2,598.70 |
| 2000 | 840 | 2,607.14 | 3,108 | 4,041.89 | 2,96.28 |
| 2001 | 1,186 | 2,784.15 | 4,214 | 6,914.19 | 2,979.94 |
| 2002 | 1,490 | 3,858.76 | 4,853 | 6,740.84 | 3,970.64 |
| 2003 | 1,837 | 4,594.99 | 4,495 | 8,557.87 | 3,377.24 |
| 2004 | 2,004 | 6,940.66 | 4,002 | 9,305.94 | 3,117.49 |
| *January–September 2005* | 965 | 4,193.47 | 2,850 | 7,013.41 | 1,576.89 |

Source: 'Table 10: Taiwan Investment in Mainland China', MAC website, http://www.mac.gov.tw/big5/statistic/em/155/10.pdf.

Note: Includes the number of registration of previously unregistered investment.

businessmen compared to the Pearl River Delta in the south as it is more dominated by Hong Kong businessmen.

Taiwan has been wary of high-tech investments in mainland China by Taiwanese companies. In particular, the Taiwanese government is concerned about the semiconductor sector; Taiwan has among the largest computer maker industries globally, with about 73 per cent of their output coming from Taiwanese-owned factories in China in 2004.[46] Taiwan Semiconductor Manufacturing (TSM) is the only Taiwanese semiconductor firm to have received a formal approval to open a semiconductor plant in the mainland. However, this could be due to the fact that TSM is using an older technology, 'trailing edge technology', and is thus not seen as posing too much of a threat to the Taiwanese economy.[47]

Nevertheless, it is unlikely that the Taiwanese government has been successful in its opposition. It is not easy for the Taiwanese government to regulate Taiwanese companies especially since they could register overseas first before investing in China. For instance, Semiconductor Manufacturing International Corporation (SMIC or Zhongxin), which is based in Shanghai, is registered as an American company but it is led by a Taiwanese businessman.[48]

This does not mean that the Taiwanese government has given up trying to restrict the flow of capital.[49] For instance, in 2005 after China passed the Anti-Secession Law, the Taiwanese government began to strengthen regulations on Taiwanese companies such as Powerchip Semiconductor and ProMOS Technologies. Powerchip Semiconductor filed for government approval to set up an 8-inch wafer plant in China in 2004 but the approval was delayed. ProMOS Technologies is also facing a similar situation.[50]

The Taiwanese government has also charged a Taiwanese businessman Robert Tsao, a former chairman of United Microelectronics Corporation (UMC) with criminal 'breach of trust' over his involvement in setting up a Chinese company, Hejin Technologies, in 2001 despite a ban on Taiwanese semiconductor investment in China.[51]

Taiwan companies previously opened shell companies in Hong Kong but now are diverting through investment companies in tax havens e.g. Virgin Islands and Cayman Islands.[52] For instance, investments from Xunda Computer and Dafeng Computer are both registered as originating from British Virgin Islands but they are also subsidiaries of Mitac Computer and Quanta Computer in Taiwan.

Nevertheless, businesses with interests in cross-Strait economic ties have probably exerted some restraint on the Taiwanese leaders who might prefer independence.[53] The various commercial associations in Taiwan have also generally called for stability in February 2006 when Chen ceased the operations of the NUC.[54] It is uncertain as to the extent to which their call for restraint is heeded by either government on both sides of the Straits.

## Taiwan policy under Chen Shui-Bian

Chen Shui-Bian seems to be adopting a gradual but obvious move towards independence. First, he added the word 'Taiwan' to the ROC passports – a sign seen by the Chinese as a step moving towards a separate entity – in his first term of office. Second, he has continued to ask for entry to the UN but as Taiwan, rather than the 'Republic of China'.

In his inaugural speech after winning his first presidential elections in 2000, he said:

> I fully understand that, as the popularly elected 10th-term president of the Republic of China, I must abide by the Constitution, maintain the sovereignty, dignity and security of our country, and ensure the well-being of all citizens. Therefore, as long as the CCP regime has no intention to use military force against Taiwan, I pledge that during my term in office, I will not declare independence, I will not change the national title, I will not push forth the inclusion of the so-called 'state-to-state' description in the Constitution, and I will not promote a referendum to change the status quo in regard to the question of independence or unification. Furthermore, there is no question of abolishing the Guidelines for National Unification and the National Unification Council.[55]

The results of the 11 December 2004 elections were widely regarded as a setback for Chen Shui-Bian and his provocative policies against China.[56] The pro-independence parties (also known as the pan-blue parties) won the elections with a slim majority of 114 seats in the 225 member Legislative Yuan. The pan-green forces won 101 seats with the remaining 10 seats going to independent candidates.

However, in 2006, Chen raised the possibility of abolishing the NUC. The NUC had not met since April 1999. Its budget had also been cut drastically.[57] Chen pointed out that the guidelines and the council were 'absurd products of an absurd era'. The US, subsequently, condemned this provocative act.

## Separate Taiwanese identity

Since the political liberalisation of Taiwan in the 1980s, the sense of a Taiwanese identity has been growing stronger.[58] This has been one of the reasons for the wariness many Taiwanese feel about Chinese moves towards greater economic integration. For instance, if we were to look at the results of polls carried out by the MAC, the percentage of Taiwanese wanting unification as soon as possible has generally been less than 3.5%, with the latest poll conducted on November 2005 showing 2.1% of the people wanting unification immediately. The percentage of respondents wanting independence as soon as possible was 10.3 per cent. Most (37.7 per cent) favoured the status quo now and a decision later.[59] Having said that, most polls seem to show that most Taiwanese favour neither immediate unification nor independence. In a way, this means that there is still some room for manoeuvre by both Taiwanese and Chinese governments.[60]

Aside from polls, other Taiwanese have used other arguments to provide justification for Taiwanese independence, including re-examination of the terms of the various declarations in the late nineteenth and twentieth century such as the Shimonoseki Treaty, Cairo Declaration, San Francisco Treaty and the Mutual Defence Treaty (between the US and Taiwan).[61]

There have been missed opportunities by the PRC to win support from the Taiwanese. For instance, in September 1999, Taiwan suffered the strongest earthquake of the century (ranking 7.6 on the Richter scale). About 2,000 people were killed and over 8,000 injured. Many more were left homeless. However, the PRC insisted that any foreign emergency humanitarian agency obtain Beijing's approval before providing aid to Taiwan. The PRC's image in Taiwan was further damaged when it did not allow a Russian relief plane to fly over the mainland to Taiwan, causing a 12-hour delay.[62] Its initial offer of assistance was also relatively insignificant – US$100,000 in disaster aid and US$60,000 worth of relief supplies.[63] These and other diplomatic errors ended up alienating the Taiwanese people.[64]

### Breaking out of diplomatic isolation

Taiwan has been trying to break out of its international isolation by 'buying' allies especially in the smaller developing countries.[65] Where possible, it has tried to join regional and international organisations. For instance, it is a member of Asia-Pacific Economic Cooperation (APEC), Asian Development Bank (ADB) and the WTO. The strategy in gaining membership, or at least legitimacy for its bid for membership, includes arguing for the right for representation by the Taiwanese people (and that Taiwan or China cannot speak for the other), contrasting the democratic credibility of Taiwan against the communist regime,[66] or simply as an economic or 'health entity'.

Although China objects to Taiwan participating in international organisations, it tolerates Taiwanese participation if 'statehood' is not a criterion. For instance, Taiwan's twelfth successive bid of joining the UN General Assembly was rejected in 2004. While Taiwan has slightly more success in joining some organisations, namely APEC and WTO, it has been unsuccessful, for the eighth time, in its attempt to join the World Health Organization (WHO) in 2004 as a 'health entity'.[67] This failure also gives an indication of the concern China has regarding creeping moves (in its own perception) towards Taiwanese independence.[68]

## China–Taiwan FTA

*Is an FTA the best way forward?*

One proposal of mitigating the conflict is to promote greater cross-Strait relations. An FTA is a possibility, or something akin to the CEPA between China and Hong Kong, or China and Macao.

The Taiwan government has recognised that closer economic integration is part of the mainland Chinese's strategy to reintegrate Taiwan. Hence Taiwan has generally been reluctant to liberalise its economic relations with China. For instance, the two countries do not yet have direct transportation links except for festive seasons and in localised areas. There are also restrictions on high-tech investments in mainland. Taiwan is wary of economic integration with mainland China. Instead, it has sought FTAs with other partners, such as the US, Japan and Singapore partially to break out of the diplomatic isolation.

*What are the other considerations for an FTA?*

There is also a case of legal ambiguity even if an FTA is signed. That is, if there were to be a commercial dispute between the two, would the dispute be settled at the WTO or at the bilateral level or in Chinese courts? Given that mainland China sees Taiwan as part of China, it is not unthinkable that the Chinese would insist that it is a domestic issue and ought to be handled by the Chinese courts rather than at the international level.

One should have realistic expectations of what the FTA can accomplish. That both China and Taiwan are members in various regional and international organisations such as ADB, APEC and WTO and yet serious tensions remain suggests that there can be occasions when political exigencies override common memberships.[69]

Despite the common membership in the WTO, Taiwan has still maintained several restrictions on trade with China. For instance, it was reported in the Taiwanese media that Taiwan would not provide China's agricultural and service products the same reciprocal treatment. It has invoked Article 13 of the WTO Agreement, arguing that its national security would be jeopardised.[70]

Cooperation between the two in the WTO is at a minimum. For instance, in a letter to the periodical *Business Week*, the director of the Information Division, Yih de Jung-Tzung of the Taipei Economic and Cultural Office was adamant in insisting that Taiwan was not a part of mainland China. He added 'it is a mischaracterization to count Taiwan among China's three votes' in the WTO. Indeed, Taiwan's representatives are there to advocate only the interests of Taiwan. They have and will exercise the right to vote differently from China's representatives in WTO decisions.[71]

China too has invoked WTO clauses against Taiwan.[72] Taiwan maintains a large trade surplus with China, which puts it in a vulnerable position.[73] For instance, in March 2001, China initiated an anti-dumping investigation against cold-rolled steel imported from Taiwan. Given that Taiwan exported 45 per cent of its total 2.6 million tons of cold-rolled steel to China, this investigation had serious economic implications for Taiwanese commercial interests. Less than a week later, China announced another anti-dumping investigation on PVC imports from Taiwan; in this case, China absorbs 80 per cent of Taiwan's total PVC exports.

China was also able to pressurise the Taiwan Plastic Industries Association to be the lead contact agency.[74] In fact, in both cases, China did not go through the Taiwanese government but consulted directly with the various commercial associations. By reaching directly to these commercial associations with direct interests, China has managed to marginalise the Taiwanese government and to force the Taiwanese government to open its market to Chinese markets.[75]

While APEC is a much looser economic forum, its annual leaders' summit provides a useful forum politically for the leaders of the members to meet. China has been insistent in preventing high-level Taiwanese representatives from attending these annual summits. If Taiwan President Chen had thought of increasing the level of political visibility through such forums, he would have to try harder.[76] For instance, only economic ministers from Taiwan are allowed at these APEC summits. Things turned quite unpleasant at the 2001 APEC summit held in Shanghai when the Taiwanese delegation withdrew from the summit after China rejected the Taiwanese choice of sending former Vice-President Li Yuan-zu for the annual summit. (China viewed Li as too political.)[77]

Perhaps, ironically, it might be easier to secure an FTA between the two if Taiwan were able to declare independence and negotiate as a sovereign state. This would allow the Taiwanese people's aspirations for international recognition to be fulfilled and reduce their fears of being subsumed into the Chinese polity. However, this scenario is likely to result in a war between the two since independence for Taiwan is likely to significantly reduce the legitimacy of the CCP leadership.

## Conclusion

It is difficult to see how an FTA would happen between China and Taiwan at least under the current Taiwanese leadership. While the implicit assumption of the research agenda is to find the best way to improve the political relationships between China and Taiwan via economic integration, such economic integration is seen as a threat by Taiwan. A formal FTA would require the political will of both governments. At the moment, this will is missing.

The bilateral relation between China and Taiwan must be seen not just at the domestic level but also at the larger geopolitical conditions of the region.

This relationship is complicated by the dynamics of other bilateral relations, particularly Sino-Japanese and more importantly, Sino-US relations.

Unless the Sino-Japanese relations improve, Taiwan would be able to count on Japanese support to keep its distance from China. Japan has a historical relationship with Taiwan as it was Taiwan's colonial master for about five decades. Japan wrested Taiwan from the then Qing dynasty after winning the Sino-Japanese war in 1894–1895. However, unlike the other Asian countries such as South Korea, China and some of the Southeast Asian states, the people in Taiwan do not seem to bear as much of a grudge against Japan for its imperial behaviour in the late nineteenth century to the end of the Second World War.[78]

The Sino-Japanese relationship itself is too complicated to be sufficiently reviewed here. Prime Minister Shinzo Abe, the successor of Koizumi, has demonstrated his interest to patch up relations with China by visiting China first after he became the new prime minister. The regular visit to the Japanese shrine by Koizumi, despite the protests of its Asian neighbours, has been one of the main reasons for the deterioration of ties between China and Japan.

Ultimately, however, it is the quality of the Sino-US relations that is the most consequential for Sino-Taiwanese relations. Taiwan needs the political support of the US in order to keep its distance from China. It is with the supply of advanced military technology as well as the presence of the US Seventh Pacific Fleet that has allowed Taiwan to maintain an independent political existence. When the Sino-Taiwanese relations deteriorated dramatically in 1996 with the Chinese conducting war games off the coast of Taiwan, the then US President Bill Clinton sent two carrier groups to the region. In June 1998, Clinton articulated his administration's Taiwan policy in what was known as the 'three nos policy'. Under this policy, the US agreed that there would be:

- no US support for independence for Taiwan;
- no support for a two-China or 'one China, one Taiwan' policy;
- no support for Taiwan's admittance into any international organisation that requires statehood for membership.

The Sino-US relations deteriorated in the early period of George W. Bush's presidency when the US State Department spokesman Richard Boucher announced that the Bush administration intended to drop Clinton's 'three nos' policy on Taiwan. However, after 9/11, Sino-US relations turned much warmer as the Chinese supported Bush in his 'war against terror'. With the six-party talks in limbo, it is likely that the US will continue to maintain a somewhat close relation with China to exert pressure on the North Koreans.

Ultimately, even if Taiwan declares independence, it is uncertain as to which major country would dare to recognise it given that China is likely to impose high political and economic costs on offending countries. It is very unlikely that any of the Southeast Asian states would do so. If China can maintain a close relationship with the US, it is unlikely that there will be a major incident over Straits.

Despite no visible prospects of a formal FTA between China and Taiwan, closer economic cooperation driven by market consideration is proceeding without much official interruptions from both sides of the Straits of Taiwan. Without doubt closer economic links between the contending parties and increasing economic stakeholders in the region has contributed to stability and the present 'status quo' equilibrium.

## Notes

1  In mainland China, names are conventionally spelt using '*hanyu pinyin*', which is the Chinese phonetics whereas names are spelt in the Wades–Giles system. Both *hanyu pinyin* and the Wades–Giles spelling are used interchangeably in this chapter depending whichever has the greater currency.

2  This period is commonly known as the 'Nanjing decade'. After the full-scale Japanese invasion of China, Chiang moved the capital to Wuhan and then to Chongqing (until the end of the Second World War).

3  See the 'History' section of the *Taiwan Yearbook 2005*. Available from http://www.gio.gov.tw/taiwan-website/5-gp/yearbook/p042.html#1 (accessed 26 February 2006).

4  Chai (1986: 1315).

5  In 2006, Chiang Kai-Shek was named responsible for the massacre. See 'Taiwan marks 1947 massacre for the first time since Chiang implicated', *Agence France Presse*, 28 February 2006. Accessed through LexisNexis.

6  This is not problematic since claims by both leaders shift over time. See Phillips (2001) for an account of the shifting claims of the KMT over Taiwan during 1941–1945. Nevertheless, for our discussion here, it suffices to say that 'China' primarily refers to the territory of mainland China and the island Taiwan.

7  Panagariya (2000: 288) defined a PTA as 'a union between two or more countries in which lower tariffs are imposed on goods produced in the member countries than on goods produced outside'. The definitions in this paragraph are taken from Panagariya (2000: 288) unless otherwise specified.

8  Brenton and Manchin (2003) provide a case of the RO in the case of the agreements the EU has concluded with its partners, particularly those in the Balkans and the least developed countries. Brenton and Manchin pointed out that these agreements have largely not been effective in increasing market access for the developing countries or the agreement partners because of the stringent conditions of the RO.

9  Especially with the current proliferation of FTAs.

10  This logic is a neofunctionalist one. See Haas (1958). Although Haas subsequently claimed that his theory was obsolete, the concept of integration via economic means with the EU as the prime example has captured the popular imagination.

11  Mallon and Whalley (2004: 7) cite Taiwan as an extreme example of countries achieving remarkable long term export growth without formal WTO membership.

12  Taiwanese President Chen Shui-Bian has recently denied that there was a '1992 consensus'. Taipei Mayor Ma Ying-Jeo has criticised Chen's denial. See 'DPP should not deny existence of "1992 Consensus": KMT Chairman', Xinhua General News Service, 23 February 2006.

13  See Cabestan (1999: 142). See also 'China and Taiwan: first steps', *Economist*, 24 October 2000. Accessed through LexisNexis.

14  For more information on the phenomenon of round-tripping, see Xiao (2004).

15 Figures in this paragraph are taken from MAC website, unless otherwise stated.

16 Figures in this paragraph are taken from http://www.mac.gov.tw/big5/statistic/em/156/9.pdf, unless otherwise stated.

17 See 'Three links mean pain before gain', *South China Morning Post*, 24 February 2006. Accessed through LexisNexis.

18 Figures taken from China National Tourist website, http://www.cnto.org/chinas tats.asp (accessed 28 February 2006).

19 The term CEPA is chosen probably because China sees CEPA as an arrangement between a customs territory and sovereign state. See Wong and Chan (2003: 1).

20 Antkiewicz and Whalley (2004).

21 See Wong and Chan (2003).

22 Hong Kong was badly affected by the SARS. Unemployment rate rose to 7.8 per cent in the three months from February to April 2003, a record level not seen since mid-2000. See http://news.bbc.co.uk/2/hi/business/3043419.stm (accessed 11 June 2008).

23 This National Assembly was only abolished in 2005.

24 This also partially explains why many Taiwanese thought that the Japanese rule (the Japanese had colonised Taiwan prior to the Second World War) was preferable to the KMT. See 'Beijing's wrath over claims of Japanese education legacy finds little echo in Taiwan', *Financial Times* (Asia Edition 1), 9 February 2006. Accessed through LexisNexis.

25 This NUC was abolished by President Chen Shui-Bian in 2006. See 'Defiant Chen scraps unity body; Beijing warns of crisis but Taiwanese president says termination of Unification Council is not aimed at changing status quo', *South China Morning Post*, 28 February 2006. Accessed through LexisNexis.

26 'SER secretary-general: 'It's time to review three nos policy', Central News Agency (Taiwan), 20 March 1993. Accessed through LexisNexis.

27 See the PRC foreign ministry's press statement, 'Chinese FM statement on US allowing Lee Teng-Hui's visit', Xinhua News Agency, 23 May 1995. Accessed through LexisNexis.

28 See 'China may escalate its fear tactics in pursuit of reunification with Taiwan to the point of an armed skirmish', *South China Morning Post*, 16 August 1995. Accessed through LexisNexis.

29 China moves to calm Taiwan strait storm', Agence France Presse, 14 March 1996. Accessed through LexisNexis.

30 As an example of the furious reaction from the Chinese media, see 'No explanation can cover up aim of "Two States"', *People's Daily* online, 1 August 1999, http://english.people.com.cn/english/199908/01/enc_19990801001002_TopNews.html (accessed 11 June 2008).

31 'Special state-to-state spell out solid truth: Chen', Central News Agency (Taiwan), 27 December 1999. Accessed through LexisNexis.

32 For an account from the PRC's perspective on the episode and Beijing's view of Lee more broadly, see Sheng (2002: 11–39).

33 See Cabestan (2000: 173).

34 Cited from Ho and Leng (2004: 734–735).

35 Ibid.: 734.

36 Cheng (1997: 49).

37 See 'Editorial says three small links with China threaten Taiwan's security', Text taken from *Taipei Times*, BBC Monitoring International Reports, 22 August 2005. Accessed through LexisNexis.

38 Cited from the question and answer section of the MAC website, http://www.mac.gov.tw/english/index1-e.htm (accessed 11 June 2008).

39 'Executive Yuan passes easing of no haste, be patient policy', Central News Agency (Taiwan), 7 November 2001. Accessed through LexisNexis.

40 'President Chen stresses need to manage China investment', Central News Agency (Taiwan), 17 January 2006. Accessed through LexisNexis.

41 This value might have included Taiwan's trade with mainland China.

42 This figure is taken from table 8 in 'The share of cross-Strait trade in Taiwan total foreign trade', http://www.mac.gov.tw/big5/statistic/em/156/8.pdf (accessed 11 June 2008).

43 See the section on 'Economic ties with China', on the GIO website, http://www.gio.gov.tw/taiwan-website/5-gp/brief/info04_8.html (accessed 11 June 2008).

44 'Yangtze River delta lures Taiwanese entrepreneurs', Xinhua News Agency, 10 December 2005. Accessed through LexisNexis.

45 'China – You give me fever: many Taiwanese making their move to the mainland', China Online, 22 May 2001. Accessed through LexisNexis.

46 'War threats from China get trumped by a corporate love story in Taiwan', Associated Press, 14 March 2005. Accessed through LexisNexis.

47 'UMC admits China proxy war; Taiwanese semiconductor maker says it uses ally He Jian to break into the mainland but denies violating regulation', *South China Morning Post*, 19 February 2005. Accessed through LexisNexis.

48 'Shanghai Park seals US$1.4b deal', *South China Morning Post*, 19 October 2000. Accessed through LexisNexis.

49 See also 'Taiwan firms slow China investment: cross strait tension cools interest in mainland as eyes turn to low-cost Vietnam', *The Nikkei Weekly* (Japan), 4 July 2005. Accessed through LexisNexis.

50 'Taiwan's powerchip still awaiting govt approval for China plant', AFX-Asia, 12 January 2006. Accessed through LexisNexis.

51 'Fettered by politics Taiwan should review its unrealistic China investment policies', *Financial Times*, 12 January 2006. Accessed through LexisNexis.

52 Ohashi (2006: 84–85).

53 Chan (2004: 55) cites the example of EVA Airways, a supporter of DPP, which had been 'particularly unhappy about the lack of progress in launching direct air travel across the Taiwan Straits'.

54 'Taiwan business groups hope for peace, prosperity', Asia Pulse, 1 March 2006. Accessed through LexisNexis.

55 See Chen (2000).

56 Chan (2004: 58).

57 'Taiwan leader calls for end of Unification Council', *New York Times*, 31 January 2006, from http://www.nytimes.com/2006/01/31/international/asia/31cnd-taiwan.html?ex=1296363600&en=e3f6e93d4ce494a0&ei=5088&partner=rssnyt&emc=rss (accessed 11 June 2008).

58 See 'The islanders are developing a distinct identity', *Economist*, 15 January 2005, Volume 374, Issue 8409.

59 The results of the polls can be seen on http://www.mac.gov.tw/english/index1e.htm (accessed 11 June 2008).

60 See also Wang and Liu (2004).

61 See, for instance, Chai (1986).

62 See remarks by ROC Foreign Minister Jason Hu in 'ROC grateful for foreign relief aid: foreign minister', Central News Agency (Taiwan), 24 September 1999. Accessed through LexisNexis.

63 See 'With subtle dig for sovereignty, China promises aid to Taiwan', Associated Press, 21 September 1999. Accessed through LexisNexis. See also Cabestan (2000: 175).

64 See 'Quake politics deals blow to Cross-straits ties', *The Straits Times*, 25 October 1999. Accessed through LexisNexis.

65 See 'The Two China woos one Pacific', *The Australian*, 13 February 2006. Accessed through LexisNexis.

66 See 'Shifting strategy', *Taiwan News*, 20 September 2004. Accessed through LexisNexis.
67 'MOFA slams China for blocking WHO bid', *China Post*, 19 May 2004. Accessed through LexisNexis.
68 See also 'Chinese paper comments on gradual Taiwan independence', Renmin Ribao website peopledaily.com, BBC Monitoring International Reports, 12 February 2004. Accessed through LexisNexis.
69 Although the ROC was one of the founding members of the GATT, it resigned from its position in 1950. It lost the observer status in 1971. On 1 January 2002, Taiwan joined the WTO as a separate customs territory of Taiwan, Penghu, Kinmen and Matsu.
70 See 'Officials urge China, Taiwan WTO talks', *Taipei Times*, 14 April 2005, http://www.taipeitimes.com/News/biz/archives/2005/04/14/2003250449 (accessed 11 June 2008).
71 Yih (2002).
72 Here we take a view that is more nuanced than Cai (2005: 592–594), who has neglected to sufficiently examine how the PRC used the WTO for political leverage over the Taiwanese. However, Cai's argument that Taiwan's interest could be 'better protected and promoted by active involvement in, rather than absence from, the process of movements toward FTA in the region' was probably correct though. Taiwan does not seem to have been successful in this aspect.
73 Indeed without its trade surplus with China, Taiwan would have been running trade deficits since the 1990s.
74 See Cho (2005: 747–748).
75 Cho (2005).
76 Wu (2002: 36–37).
77 See 'Premier regrets Beijing's refusal to invite Taiwan to APEC summit', Central News Agency (Taiwan), 19 October 2001. Accessed through LexisNexis.
78 For a review of the issue of Taiwan in Japan's security consideration, see Yoshihide (2001). Yoshihide's argument that Japan's policy towards Taiwan has been driven more by its US security arrangement and its reluctance to be involved in Cold War major powers' strategic issues overstates the passivity of Japan's Taiwan policy.

## References

Antkiewicz, A. and Whalley, J. (2004) 'China's new regional trade agreements', NBER working paper no. 10992, Cambridge: National Bureau of Economic Research.
Brenton, P. and Manchin, M. (2003) 'Making EU agreements work: the role of rules of origins', *World Economy*, 26:5, 755–769.
Cabestan, J.-P. (1999) 'Taiwan in 1998: an auspicious year for the Kuomintang', *Asian Survey*, 39:1, 140–147.
Cabestan, J.-P. (2000) 'Taiwan in 1999: a difficult year for the island and the Kuomintang', *Asian Survey*, 40:1, 172–180.
Cai, K. (2005) 'The China–ASEAN free trade agreement and Taiwan', *Journal of Contemporary China*, 14:45, 585–597.
Chai, T. (1986) 'The future of Taiwan', *Asian Survey*, 26:12, 1309–1323.
Chan, S. (2004) 'Taiwan in 2004: electoral contests and political stasis', *Asian Survey*, 45:1, 54–58.
Chen, S.B. (2000) 'Taiwan stands up: advancing to an uplifting Era', English translation of inauguration speech by Republic of China President Chen Shui-Bian,

Office of the President, Republic of China. Available from http://www.gio.gov.tw/taiwan-website/5-gp/rights/general_01.htm. Accessed 19 June 2008.

Cheng, T.-J. (1997) 'Taiwan in 1996: from euphoria to melodrama', *Asian Survey* 37:1, 43–51.

Cho, H.-W. (2005) 'China–Taiwan tug of war in the WTO', *Asian Survey* 45:5, 736–755.

Copeland, D. (1996) 'Economic interdependence and war: a theory of trade expectations', *International Security*, 20:4.

Haas, E. (1958) *The Uniting of Europe: Political, Social and Economic Forces 1950–1957*, Stanford, CA: Stanford University Press.

Ho, S.-Y. and Leng, T.-K. (2004) 'Accounting for Taiwan's economic policy towards China', *Journal of Contemporary China*, 13:41, 7433–7462.

Mallon, G. and Whalley, J. (2004) 'China's post accession WTO stance', NBER Working Paper, 10649, Cambridge: National Bureau of Economic Research.

Ohashi, H. (2006) 'China's regional trade and investment profile', in David Shambaugh (ed.) *Power Shift: China and Asia's New Dynamics*, Berkeley, CA: University of California Press.

Panagariya, A. (2000) 'Preferential trade liberalisation: the traditional theory and new developments', *Journal of Economic Literature*, 38:2, 287–331.

Phillips, S. (2001) 'Confronting colonisation and the national identity: the nationalists and Taiwan: 1941–1945', *Journal of Colonialism and Colonial History*, 2:3.

Sheng L. (2002) *China and Taiwan: Cross-Strait Relations under Chen Shui-Bian*, Singapore: Institute of Southeast Asian Studies.

Wang, T.Y. and Chou Liu, I. (2004) 'Contending identities in Taiwan: implications for cross-strait relations', *Asian Survey*, 44:4, 568–590.

Wong, J. and Chan, S. (2003) 'China's closer economic partnership arrangement (CEP) with Hong Kong: a gift from Beijing?' EAI background brief, no. 174, Singapore: East Asian Institute.

Wu, Y.-S. (2002) 'Taiwan in 2001: stalemated on all fronts', *Asian Survey*, 42:1, 29–38.

Xiao, G. (2004) 'People's republic of China's round-tripping FDI: scale, causes, and implications', Asian Development Bank Institute, discussion no. 7. Available from http://www.adbi.org/files/2004.06.dp7.foreign.direct.investment.people.rep.china.implications.pdf. Accessed 11 June 2008.

Yih J.-T. (2002) 'At the WTO, Taiwan's is an independent voice', *Business Week*. Accessed through LexisNexis.

Yoshihide, S. (2001) 'Taiwan in Japan's security considerations', *China Quarterly*, 165, 130–146.

# 10 Conclusion

## The role of regional trade integration in conflict prevention

*Oli Brown, Mzukisi Qobo and Alejandra Ruiz-Dana*

### Trading enemies for partners

Our world is being reshaped by the competing forces of globalisation and regionalism. As new economic and political powers emerge, the centre of gravity of the world's economy is shifting away from the old pact of economic strength that straddled the north Atlantic. Trade is one of the principal drivers of that change.

Since the General Agreement on Tariffs and Trade (GATT) was signed in January 1948, the international community has launched successive rounds of negotiations to reduce the barriers to the trade in goods and services and to harmonise the numerous regulations that govern international trade. As the easily negotiated 'low-hanging fruit' was picked off, the negotiations became more protracted and complex. Meanwhile, the sense (and plentiful evidence) that international trade liberalisation has not benefited all countries equally has made those negotiations more acrimonious.

The latest round of trade talks was dubbed the 'Doha development agenda' when launched by the members of the World Trade Organization (WTO) in November 2001. It has since foundered on the intransigent negotiating positions of both sides, and is likely to stutter on for a few more years before completion. However, pro-liberalisation countries are not kicking their heels waiting for the Doha round to finish. The difficulty of reaching multilateral agreement, and the intense media spotlight that shines on each ministerial meeting of the WTO, means that the trade liberalisation agenda is increasingly being pursued behind closed doors in bilateral and regional agreements rather than under the uncomfortable glare of multilateral negotiation. In other words, the WTO is no longer the only game in town – if, indeed, it ever was. There is a fundamental tension between multilateralism and unilateralism to which regionalism offers a 'third way'.

Received wisdom suggests that trade fosters interdependence between countries, that trade agreements can help to manage disagreements between countries and that trade integration can bind countries' divergent national interests to a common future. The European Union (EU) was an explicit experiment in trying to 'design' conflict out of a system. Regardless of its political effectiveness, as a form of internal conflict prevention it has been wildly successful. Nearly 60 years after the creation of the European Coal and Steel Community, European trade integration has transformed a continent that had previously started many of the world's bloodiest wars into a stable, democratic grouping of 27 nations – with more queuing to join.

But as the studies within this volume underline, peace is by no means an automatic outcome of trade integration. The EU experiment is not universally applicable; the driving forces of regionalism will vary from region to region. Integration is a political as well as an economic process. It is almost always about more than just functional trade complementarities and there are always more political and strategic interests at work. However, the political economy of trade integration is still poorly understood.

This book is the culmination of an 18-month multi-continent comparative research project, which has tried to assess the impact of regional trade integration on conflict prevention and management. Throughout the project two core questions have guided the research. The first is of the 'chicken and egg' variety: is peace a product of trade or does trade flow from peace? More specifically, what are some of the conditions under which trade can help (or hinder) political rapprochement? The second is more institutional and functional: namely what sort of institutions and mechanisms need to be in place for trade integration to be supportive of conflict prevention and dispute resolution? The rest of this concluding chapter tackles each of these questions in turn.

## Finding sequential meaning in the trade conflict relationship

### *The trade–conflict linkage*

The idea that trade promotes peace is attributed to several classical liberal thinkers. In his monumental work, *The Spirit of the Laws*, French political philosopher Charles de Secondat, the Baron of Montesquieu (1689–1755), declared that 'the natural effect of commerce is to bring about peace. Two nations which trade together render them reciprocally dependent: if one has an interest in buying the other has an interest in selling; and all unions are based upon mutual needs' (Cohler *et al.* 1989).

Later, the concept of trade diplomacy came to be known as Cobdenism. It was named after Richard Cobden, the British politician who, together with John Bright, led the Anti-Corn Law movement[1] and formed the Manchester School.[2] Cobden defined trade as a moral issue, as it upholds the right of people to exchange the fruits of their labour and, consequently, draws 'men together, thrusting aside the antagonism of race, and creeds and language, and uniting us in the bonds of eternal peace' (Cohler *et al.* 1989).

Similarly, French economist Frédéric Bastiat (1801–1850) emphasised the political benefits of trade. He observed that when borders impede the flow of goods, armies will cross borders. Later, Ludwig von Mises, an influential

Austro-Hungarian economist and one of the staunchest defenders of capitalism (1881–1973), argued that government interference was the main culprit in the incidence of conflict amongst nations. Interference 'creates conflicts for which no peaceful solution can be found' (Von Mises 1996) by setting up trade and migration barriers or, more specifically, by engaging in mercantilism.[3] In this sense, he agreed with Adam Smith's (1723–1790) invisible hand concept; the market would work itself out without the need for government to intervene. People, as rational actors, will choose to exchange goods to improve their lot since no one is fit to produce everything.

Along with Adam Smith, David Ricardo (1772–1823) provided much of the material upon which liberal economic and political theories are based. According to him, trade is a positive-sum game for all interested actors as it allows them to focus on their comparative advantages. By opening up to trade, nations improve their well-being as they are able to purchase goods whose production is cheaper elsewhere, while expanding the market for their own products. Protectionism, on the other hand, only benefits a minority at the expense of the majority.

Recently, classical liberal thinking has sparked empirical studies to determine whether there is a positive connection between trade and conflict. Oneal and Russet (1997) have found that bilateral trade flows reduce the risk of war, particularly if the level of these trade flows is high, as this augments the opportunity cost of conflict. Mansfield and Pevehouse (2000) argue that the institutional context (trade agreements, regional integration schemes, etc.) influences the effect trade has on bilateral relations. Countries that belong to the same trading bloc (or preferential trade agreement (PTA)) are less likely to engage in disputes than non-trading countries.

Other studies have found that trade constitutes a stronger disincentive to engage in conflict when it occurs between contiguous states, which are usually more conflict-prone (Gartzke 2000). More recently, Gartzke and Li (2005) have estimated that capitalism's contribution to international peace far outweighs that of politics or democracy. They argue that nations with very low levels of economic freedom are 14 times more likely to experience conflict than the freest states.[4] Polachek and Seiglie (2006) find that any unfavourable gains from trade reduce the marginal cost of conflict, and that, 'only through mutual dependence can an equilibrium come about where peace remains solid and secure, so that neither party is motivated to change the status quo'.

Other variables have been (and have to be) taken into account. Democracy is considered a necessary ingredient by some; together with trade, it constitutes much of the liberal peace theory.[5] In particular, democracy allows those interest groups that have much to lose from a potential conflict to influence foreign policy with their vote (Russett and Oneal 2001). Others argue that democracy might come after trade; that is, trade promotes economic development, which ultimately results in democracy.

Criticisms include that of Barbieri (1996, 2002) who argues that trade can actually cause conflict. Yet, according to Oneal *et al.* (2003), this conclusion

234 Oli Brown, Mzukisi Qobo and Alejandra Ruiz-Dana

does not take diverging military capabilities into account; less capable states are unlikely to attack those with superior capacity to engage in warfare. Seiglie (2002) points out that trade-generated wealth allows countries to purchase military equipment, which can provoke tensions between partners. Polachek and Seiglie (2006) find that this connection between increased military spending and conflict is unclear; military equipment is more likely to be used against non-trading partners to protect gains from trade.

These studies principally focused on the likelihood of conflict erupting between trading partners. Quite apart from significant selection bias (countries that trade already are likely to have solved many of their disputes already), they do not specifically address the difficulty or likelihood of countries resolving disputes in order to trade. They might consider the potential gains from trade, but often these are not enough when the political and/or ideological views are too divergent, as in the case of India and Pakistan, for example. Thus, the peace-building potential of trade remains unproven.

The capacity of trade to foster prosperity remains unquestioned. In doing so, trade reduces the need for countries to utilise force to achieve desired ends (such as getting new supplies of resources). But trade and conflict are not necessarily incompatible. Wars can encourage certain types of trade – in arms, for example. Trade can also underpin conflict as a source of funds; both for rebel groups or the state, and can perpetuate violence should the profits to be made from war by the belligerents exceed those available to them in times in peace. Conflict diamonds are one recent, headline-grabbing example, though many others exist.

Trade can also provoke conflicts of interest at the intra-state level. WTO negotiations and bilateral trade discussions, such as the ones between the United States and the former beneficiaries of the Andean Trade Preference Act (ATPA),[6] have caused public uproar. Protesters believe that the gains from free trade only benefit those countries with the greatest negotiation leverage (i.e. the wealthy nations) and the small minority in the developing countries that accept their terms. In some cases, this discontent has resulted in armed rebellion such as the Zapatista movement in Mexico.[7]

The relationship between trade and conflict remains a complicated one. Still, attempting to understand it is worthwhile in order to understand whether trade can be a viable form of conflict prevention.

### Lessons drawn from the case studies

Trade alone is not sufficient to hinder conflict. The case studies in this book indicate that there are other variables that contribute to creating an atmosphere of peace and stability. These include internal stability, strong institutions, like-minded governments, compatible market economies, well-defined borders and mutual interdependence. While a variable's importance might change according to the case under discussion, they are all necessary for true trade integration to take place.

In South Asia, country leaders hoped that by achieving economic integration through the South Asian Association for Regional Cooperation (SAARC) the groundwork for achieving peace would be laid (see Chapter 4). But internal strife and inter-state tensions have continued to block such peace. Furthermore, intra and inter-state conflicts prevent SAARC members from pursuing the internal reforms needed to complete the integration process; they need political stability to do so.

The ongoing conflict over Kashmir[8] between India and Pakistan illustrates how trade flows are effectively hostage to conflict. This unresolved dispute prevents both regional integration and cooperation; profound nationalistic sentiment has made bilateral reconciliation difficult, and the dispute has thus far resulted in two armed conflicts and three crises. The severity of the dispute makes it 'the single largest constraint' for regional aspirations (see Chapter 4).

Despite their ongoing disagreements, India and Pakistan do still trade with each other, albeit at sub-optimal levels. But various impediments remain. For instance, Pakistan has not granted most favoured nation (MFN)[9] status to India, while India maintains, on average, higher tariff levels than Pakistan. Were these two countries to normalise their diplomatic relations and establish a free trade agreement (FTA), some analysts estimate that bilateral trade flows would, in ten years, increase ninefold (Burki 2004: 24). This potential was first observed between 1948 and 1949, when India received 56 per cent of Pakistan's exports and Indian goods made up 32 per cent of Pakistan's imports. In contrast, today Pakistan's exports to India hover between 0.4 and 2.5 per cent of total exports, and India's exports to Pakistan are less than 0.5 per cent (see Chapter 6).

Given the trade restrictions and shared border between Pakistan and India, informal trade has flourished. Indeed, 'informal trade exceeds formal trade by over US$150 million. The combined value of trade is close to US$1.0 billion' (see Chapter 6). The elimination of trade barriers would eliminate the need to resort to informal trade channels and could result in annual trade flows of at least US$2.62 billion. Given that the average annual trade between 1999 and 2005 did not exceed US$250 million, the potential gains from free trade become evident (see Chapter 6).

Another case of neighbourly hostilities occurred between Peru and Ecuador. Like India and Pakistan, these countries continued to trade with each other (at reduced levels) despite an ongoing territorial dispute. The scale of this trade varied with diplomatic relations; in times of conflict, trade was at its lowest. A study by Simmons found that actual average yearly trade during the dispute was US$74.94 million and actual average yearly trade in times of peace amounted to US$182.67 million (Simmons 1999: 14). However, the level of economic interdependence between the countries was so low that, at one point, they closed the border between them for eight months with no significant economic repercussions (Ruiz-Dana *et al.* 2007: ch. 2).

Ecuador and Peru eventually resolved their dispute to promote the benefits of the Andean Community (CAN). A 'clearly defined jurisdiction over borders' was necessary to avoid the curtailment of commercial transactions; without it, the integration process could not move forward (Ruiz-Dana *et al.* 2007: ch. 8). Therefore Andean integration required a peaceful agreement between the two countries. As noted, Ecuador and Peru were both experiencing significant yearly losses in bilateral trade; by resolving their differences, both could achieve greater gains from bilateral and regional trade. Indeed, it was followed by an upsurge in exports from both countries to the CAN.[10] Similarly, bilateral trade jumped to US$310 million in 1999 (*La Oferta* 2005).

There seems to be a clearer trade–conflict link in Latin America with regard to intra-state, rather than inter-state, conflict. To begin with, most inter-state conflicts have been caused by territorial disputes. These have largely been resolved. Intra-state conflicts, on the other hand, continue to haunt countries such as Colombia and Bolivia. In the former's case, trade liberalisation has been accompanied by the illegal trade in arms and narcotics. In Bolivia, a fight over resources, especially natural gas, has pitted an elite minority against a majority of indigenous peasants. Some of these peasants believe that gas exports undermine Bolivia's sovereignty; estimates indicate that these exports would fetch up to US$500 million in annual earnings (International Crisis Group 2004: 32).

These situations occur in the presence of a weak state apparatus. In both countries, the state has been unable to put an end to the internal conflicts, a failure that has indirectly jeopardised potential gains from trade. In addition, the CAN has not come up with a regional approach to the conflicts. This has been particularly harmful to Colombia, as its neighbours (Ecuador, Peru and Venezuela) have not fully cooperated to halt the flow of illicit goods and rebel groups.

Despite their weaknesses, South America's two trading blocs (Southern Common Market (MERCOSUR) and the CAN) have evolved from security concerns to commercially viable arrangements. It remains limited, however: while the level of intra-regional trade has grown since the inception of both blocs, regional trade does not exceed that of individual members' trade with their traditional partners (i.e. the US and the EU). Yet, in the absence of adequate substitutes in the region, this is not necessarily a bad thing. Common economic interests have already been forged, and future improvements in competitiveness among the members are likely to benefit the blocs by tightening this trade gap. These shared interests also make the potential for future conflicts unlikely.

The study by the South African Institute of International Affairs (SAIIA) suggests that weak institutions, both at the domestic and regional level, obstruct economic integration in Southern Africa. Instead, they 'create fertile conditions for conflict', for this is a context where 'the pursuit of power lies at the core of defining relations between states' (see Chapter 3). The Great Lakes conflict is cited as an example of this. Zimbabwe took advantage of its presiding role over the Organ for Politics, Security and Defence (OPSD) to intervene in the conflict. In doing so, it sought to tip the balance of power in its favour vis-à-vis South Africa's predominant role in the Southern African Development Community (SADC).

Whereas formal trade has not met expectations,[11] informal trade rises and falls with the security situation. In Zimbabwe, a country that has been immersed in internal turmoil since its independence in 1980, the economy subsists on this informal trade (see Chapter 7). The ongoing conflict has eroded formal market mechanisms and institutions, particularly due to corruption. The informal economy has become the preferred exchange medium; at least 80 per cent of households currently participate in it (see Chapter 7). Since informal trade greatly affects the entire region, the SAIIA argues that it is eroding the potential for formal trade. The SADC has not come up with a direct response to this. Institutional overhaul is a necessary first step to ensure that it plays a meaningful role in conflict prevention and trade integration.

Economics proved to be the main driver behind Southeast Asia's integration, which became more formalised with the creation of the Association of South East Asian Nations (ASEAN) in 1967.[12] The 1992 establishment of the ASEAN free trade area (AFTA) resulted in lowered tariffs that have, in turn, boosted intra-regional trade and fostered interdependence. Total intra-ASEAN trade increased from US$44.2 billion in 1993 to US$174.39 billion in 2003. This result has raised the cost of regional or inter-state conflict, particularly as the region grew more competitive vis-à-vis the EU and the North American Free Trade Agreement (NAFTA) (see Chapter 5).

The Singapore Institute of International Affairs (SIIA) argues that the Southeast Asian picture is not entirely rosy. AFTA's non-binding and non-punitive nature has sometimes resulted in entrenched interests and economic nationalism that encourage exceptions that go unpunished, as neighbours with similar resource inputs and export products compete with each other. To date, no ASEAN member has invoked the dispute settlement mechanism (DSM) for fear of jeopardising intra-regional relations. However should disparities continue this acquiescence could be shaken up and result in heightened tension amongst ASEAN members. In the face of the aforementioned threat, as well as existing intra-state conflicts and non-traditional security threats, cooperation within ASEAN will have to move beyond commercial interests in order to set up the institutions and mechanisms needed to forge stronger political and cultural ties in the region (see Chapter 5).

## The institutional angle: regional trade agreements (RTAs) and conflict prevention

The case studies demonstrate that political stability and compatible views are a prerequisite to solid and formal trade relations. At the same time, potential gains from trade can encourage the resolution of a dispute, as in the case of

Peru and Ecuador. Once trade flows have been established, they are likely to deter future conflict.

Nevertheless, economic gains are not always an incentive. India and Pakistan are unwilling to put their differences aside to achieve full trade benefits. In southern Africa, there are too many vested interests in maintaining informal trade flows. Also, similarities or common bonds do not necessarily foment harmonious relations. Shared boundaries, particularly if undefined, can be a source of conflict (e.g., India and Pakistan, Peru and Ecuador). The Southeast Asian case demonstrates that similar product bases and resource inputs can result in cut-throat competition. The link between trade and conflict is, therefore, not always obvious; there are other dynamics that play out in distinct disputes. Hence the importance of weighing differing contexts individually. Each necessitates a unique approach and, where conflict exists, a unique solution.

The causality of the trade–conflict relationship is not unidirectional. There are a number of intervening variables, including: the history of conflict in an integrating area, the role of formal and informal rules in integration, the domestic political setting and the role played by political economy forces in the regional integration process. One of the conclusions drawn from this study is that the design of institutions shapes the nature of regional relations and the economic and political success of trade integration.

But as to exactly how such institutions should be structured to support stability more is hardly an obvious matter. Since conflicts stem from disagreements between two or more states or within states, institutions designed to limit such conflicts should be properly designed and managed (World Bank 2005: 57). Faulty design and implementation seems to plague most regional integration schemes in the developing world. Yet regional institutions are an important part of governance alongside domestic and global governance institutions. They have the potential to manage conflicts and buffer risks associated with instability, promote trade and investment, contribute to better political governance and enhance economic development.

### Creating a positive association between trade and peace

While there is evidence of deeper integration in parts of the developing world, especially Southeast Asia, it is still hard to find examples of integration that have reached a high level of institutionalisation. Europe, which has one of the most successful integration mechanisms in the world, prides itself on having achieved a high degree of internal integration and high level of institutionalisation.

Europe's relative success has been achieved largely through fostering interdependence and healthy resource competition within the integrating area. From this example, there is no doubt that both formal and informal constraints are important in governing the behaviour of actors. Formal constraints are those that are codified in rules and institutions, whereas informal constraints are tacitly understood. The latter are difficult to define in concrete terms since by their very nature are soft, and hard to measure.

One of the most common features of regional integration initiatives in the developing world is the pre-eminence given to narrowly defined political objectives, without clear linkages to important aspects such as trade and development. For Africa, this was recently made evident in the efforts led by Libya's Muammar al-Gaddafi and Abdoulay Wade of Senegal to create a 'United States of Africa', to be made up of federated states under a central government. This was blocked by a group of countries led by South Africa who preferred an option based on gradually strengthening regional economic communities (RECs) and their associated institutions. The regional institutions that can better facilitate peace and stability are those that are carefully designed and make an explicit linkage between the peace and security agenda with issues of trade and development cooperation.

But an unwieldy continental government that is not constituted by strong regional or sub-regional building blocks founded on common values and objectives will not have much success in creating conditions for sustainable peace. Most regions in the developing world have not as yet reached the maturity to expand as Europe for example has, through various phases, over the last five decades. Neither are they established with a similarly strong institutional framework. Since the regions that we examined are developing regions this should not come as a surprise, but especially for three reasons.

First, the state has not achieved a level of confidence that is characteristic of modern Western states; consolidating the state and defending its sovereignty thus becomes a preoccupation for most developing regions. This is strongly the case in most parts of sub-Saharan Africa and, to some degree, for Southeast Asia. The fundamental difference with the relatively developed regions that have attained high levels of institutionalisation lies in deeper internal integration that has encouraged healthy resource cooperation between states.

Weak sovereignty in the countries constituting regional communities partly explains the reluctance of these organisations to interfere in the internal affairs of their member countries, even when human rights abuses are rampant. Weak internal institutions and underdevelopment lend these states a weak form of sovereignty. This also means that successful regional integration hinges on the availability of strong institutions and convergence around democratic norms.

The second reason has to do with the recent history of inter and intra-state conflict in these regions. In most of these cases militarised conflicts were present as recently as the 1980s, with some regions witnessing a series of military rulers. This history has created a social milieu of economic nationalism and military–industrial complexes. Perceptions of insecurity and the need to increase the aggregate power of the state remains a problem for deepening integration. Yet it is only when intra-regional integration is deepened and the region pursues external integration that the risk of militarised conflict can be significantly reduced.

Consider the case of southern Africa. In this area, regionalism began in the late 1970s as a political project aimed at reducing dependence on apartheid South Africa, and structuring relations that would thwart South Africa's efforts to encroach upon the region north of its border. There was very little in common between the countries that began what was then called the Southern African Development Coordinating Conference (SADCC) and now called the Southern African Development Community (SADC), other than the common enemy of apartheid South Africa. This area has a long and deep history of conflict, including the civil wars in Angola and Mozambique, beginning in 1975 and lasting until the early 1990s.

The insurgent movements in these countries received support from South Africa as part of its war effort against the liberation movement. Cross-border attacks by South Africa in its neighbouring countries were a common feature in the 1970s, ostensibly to drive out 'terrorist' elements. There were weak trade ties in this area. The establishment of the formal regional organisation in the form of SADC, with trade as one of the prominent agendas, was not preceded by increased commercial relations between countries.

Other conflicts in the area include the more recent Great Lakes conflict between 1998 and 2002, which also involved four SADC countries – Zimbabwe, Angola, Namibia and the Democratic Republic of Congo (DRC). The DRC had joined SADC in 1997 driven largely by security considerations rather than any strong economic ties with other SADC countries.

Whereas in the case of Southeast Asia there are no militarised inter-state conflicts, intra-state tensions abound, and these are linked to income inequalities and poverty or marginalisation. In essence these are socio-economic grievance-based tensions. Even the historical tensions between China and Taiwan have gradually de-escalated with little sign that this could become an actualised conflict. The dense commercial networks and economic integration between the two make it unlikely, though not impossible, that conflict could break out in the future. Other conflicts in this region include those in Aceh in Indonesia, southern Thailand and southern Philippines.

Trade integration that inhibits conflict is, to a degree, evident in South Asia. There is a sense that to some degree integration within the context of the South Asian Preferential Trade Agreement (SAPTA) has contributed to the thawing of tensions between India and Pakistan. This is the case where growing trade relations have a potential to create a zone of peace in this area in the future. In the past, the persistence of conflict – especially between India and Pakistan – in this region hindered meaningful trade integration. In a general sense, the complex nature that conflict has assumed – with intra and inter-state tensions feeding each other – has made it difficult to develop confidence building measures (CBMs) that could guarantee long-term stability.

The tensions here include the long-standing India–Pakistan tensions; the Kashmir insurgency, which is believed by India to be supported by Pakistan; the India–Sri Lanka tensions, which articulate with the internal conflict involving Tamil Tigers within Sri Lanka; as well as territorial disputes between India and Bangladesh. Trade alone cannot be sufficient in addressing these tensions, some of which can be traced to history and touch deep on issues of identity. However, as a CBM and as a platform to foster commercial linkages and cooperation, trade integration could in the long run ensure convergence of the interests of various actors and limit further escalation of tensions.

Limiting the escalation of tensions depends not only on what happens at the regional level but also on the domestic political setting. Regional relations on issues of trade and security cannot be understood in isolation from domestic level forces, including the nature of institutions, the political culture, and the character of relationships between various societal actors. Willingness of various states to cooperate both at the political and economic level is an important success factor.

Third, most of these regions have the highest incidence of poverty. Sub-Saharan Africa, for example lags far behind with respect to economic development. Even in the promising region of Latin America, the incidents of poverty are very high. While Southeast Asia has significantly reduced overall poverty levels, Cambodia and Laos are performing poorly (World Bank 2005: 22). As the case study of Southeast Asia highlights, some of the intra-state conflicts are linked to poverty and economic marginalisation.

### *The role of formal and informal constraints in creating positive associations*

Both formal and informal constraints help to inhibit conflict and force actors to take integration seriously and commit themselves to agreed objectives. Informal constraints, as Douglas North observes, encapsulate acceptable norms that are not necessarily codified, which provide solutions to coordination problems (North 1997). In this respect, it is not only the formal rules that matter, but also softer variables such as culture, tradition and beliefs that play a significant role in shaping economic performance.

This can also be expressed in growing cross-border commercial linkages that are not mediated by formal institutions. For example, in Southeast Asia, regionalism in a formal institutional sense played no role in fostering trade between 1985 and 2000, and the role of AFTA – after it was established in 1992 – was minimal. It did however help as a CBM and a formal institutional mechanism to strengthen commercial linkages.

Across all the case studies that we have looked at, shared understanding, inter-subjective norms, common values and political orientation play a critical part in regional relations. Where these are lacking, tensions abound, especially of the inter-state nature. This is evident in sub-Saharan Africa and South Asia. It is clear that a shared political culture is a major CBM, without which coordination among the actors would be difficult.

Consider, for example, the case of South Asia, where the actors exhibit fundamental differences along cultural, religious, political system and ethnic lines. In this region the index of political stability is low, and tensions have hindered the development of a progressive regional integration mechanism. Moreover, inter and intra-state conflicts intersect considerably, and throw the region into a perpetual state of hostility. This contrasts markedly with South-east Asia, where the incidents of inter-state conflict are rare, though certain parts of the region are marred by intra-state conflict.

The limited occurrence of inter-state conflicts in Southeast Asia can be explained by the existence of informal constraints by state elites, which in turn limits the propensity towards inter-state conflict. In this region, the long tradition of informal relationships dating back to the establishment of ASEAN in the wake of the Vietnam War seems to have had a constraining effect on actor behaviour. It is the more formal institutions such as ASEAN that are weak (especially for their lack of restraining capacity), and it is here that more buttressing is needed.

### *From informal to formal constraints: developing strong institutions*

Informal constraints are not, on their own, sufficient to create sustainability. As noted earlier, informal constraints include, but are not limited to, inter-subjective and tacit norms that are not necessarily codified, as well as com-mercial relationships that are not mediated by formal structures. The latter, for example, includes trade flows that take effect even in the absence of for-mal structures governing trade. Over and above informal constraints, a set of formal rules governing the conduct of actors with respect to both trade and security issues is required, especially to lend credibility to regional inte-gration efforts. Regional integration has to have explicit declarations on what is expected from various member countries.

An instructive example can be seen in the 'Declaration on Security' made by the Organization of American States (OAS) in 2003.[13] This Declaration highlights a commitment to cooperating on the combat of: transnational organised crime; corruption; asset laundering; illicit trafficking in weapons; extreme poverty and social exclusion; health issues; and environmental degradation.

MERCOSUR put in place 'club rules' (explicit rules of political conduct for member states) when the commander of Paraguay's armed forces was suspected of harbouring intentions of a coup in 1996. This resulted in the four presidents of the MERCOSUR member states signing a declaration on democratic commitment in Argentina in June of that year, making dem-ocracy a precondition for membership. This was later extended to the FTAs between MERCOSUR and Bolivia and Chile in the Protocol of Ushaia in June 1998 (Schiff and Winters 2003: 199). This is a good, although by no means perfect, accountability mechanism.

Indeed, as Maurice Schiff and Alan Winters (2003: 188) observe, integration schemes are most effective when they impose 'club rules' such as democracy and human rights. The dilemma often faced by regional integration schemes is that members cannot possibly impose strictures or conditions at the regional level that are non-existent in their own countries. Hence infrastructure of democratic governance, adherence to the rule of law and protection of human rights are essential in various member states if the regional project is to be a success. Formal rules exist, in part, to encourage member states in regional organisations to develop democratic norms at the national level.

In the case of SADC the formal rules aimed at dealing with conflict are captured in what is known as the OPSD, established in Windhoek in July 1996 (Cilliers 1996). Although this sought to accord importance to security coordination, conflict mediation and military cooperation, the manner in which the OPSD has functioned has not been optimal. There has been lack of policy coherence or clear linkage between this structure and those dealing with economic or trade relations. For better functionality, it is important to establish strong linkages between issues of regional security and trade and development.

For many years, the OPSD has been weakened by lack of leadership, particularly tensions between Nelson Mandela and Robert Mugabe (the former chairing the SADC summit and the latter chairing the OPSD in 1996). The absence of commonly agreed values at the regional level compounded the difficulties experienced by this body. Recently this has been restructured to give it a better focus, but coordination problems persist. Nonetheless, it is an important CBM in the sub-region and, with the very significant exception of the Great Lakes conflict of the late 1990s, there have not been other inter-state conflicts.

In its recent restructuring, with the adoption of the Strategic Indicative Plan for the Organ for Politics, Security and Defence (SIPO) in 2001, the OPSD sought to shift its emphasis from narrow military/security issues towards emphasising democratisation, institution-building, human rights, political pluralism and inclusion of civil society. At its core it has two important articles: a protocol on politics, defence and security; and a mutual defence pact.

In Southeast Asia, CBM such as the Treaty of Amity and Cooperation set out to promote mutual respect for the independence, sovereignty, equality, territorial integrity and national identity of all nations. Significantly, this Treaty also establishes a code of conduct for peaceful settlement of dispute: the High Council arbitrates and determines the best course of dispute settlement. This formal framework encourages mediation before the more formal and legalistic arbitration route.

There is also the ASEAN Troika, which exists at a higher level and is made up of the past president, the outgoing president and the incoming president of the Troika. This is another instrument that is used to mediate conflict, and can be activated by ASEAN ministers of foreign affairs. The Troika, however, lacks any decision-making capacity and cannot encroach into the internal affairs of member countries. Because of this, some ASEAN members tend to rely on external security provision, and this helps to keep stability. As such, both ASEAN and SADC need to strengthen the capacity of their security institutions.

The SAARC is an overarching RTA with both an economic and political mandate. While SAARC's charter promotes active collaboration and mutual assistance in the economic, social, cultural, technical and scientific fields, the main thrust of regional efforts has been directed towards economic integration. All activities to be undertaken within the SAARC framework are governed by the overarching principles of 'sovereign equality, territorial integrity, political independence and non-interference in the internal affairs of other states'. On the one hand, mutual benefit is a primary consideration; the sovereign equality condition weighs in against powerful countries leveraging their power against weaker countries. On the other hand, member states can not involve themselves in bilateral conflicts within the region. For the moment, the clauses on territorial integrity and non-interference in member countries' internal affairs rules out SAARC's role as a peacekeeper.

However, the absence of recourse to deliberate upon bilateral political relations has become a major concern for member states. Realising the negative impact of political tensions on trade arrangements in the region, some analysts have called for a regional institutional mechanism to contain conflict among members. Others have even suggested the need to amend the SAARC charter to allow it to deliberate upon bilateral issues. As early as 1990, Sri Lankan analyst Ravinatha Ariyasinghe had proposed a 'strategic regional security framework' designed to ensure regional security in South Asia (Ariyasinghe 1990). No progress has been made on this front, and realistically such a development is not on the cards any time soon. Member states, particularly Pakistan and India, must find means outside the SAARC arrangement to resolve their differences.

While none of these cases are necessarily models to be replicated, they provide useful examples from which important lessons can be drawn. One such lesson is that there may not be a need to design new institutions or to impose a one-size-fits-all approach. However there are necessary processes that regional institutions need to set in motion. The existing institutions need to evolve organically to deeper levels of institutionalisation as trade integration deepens. Hence, even in the ongoing discussions about establishing the pan-African government there was simply no support for imposing institutions that did not organically evolve. In some instances existing institutions may need to be restructured and better capacitated in order to function optimally.

### *Creating strong regional–global linkages*

Global linkages can enhance the conflict-inhibiting potential of RTAs. Inward-looking and shallow integration schemes can easily generate tensions between the integrating countries. In this respect, RTAs may need to exhibit depth in the percentage coverage of traded goods as well as in the scope of products that are traded. Some integration schemes – such as MERCOSUR – are customs unions in a shallow sense but have sectors that are excluded on the basis of them being designated sensitive.

Other regional integration schemes, as the case of SADC shows, are characterised by slow implementation or their benefits are eroded by bureaucratic impediments, such as the occasionally complex provisions to meet rules of origin (RO) requirements (which demonstrate that a good is produced within a particular region and so qualifies for lower tariffs). In a sense, countries would have to engage in deeper integration that promotes open regionalism or that is WTO-consistent. This lays at the heart of what Richard Baldwin (Baldwin and Krugman 2002) calls the 'juggernaut effect' of regional integration.

In the ongoing WTO negotiations an emphasis is laid on having both a quantitative and qualitative benchmark for RTAs. A qualitative benchmark would ensure that in future no sector would be excluded in the tariff liberalisation schedule, except those that are deemed security sensitive – especially agriculture and textiles, which are often deemed sensitive sectors. Quantitative benchmarks set acceptable percentage thresholds for tariff liberalisation for products in the tariff schedule.

This may not necessarily address issues of conflict or establish the necessary confidence to overcome tensions, but it may help to build a critical mass of trade between two or more countries in a way that increases the cost of conflict. Dynamics such as the 'agglomeration effect' inherently generate tensions. Agglomeration happens when, as a result of regional integration, firms gravitate towards central (as opposed to peripheral) locations that offer attractive features such as trade cost advantages and proximity to other industrial activities and suppliers. This problem could be mitigated by increased developmental cooperation through the establishment of regional value chains in certain sectors, or through developmental funds to improve the competitiveness of peripheral countries. Such measures could go some way in mitigating the tensions that arise from an asymmetric distribution of economic benefits.

### *Creating the right climate for trade to reinforce stability: the necessary conditions for success*

Rather than describing the types of institutions that may help to facilitate peace, we will highlight some of the conditions that are necessary for the emergence of better regional institutions of trade and security. There are five key dimensions that we would like to highlight.

The first dimension has to do with the relationship between the domestic and regional level processes. There is little doubt that the two have to be mutually reinforcing if regional integration is to create stability. Furthermore, if the relationship between regional trade and security is to be a positively reinforcing one it would need to be supported by normative values that capture a commitment to democratisation, upholding of the rule of law and respect for human rights. More than anything else this would require far-reaching political and economic reforms at the domestic level. This, along with greater integration with developed countries in the North, will help create the necessary agency of restraint that will guard against reversal or slips into instability.

Second, the design of regional integration schemes have to be sensitive to latent historical tensions or perceptions that trade agreements could be skewed in favour of dominant countries. While in most instances trade integration schemes were created with a view to ensuring political cooperation and stability, these could also create the opposite effect. As Maurice Schiff and Alan Winters observe, this could be the case where 'tariff preferences created to induce regional trade can create powerful income transfers within the region and can lead to the concentration of industry in a single location' (Schiff and Winters 2003: 194). A strong focus on 'developmental regionalism' could considerably reduce the scope for tensions.

Developmental regionalism emphasises the removal of supply-side constraints and infrastructure development and views trade in a more integrated manner, linked to domestic developmental challenges. Some of the examples of developmental oriented regionalism include infrastructure-related or project-based regional cooperation to manage regional public goods such as forestry, shared water resources, energy and transport infrastructure.

In South Asia, where there are pre-existing political tensions, the design of RTAs should take into consideration these sensitivities, especially the antipathies of smaller countries towards more powerful ones. One way of overcoming this is to put in place a mechanism – in the form of a developmental fund – to compensate for any possible losses. This development fund would act as a mechanism to compensate for any loss of revenue and mitigate any possible risk to integration. In the MERCOSUR, this US$100 million development fund is known as the Fund for Structural Convergence of MERCOSUR (FOCEM), and is hardly sufficient in an area with 95 million people – the majority of whom are poor.

FOCEM is aimed at structural convergence, developing competitiveness, encouraging social cohesion and strengthening the integration effort. Ideally, in such a developmental mechanism, member countries should make contributions that reflect their level of economic development and the extent of their benefit from regional integration. Larger countries would thus contribute more.

This asymmetrical contribution will help limit the tensions that are likely to arise between the core and peripheral countries in an RTA. The developmental fund could also be further explored in the context of the economic partnership agreements (EPAs) between the EU and various African sub-regions, where the EU makes developmental allocations as part of enhancing competitiveness of smaller economies and encouraging them to deepen integration.

Recently, African ministers launched the Pan-African Infrastructure Development Fund, which currently stands at US$625 million with the goal of raising US$1.2 billion, to provide long-term financing for developmental projects in the areas of cross-border energy, transport, telecoms, water and sanitation.[14] This is one example of strengthening regional integration to become more development-focused and to reduce economic imbalances that could be fertile ground for tensions within the region.

The third dimension is the need to broaden the capacity of regional integration mechanisms. For example, structures such as the SAARC and the South Asian Free Trade Agreement (SAFTA) need to be institutionally equipped so that they can address trade disputes when they arise. They should also do so proactively, so that in regions with sensitive security situations (i.e. South Asia), disputes are resolved before they escalate. Without an appropriate mechanism for addressing trade-related disputes, trade integration could exacerbate existing political tensions in a given region.

The architecture of such a conflict-resolution mechanism should include a standardisation of conflict indicators; developing early warning systems in member countries; enhancing the capacity for conflict prevention, management and resolution; and a regular assessment of factors that have a potential to lead to conflict, including imbalances in welfare and poverty.

Fourth, regions need to fully exploit or develop product complementarities across all sectors, including services, as this could help to deepen regional trade integration and lessen the propensity towards competition – and conflict. As with the instruments that deal with security issues, similar DSMs in the trade arena could help deal with disputes that might arise.

RTAs that are of the open regionalism type, aimed at harmonisation and the deepening liberalisation of trade and investment regimes, have better chances for success than those that are inward-looking. It is here that harmonisation with multilateral trade liberalisation becomes important. At a broader level, integration should be aimed at tariff reduction rather than creating a gridlock of import-substitution policies overlaid with complex RO, as is the case with SADC.

RO should be kept simple, and should not be used for protectionist reasons under the guise of curtailing transhipment. In addition, particular attention needs to be paid to non-tariff barriers, including those issues that have a bearing on trade facilitation, such as customs procedures and standards. In comparison to other regional efforts, ASEAN seems to have been most successful in this respect; it has pursued external openness in tandem with the expansion of intra-regional trade (World Bank 2005: 60).

Fifth, regional infrastructural cooperation, especially over scarce and shared resources such as water, could help prevent potential conflicts. In Latin America a resource-based conflict erupted when Peru and Ecuador clashed over a section of the Amazon River basin. Cooperation in this area could be governed in the form of protocols that are built into the regional integration scheme. Some of the other areas where cooperation could be facilitated include energy, transport, environment and health. A focus on infrastructure cooperation and development-oriented regionalism can help build confidence, since many conflicts are linked to real or perceived economic marginalisation.

Finally, porous borders present a challenge, as incidents of drug trafficking, the illegal arms trade and the movement of criminals between countries remain prevalent. In southern Africa, the political and economic situation in Zimbabwe, which has arisen largely from political mismanagement and the recession of democracy, has accentuated these border leaks, with security implications for South Africa and other neighbouring countries. In Latin America, internal strife in Colombia has had a spill-over effect, including a narcotics problem in Colombia that affects its neighbouring countries. This again points to the importance of fostering cooperation beyond simple trade integration. Such expanded cooperation could lead to protocols on cross-border movements of people, illegal arms trafficking and trade in illicit goods and so on. SADC has various protocols dealing with these and other areas. However, it is one thing to have such protocols on paper, and quite another for member states to ratify them and to ensure that implementation and surveillance mechanisms are in place.

## Concluding remarks: implications for policy-makers

The fundamental conclusion of this research is not revolutionary. It is that the nature of the economic connections between countries affects the evolution of their political relationship, and vice versa. RTAs are as much political as economic agreements. As such, they can play an important role in developing *informal* constraints on conflict (both inter and intra-state), such as interdependence and 'constituencies for peace', as well as institutionalising *formal* constraints on conflict, such as channels for political dialogue and dispute resolution.

The relative fall in inter-state conflict in recent years has been mirrored by a growth in RTAs. These trends seem inter-linked – but which is 'cause' and which is 'effect' is unclear. Evidently, countries experiencing latent or overt conflict will be unwilling to sit down over a trade negotiating table. To even consider trade integration, countries have to have reached a certain level of institutional maturity and stability. As such, universally ascribing a 'peace dividend' to regional trade integration risks a serious selection bias. Nevertheless, it is clear that regional trade integration can be a very important aspect of regional governance mechanisms, economic welfare and conflict avoidance.

The question for policy-makers is whether there is enough of a rationale for promoting regional trade integration as a mechanism for conflict prevention in the absence of clear trade complementarities. In other words, is there enough of a peace dividend from trade integration to justify externally encouraging trade integration on fragile states (as the EU has been keen to do)? Or is the momentum for trade integration something that has to develop endogenously?

Our research underlines the fact that trade links alone are not sufficient to hinder conflict. Many other variables contribute to creating an atmosphere of peace and stability. Economic gains are not enough of an incentive to avoid conflict – but they can help. India and Pakistan, for example, are unwilling to put their differences aside to achieve the full benefits of trade. In Africa, there are too many vested interests in perpetuating informal trade. Similarities or common bonds do not necessarily result in harmonious relations. The Southeast Asian case demonstrates that similar product bases and resource inputs can result in cut-throat competition.

Trade agreements are typically concluded between asymmetric powers. Trade integration inherently involves ceding a portion of sovereignty to regional institutions, something which many developing countries, still in a process of state building, are unwilling to do. RTAs are likely to be more successful where the larger power recognises its enlightened self-interest in not pushing an unbalanced agreement. However, in southern Africa at least, it seems that a neo-mercantilist approach to RTA negotiation is prevalent. In Latin America inherent asymmetries highlight the fact that the integration process has yet to be completed. And members' unwillingness to subject themselves to strong legal mechanisms and instead resolve problems through diplomatic engagement hinders progress.

The case studies demonstrate that political stability and compatible views are a prerequisite to stable, formal trade relations. However, as a CBM and a platform to foster commercial linkages and cooperation, trade integration can, in the long run, ensure convergence of the interests of various actors and limit the further escalation of tensions.

## Notes

1 A movement to abolish tariffs on corn, which were equivalent to taxes on bread.
2 Term used to refer to the free trade movement and laissez-faire thinking in England during the nineteenth century.
3 Government's actions to block free trade.
4 Economic freedom indicates how much economic liberalisation a given country has experienced. See Gartzke (2005: 34).
5 Based on Immanuel Kant's ideas, as expressed in his work, *Perpetual Peace*, the theory suggests that democracies are, in principle, less conflict prone and trade reinforces their mutual dependence. Thus, it is in their best interest to maintain the peace.
6 The beneficiaries are Peru, Ecuador, Colombia and Bolivia. The Act expired in December 2006 and it granted unilateral trade advantages to these countries; they were allowed to export over 5,000 products without paying duties. The Act was part of the fight against drug production and trafficking in the Andean region.
7 The armed movement came into existence in 1994, on the very same day that NAFTA, Mexico's free trade agreement with the US and Canada, became effective. It is based in Chiapas, one of Mexico's poorest states, and its members are mostly indigenous peasants. The Zapatistas have declared themselves against

neo-liberalism and globalisation. Although the movement started off with an armed uprising, the Zapatistas have, in recent times, resorted to more diplomatic means for presenting their demands to the Mexican government.

8  The Kashmir conflict dates from 1948, the year after both countries' independence.

9  MFN status indicates that one nation is accorded the same treatment as other nations trading under the WTO, thus benefitting from lower tariffs and trade barriers; it signals open trade with that particular nation.

10 Negotiations concluded in 1998 and the definition of the boundary was finalised in May 1999.

11 South Africa's regional partners hoped that trade with South Africa, given its dominant economy, would result in complementarities and, consequently, prosperity. Thus far, the outcome of such trade indicates that South Africa has benefited the most from the trading arrangement; the rest of the region has not benefited from similar export–import complementarities.

12 ASEAN was established on 8 August 1967 in Bangkok by the five original member countries: Indonesia, Malaysia, Philippines, Singapore and Thailand. Brunei Darussalam joined on 8 January 1984, Vietnam on 28 July 1995, Laos People's Democratic Republic and Myanmar on 23 July 1997, and Cambodia on 30 April 1999, http://www.aseansec.org/64.htm (accessed 5 June 2008).

13 The original document can be found at, http://www.oas.org/documents/eng/DeclaracionSecurity_102803.asp (accessed 5 June 2008).

14 'Africa Fund backs unity drive with cash', *Engineering News*, 2 July 2007.

# References

Ariyasinghe, R.P. (1990) *South Asian Association for Regional Co-operation (SAARC), The Potential for Regional Security*, Colombo: Bandaranaike Centre for International Studies.

Baldwin, R.E. and Krugman, P. (2002) *Agglomeration, Integration and Tax Harmonization*, NBER Working Papers no. 9290, National Bureau of Economic Research, Inc.

Barbieri, K. (1996) 'Economic interdependence: a path to peace or source of interstate conflict?', *Journal of Peace Research*, 33:1, 29–49.

Barbieri, K. (2002) *The Liberal Illusion: Does Trade Promote Peace?* Ann Arbor: University of Michigan Press.

Burki, S.J. (2004) *Prospects of Peace, Stability and Prosperity in South Asia: An Economic Perspective*, Islamabad: Institute of Regional Studies.

Cilliers, J. (1996) 'The SADC organ for defence, politics and security', occasional paper, no. 10, Pretoria: Institute for Defence Policy.

Cohler, A.M., Basia, C.M. and Stone, H.S. (eds) (1989) *Montesquieu: The Spirit of the Laws*, Cambridge: Cambridge University Press.

Gartzke, E. (2000) 'Preferences and democratic peace', *International Studies Quarterly*, 44:2, 191–212.

Gartzke, E. and Li, Q. (2005) 'Mistaken identity: a reply to Hegre', *Conflict Management and Peace Science*, 22:3, October, 225–233.

International Crisis Group – Las Divisiones en Bolivia (2004) 'Demasiado Hondas para Superarlas', *Informe Sobre América Latina No. 7*. Available from http://www.crisisweb.org. Accessed 22 November 2005.

*La Oferta* (2005) 'Ecuador y Perú impulsan proyectos fronterizos comunes'. Available from http://www.laoferta.com. Accessed 15 June 2006.

Mansfield, E.D. and Pevehouse, J.C. (2000) 'Trade blocs, trade flows, and international conflict', *International Organization*, 54:4, 775–808.

North, D. (1997) *The Contribution of the New Institutional Economics to an Understanding of the Transition Problem*, Helsinki: United Nations University/World Institute for Development Economics Research, Annual Lectures.

Oneal, J. and Russett, R. (1997) 'The classical liberals were right: democracy, interdependence and conflict: 1950–1985', *International Studies Quarterly*, 40:2, 267–294.

Oneal, J., Russett, R. and Berbaum, M.L. (2003) 'Causes of peace: democracy, interdependence, and international organizations, 1885–1992', *International Studies Quarterly*, 47:3, 371–393.

Polachek, S.W. and Seiglie, C. (2006) 'Trade, peace and democracy: an analysis of dyadic dispute', discussion paper no. 2170, Bonn: Institute for the Study of Labor.

Russett, R. and Oneal, J. (2001) *Triangulating Peace: Democracy, Interdependence, and International Organizations*, New York: W.W. Norton.

Ruiz-Dana, A. *et al.* (2007) 'Peru and Ecuador: a case study of Latin American integration and conflict', Santiago: Recursos e Investigacion para el Desarrollo Sustentable (RIDES).

Schiff, M. and Winters, L.A. (2003) *Regional Integration and Development*, London: Oxford University Press.

Seiglie, C. (2002) 'Arms races in the developing world: some policy implications', *Journal of Policy Modeling*, 24:7–8, 693–705.

Simmons, B.A. (1999) 'Territorial disputes and their resolution: the case of Ecuador and Peru', Washington, DC: United States Institute of Peace. Available from http://www.usip.org/pubs/peaceworks/pwks27/pwks27.html. Accessed 23 July 2006.

Von Mises, L. (1996) *Human Action: A Treatise on Economics*, 4th revised edn, San Francisco, CA: Fox and Wilkes.

World Bank (2005) 'Global economic prospects: trade, regionalism, and development', Washington DC: World Bank.

# Index

Note: *italic* page numbers denote references to Figures/Tables.